D0881376

UNDERSTANDING CONCURRENCY IN ADA

Ken Shumate

Hughes Aircraft Company

Intertext Publications
McGraw-Hill Book Company
New York, N.Y.

Library of Congress Catalog Card Number 88-80271

10 9 8 7 6 5 4 3 2 1

ISBN 0-07-057299-2

Intertext Publications/Multiscience Press, Inc.
McGraw-Hill Book Company
11 West 19th Street
New York, NY 10011

Preface

This book provides a detailed understanding of concurrency in the programming language Ada. Although it contains a great amount of detail, it explains Ada tasks in a simple and tutorial manner. The reader is expected to have a basic understanding of the Ada language.

The book is an outgrowth of an advanced Ada course dealing with concurrency and real-time systems that I have taught within Hughes Aircraft Company. It deals not only with how Ada approaches concurrency, but also with how a programmer should use Ada tasking features. The latter topic is primarily addressed in a series of five case studies.

The case studies are an important component of the book. They are essentially simplified real-time systems. The simplification is in the algorithms internal to the tasks; the interaction between the tasks is quite realistic. Each case study starts with a statement of a problem to be solved. The problem, presented as a software requirements specification, is followed by top-level and detailed design of the task interactions, complete code of the tasks, and a discussion. The case studies were prepared using the Digital Equipment Corporation validated Ada compiler.

There are a large number of exercises in addition to the case studies. Among the exercises is a series of problems that deal with a single topic. The basic problem is slowly made more complex, requiring more complex aspects of tasking for its solution. Alternative solutions are presented. During the series of problems, the major paradigms for using tasks to handle client-server interactions are discussed.

The book is suitable for both individual study and for classroom use. It could serve as the foundation for an advanced Ada course dealing with real-time systems, or as a text for an undergraduate course with a focus on concurrency and design of software systems.

Ken Shumate

San Diego
July 1987

Acknowledgements

Many people made important contributions during the preparation of this book. I particularly wish to acknowledge the contributions of Kjell Nielsen. Many of the ideas in this book have been refined through our daily discussions and influenced by our shared real-time software development activities, in Ada and other languages. Bryce Bardin and Tom Burger also contributed significant ideas. George Cherry's methods of using process abstraction for system design have influenced my thoughts on concurrency for several years. He introduced me to the example that inspired the final case study in the book.

Very special thanks to the students who sat through several early sessions of an advanced course on tasking at Hughes Aircraft Company and made valuable comments and clarifications to early versions of the manuscript. Finally, a special thank you to Corinne Finney for doing the artwork, both for the classes and for the text of the book.

Contents

Part 3 Task Manipulation

Part 4 Tasks in Real-Time Systems   385

Background

Part 1 is an overview of the book and its major subject. Chapter 1 introduces some of the concepts and notation to be used throughout the book. Chapter 2 is an overview of tasking in Ada. This serves as both a review of topics familiar to the reader and a brief introduction to topics that will later be discussed in detail. Chapter 3 is a case study presented to establish the architecture of a concurrent Ada program.

Introduction

Objective: To define the subject matter of the book, to introduce certain concepts and graphical notations that will be used throughout the rest of the book, and to provide an overview of its contents

1.1 Purpose

The purpose of this book is to provide a detailed understanding of concurrency in Ada. It explains Ada tasks in a simple and tutorial manner.

1.2 Background

To begin to understand concurrency in Ada, we must establish a starting point. This section lays the foundation for that understanding by explaining the relationship between sequential and concurrent programs, relating concurrency to Ada and real-time systems, and describing how the Ada tasking model differs from traditional approaches to concurrency.

1.2.1 Sequential and Concurrent Programs

A *sequential program* specifies a step-by-step sequence of execution of a list of instructions. The execution of the program results in a *process* or a *task*. A *concurrent program* specifies two or more sequential programs that may execute at the same time; the result is two or more *threads of control*. This concurrency may be actual, having two or more processors, or only apparent, with interleaved execution on a single processor.

A *process* is a (abstract) program, either sequential or concurrent. At a certain level of design abstraction a process can be considered to be sequential, while at a lower level of abstraction it can be considered to be a concurrent program of several cooperating processes. Thinking about processes abstractly (a focus on *what* the processes accomplish) while considering what things must occur concurrently is an application of *process abstraction.*

Concurrency is a difficult topic. It finds its most important use in real-time systems, where the multiple interactions with the external world require consideration of multiple, concurrent, asynchronous processing.

Ada specifies a specific model of concurrency, one based on tasks operating asynchronously, as though each had its own processor. In contrast with the *asynchronous* model of *processing*, the intrinsic model of task *communication* is *synchronous*. It is based on the notion of a *rendezvous* between two tasks, at which point they exchange information while their execution is combined into a single thread of control—they are synchronized. In taking this approach, Ada integrates the concepts of synchronization and communication.

The synchronous or unbuffered communication is consistent with modern thought. For example, Hoare [HOA85, p. 238] states that "For a number of years now, I have chosen to take unbuffered (synchronized) communication as basic." The combination of synchronous communication combined with an asynchronous model of processing is different from more traditional models of concurrency. It is particularly in sharp contrast to the traditional "cyclic executive," where the order in which tasks are invoked is fixed, each task runs to completion, and each task has exclusive access to all global data [MAC83].

1.2.2   Concurrency and Real-Time Systems

Concurrent systems are those in which two or more activities occur, or appear to occur, at the same time. Concurrency arises naturally in situations in which there are two or more processors, whether both act independently or one acts as a slave to the other—as is the case in a system with an input/output processor.

Real-time systems (often called embedded systems) are computer hardware and software systems incorporated into larger systems such as ships, airplanes, radar, command and control systems, automated factories, and robots. They must respond in "real time" in order to, for example, adjust the control surfaces of an aircraft in response to a sensed change in attitude, or halt the movement of a robot's fingers as they touch a teacup. Real-time systems typically interface with external devices, reading signals from sensors and signaling commands to electrical and electromechanical devices.

This interaction with external devices in real-time systems forces consideration of concurrency even when there is only a single processor. Since there is true concurrency in the actions of the external world, the single processor must have multiple threads of control in order to cope with those actions (often manifested as interrupts from external devices). Since the multiple external actions are asynchronous and potentially simultaneous, we face potential problems when programs attempt unsynchronized responses such as simultaneous access to data.

In any concurrent system, provision must be made for the coordination and synchronization of the concurrent processes.

1.2.3   Ada Is a New Approach to Concurrency

The traditional approach to control of concurrent processes has been through the use of a real-time executive, typically based on the model of many tasks executing on a single processor. The executive is the program that looks at the current state of the system and decides which task shall execute next. Tasks are alternately "running" (are executing on the processor), "blocked" or "suspended" (do not have resources needed to execute), or "ready" (have resources, but are waiting for the processor). The change from ready to running is a "dispatch" operation. The ready and running states are also referred to as "executable." In a system with as many processors as tasks, there would be no need to distinguish ready and running; tasks would transition from blocked to running. This set of states for tasks is shown in Figure 1-1.

In the traditional approach, the mechanism for task cooperation and synchronization is typically either:

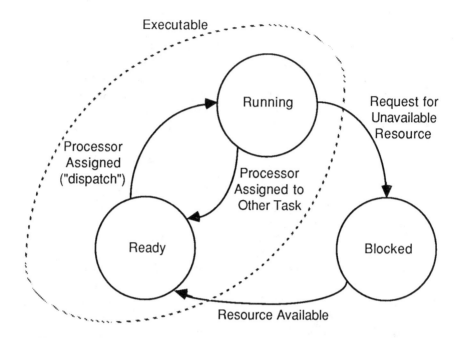

Figure 1-1. Task states and transitions

- Based on a message-passing model, in which tasks communicate by sending messages through services provided by the executive

- Or based on use of explicit synchronization, in which tasks signal and wait for each other through services provided by the executive

In either case, the services provided by the executive are often accessed by what are called "Executive Service Requests," or ESRs. Such requests are explicit and visible to the tasks, as shown in Figure 1-2. The methods of synchronization may include semaphores, critical regions, monitors, and other approaches [AND83].

Ada is different. Its view of multitasking is that tasks are concurrent, asynchronous processes, potentially each with its own processor. Its single, unified feature for task communication and synchronization is the rendezvous, an approach never before used in a real-time system. Because the rendezvous is intrinsic to the language, Ada has no need for a real-time executive and associated services. Instead, there is a hidden run-time system that underlies the Ada tasking model, but it is not visible to the programmer. This is shown in Figure 1-3.

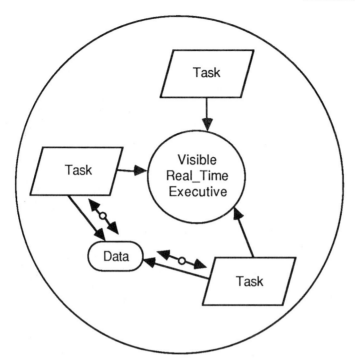

The tasks may use ESRs to coordinate access to data,
as shown, or the Executive may have internal buffers for data.

Figure 1-2. Conventional language and real-time executive

1.3   Graphical Notation

Graphical representation of complex programs is essential. This is
particularly true of concurrent systems, in which it is important to
picture the separate threads of control. We use four graphical tools:
context diagrams, process graphs, dependency graphs, and structure
graphs. The context diagram shows data flow with the world outside the system being designed, the process graph is a design tool
used to represent concurrency in an abstract way, the dependency
graph shows the Ada "withing" relationships of library units, and
the structure graph is a detailed *road map* to an Ada design.

1.3.1   Context Diagrams

A context diagram is shown in Figure 1-4. It is very simple, representing a top-level view of the data flow of the system to be developed; the only data shown is that which is exchanged with devices
external to the system. The direction of data flow is shown by the

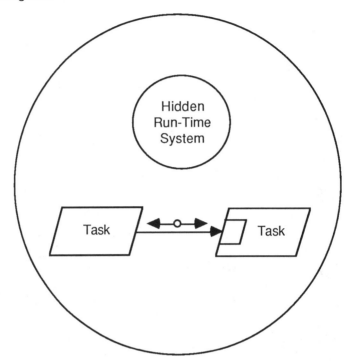

Rendezvous is single mechanism for
data access and other synchronization.

Figure 1-3. Ada

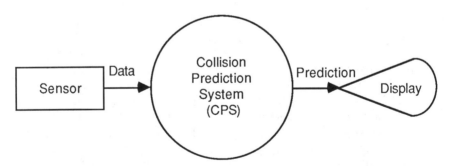

Figure 1-4. A context diagram

arrows. The context diagram can be decomposed into either traditional data flow diagrams [YOU79] or process graphs.

1.3.2 Process Graphs

A process graph is a picture of a concurrent system; it shows the individual sequential processes and their interactions. Each process, at the level of abstraction shown, represents a single, sequential thread of control. The processes together are concurrent, defining multiple threads of control. Figure 1-5 is a process graph.

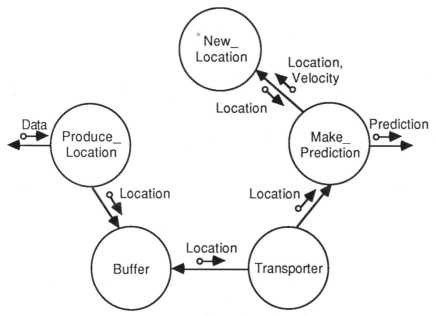

Figure 1-5. A process graph

Each process is represented by a circle. The arrows (directed arcs) between circles represent process interactions. The base of the arrow denotes the *calling* task, the one that issues a call to an entry of the *called* task. The arrowhead touches the called task, the one that declares an entry and accepts the entry call. The small arrow represents the direction of flow of data. The name of the data is near the small arrow. The direction of flow of the data is independent of the direction of call. There may be data flow in both directions.

Process graphs are sometimes called *abstract* process graphs since they are an abstract representation of processes; they are sometimes called *concurrent* process graphs since they represent concurrency; and they are sometimes called *hierarchical* process graphs since they may be further decomposed in a hierarchical manner, much like the data flow diagrams they resemble. We may use any of these names, depending on which process graph feature we want to emphasize.

The process graph, because of its simplicity, is ideal for the sort of evaluation, rethinking, and modification that goes on during the design of concurrent systems. It helps focus on abstract notions of concurrency, while ignoring detail that is not important at an early stage of design. It allows teams of people to discuss and cooperate on the design of task interaction. Further, its simplicity makes it easy to use as a pencil and paper method (although automation would be useful).

We will use the process graph to represent the graphical portion of the top-level design for case studies in the book. We will also use it to help explain concurrency by illustrating specific paradigms of task interaction and providing pictures of small programs. Refinements to the basic concept of the process graph will be introduced as they are required.

1.3.3 Dependency Graphs

The dependency graph shows all the library units in a software design, and the "withing" dependency. Figure 1-6 is a dependency graph. The arrows originate in the dependent unit, while the arrowheads touch the "withed" unit. The picture distinguishes whether the dependent unit has the context clause preceding its specification or body. If the context clause is associated with a subunit of the body, it is shown as being with the body.

It is not the intent of the dependency graph to give a complete illustration of compilation or logical dependencies, but rather to give an overall picture of the Ada units.

1.3.4 Structure Graphs

A structure graph is a picture of Ada tasks, subprograms, and packages. It identifies tasks, their entries, and their calls; it shows tasks as encapsulated in packages; it identifies procedures; and it illustrates the data flow between and within packages. Figure 1-7 is a structure graph. The large rectangles are packages; the small rectangles on the inside edges of the packages are procedures declared in the package specification; the parallelograms are tasks, with their entries shown as small, labeled parallelograms on the inside edges of the task. The data flow is shown in a manner similar to that in process graphs.

Structure graphs were first illustrated by Buhr [BUH84] and are sometimes called "Buhr charts." We later describe refinements to the basic notions presented above, but we shall not use all of Buhr's

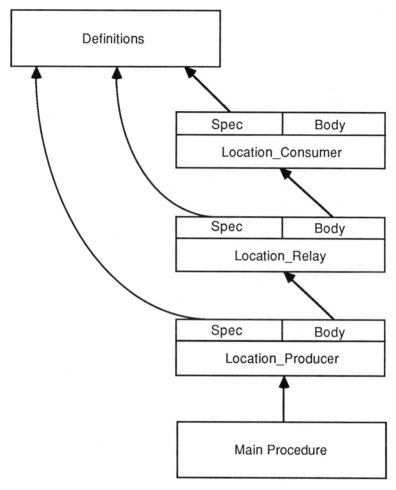

Figure 1-6. A dependency graph

notation; his notation is considerably more complete and complex than required for the case studies in this book.

The structure graph is isomorphic to the Ada detailed design and resulting code; there is a one-to-one correspondence between the structure graph and the portions of the Ada code dealing with process interfaces and interactions. The structure graph reflects packaging decisions, identifies specific program units and entries, and indicates specific calling relationships and data flows. It provides a compact picture of the organization of the actual program.

We use the structure graph to introduce the detailed design of the case studies in the book. It provides a picture of the design and helps to organize discussion and thought about the design.

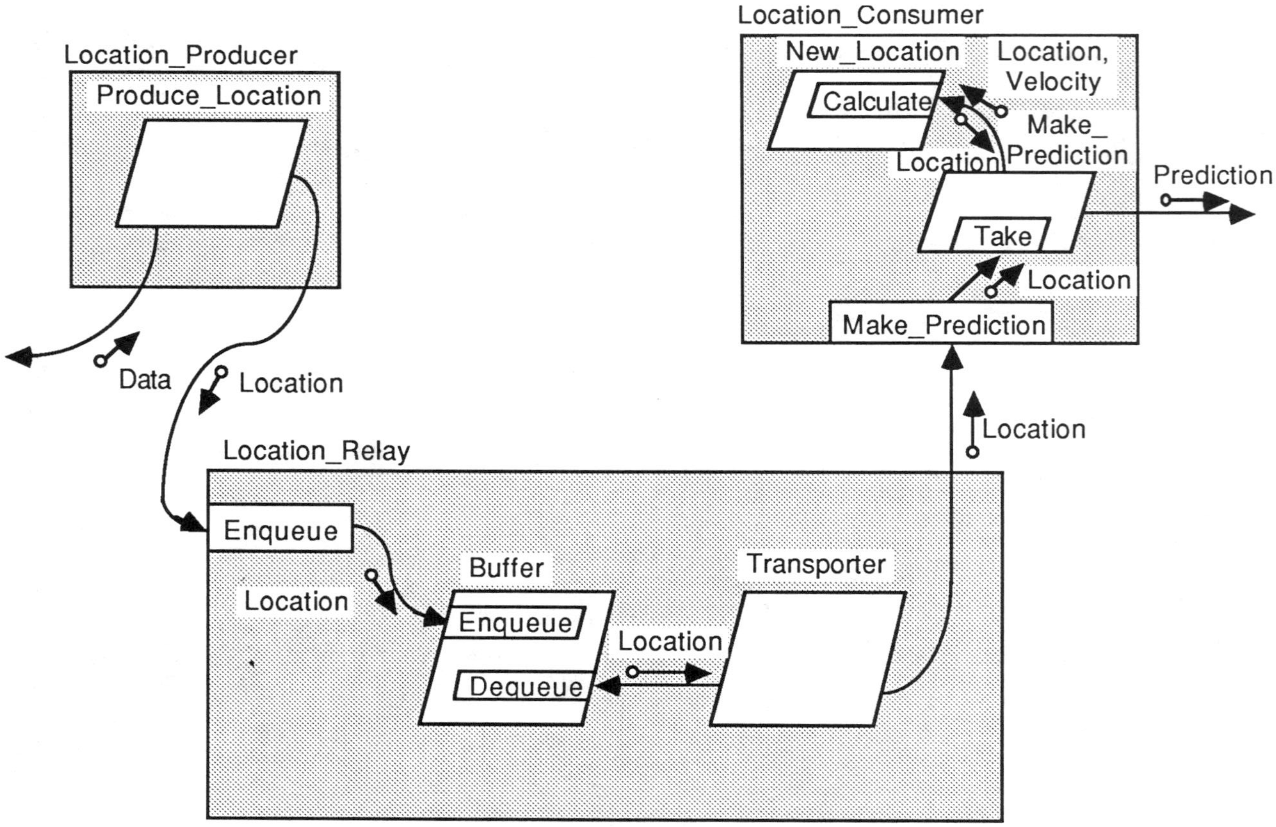

Figure 1-7. A structure graph

1.4 Exercises

There are three sorts of exercises in this book: individual problems to be solved at the end of chapters, exercises at the end of case studies that extend or modify the solution presented, and a series of related problems grouped together in an appendix. These are the "cobbler" problems. They start as a simple exercise, then evolve into more complex problems. Alternate solutions to the problems are presented. Many chapters in the book refer to the problems in the appendix.

The exercises are an inherent part of the text of the book. All short exercises are solved and discussed. Some of the exercises at the conclusion of the case studies are solved. The exercises are not presented merely to expand on earlier material; they often introduce new material. Even if you do not wish to attempt the exercises yourself, it is important to read the problem and analyze the solution presented.

1.5 Case Studies

A major feature of this book is the five case studies. They are simplified versions of large real-time systems. The simplification is largely in the algorithms and the internal details of the tasks; the task interactions themselves are nearly as complex as those in an actual real-time system.

The case studies are intended to help you understand the concurrent features of Ada and how tasks are used to solve problems. Only a large problem, or a model of a large problem, can give insight into how the tasking features interact to allow effective task synchronization, communication, and concurrent operation.

Each case study consists of:

- A statement of the problem to be solved
- The top-level design
- The detailed design
- The coded tasks
- A discussion
- Additional exercises, some with partial solutions

Frequently you will be given information about certain system components or told to assume their existence. This is particularly true for the first two case studies, where the problem is even more simplified. Because the algorithms have been simplified for each case study, you should be able to develop all required code to meet the stated requirement.

You should read the material even if you do not solve the problem yourself, since the discussion is often used to emphasize material presented earlier or to introduce new material that is best presented in the context of a real problem.

Each case study will follow the format specified below.

Case Study Format

Each case study will have both a full title, such as "Hot Line Communication System," and a short title, such as "HLCS."

Software Requirements Specification

The first paragraphs of the case study will present the software requirement (i.e., the statement of the problem to be satisfied). Figure 1 (of the case study) will provide an illustration of the problem.

The requirement will occasionally be moderately directive in terms of how the problem is to be solved. This is to ensure that the learning objectives of the case study are satisfied.

Following the requirement itself is the environment or context for the system to be developed. This may be a discussion of the hardware interfaces, or a description of already existing packages of software that provide the interface to the hardware. Figure 2 of the case study will be a context diagram. The environment is considered to be part of the explanation of the problem to be solved.

After carefully reading the requirements specification and the environment section, you should attempt to develop a complete solution—or at least a top-level design that deals with concurrency issues and data flow between tasks. You should focus your attention on the task interactions.

Top-Level Design

This section will provide a solution to the requirement at an abstract level using process graphs, written descriptions of what each process does, package specifications that define the interface between major program units, and an abstract outline of the algorithm that describes the functioning of each process. The design will be presented in two sections:

- *Graphical design.* Process graphs and "minispecs" that describe the functions accomplished by each process

- *Package specifications.* The interfaces between major units, and a high-level description of the algorithms of the major components of the package

The graphical design will be completed for all packages, followed by the specifications for all packages. The graphical design will be accompanied by case study Figure 3 to provide process graphs, while the package specifications will be introduced by case study Figure 4, a dependency graph.

Detailed Design

The detailed design also consists of two steps:

- *Package bodies.* The code of package bodies, with tasks and procedures being declared as separate
- *Subunits.* The bodies of the separate tasks and procedures, containing pseudocode to describe algorithms

Both steps will be completed for each package, before presenting the design of the next package. The detailed design will be introduced by providing a structure graph (as case study Figure 5), the road map to the design.

The detailed design begins with the development of the package bodies. Here we will see the task specifications, procedure specifications for hidden functions performed in the package body, and any data structures that are hidden within the package body. The task and procedure bodies will be declared as stubs, using the "separate" clause. Certain types of procedures (which we call "entrance procedures") are used merely to provide access (for processes outside the package being designed) to tasks hidden in the package body. These procedures will be completely specified.

The next step of the detailed design is the refinement of both the task and procedure bodies. The data structures are at least partially defined, and algorithms of the sequence of statements of the bodies are given in detail. Ada constructs will be used to indicate the major flow of execution in the task or procedure body (loops, if-then-else, accepts, select statements, and so on), but not at a coding level. The algorithms are complete in terms of how a function is to be performed, but coding details are omitted; the algorithms are presented in an abstract form as pseudocode. Calls to external procedures and entries may be completed at this stage, or simply be indicated as abstract calls.

Code

The final step in the solution of the stated problem is the refinement of the pseudocode into complete Ada. Coding details not provided in the pseudocode description of the algorithm are added, data structures are completed, and the remaining procedure and entry calls are added.

NOTE

The overall process of top-level design, detailed design, and code is summarized in Figure 1-8.

Discussion

The final section discusses the overall solution and introduces possible alternative approaches.

Additional Exercises

Additional exercises will be provided, building on the case study and pointing out additional aspects of the software requirement. Some of these exercises will be partially solved. Here is a summary of the five case studies.

- *Hot Line Communication System (HLCS)*. Illustrates the overall architecture of an Ada concurrent program. It introduces notions of how intermediary tasks are used.

- *Air Track Display System (ATDS)*. Illustrates a more complex model of task interaction. It is a large problem that hints at the complexity of real-time systems.

- *Message Transmission System (MTS)*. Illustrates a specific paradigm for a user-server relationship.

- *Multiple Keyboard Handler (MKH)*. Illustrates interaction with an external device.

- *Remote Temperature Sensor (RTS)*. Illustrates a complex system that interacts with several external devices using interrupt handlers.

1.6   Organization of the Book

It is important to understand how the different portions of the book interrelate. The sections below discuss the structure of the book, then the general contents of the parts and chapters.

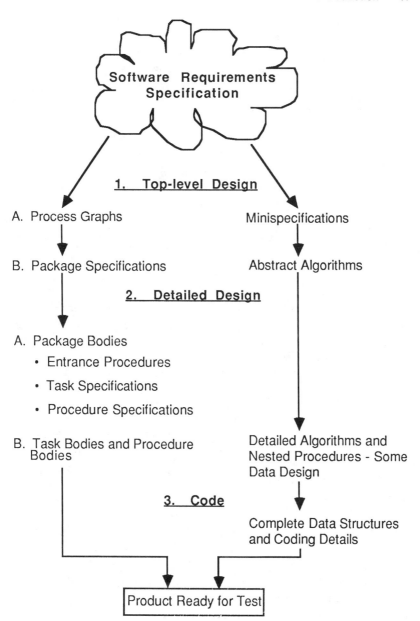

Figure 1-8. From SRS to complete code

1.6.1 Structure

The book has four parts. Each concludes with a case study. (Part 4 has two case studies.) The parts are composed of separate chapters organized around different aspects of the language and how it is used. Each chapter starts with the objective of the chapter. The chapter is decomposed into as many sections as necessary to make its point. Many of the chapters contain exercises and associated discussions. The series of cobbler problems, presented in the appendixes, is a thread connecting many of the discussions. Each chapter concludes with a summary of important issues; we call these "Keys to Understanding."

1.6.2 The Parts and Chapters

Part 1, Foundation, is introductory. Chapter 2 provides a complete overview of Ada tasking. The case study in Chapter 3 serves as an example of a complete Ada system.

Part 2, Task Intercommunication, deals with information flow between tasks and introduces several important models of asynchronous message passing. Chapter 4 addresses the rendezvous in great detail, with particular emphasis on the mechanisms by which tasks control and participate in a rendezvous. Chapter 5 distinguishes between tasks that issue entry calls and tasks that declare entries and accept calls. It points out that a degree of asymmetry in the capabilities of calling and called tasks makes the distinction important. Chapters 6 through 8 introduce intermediary or "third-party" tasks that allow the programmer to control the degree of synchronous-asynchronous behavior. The case study in Chapter 9 illustrates the methods of task intercommunication described.

Part 3, Task Manipulation, deals with some very detailed issues of how tasks operate and how they can be used. Chapter 10 introduces the idea of a task object created through the use of a task type and shows how task objects can be manipulated. Chapters 11 and 12 tell how tasks start and stop, based on the normal Ada visibility and elaboration rules. They do not discuss the rules concerning activation and termination of tasks created through the use of allocators. These topics are presented in Chapter 13, which centralizes all the information about such tasks. The case study in Chapter 14 involves the use of arrays of tasks. A solved exercise uses an agent task created through the evaluation of an allocator.

Part 4, Tasks in Real-Time Systems, addresses low-level issues that are of particular importance for real-time systems. It includes two case studies in order to provide additional illustration of all the aspects of concurrency covered in the book. Chapter 15 gives details about machine-level issues other than interrupt handling. The case study in Chapter 16 addresses a task as a device driver for a set of keyboards that do not interrupt the processor, but rather interact through a hardware buffer. The use of tasks to handle interrupts is addressed in Chapter 17. Examples about the use of tasks as handlers for interrupt-driven devices are given in the context of an earlier case study. The case study in Chapter 18 uses interrupts to manage several external devices. It illustrates additional topics related to the design of a realistic real-time system.

Keys to Understanding

- This book is about Ada tasks and how they can be used in the development of real-time systems. Ada's facilities for concurrency are an integral part of the language.

- Each chapter starts with "Objective" and ends with a summary of important issues: "Keys to Understanding."

- The problems at the end of chapters are an integral part of the chapter material.

- Graphical methods are vital to understanding the design of a concurrent system. We use four tools:

  Context diagrams to show interfaces to the world outside the system to be developed

  Process graphs to illustrate the top-level design in an abstract fashion

  Dependency diagrams to provide a simplified overall view of the system software architecture

  Structure graphs to provide a detailed road map to the interfaces and data flow of the final program

- The case studies are a major part of the book. Although simplified, they are representative of actual real-time systems. They are solved through use of a methodical design process. Each case study includes:

  Software requirements specification

  Top-level design

  Detailed design

  Code

Discussion

Additional exercises and partial solutions

- The Cobbler problems in the appendixes provide a set of graduated examples to illustrate the major client-server models of interaction.
- Together, the four parts of the book and the appendixes provide detailed coverage of tasks in Ada.

2

Overview of
Concurrency in Ada*

> Objective: To review some elementary tasking concepts, to provide a brief background on historical methods for control of concurrent processes, and to summarize the main concepts of tasks in Ada

The programming language Ada is likely to become the most widely used language for the programming of real-time systems, and will also become important as a general-purpose language. It is the standard language for the development of U.S. Government software, and it is an ANSI and ISO standard. An important aspect of Ada for its use in real-time systems is its model of concurrency: the

---

*Material in this chapter has been adapted from the author's Portfolio 13-02-65, "Ada Tasks: Concurrency for Real-Time Systems." Copyright 1987 Auerbach Pub. Inc. Computer Programming Management. Used with permission.

Ada task. Further, the Ada tasking model, particularly the rendezvous for mutual exclusion and synchronization, is of considerable theoretical interest in that it has not before been available in a widely used language. This chapter introduces the concept of tasking in Ada in a simple way but also provides a thorough discussion of Ada's mechanisms for task control.

2.1   Introduction

The purpose of this chapter is to provide a general understanding of tasks in Ada, and to explain how tasks can be used in real-time systems. It includes an introduction and background on some general topics related to concurrency and mutual exclusion.

The sections that follow first introduce the basic notions of the Ada tasking model and provide an overview of some issues and problems related to concurrent execution of processes. Then the details of Ada tasking are presented, by covering interprocess communication via the rendezvous, methods to control the rendezvous, activation and termination of tasks, and use of task types. The final major section introduces the use of tasks in conjunction with machine-level constructs for programming a device driver for a real-time system.

2.2   The Ada Tasking Model

Tasks provide a means of expressing concurrent (simultaneous or parallel) execution. The concurrent execution may be actual (with two or more processors) or apparent (with interleaved execution on a single processor). We can illustrate the idea of concurrency with an abstraction of a business problem.

Suppose that the accounting office of a small firm is responsible for carrying out these functions or tasks:

Ordering supplies

Paying bills

Preparing invoices

With one accountant, the process might be represented as:

```
procedure Accounting is
begin
  Order_Supplies;
  Pay_Bills;
```

```
    Prepare_Invoices;
  end Accounting;
```

With three accountants, however, the tasks could be performed in parallel. A typical Ada representation of such a situation might be:

```
    procedure Accounting is

        task Order;
        task body Order is
        begin                        declarative
          Order_Supplies;
        end Order;

        task Pay;                    part
        task body Pay is
        begin
          Pay_Bills;
        end Pay;

      begin          ←——— here all parallel
        Prepare_Invoices;
      end Accounting;
```

Notice that there is a distinct and separate specification for each task. For example,

```
    task Order;
```

The specification is followed by a body or implementation describing what the task does. For example,

```
    task body Order is
    . . .
    end Order;
```

The task specification is used to describe the interface presented to other tasks. In this case the tasks present no interface, so the declarations involve only the statement of the name.

The way we organized the tasks in procedure Accounting, which is the *master* of the tasks and also called the *parent*, has the effect of assigning the invoice function to the chief accountant, with ordering supplies and paying of bills being left to the assistants. Of course, the chief accountant first assigns the assistants to work. Hence, in Ada, tasks are declared in the declarative part of the parent procedure. Then, upon reaching the *begin* of the parent procedure, they are set active in parallel ("assigned to work"). The statements of the parent procedure (which carry out the invoicing) are then activated and execute in parallel with the other tasks.

It is also permissible to declare all three processes as tasks. In this case, the executable part of procedure Accounting would contain a *null* statement, and serve only to activate the three processes that perform the work.

The net effect, with either style of declaring the tasks, is that there are three separate threads of control: all three processes execute at the same time. This is shown in Figure 2-1.

begin -- Accounting

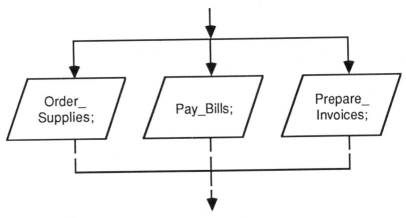

end Accounting;

Figure 2-1. Three accounting tasks accomplished in parallel

Each task terminates normally when it completes execution. However, the master cannot be left until all the dependent tasks have terminated. The master can be a subprogram, a block, a task body, or a library package. It is a construct in which tasks have been declared. This termination rule is important, since it implies that tasks are not completely autonomous agents, but are nested within, and depend upon, some other unit. The rule ensures that the resources necessary to the task, likely to be declared in the parent unit, will be in scope during the lifetime of the task. For our example, this means that if invoicing is complete prior to completion of the tasks Order and Pay, procedure Accounting waits for termination of the subordinate tasks before it completes.

Although the example above illustrates concurrency, it does not require any cooperation among the tasks; they simply execute independently. After we introduce some basic notions and problems of process coordination, we will introduce the Ada mechanism for task synchronization and mutual exclusion.

2.3 Concurrent Process Coordination

There are a number of difficult synchronization problems that can arise in the coordination of concurrent programs. We will focus on the type of problem that deals with mutual exclusion and present several methods of solution.

Concurrent processes that share data face potential problems in access to the data; without special consideration, the processes may be incorrect as a result of simultaneous access to the data. Preventing simultaneous access is not easy.

The sections below first provide some definitions dealing with concurrent access to data, demonstrate why concurrent systems have a problem dealing with shared data, and then introduce mechanisms for safe access to shared data.

This is by no means an exhaustive discussion of this topic; it is the barest overview to introduce this fundamental issue of concurrency in order to lay the foundation for the following discussion of Ada tasking. The references provide additional information on these topics.

2.3.1 Definitions

The words and phrases we will define are:

- Sequential program
- Concurrent program
- Interleaved
- Race condition
- Atomic/indivisible
- Mutual exclusion
- Critical section
- Safety
- Deadlock and starvation
- Liveness

- Semaphore
- Critical region
- Monitor

Although we will group all definitions here, these definitions will be restated/elaborated as they are used in the context of specific examples throughout the chapter.

We must first distinguish between a sequential program and a concurrent program.

A *sequential program* executes a list of statements one after the other. Iteration and selection among alternatives is accomplished by appropriate control constructs.

A *concurrent program* specifies two or more separate threads of control (each being a sequential program) that execute concurrently.

We will call the two threads of control, the two processes, P1 and P2.

The execution of P1 and P2 is said to be *interleaved* if the instructions of P1 and P2 can be considered to be more or less alternately executed (i.e., a few instructions of P1, a few instructions of P2, a few of P1, and so on).

This is easy to see if there are two processors (since the execution of P1 and P2 are actually concurrent or simultaneous), but the same effect may prevail on a single processor. You can imagine that a coin is flipped before each instruction to be executed. If the coin is heads, the instruction to be executed is the next instruction in P1. If the coin is tails, the instruction is from P2. Thus we get the effect of interleaving.

Of course, this is not the way systems really work. But the occurrence of asynchronous interrupts from external devices (and the nondeterministic scheduling of processes resulting from the effect of the interrupt) gives essentially the same effect in terms of how we must think about real-time systems.

Since the two processes are proceeding independently and potentially at different rates (many heads or tails in a row as a result of random variation or a coin that is not fair), they might be considered as "racing" toward some destination. A *race condition* is a situation in which different results are obtained, depending upon which process wins the race.

If there is a certain block of code that we wish to not participate in the race, we must ensure that the code is executed indivisibly. A statement or sequence of statements that is executed in an *atomic* or *indivisible* manner is *not* interleaved with some other specific sequence of statements in a different process (or several different processes).

This notion deals with blocks of code in different processes that are intimately related, typically because they are dealing with the *same data structure.* A block of code in P1 might be executed indivisibly with respect to a *specific* block of code in P2, but still be interleaved with other statements in P2 (or with statements from some other process).

We can restate the above somewhat more formally in a definition of *mutual exclusion.* Suppose that action A1 (in process P1) and action A2 (in process P2) are related in such a way that we do not wish the statements that accomplish A1 to be interleaved with the statements that accomplish A2. (That is, we wish A1 and A2 to be atomic or indivisible actions.)

If we arrange things so that P1 and P2 cannot simultaneously execute A1 and A2, then A1 and A2 are said to be executed in *mutual exclusion.* By simultaneous execution of A1 and A2, we specifically mean interleaved execution in the sense defined earlier.

What is meant by "arrange things" so there is no interleaving? If P1 and P2 attempt to simultaneously execute A1 and A2, we must guarantee that only one of them succeeds. The process that first reaches its action (wins the race, so to speak) will continue execution; the other process must block, or suspend, execution. It will be allowed to proceed when the first process finishes (we say "departs" the sequence of statements of the action). Methods for accomplishing mutual exclusion are discussed later in the chapter and in the exercises at the end.

A shorter definition is that *mutual exclusion* is the mechanism by which a task gains exclusive access to a shared resource.

A *critical section* is a sequence of statements of a process that must be executed in mutual exclusion. The actions A1 and A2 in the definition of mutual exclusion are accomplished by a sequence of statements in a critical section. We say that the sequence of statements to accomplish A1 is a critical section of P1, while the sequence of statements to accomplish A2 is the corresponding critical section of P2.

The code of a critical section accesses some shared resource (such as a shared data area). If the shared data were accessed by two or more tasks in a interleaved fashion—i.e., simultaneously—we might have erroneous access to the data. Remember that it is *not* the case that the code of the critical section cannot be interleaved—it just must not be interleaved with the code of the corresponding critical section.

A process is said to be *safe* if its critical section (actually, all its critical sections) are executed in mutual exclusion. Otherwise, *safety* is violated.

Deadlock is a situation in which processes are waiting for resources that will never be released. Imagine a circumstance in which *each* of P1 and P2 require *both* R1 and R2 in order to proceed. We have deadlock if the sequence of actions is:

- P1 acquires exclusive access to R1 (by entering a critical section).

- P2 acquires exclusive access to R2.

- P1 attempts to acquire exclusive access to R2—but blocks since it has been acquired by P2.

- P2 attempts to acquire exclusive access to R1—and also blocks since it has been acquired by P1!

Each process will wait forever for the other. Deadlock can be more complex, including the general case in which all processes are blocked. In this general case, the computer is no longer doing any useful work.

A subcategory of deadlock is *starvation*, a situation in which a single process is blocked for an arbitrarily long time. We consider a process to be *starved* unless we can guarantee that it will eventually proceed. (A related problem is not true starvation, but arises when a task is delayed so long that it cannot accomplish its function; we might think of such a task as being *hungry*. This sort of timing issue is a serious problem in real-time systems.)

Liveness is the property of a system that will not demonstrate deadlock or starvation.

The key definition of those given above is that of *mutual exclusion*. The other definitions were helping us define mutual exclusion and explaining why it is important. Now that we have all the definitions at our disposal, we can combine some of them in a restated definition of mutual exclusion. "Mutual exclusion is the mechanism for preventing race conditions and ensuring safety and liveness."

The next three definitions are short explanations of methods for implementing mutual exclusion, for controlling access to critical sections. The methods will be discussed at length later in the chapter.

A *semaphore* is a special-purpose integer used to keep track of the number of processes in a critical section. The only operations on the integer, called P- and V-operations, are used to announce entry into the critical section and signal departure from the critical section.

A *critical region* is a program construct that associates a shared variable with a region of code (a critical section) and ensures that the code is executed in mutual exclusion. The process incorporates compile-time checks on access to the shared variable that make it safer than the use of semaphores.

A *monitor* is a program construct that enforces a protocol of using procedures for access to shared data; the procedures are executed in mutual exclusion. We say that the monitor "encapsulates" the data and the procedures that access the data.

These definitions will be used, and expanded upon, in the sections to follow.

2.3.2 Problems with Unprotected Access to Data

We will use the single example of two processes sharing an integer variable. They will each increment the variable. This is a simplification of the more general problem of sharing a buffer area that contains signals and data. The same principles apply to the general problem.

We first illustrate how interleaving of statements of high-level languages can lead to errors. We then make the point that even high-level language statements are not executed atomically, but are potentially executed as a series of assembly language statements. We then illustrate how even very simple assignment statements can lead to incorrect programs because of interleaving at the assembly language level.

2.3.2.1 High-Level Language.
One way that two separate sequential processes may communicate is by using shared variables. They may use the value of the shared variable in some calculation, or they may use the shared variable to synchronize their actions. Here we will illustrate a simple (and incorrect) way to access a shared variable without considering the requirements of mutual exclusion.

Suppose we have two processes, P1 and P2, that access a shared variable, Item, with an initial value of 17.* P1 and P2 both print and update Item. The processes are:

```
ACTION OF P1                          ACTION OF P2

Put (Item);      -- statement 1    Put (Item); -- statement 3
Item := Item + 1; -- statement 2    Item := 0;  -- statement 4
```

We must make no assumption about the relative speeds of the processes P1 and P2; they may be executing on separate processors, with Item in shared memory, or they may be executing in an

---

*This example is adapted from CEN84, page 1-4.

indeterminate interleaved fashion on a single processor—the effect is the same.

If the order of the statements is (1, 2, 3, 4), then a 17 and 18 are printed, and Item is set to 0.

If the order is (3, 4, 1, 2), then a 17 and a 0 are printed, and Item is set to 1. If the order is (3, 1, 4 2), then a 17 and a 17 are printed, while Item is again set to 1.

You can see that the result of the execution of the two processes is unpredictable. Furthermore, it is not typically reproducible, since the result depends upon the underlying mechanism of concurrency and, in real-time systems, interaction with external devices.

The example illustrates what is called a *race condition*. A race condition is a set of circumstances in which the relative speeds of two processes influences the result of program execution. Race conditions, with their typical irreproducibility of results, are what make the construction of reliable, error-free, concurrent systems so difficult.

The above example made the implicit assumption that the increment statement was *atomic*, that is, it was performed as an indivisible action. In reality, on many processors the statement would compile to several machine-level statements. We illustrate the associated problems below.

2.3.2.2 Assembly Language.

Suppose the two processes, P1 and P2, were each incrementing the shared variable Item, still initially set to 17. The situation is:

STEP	ACTION OF P1	ITEM	ACTION OF P2
1.		17	
2.	Item := Item + 1;	18	
3.		19	Item := Item + 1;

This works fine if we are lucky. But it is easy to get unlucky. Remember that the assignment may not be an indivisible (uninterruptible) process. Specifically, the incrementing of Item may involve, at the assembly language level, three instructions:

Load Item   (to a local register)
Add 1   (to register)
Store Item   (register contents to Item)

The interleaving may now occur as shown below.

STEP	ACTION OF P1	ITEM	ACTION OF P2
1.		17	
2.	Load Item (to P1's local register)	17	
3.		17	Load Item (to P2's local register)
4.	Add 1 (to P1's local register)	17	
5.		17	Add 1 (to P2's local register)
6.	Store Item	18	
7.		18	Store Item

If we are unlucky in terms of how the instruction interleaving takes place, we can increment Item twice, but only raise it from 17 to 18. This happens because the incrementing (in this example) is to the local values of Item in each of P1 and P2. Since they each increase the value of Item to 18 and then store that value, Item does not receive the correct value of 19.

The underlying problem illustrated in the two examples above is that, whether we view the situation from the high-level or assembly language position, the assignment

```
Item := Item + 1;
```

is a *critical section*. A critical section is a part of a program that must be executed in *mutual exclusion* in order to ensure correct operation.

Mutual exclusion is a property of an activity (such as incrementing Item) of some process (say, P1) that is guaranteed to not overlap (i.e., have interleaved execution with) some specified activity of some other process (say, P2). If P1 and P2 attempt to simultaneously execute their respective activities, one of the processes must block.

This is another way of saying that the code in the critical section must be executed atomically, or indivisibly. Note that the ideas of mutual exclusion and atomic/indivisible execution are relative to some other *specific activity* of some other *specific process*. (This typically has to do with access to some resource.) We do not care if the critical section's execution is interleaved with some other process's function that is unconnected with the critical section.

The idea of mutual exclusion, of two processes synchronizing their activities or access to some data, is fundamental to understanding concurrency. In fact, Ben-Ari [BEN84] contends that, "The basic concurrent programming problem is mutual exclusion."

An alternative to viewing the problem as that of mutual exclusion is to state that the processes P1 and P2 must *synchronize* their access to the shared variable. One might even view synchronization as a more general principle than mutual exclusion. Gehani's position is that "A special case of synchronization is mutual exclusion" [GEH84]. We will focus on the critical section problem with the viewpoint of mutual exclusion, but understanding that we are also dealing with synchronization.

2.3.3 Traditional Methods of Ensuring Mutual Exclusion

This section presents a simplified version of three approaches to sharing data. They are:

- Semaphores
- Critical regions
- Monitors

2.3.3.1 Semaphores. Dijkstra [DIJ68] introduced the notion of semaphores. A semaphore is:

- A special purpose, nonnegative integer with two primitive special-purpose operations, P and V.

With S (the semaphore) initialized to 1, the operations are defined as:

- P: For P (S),

```
if S = 0 then
    block the process that called P;
```

```
        else
          S := S - 1;
        end if;
```

- V: For V (S),

```
        if <some process is blocked as a result of P(S)> then
            unblock (transition state to ready) the process;
        else
          S := S + 1;
        end if;
```

The initials P and V are from the Dutch (Dijkstra's native language) words "Passeren" (to pass) and "Vrygeven" (to release). The P- and V-operations themselves must be indivisible operations executed in mutual exclusion. Two processes can use the semaphore to cooperate upon access to a critical section. Each process does a P-operation before entering a critical section and a V-operation when leaving a critical section. This guarantees that the critical section (for example, Item := Item + 1;) is executed indivisibly.

Figure 2-2 illustrates the use of semaphores to provide for mutually exclusive access to a critical section. (Some of the uses illustrated to show what problems may arise by using semaphores are incorrect.) In Figure 2-2, the critical section is a one-person sauna that is in great demand. It has a sign that indicates whether the sauna is in use. When someone wishes to use the sauna, he sets the sign to "In Use"—this is the same as a P-operation on a semaphore. When he is finished with the sauna, he sets the sign to "Available"—this is the same as a V-operation on the semaphore.

The people who wish to use the sauna are tasks or processes that are executing concurrently and wish to use the critical section. If everyone uses the sign correctly, the sauna will be enjoyed in mutual exclusion.

The steps below explain the 13 conditions illustrated in Figure 2-2.

1. The sign is initially set to available and the sauna is empty.

2. A person starts to use the sauna, setting the sign to "In Use."

3. Another person arrives and wishes to use the sauna, but waits since he sees that the sauna is in use.

4. The first person finishes, resets the sign to "Available,", and slips out the back "exit only" door.

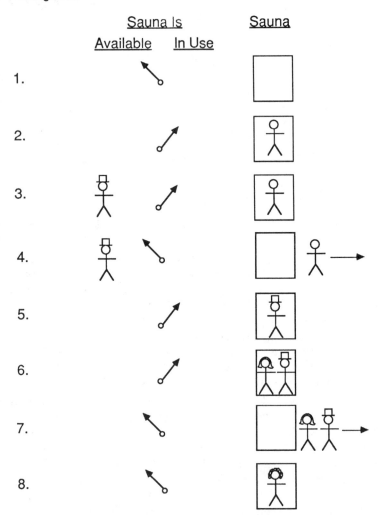

Figure 2-2. Use of the semaphore

5.   The first person in line enters the sauna and changes the sign. (If there had been many people in line, the first would have entered while the rest continued to wait.)

6.   Someone comes along, forgets to check the sign, and enters the sauna. We now have a problem: two people are in the sauna at the same time. (This is against the rules.) Note that even if other people had been waiting, this person would have gone immediately into the sauna.

7.   The original person finishes using the sauna, changes the sign, and departs through the rear exit. The person who forgot to

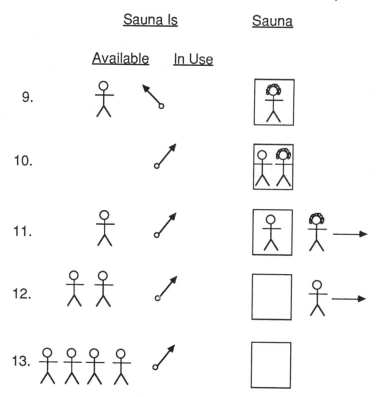

Figure 2-2. (continued)

check the sign also leaves. (They have gotten to be good friends while in the sauna.)

8. Another person comes along and begins to use the sauna, but has forgotten to change the sign to "In Use."

9. The next person comes along and sees that the sauna is available.

10. The person enters the sauna. We again have a problem with two people in the sauna at the same time. At least the last person to enter the sauna remembered to change the sign, or more people might arrive and enter the sauna.

11. Someone does arrive, and waits in line. One of the people leaves the sauna by the back door.

12. The other person in the sauna leaves, but forgets to change the sign.

13. A very long line is going to form.

Let's look at some additional characteristics of semaphores, and then a complete example, revisiting our attempt to have two processes correctly increment a shared variable.

- P and V are the only allowable operations.
- If S initially is 1 and is used only for mutual exclusion, i.e., a series of (P (S) . . . V (S)), it only assumes values of O and 1 (i.e., a *binary* semaphore). Otherwise it is a general semaphore.
- Many semaphores—S1, S2, etc.—may be defined.
- *P/V illustration.* Here are some typical situations, using the two processes P1 and P2. Assume S is initially 1:

    P1 calls P (S) = > S := 0;

    P1 calls V (S) = > S := 1;

    P1 calls P (S) = > S := 0;

    P2 calls P (S) = > S = 0 (already) = > P2 sleeps

    P1 calls V (S) = > P2 awakes (S still 0)

    P2 calls V (S) = > S := 1;

Here is a complete example program using Ada syntax. We assume the P- and V-operations are provided externally and that the type Semaphore has been defined elsewhere. Ada does not provide P- and V-operations itself (although we could construct them); we are simply using Ada syntax to illustrate the use of semaphores.

```
procedure Mutual_Exclusion is

   Item : Integer   := 17;
   S    : Semaphore := 1;

   task P1;
   task P2;

   task body P1 is
   begin
      loop
         ... -- code before critical section
         ...
```

```
P (S); -- here is the critical section
   Item := Item + 1;
V (S); -- this ends the critical section

... -- code after critical section
...
   end loop;
end P1;

task body P2 is
begin
   loop
     P (S);
        Item := Item + 1;
     V (S);
   end loop;
end P2;

begin -- Mutual_Exclusion
   null;
end Mutual_Exclusion;
```

Suppose P1 reaches the P-operation before P2 does. It enters the critical section. Suppose that in the middle of P1's execution of the critical section, the instruction interleaving causes P2 to execute the P-operation. Since S is 0, P2 is suspended. Its execution ceases. When P1 executes the V-operation, P2 becomes eligible for execution again. Of course if there are other processes in the system, they may get to execute before P2.

Although the semaphore provides a simple mechanism for ensuring mutual exclusion, there are potential problems. The programmers writing P1 and P2 could forget to use the P- and V-operations; they could interchange the P and V; they could directly branch into a critical section; or they could commit other errors. Some of these errors would violate *safety* (simultaneous execution of a critical section); others would violate *liveness*. Liveness is lost when a program reaches a stage of *deadlock*—a situation in which a system having two or more tasks is forever unable to proceed because each task is waiting for another to do something first, typically free some resource.

To overcome these problems, Hoare and Brinch Hansen proposed the *critical region*.

2.3.3.2 Critical Regions. An important ingredient in the potential misuse of semaphores is that the compiler cannot assist the programmer. It does not have the information to recognize that a semaphore is related to a shared variable and has no mechanism to enforce consistent use of the P- and V-operations.

It is to improve this situation that Brinch Hansen [BRI73] suggested what he calls a "structured notation for shared variables and critical regions." The *critical region* is the mechanism for ensuring mutually exclusive access to the critical section. The critical region is part of a program associated with a shared variable that will be executed atomically, or in mutual exclusion. The critical region guarantees that a critical section will not be violated.

(We are simplifying the notion of the critical region; there is much more to the concept, including *conditional critical regions* to address the issue of synchronization.)

For our P1/P2 example, Brinch Hansen's notation is:

```
var Item :  shared Integer;
```

In both P1 and P2 the only way to access and change the shared variable is:

```
region Item do
  Item := Item + 1;
end;
```

The statements (there may be more than one) within the critical region from "region . . . end;" have exclusive access to the shared variable. By explicitly associating the critical region and the associated variable Item, the compiler has the information to ensure that the value is not accessed outside the critical region. Furthermore, it can guarantee that the critical region is properly opened and closed, and that no branches are taken into (or out of) the critical region.

Brinch Hansen feels that, "It is perfectly reasonable to use semaphores in the underlying implementation of this language feature, but at higher levels of programming the explicit use of semaphores to achieve mutual exclusion is debatable." Ada does not directly support the critical region (there is no "shared" or "region" construct); we are simply using an Ada-like syntax to illustrate the critical region.

2.3.3.3 Monitors. An even higher level, more abstract mechanism for guaranteeing mutual exclusion is the *monitor*. A monitor is a module that protects some shared data by only allowing access to the data via procedures controlled by the monitor.

The basic feature of a monitor is that it includes (or encapsulates) two things:

- A collection of shared data
- The procedures that access the data

The critical sections are within the monitor procedures.

The monitor ensures that only one process may be executing in the monitor (i.e., executing one of the procedures) at any one time, and ensures that the shared data are not accessed outside the monitor. Hence mutual exclusion is ensured. The monitor was proposed by Brinch Hansen [BRI73b] and further developed by Hoare [HOA74]. A monitor for our P1/P2 example is:

```
monitor Item_Section is -- ** this is not Ada

   Item : Integer;

   procedure Add (Amount : in Integer) is
   begin
     Item := Item + Amount;
   end Add;

begin -- initialization of the monitor
   Item := 17;
end Item_Section;
```

(Ada does not directly support a "monitor" construct. We are just using an Ada-like syntax to represent the monitor.)

The effect of the monitor is that calls are serialized so that the procedure Add is executed in an indivisible manner on behalf of each caller. The initialization portion of the monitor is executed only once—prior to the monitor's accepting any calls to the monitor procedure. The result is that Item is properly incremented by calls in P1 and P2 as:

```
         P1                              P2

Item_Section.Add (1);          Item_Section.Add (1);
```

The monitor will ensure that the two simultaneous calls are executed serially and indivisibly, so that the result is Item = 19.

2.3.4 Summary

The use of semaphores, critical regions, and monitors is considerably more complex than is shown above. The intent of the presentation has been to provide an overview of earlier methods of mutual exclusion in order to lay the foundation for the Ada approach presented in following sections.

The examples focused on the incrementing of a single variable. This is a simplification of the more general case of access to a record, access to a more complicated buffer area (perhaps containing signals and messages), and access to resources such as external hardware. Section 2.4 below addresses the general issue of interprocess communication in Ada. The specific issue of the critical section in Ada is addressed by the exercises at the end of the chapter, using an example of access to a record.

There are many other ways to provide for mutual exclusion and synchronization. One of the important ones, since it was partially the basis for the Ada rendezvous, is called Communicating Sequential Processes (CSP). It was developed by Hoare [HOA78]. It provides for interprocess communication by a mechanism of exchanging data between processes at a synchronization point. There are real-time executives based on a somewhat similar philosophy of passing messages between processes, but they usually do not combine message passing and synchronization in an intimate way. A survey of additional concurrent programming concepts is provided by Andrews [AND83] and many concepts are directly related to Ada by Ichbiah [ICH79].

2.4 Interprocess Communication

In the accounting example of Section 2.0, the tasks had no need to coordinate their actions in time and no need to pass information while they were executing—capabilities most parallel-processing applications require. We will illustrate Ada capabilities for task interaction, based on the *rendezvous*, through an example of a message-processing system. We will refer to this example throughout the remainder of the chapter.

The message-processing system has two components: 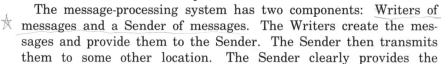 Writers of messages and a Sender of messages. The Writers create the messages and provide them to the Sender. The Sender then transmits them to some other location. The Sender clearly provides the service here and must have an entry into its process by which it can accept a message. Here is an example of a task specification that shows the entry being offered as an interface.

```
task Sender is
   entry Take_Message (Message : in Message_Format);
end Sender;
```

The task specification is essentially a contract. It may not contain type definitions, but it may contain entry declarations to establish an interface to the services provided by the task body. The entry declaration is much like a procedure declaration. The entry has the same format as a procedure and may have *in*, *out*, and *in out* parameters. The corresponding task body defines the processing done in the task, including an *accept statement* to fulfill the promise of the entry specification. The body of Sender is

```
task body Sender is
   Out_Going : Message_Format;

   procedure Transmit_Message (Message : in Message_Format) is
   . . .
   end Transmit_Message;
begin
   loop
     accept Take_Message (Message : in Message_Format) do
       Out_Going := Message;
     end Take_Message;

     Transmit_Message (Out_Going);
   end loop;
end Sender;
```

The general form of the accept statement,

```
accept Take_Message (. . .) do
   . . .
end Take_Message;
```

repeats the specification provided in the corresponding entry. The body of the accept statement consists of a sequence of statements with no declarative part. The entry is called by another task:

```
Sender.Take_Message (X);
```

in which the Task_Name.Entry_Name is used as in selected component notation. Note that the calling task must know the name of
the task providing the entry. The called task, however, does not
know the name of tasks that call its entries. In Writer the entry
call might appear as:

```
task Writer;
task body Writer is
  Story : Message_Format;

  procedure Create_Message (Message : out Message_Format) is
  . . .
  end Create_Message;
begin
  loop
    Create_Message (Story);
    Sender.Take_Message (Story);
  end loop;
end Writer;
```

The call Sender.Take_Message (Story) looks like a procedure call.
However, remember that Writer and Sender are operating in parallel. This has two important consequences for the interaction of the
rendezvous.

First, the rendezvous does not occur (the information is not passed
from one task to another) until a task calls the entry and the task
containing the entry reaches the accept statement. If the entry call
occurs first, the calling task (Writer) is suspended. It waits for the
called task to reach the accept statement. If the task providing the
entry (Sender) reaches the accept statement first, it waits until the
entry is called. When both conditions have been satisfied, the tasks
are synchronized and the information in the parameter list is
exchanged.

Second, the sequence of statements contained in the accept is considered to be executed by the called task on behalf of both tasks.
The tasks stay synchronized until the accept statement is complete.

There is a fundamental difference between a procedure call and a
call to an entry of a task. A procedure is executed upon demand,
and as part of the thread of control, of the caller. An accept statement, on the other hand, is under the control of the called task; the
called task may choose when (and whether) to accept the call, can
accept the call at different points in its thread of control (since there

may be many accept statements for a single entry), and may execute different code in each of the alternate accept statements. The called task is an autonomous entity, not a static section of program. These issues are discussed further in Chapter 4, Rendezvous.

The rendezvous joins together, into a single synchronized thread of control, what had been two separate threads of control. Information may be transmitted while the tasks are executing as a single thread of control. Hence the rendezvous is the Ada mechanism both for task coordination and for sharing of information. The joining of the threads of control is shown in Figure 2-3.

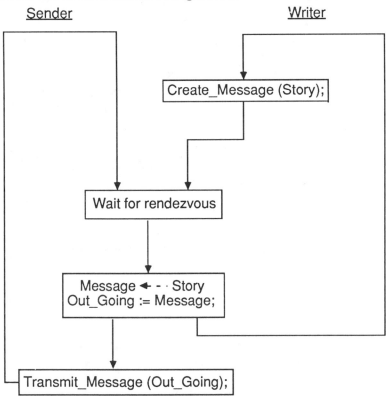

Figure 2-3. Sender/Writer task interaction

Initially, Sender must wait for Writer to complete the Create_Message. Then they rendezvous. This is followed by parallel processing of Transmit_Message and Create_Message.

If multiple processors were available, Transmit_Message and Create_Message could actually be executing at the same time. On a single processor the execution may be interleaved for an apparent concurrency. Whichever task completes its message processing first waits for the other. Then they rendezvous, and the cycle repeats.

To increase the amount of parallel processing by decreasing the amount of time spent waiting for a rendezvous, we might use a separate task as a buffer. Here is a task that can buffer a single item:

```
task Message_Box is
  entry Store_Message    (Message : in  Message_Format);
  entry Retrieve_Message (Message : out Message_Format);
end Message_Box;

task body Message_Box is
  Hold : Message_Format;
begin
  loop
    accept Store_Message (Message : in Message_Format) do
      Hold := Message;
    end Store_Message;

    accept Retrieve_Message (Message : out Message_Format) do
      Message := Hold;
    end Retrieve_Message;
  end loop;
end Message_Box;
```

In this case the Writer task would no longer call an entry in Sender, but would use the call,

```
Message_Box.Store_Message (Story);
```

and the Sender task would no longer have an accept statement. Instead, whenever it was ready to send another message, Sender would also call an entry in Message_Box:

```
Message_Box.Retrieve_Message (Out_Going);
```

Message_Box is designed to alternate between Store_Message and Retrieve_Message. It can buffer only one message, and after a Store_Message, will wait until a call to Retrieve_Message has occurred before it is prepared for another rendezvous with a call to Store_Message. Therefore, either Sender or Writer could still be waiting for a rendezvous.

The reason that the use of Message_Box improves concurrency is that the Writer can produce a message, pass it to Sender (through

Message_Box), prepare a second message, place it in the box, and start preparation of a third message *while Sender is still transmitting the first message.* If it were not for the intervening buffer of Message_Box, the Writer would be blocked instead of being able to create the third message. If the Writer finishes the creation of the third message before the first is transmitted, he will then block since the buffer is full. (This hints that a larger buffer will further increase the opportunities for concurrent operation. We will see much more of this issue, particularly in Chapter 7, The Bounded Buffer.)

So far we have considered only a single Writer and single Sender. Suppose, however, that there are several Writer tasks, each of which issues calls to Message_Box. The Store_Message entry may be called several times while Message_Box is waiting to rendezvous with Sender. In this case the calls are queued on a first-come–first-served basis. Of course, there might also be multiple Sender tasks that could issue calls to be queued for the Retrieve_Message rendezvous. Within the body of the task providing the entries, there is an attribute, 'Count, that allows the determination of how many tasks are on the queue for an entry. The attributes Store_Message'Count and Retrieve_Message'Count are the number of tasks queued for each of the two entries. Knowledge of the queue length might be used to choose among alternate accepts. Ada also provides some built-in mechanisms for selecting among accepts and for controlling entry calls. These are discussed in the next section.

Before leaving the rendezvous concept, we should pause and point out the asymmetric nature of the rendezvous and differentiate between "caller" and "called" tasks.

The rendezvous is asymmetric in two major ways:

1. The calling task must know the name of the called, or accepting, task as well as the specification of the entry point. The called task does not know the name of the caller. The task providing the entries and accepts is a server. It is essentially passive: it provides a service to any task that knows its name.

2. A task calling an entry point may be on only one queue at a time. It may choose between calls to alternate tasks, but is not allowed to wait for two entries in order to be served by the first one ready for rendezvous. On the other hand, a task providing entries may have a number of tasks queued waiting for service, at a number of different entry points.

In addition, a calling task may issue an entry call in a procedure nested within (or otherwise available to) the task. However, the called task may not accept a call in a nested procedure. All accept statements must be directly in the task body (between the *begin* and the *end*) of the task that declares the entries. This has implications for modularity: a calling task can have a functional decomposition into procedures that include calls to other tasks; a called task cannot have a functional decomposition into procedures that include accept statements.

Chapter 5, Calling and Called Tasks, discusses some minor additional differences and further implications for using tasks to build concurrent programs.

2.5   Control over the Rendezvous

Each of the two types of tasks we have been considering, the calling task and the called task, has a mechanism for controlling the rendezvous. For the called task it is the selective wait, and for the calling task it is conditional and timed entry calls. These mechanisms are described in the context of the message-processing system of the previous section.

2.5.1   Selective Wait

The selective wait provides a mechanism for a called task to select among alternative entry calls. It also has the option to selectively wait for a rendezvous (delaying a specified time interval), or to continue execution if no rendezvous is immediately available.

To improve the capabilities of the task Message_Box, we will allow it to accept either a Store_Message or a Retrieve_Message, whichever is available. This implies that two or more Store_Message entry calls without an intervening Retrieve_Message will cause overwriting of old messages, and multiple Retrieve_ Message calls without an intervening Store_Message will receive the same information. For systems passing perishable information such as aircraft location, this is a realistic situation.

Task Location_Message will select either a Store_Message or a Retrieve_Message.

```
task Location_Message is
  entry Store_Message    (Message : in  Message_Format);
  entry Retrieve_Message (Message : out Message_Format);
end Location_Message;
```

```
task body Location_Message is
  Hold : Message_Format;
begin
  accept Store_Message (Message : in Message_Format) do
    Hold := Message;
  end Store_Message;

  loop
    select
      accept Store_Message (Message : in Message_Format) do
        Hold := Message;
      end Store_Message;
      ... -- optional sequence_of_statements
    or
      accept Retrieve_Message (Message : out Message_Format) do
        Message := Hold;
      end Retrieve_Message;
      ... -- optional sequence_of_statements
    end select;
  end loop;
end Location_Message;
```

Location_Message does not accept only alternating Store_Message and Retrieve_Message calls as did Message_Box. It will accept *either* a call to Store_Message *or* a call to Retrieve_Message. This is the *selective wait*.

Location_Message ensures that it first accepts a Store_Message in order to provide a value for Hold. Location_Message will then accept multiple calls to the same entry to prevent queueing of calling tasks while it awaits a call to the other entry. However, if Location_Message entries are called at a faster rate than they can be serviced, there may still be a queue for each of the two entries in the select statement.

The method of choosing among the alternatives depends on the implementation. The language definition states that the selection is arbitrary, by some method not defined by the language.

Suppose we have a message-processing requirement in which the task Sender (or group of similar tasks) wishes only to send unique Messages. That is, if "Hold" in Location_Message has not received a new message, the task does not wish a rendezvous. However, the information is still perishable, so Store_Message entries will always be accepted. This is exactly the situation in aircraft tracking situations in which a number of sites share ("cross-tell") information on tracks. We can accomplish this type of processing by using the selective wait with a condition. Thus modified, Location_Message becomes Unique_Message:

```
task Unique_Message is
  -- Same entry declarations
  . . .
end Unique_Message;

task body Unique_Message is
  Hold         : Message_Format;
  New_Message : Boolean := False;
begin
  loop
    select
      accept Store_Message . . .
        . . .
      end Store_Message;

      New_Message := True;
    or
      when New_Message =>
       accept Retrieve_Message . . .
        . . .
        end Retrieve_Message;

       New_Message := False;
    end select;
  end loop;
end Unique_Message;
```

The *when* clause stipulates that the condition New_Message must be True for the Retrieve_Message entry to be available for rendezvous. New_Message is a *guard* on Retrieve_Message. If the guard is true, the entry is *open*. The operations on New_Message ensure the correct ordering of rendezvous. Note that the assignments to New_Message are not part of the rendezvous. The calling task does not have to wait for their completion. However, they do have to be completed before Unique_Message is ready to loop and again execute the select statement. The task Unique_Message meets the stated requirement and also, by initializing New_Message to False, prevents the retrieving of a message before one has been stored.

The selective wait can also be used to limit the time that a task will wait for a rendezvous. We will call this a *timed* selective wait. It is:

```
select
    accept Store_Message . . .
        . . .
    end Store_Message;
or
    delay 10.0; -- seconds
    ... -- optional sequence_of_statements
    ...
end select;
```

The task will wait only 10.0 seconds for a rendezvous, then proceed. That is, if a call to the entry Store_Message is issued within 10.0 seconds, a rendezvous will take place. If no call is issued within 10.0 seconds, the task containing the timed selective wait statement becomes unblocked (sometime after the 10.0 second period has expired). It continues its execution with the optional statements following the delay alternative, and then the statements following the select statement.

We can also create a situation in which the rendezvous would occur only if a calling task were waiting on the Store_Message queue: that is, only if a rendezvous were immediately available. We will call this a *conditional* selective wait. It is:

```
select
    accept Store_Message . . .
        . . .
    end Store_Message;
    ... -- optional sequence_of_statements
else
    ... -- at least one statement
    ...
end select;
```

If the entry Store_Message has been called, a rendezvous takes place. If the entry has not been called, the statements following the "else" are executed, and the task continues.

Ada also provides a mechanism, based on the idea of a "family" of entries. One use is to control the priority of entry calls. We first define the priority as:

```
type Msg_Priority is (Low, Medium, High);
```

Then the entry specification, using Retrieve_Message in task Location_Message as an example, is

```
entry Retrieve_Message (Msg_Priority)
                (Message : out Message_Format);
```

This declares the family of Retrieve_Message entries. An entry would be called from another task by (for a high priority call):

```
Location_Message.Retrieve_Message (High) (Out_Going);
```

The task body of Location_Message would have code such as the following to give precedence to high priority calls.

```
select
  accept Retrieve_Message (High) ( . . .
    . . .
  end Retrieve_Message;
or
  when Retrieve_Message (High)'Count = 0 then
    accept Retrieve_Message (Medium) ( . . .
      . . .
    end Retrieve_Message;
or
  when Retrieve_Message (High)'Count   = 0 and
       Retrieve_Message (Medium)'Count = 0 then
    accept Retrieve_Message (Low) ( . . .
      . . .
    end Retrieve_Message;
end select;
```

The Medium member of the entry family is available for a rendez-vous only if there are no pending calls to the High member of the entry family. The Low member is available only if there are no calls to either High or Medium.

2.5.2 Conditional and Timed Entry Calls

The calling task has two tools that allow it to control the conditions under which a rendezvous may occur. One control mechanism is to issue an entry call only if a rendezvous is immediately available. This is a conditional entry call. For example, in task body Writer the entry call Message_Box.Store_Message (Story) could be replaced by:

```
select
  Message_Box.Store_Message (Story);
    ... -- optional sequence_of_statements
else
    ... at least one statement
end select;
```

The result is that the rendezvous will occur only if no other entry calls are queued (or being serviced) for Message_Box.Store_Message. If the rendezvous cannot take place immediately, the alternative sequence_of_statements is executed. The calling task cannot perform the alternative action and at the same time be on the queue for the entry.

The second control mechanism allows the calling task to enter the queue for an entry. If the rendezvous does not occur within a specified time, the calling task leaves the queue and continues execution. This is a timed entry call. For example,

```
select
  Message_Box.Store_Message (Story);
    ... -- optional sequence_of_statements
or
    delay 5.0; -- Seconds
    ... -- alternate optional sequence_of_statements
end select;
```

This code says that the task Writer will wait for a rendezvous for 5.0 seconds. If the called task is prepared for a rendezvous before 5.0 seconds has passed, Writer will participate in the rendezvous, execute the optional sequence_of_statements, and then exit the select statement. If no rendezvous occurs within 5.0 seconds, the alternate optional sequence_of_statements will be executed when the task again becomes a running process. Unless a rendezvous occurs, the task is delayed *at least* 5.0 seconds. The delay statement always specifies a *minimum* time of delay.

2.6 Activation and Termination

The paragraphs below discuss the basic issues of task activation and termination.

2.6.1 Task Activation

Task activation in Ada is *implicit*. There is no explicit command to initiate or activate a task. A task is activated after the declarative part of the enclosing construct, either a block, subprogram, task body, or package. There are a number of complex activation issues related to nested packages and to exactly how and where the tasks are declared and created. However, the rule stated above is the key to a basic understanding of task activation concepts.

2.6.2 Task Termination

In order to understand task termination, we must introduce the idea of the *master*, also called the *parent*, of a task.

The master of a task is the block, subprogram, task, or library package that defines the task. (A package nested in some other unit's declarative part cannot be the master of tasks, although it may cause their activation.)

A task is said to be *dependent* upon its master. The flow of execution may not leave a master until all its dependent tasks have terminated. This is so since the master defines the context in which the task executes. For example, the master may contain type definitions, procedures, and other declarations necessary for the continued execution of the dependent task. The master is often the construct that contains the task and causes it to activate.

(There are some differences between the master of a task and the construct that activates the task—these are explained in Chapters 11, Activation; 12, Termination; and 13, Pointers to Tasks.)

The basic rule for task termination is: if a task has no dependent tasks, it may terminate when it completes the sequence of statements that define its execution.

Completion of its execution may be a consequence of the normal flow of control or in response to an *exception* (an error, such as divide by zero, or other unusual circumstance).

If the exception is handled at the outer level of the task body (i.e., the exception handler is immediately before the *end* of the task), then the execution of the handler completes the execution of the task.

If the exception is not handled, execution is considered to be immediately completed. Unhandled exceptions are not further propagated; they simply cause completion of the task.

A task may also terminate as a result of being aborted by some other task. For example, task Writer could *abort* task Sender by executing the statement:

```
abort Sender;
```

An aborted task can be considered to be immediately terminated. Aborting a task also aborts all its dependent tasks.

Use of abort should be restricted to extreme circumstances.

In each of the cases above (normal completion of sequence of statements, exception, abort), a master task still does not terminate until all its dependent tasks have terminated.

The final way to terminate is of particular importance since it allows a group of tasks to cooperatively end execution when they have nothing more to do. A select statement is allowed to have a *terminate alternative* as in:

```
select
  accept Store_Message . . .
    . . .
  end Store_Message;
or
  accept Retrieve_Message . . .
    . . .
  end Retrieve_Message;
or
  terminate;
end select;
```

A task containing a select statement with a terminate alternative will terminate if both of the following conditions are true.

- The master of the task has completed execution (and hence is waiting to terminate).

- All other tasks depending on the same master are either terminated or waiting at a terminate alternative of a select statement.

If both conditions are true, all the "related" tasks will have completed their function, will not be able to move from their current status, and hence can cooperatively terminate. Except for tasks declared in library packages, a consequence of the rules is that there are no pending calls on any of the entries.

The effect of the terminate alternative in a selective wait is difficult to understand since it involves interactions among a number of tasks. We cannot look at a single task in isolation and determine whether or not it is prepared to terminate; we must simultaneously consider all tasks of a given master (and the master itself). The effect of the terminate alternative will be discussed further in Chapter 12, Termination.

These rules do not apply to tasks in library packages, as Ada does not define how or when such tasks terminate. For such tasks, the effect of the terminate alternative is implementation-dependent.

2.7 Task Types

Ada provides for the definition of task types, allowing the later declaration of multiple objects of the same type. The only change from what we have done so far is to change the task specification by adding the word *type*, replacing "task Message_Box is" by:

```
task type Message_Box is
   . . .
```

Later declaration of task objects are:

```
Mailbox, PO_Box : Message_Box;
```

Then calls to the new tasks would be:

```
Mailbox.Store_Message (Story);
PO_Box.Retrieve_Message (Out_Bound);
```

It is also possible to declare an array of tasks:

```
Mail_Slot : array (1 .. 100) of Message_Box;
```

This declaration creates 100 tasks, all executing concurrently. One of the entries is called by:

```
Mail_Slot (77).Store_Message (Story);
```

It is also possible to declare a pointer to a task type and then create tasks dynamically with an allocator. For example,

```
type Point_To_Message_Box is access Message_Box;
New_Box : Point_To_Message_Box;
```

The method of dynamically creating a new task (pointed to by New_Box) during execution of a sequence of statements is based on the evaluation of an allocator—the use of "new".

```
New_Box := new Message_Box;
```

The call to an entry is:

```
New_Box.Store_Message (Story);
```

This call to an entry of a task created by the evaluation of an allocator is no different from entry calls to other tasks.

The use of task types and objects can be complex. Occasionally rules for their use are different from rules governing use of other tasks. For example, the master of a task created by an allocator is the program construct that contains the *access type definition*, rather than the construct that causes the task to activate.

2.8   Tasks as Device Drivers

An important aspect of programming for real-time systems is communication with system hardware. The communication frequently involves handling interrupts from external devices.

The example below uses address clauses referring to memory locations given in octal (base 8). The address clauses link a variable name and a task entry to memory locations. Hardware_Buffer is associated with a memory location that receives information from an external device such as a keyboard. The external hardware places the information in the buffer and then generates an interrupt. The example below handles the interrupt by moving the information from the buffer to the presumed (globally visible) variable Input_Char.

```
task Interrupt_Handler is
  entry Device_Interrupt;
  for Device_Interrupt use at 8#40#;
end Interrupt_Handler;

task body Interrupt_Handler is
  Hardware_Buffer : Character;
  for Hardware_Buffer use at 8#177562#;
begin
  loop
    accept Device_Interrupt do
      Input_Char := Hardware_Buffer;
    end Device_Interrupt;
  end loop;
end Interrupt_Handler;
```

The address clause "for Hardware_Buffer use at 8#177562#;" causes the object Hardware_Buffer to be located at the given address.

The address clause "for Device_Interrupt use at 8#40#;" identifies the entry Device_Interrupt as an entry "called" by what may be thought of as a hardware task. The address clause links the entry to the interrupt.

When the interrupt occurs, the effect is as though a call was made on the entry Interrupt_Handler.Device_Interrupt by a "mythical hardware task." The implementation and exact effect of tasks as interrupt handlers is highly implementation-dependent.

Ada has many additional features for mapping machine-level representations onto high-level language constructs. They will be discussed in Part 4, Tasks in Real-Time systems.

2.9 Summary

Tasking in Ada, and task use in real-time systems, is a complex topic. The reason for this complexity is that concurrency is complex. The Ada tasking model of concurrent execution is intended to allow software designers to master the complexity of concurrent real-time systems, and to write correct programs.

This chapter has touched on the major topics in Ada tasking; it does not exhaust the complexity of the topic or address all the issues or ramifications of tasking. The *Ada Language Reference Manual* [ANS83] is the basic reference and definition of tasking.

In the following chapters we provide a detailed discussion of all the topics covered in this overview of concurrency in Ada.

2.10 Exercises

These exercises are designed to illustrate the problems of uncontrolled access to a shared data structure, and to demonstrate three mechanisms for controlling access by ensuring mutual exclusion. The data structure that will be shared is a record.

Exercise 2.1. Unprotected_Shared_Record

Purpose: To illustrate the problems of unprotected access to shared data

Problem: Create a procedure with a global record of type:

```
Shared_Record_Type is
  record
    First  : Character;
    Second : Character;
    Third  : Character;
  end record;
```

Create a record (a variable, an object) of the type.

The procedure is to contain four tasks, three that write to the record and a fourth that reads the record and writes its contents to the standard output. The three writing tasks should write, component by component, different characters to the record. (e.g., one task could write three A's, the second task write three B's, and the third write three C's.)

The access to the data, reading and writing, is a critical section. If we do not ensure mutual exclusion, the results depend upon the "race" for access by the four tasks. The four tasks are to execute concurrently (and presumably asynchronously). Run the program several times to observe the different output. What you should observe is output such as:

```
AAC BCA BBB CAB BBA CAC ...
```

This demonstrates the results of uncontrolled data access. What is actually desired is:

```
BBB AAA CCC BBB CCC BBB AAA AAA ...
```

We don't care about the order in which the groups of three are written, only that each group of three contain only a single character.

Note: Since this is a time-dependent (and to some extent implementation-dependent) error, you may not observe the inconsistent behavior. Then a part of the problem becomes "forcing" asynchronous behavior for the four tasks, in order to observe the inconsistent data access. You can do this by placing random delays in the tasks, at the points before and after access to the data.

Solution:

```
with Text_IO;          use Text_IO;
procedure Unprotected_Shared_Record is
```

```
type Shared_Record_Type is
  record
    First  : Character;
    Second : Character;
    Third  : Character;
  end record;

-- THIS IS THE OBJECT THAT IS BEING SHARED -- UNPROTECTED
------------------------------------------------------------
Unprotected : Shared_Record_Type := ('*', '*', '*');
------------------------------------------------------------


task Write_Letter_A_To_Record;
task Write_Letter_B_To_Record;
task Write_Letter_C_To_Record;

task Access_Record;

task body Write_Letter_A_To_Record is
  Letter : constant := 'A';
begin
  loop
    Unprotected.First  := Letter;
    Unprotected.Second := Letter;
    Unprotected.Third  := Letter;

    exit when <some condition>;
  end loop;
end Write_Letter_A_To_Record;

-- the tasks below are similar to Write_Letter_A_To_Record

task body Write_Letter_B_To_Record is ...
                        end Write_Letter_B_To_Record;
task body Write_Letter_C_To_Record is ...
                        end Write_Letter_C_To_Record;

task body Access_Record is
  Local_First  : Character;
  Local_Second : Character;
  Local_Third  : Character;
```

```
begin
   -- start reading the shared record
   loop
     Local_First  := Unprotected.First;
     Local_Second := Unprotected.Second;
     Local_Third  := Unprotected.Third;

     -- output the local values
     Put (Local_First);
     Put (Local_Second);
     Put (Local_Third);

     -- provide control for carriage return (not shown here)

     exit when <some condition>;
   end loop;

   end Access_Record;
end Unprotected_Shared_Record;
```

Discussion: The three tasks write to the record, asynchronously, while the fourth task reads from the record, asynchronously. (The solution shown ignores some details of control of the looping and format of output; we are concerned with the issue of simultaneous access.)

Since the access is interleaved, at any time the data in the record are apt to be inconsistent, i.e., not AAA or BBB or CCC, but ACC, BCA, and so on. Alternatively, the reading task may read the first character when the record contains AAA, the second character when the record contains CCC, and so on. The end result in either case is that the data values read, and written out, are inconsistent. Here is the output from a sample run.

```
$ run unprotected_shared_record

AAC AAC AAA ACA ABB BBC CVA BBB BBB BBC CBC
CBC AAA ACA ACC CAA CAA CAA ACA AAA CAA CAA
AAA AAA ACA AAC AAA BBB BBA CBB BBB BBA BCB
```

If the desired result was triplets, all of the same letter (AAA, CCC, and so on), this would be very bad. The exercises below show how we can achieve consistent data.

NOTE

Some compilers will generate code that, in the absence of external interrupts or delays in the tasks themselves, will not actually share the processor in an asynchronous manner. The data above are from a version of Unprotected_Shared_Record that contains random delays that cause asynchronous sharing of the processor in a way typical of a system that is being interrupted by external devices.

Exercise 2.2.   Protected_Shared_Record

Purpose: To illustrate use of semaphores

Problem: Use a semaphore to ensure that the critical section is accessed in mutual exclusion. Since Ada does not have a semaphore, you will have to implement a semaphore using Ada tasks. (This is a secondary purpose of the exercise—it is very easy and short to do this, once you think of the solution. The P- and V-operations do not need to take a parameter since we are using the semaphore only for simple signals.)

By modification to the program of the previous exercise, protect access to the shared record by implementing a semaphore and using the semaphore to provide mutual exclusion for access to the critical section. Create a task called Semaphore, then use Semaphore.P and Semaphore.V as the P- and V-operations to provide mutual exclusion. Since we are using what is essentially only a binary semaphore, it is not necessary to have a parameter. This simplifies the Ada code to implement the semaphore.

There are really two parts to this exercise: (1) Create a semaphore using an Ada task, and (2) use the semaphore to provide mutually exclusive access to a critical section.

Solution:

```
-- The solution is presented as modifications to the first problem.
-- Here is the record, now to be protected by use of semaphores.

-- This is not really a safe form of protection
-- since semaphore may be misused,
-- and not in the Ada style at all.

-- This is done only for illustration of use of semaphores.
```

```
-- THIS IS THE OBJECT THAT IS BEING SHARED.
-- IT IS NOW PROTECTED BY USE OF SEMAPHORES.
-----------------------------------------------------------
  Protected : Shared_Record_Type := ('*', '*', '*');
-----------------------------------------------------------


-- here is the semaphore task

task Semaphore is
  entry P;
  entry V;
end Semaphore;

task body Semaphore is
begin
  loop
    accept P;
    accept V;  -- after a P we wait for a V

    -- and then we wait for a P
  end loop;
end Semaphore;


-- Here is how we protect writing to the record (which we now
-- call Protected, rather than Unprotected).

-- This is in the task Write_Letter_*_To_Record.
-- The * stands for A or B or C.

    Semaphore.P;
      Protected.First  := Letter;
      Protected.Second := Letter;
      Protected.Third  := Letter;
    Semaphore.V;

-- and here is how we protect the critical section for
-- access to the record, in the task Access_Record

    Semaphore.P;
      Local_First  := Protected.First;
      Local_Second := Protected.Second;
      Local_Third  := Protected.Third;
    Semaphore.V;
```

Discussion: When the call Semaphore.P is issued, a rendezvous takes place, the calling task proceeds into the critical section, and the semaphore task now waits for a call to Semaphore.V. Any other task, attempting to enter the critical section by calling Semaphore.P, will be blocked. The queueing discipline for those blocked tasks is strictly first-in first-out, in accordance with the usual Ada protocol for the rendezvous.

When the initial task has completed its processing in the critical section, it calls Semaphore.V, has a rendezvous with the semaphore task, and goes on about its business. The semaphore task loops back for a rendezvous with its "P" entry, thereby allowing some other task to enter the critical section.

This mechanism ensures mutually exclusive access to the critical section. It suffers from the usual problems related to potential misuse of semaphores. If we really did desire to use this protocol in an Ada tasking situation, it would be possible to at least ensure that only the task that issued Semaphore.P could issue Semaphore.V. (This would give us some additional security over the plain use of semaphores shown.) We could do this by providing the caller a "receipt" or "admission slip" to the critical section. He would have to return the receipt when he leaves the critical section.

If we wish to provide for termination of the semaphore task when it is not longer needed, we would add a terminate alternative as:

```
task body Semaphore is
begin
   loop
     select
       accept P;
     or
       terminate;
     end select;

     accept V;
   end loop;
end Semaphore;
```

Exercise 2.3. Task_Shared_Record

Purpose: To provide for mutually exclusive access to the shared data by encapsulating the data in a task

Problem: Create a task with the specification:

```
task Protect is
   entry Write_To_Shared_Record (F, S, T : in  Character);
   entry Read_From_Shared_Record (F, S, T : out Character);
end Protect;
```

In the context of the previous problems, use the task to provide mutual exclusion for access to the shared data.

Solution:

```
task body Protect is
   type Shared_Record_Type is
     record
       First  : Character;
       Second : Character;
       Third  : Character;
     end record;

   -- THIS IS THE OBJECT THAT IS BEING SHARED
   -- IT IS NOW PROTECTED SINCE IT IS INSIDE A TASK
   -- THE ONLY ACCESS TO THE RECORD IS VIA THE TASK ENTRIES
   ------------------------------------------------------------
   Protected : Shared_Record_Type;
   ------------------------------------------------------------

begin
   -- ensure the record will be initialized
   accept Write_To_Shared_Record (F, S, T : in Character) do
     Protected.First  := F;
     Protected.Second := S;
     Protected.Third  := T;
   end Write_To_Shared_Record;

   -- accept either accesses or updates
   loop
     select
       accept Write_To_Shared_Record (F, S, T : in Character) do
         Protected.First  := F;
         Protected.Second := S;
         Protected.Third  := T;
       end Write_To_Shared_Record;
     or
```

```
      accept Read_From_Shared_Record (F, S, T : out Character) do
         F := Protected.First;
         S := Protected.Second;
         T := Protected.Third;
      end Read_From_Shared_Record;
   or
      terminate;
   end select;
 end loop;
end Protect;
```

Inside the task Write_Letter_*_To_Record we have

```
Protect.Write_To_Shared_Record (Letter, Letter, Letter);
```

Inside the task Access_Record we have

```
Protect.Read_From_Shared_Record (Local_First,
                                 Local_Second,
                                 Local_Third);
```

```
Put (Local_First);
Put (Local_Second);
Put (Local_Third);
```

Discussion: The object that is to be protected is now encapsulated in the task Protect. In fact, we have even put the record type definition inside the task body. There is no reason why the using tasks need to know that the information they are accessing is actually in a record.

The only access to the object is via calls to the entries of the task. The execution of the accept statement is now the critical section. It is guaranteed to be done in mutual exclusion because there is only one thread of control that has access to the protected data.

No task can misuse this mechanism by forgetting or incorrectly calling the semaphore task. This is a good way to protect shared data in Ada programs.

Exercise 2.4. Monitor_Shared_Record

Purpose: To provide for mutually exclusive access to the shared data by encapsulating the data in a monitor

Problem: Create a package with the specification:

```
package Protect is
  procedure Write_To_Shared_Record  (F, S, T : in  Character);
  procedure Read_From_Shared_Record (F, S, T : out Character);
  pragma Inline (Write_To_Shared_Record,
                 Read_From_Shared_Record);
end Protect;
```

This is essentially an Ada implementation of a simple monitor. Use the package to ensure mutual exclusion for access to the shared data. Of course there must be a task inside the package, but it is hidden.

In the context of the previous problems, use the package to provide mutual exclusion for access to the shared data.

Solution:

```
package body Protect is
  task Mutual_Exclusion is
    entry Write_To_Shared_Record  (F, S, T : in  Character);
    entry Read_From_Shared_Record (F, S, T : out Character);
  end Mutual_Exclusion;

  -- the task body of Mutual_Exclusion is identical to the
  -- earlier task Protect

  task body Mutual_Exclusion is ... end Mutual_Exclusion;

  procedure Write_To_Shared_Record  (F, S, T : in  Character) is
  begin
    Mutual_Exclusion.Write_To_Shared_Record (F, S, T);
  end Write_To_Shared_Record;

  procedure Read_From_Shared_Record (F, S, T : out Character) is
  begin
    Mutual_Exclusion.Read_From_Shared_Record (F, S, T);
  end Read_From_Shared_Record;
end Protect;
```

```
with Protect;
procedure Monitor_Shared_Record is
-- contains the tasks to write and read the shared data
-- they are identical to the tasks in the last example
end Monitor_Shared_Record;
```

Discussion: The interface to the shared data is now through the procedures in the package specification. They are "Inline" in order to not incur the actual overhead of a procedure call. (The pragma Inline is a suggestion to the compiler to expand the code inline, rather than actually implementing a procedure call.) The package body reveals that they do nothing but call the appropriate entries in the task "Mutual_Exclusion". We call these "entrance procedures," and will see them used and discussed in the case studies.

The Mutual_Exclusion task is the same as the task Protect in the previous exercise. It provides the same sort of protection. The difference between this and the previous exercise is that now we have a package/procedure interface, rather than a task/entry interface. It makes no difference to the calling tasks; their call for service is exactly the same in either case. (This is so since we have chosen not to use the "use" clause to provide immediate visibility into the package specification.)

The importance of this approach over the previous exercise is that the package is now a library unit. Its capability can be made available to many users by "withing" the package in a context clause. This is an appropriate way to construct and use a monitor, and is the proper way to protect shared information in Ada. We will use this approach extensively.

Keys to Understanding

- The design of concurrent systems must take into account issues of mutual exclusion and synchronization in order to prevent race conditions.

- Code that must be executed in mutual exclusion is said to be a critical section.

- Traditional methods of process coordination include semaphores, critical regions, and monitors.

- Tasks provide for concurrent execution in Ada programs.

- The rendezvous is the single mechanism for task coordination and communication. It replaces the traditional methods of process coordination. The execution of code in the rendezvous occurs as a critical section.

- Ada provides a number of facilities for when and how a rendezvous occurs. The facilities are asymmetric for calling and called tasks.

- Ada provides all language features necessary for the development of real-time systems, including interfacing with hardware through the use of interrupt handlers.

3

Case One: Hot Line
Communication System (HLCS)

> Objective: To establish the overall architecture
> of an Ada program in the context of a
> simple but realistic real-time system

This is the first case study of the book. As such, it also introduces
some additional terminology and the mechanics of presenting the
case studies. Further, certain aspects of the solution use methods
and techniques that we have not yet covered in a tutorial manner;
the major situations of this sort will be pointed out. You may find it
desirable to reread this case after reading Part 2 of the book.

The case study is an illustration both of the case study method
and of how Ada is used for the construction of a complete program.
It makes a number of observations on the determination of whether
a task should be a caller or should be called, and introduces the
methods by which intermediary tasks can be used to uncouple task
interactions.

The second case study (Chapter 9) will point out additional style
and design issues and case study methodology approaches. This case

study does not deal with machine-level topics, but it will be expanded in Chapter 17, Tasks as Interrupt Handlers, to deal with how the tasks would serve as device drivers.

The following sections present a software requirements specification, the environment for the HLCS software development, a top-level and detailed design, code, discussion, and additional exercises. You may wish to review the discussion in Chapter 1 of the case study format, including Figure 1-8.

3.1 Software Requirements Specification

The Hot Line Communication System (HLCS) provides for two-way communication between two communication centers, Red and Blue. Figure 3-1 illustrates the HLCS problem.

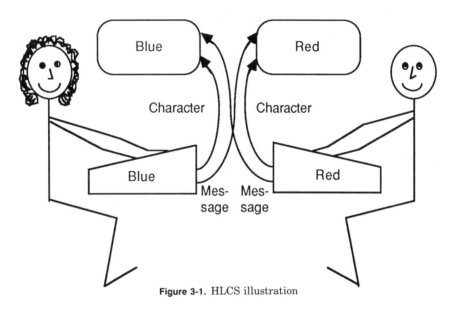

Figure 3-1. HLCS illustration

Red types one-line messages at the keyboard Keyboard_Red. Messages are limited to a maximum of 64 characters. There may be fewer characters, being terminated by the operator's entering a carriage return. The messages are displayed for Blue at Display_Blue. Similarly, Blue types messages at Keyboard_Blue for display at Display_Red. Each character typed at one of the keyboards (say, Keyboard_Blue) is also displayed on the corresponding display (Display_Blue).

The messages are sent one at a time in accordance with the following protocol. A message will not be interrupted as it is being typed. When the message is completed (i.e., the operator types a carriage return), all available incoming messages from the other color keyboard are displayed. Available messages consist of pending messages plus all messages created by the other color keyboard while the operator is reading his messages.

A sender of messages does not have to wait for an earlier message to be received before creating and sending additional messages. The HLCS can store 100 messages, 50 in the red-to-blue direction and 50 in the blue-to-red direction. Then old messages begin to be over-written by the newer messages.

We will not be concerned with the hardware controlling the keyboard and display; the HLCS environment will provide a package of services for displaying characters and receiving characters from the keyboard. However, we must know that neither the hardware nor the package providing our interface to the hardware generate line feed controls. The HLCS software must generate a line feed (LF) for each operator-generated carriage return (CR).

3.2 HLCS Environment

Figure 3-2a is a context diagram for the HLCS. Since the HLCS interfaces with four external devices, there would normally be one task per device. However, part of the HLCS software has already been designed by the company that is building the hardware inter-faces to the new HLCS-specific (and state-of-the-art) keyboard and display. This software is the HLCS Executive services; it hides the details of the hardware interaction from the HLCS application soft-ware that we are going to design as part of this case study.

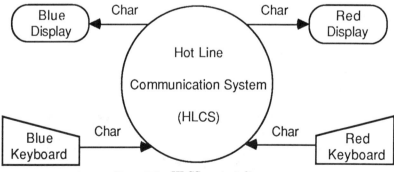

Figure 3-2a. HLCS context diagram

Figure 3-2b shows the context for the HLCS application software; the red and blue Keyboard and Display handlers pass the data back and forth between the application software and the external devices.

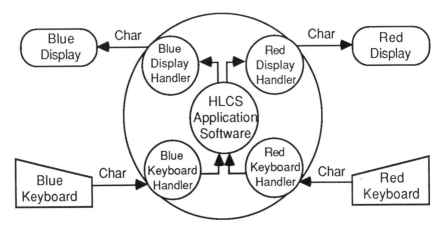

Figure 3-2b. HLCS context diagram and executive services

The handlers are encapsulated in appropriate packages. They essentially constitute an HLCS Executive. Here are the packages for interaction with the devices:

Executive Services Packages

```
package Blue_Devices is
   procedure Display          (Char :  in Character);
   procedure Keyboard_Input (Char : out Character);
end Blue_Devices;

package Red_Devices is
   procedure Display          (Char :  in Character);
   procedure Keyboard_Input (Char : out Character);
end Red_Devices;
```

When the HLCS application software wishes to use the blue display handler to display a character on the blue display, it calls Blue_Devices.Display. The calling task is blocked until the character is displayed, typically on the order of ½ ms. When the HLCS application software wishes to use the blue keyboard handler to receive a character from the blue keyboard, it calls the procedure Blue_Devices.Keyboard_Input. The calling task is blocked until a character is received, with the timing dependent upon the operator, but never less than 10 ms.

3.3 Top-Level Design

We distinguish between two parts of the top-level design: graphical design and Ada package specifications. The graphical design generally comes first, but the two phases iterate and interact with each other as well as with the later detailed design phase. The graphical design includes narrative descriptions of the processes represented in the graphic figures. The Ada package specifications will be accompanied by an abstract description of the algorithms of the tasks and procedures internal to the packages.

Design at this level makes use of *process abstraction*, an emphasis on system decomposition based on what processes (functions, actions, things) must occur concurrently or simultaneously. We noeed not be concerned with *how* the actions are accomplished, only *what* is to be accomplished. (That is why the processes are abstract.) Process abstraction, with the associated graphic illustration of the process graph, is important. It will be the method by which we design concurrent Ada systems. Process abstraction will be discussed further in later case studies.

The package specifications will be complete Ada code. This is appropriate during the design phase since the package specification is also a design tool; it defines major data types and the interfaces between the system components.

3.3.1 Graphical Design

The first task of graphical design is to identify the major concurrent elements of the system. It is natural to have the software design reflect the concurrency of the actual problem.

Almost always, we will wish to have one task for each external device. This is reinforced in this case, since a call for a character from a keyboard causes the caller to block until the character is input. We cannot afford to have the entire HLCS waiting for the character, so we establish a separate task to interact with the device.

Figure 3-3a is a process graph, as explained in Chapter 1. Decisions as to which task will provide entries and accept calls ("called tasks"), and which tasks will call entries in other tasks ("callers") are made at this time. This issue is addressed at length in Chapter 5, Calling and Called Tasks.

The keyboards alternately interact with the the same color display and the keyboard handler. They never enter a state in which they need to be prepared to interact with either of the handler or the display. It is, therefore, easy for the keyboards to be callers, alternately calling the keyboard handler to receive a character, and the

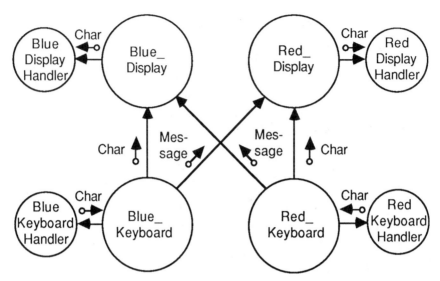

Figure 3-3a. Initial HLCS process graph

same color display to output the character. After a message is built, the keyboard may make a call to deliver the message.

In summary, the keyboards have a cycle of a series of calls to the keyboard handlers and the display while they build a message, followed by sending the message to the other color display. Sending the message can easily be a call. The cycle is:

```
loop -- outer cycle
  loop -- inner cycle to get a message
    get a character;
    display the character;
    add the character to the message;
    exit at the end of the message;
  end loop; -- to get a message

  send the message to the other display;
end loop -- outer cycle for keyboard task
```

The displays have an important characteristic that is different from the keyboards. An important part of the displays is that when no messages are pending, and the operator is not typing a new message, the display must be ready to accept *either* a message (from the other color keyboard) or a character (from the same color keyboard). It is this characteristic of wishing to interact nondeterministically with either of two other tasks that makes it desirable for a task to be called rather than a caller. We, therefore, will choose to make the displays "called" tasks, except for their calls to the display handlers in order to output characters.

The closely coupled interaction described raises a potential problem. If a (same color, say, blue) display/keyboard combination is busy handling a message being typed by an operator, the other color keyboard (red) will be blocked when it tries to send a message to the (blue) display. We can uncouple this interaction, while maintaining the caller/called relationship, by using an intermediary process. The sort of intermediary we need is called a "relay." A relay is a process that is *called* by one task, say, to store an item, and *calls* another task to deliver the item. The relay will accommodate the buffering of the messages required by the specification. The relay that we provide must have the characteristic that it does not block the calling task. The relays are shown in Figure 3-3b. The relay is discussed in detail in Chapter 8, Buffer-Transporter Model of Task Interaction.

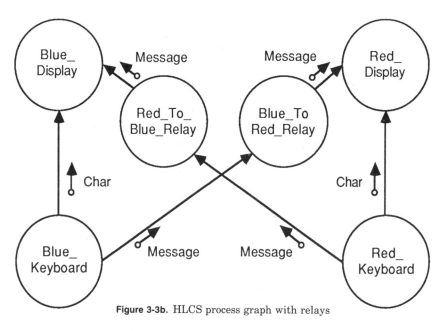

Figure 3-3b. HLCS process graph with relays

We will no longer show the device handlers in our process graphs since we wish to focus on the task interactions of the application software. The relay in this problem is actually two tasks, as will be shown on later process graphs.

At this point we are prepared to write minispecifications (or minispecs) for each function. Minispecs are narrative descriptions of the processing of each task. The description has a primary focus on what the task does, but also begins to bridge to how it accomplishes its function. From now on, we will focus only on the blue point of view, since the red is merely a mirror image of the blue processing.

This section presents minispecifications for:

- Blue_Keyboard
- Blue_To_Red_Relay
- Blue_Display

The process interactions are shown graphically in Figure 3-3b.

Minispecifications for Processing of Blue Messages

Blue_Keyboard

The Blue_Keyboard obtains characters from the keyboard, sending them to the Blue_Display as they are received. It builds a message from the characters, sending complete messages to the Blue_To_Red_Relay. The indicator of a complete line (i.e., a message) is the receipt of a carriage return. The carriage return is sent to the display and inserted in the message sent to the relay.

The keyboard does no checks on the characters received or to ensure that a carriage return is received before the end of a line. (This is just a simplification for the purpose of the case study.) The keyboard blocks while waiting for a character, but does not expect to block when putting something into the relay or the display. (Recall that we are using "block" to mean "suspended while waiting for a rendezvous.")

Blue_To_Red_Relay

The Blue_To_Red_Relay accepts messages from the Blue_Keyboard and delivers them to the Red_Display. The relay consists of two threads of control: a buffer and a transporter. The transporter takes messages out of the buffer. These will be shown as separate processes in later figures. The relay accepts messages by being *called* (i.e., a call to the buffer), and delivers messages by *calling* (i.e., a call by the transporter) The calling keyboard never blocks on a full buffer; old messages are overwritten when the buffer is full. The keyboard also never blocks while the transporter is waiting for the display to accept a message. The keyboard can still put messages in the buffer. The relay tells the display when the message being delivered is the last one in the buffer.

Blue_Display

The Blue_Display accepts either a message from the Red_To_ Blue_Relay or a character from the Blue_Keyboard. Preference is given to the display of messages from the Relay.

Once a message is received, the entire message is displayed. The remaining contents of the buffer are accepted and displayed before any consideration is again given to the display of a character from Blue_Keyboard. (Note that the need to empty the buffer implies that there is some extra communication between the Relay and the display; we will handle this with an extra parameter, Last, that tells the display when the current message is the last one in the buffer. This parameter will show up in the next figure. This sort of consideration, requiring data to be communicated between the processes, is the bridge between what is to be done and how the function is to be implemented.)

Once a character is received from the keyboard task, the display only serves the keyboard task until the message (one line) is complete. It recognizes the end of line by a carriage return, and then also displays a line feed on the display. It then once again is prepared to accept either a character or a message.

The process graph for the above functions and interactions, including the two tasks for the relay, is shown in Figure 3-3c.

There are many possible ways to package the tasks. We will take a very simple approach, placing each of the major functional tasks in its own package. The two tasks comprising the relay will be in the same package, reflecting their common action as an intermediary between the tasks performing the functions of the HLCS.

3.3.2 Package Specifications

The presentation of package specifications will include an abstract algorithm of the processing in the corresponding body. This is necessary in order to illustrate our (at least partial) understanding of how the task performs its function. You should compare the abstract algorithms to the minispecs presented earlier. This will help your understanding of the functioning of the system.

This section presents the specifications for:

- Definitions
- Blue_Keyboard
- Blue_To_Red_Relay
- Blue_Display

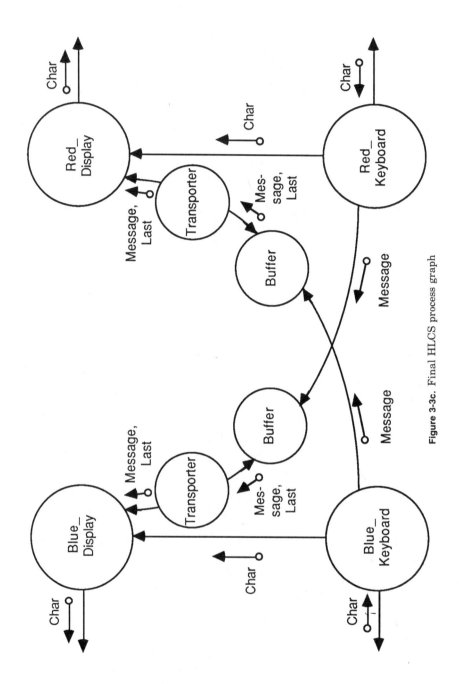

Figure 3-3c. Final HLCS process graph

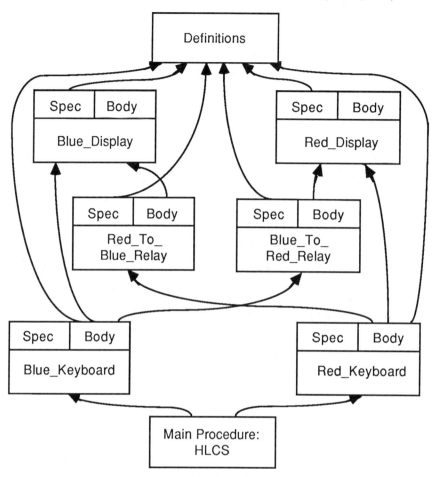

Figure 3-4. HLCS dependency graph

Their relationship is shown in Figure 3-4. This is a "dependency graph." It shows the "withing" relationships among the various library units in the system. For completeness, we include the Red, as well as the Blue, components.

We also include the main procedure. It is the withing of the two keyboard packages by the main procedure that actually initiates the activity in the system. It causes elaboration of all the packages, and hence the activation of all the tasks. This process is explained further in Chapter 11, Activation.

The dependency graph distinguishes a withing that occurs by the specification of a package from the withing that occurs by the body of the package. (Withing by the body includes withing by subunits of the body.) In general, it is good practice to with a library unit as "low" in the design as possible, i.e., in the body rather than the specification, in a subunit rather than the package body. This both hides dependencies lower in the design, and also limits recompilation effects from rippling through the system.

3.3.2.1 Definitions.

```
package Definitions is
   Message_Length : constant := 64;
   Max_Messages   : constant := 50;
   -- the messages include the carriage return (ASCII.CR)
   subtype Index       is Positive range 1 .. Message_Length + 1;
   subtype Message_Type is String (Index);
end Definitions;
```

3.3.2.2 HLCS Executive.

```
package Blue_Devices is
   procedure Display        (Char :  in Character);
   procedure Keyboard_Input (Char : out Character);
end Blue_Devices;
```

```
package Red_Devices is
   procedure Display        (Char :  in Character);
   procedure Keyboard_Input (Char : out Character);
end Red_Devices;
```

We will not consider the functioning of these packages any further.

3.3.2.3 Blue_Keyboard.

Abstract Algorithm:

```
loop
   loop to build a message
      get a character;
      add the character to the message;
      send the character to the blue display;
      exit when the character is a carriage return;
   end loop to build a message;

   send the message to the blue to red relay;
end loop;
```

Specification:

```
package Blue_Keyboard is
  -- Calls
    -- Blue_Display.Display_Char
    -- Blue_To_Red_Relay.Enqueue
    -- Blue_Devices.Keyboard_Input
end Blue_Keyboard;
```

3.3.2.4 Blue__To__Red__Relay.

Abstract Algorithm: The relay contains a buffer to store messages. It also contains an extra task, called a transporter, to take messages from the buffer and pass them to the blue display. This process, and the complete algorithm, will be explained further in Chapter 8, Buffer-Transporter Model of Task Interaction.

Specification:

```
with Definitions; use Definitions;
package Blue_To_Red_Relay is
  procedure Enqueue (Message : in Message_Type);
  -- Calls
    -- Red_Display.Display_Message
end Blue_To_Red_Relay;
```

3.3.2.5 Blue__Display.

Abstract Algorithm:

```
loop
  select
    accept a message;
    loop to display all messages in the buffer
      display the message;
      exit when the last message has been displayed;
      accept a message;
    end loop to display all messages in the buffer;
  or
```

```
    when no messages are ready to be accepted
      accept a character;
      display the character;
      while the character is not a carriage return
        loop to display all the characters in a message
          accept a character;
          display the character;
        end loop to display all the characters in a message;
      display a line feed;
  or
    terminate;
  end select;
end loop;
```

Specification:

```
with Blue_Devices; use Blue_Devices;
with Definitions; use Definitions;
package Blue_Display is
  procedure Display_Message (Message : in Message_Type;
                             Last    : in Boolean);
  procedure Display_Char (Char : in Character);
  -- Calls Blue_Devices.Display
end Blue_Display;
```

3.4 Detailed Design

The detailed design consists of two steps of refinement: (1) completion of the package bodies (with major tasks declared with stubs)
and (2) the specification of the abstract algorithms in the separate
task bodies.

One final component of the package bodies is the complete development of the procedures that are defined in the package specification. For packages whose primary function is the encapsulation of
tasks, these will typically consist only of minor processing associated
with calls to entries of tasks declared in the package body. The purpose of these procedures (we will call them "entrance procedures") is
to provide for data flow from tasks outside the package into or out of
tasks in the package.

Why do we use entrance procedures instead of making the task
specifications visible in the package specification? The short answer
is that the method is a form of information hiding, a well-known
general principle [PAR72] that basically says that you should hide
implementation details whenever you can. We will comment more

on the use of entrance procedures at various points during the additional case studies.

At the completion of the first level of refinement, the package bodies are completely coded in correct, compilable Ada. This is still appropriately part of the design phase, for all the package bodies contain at this point are task and procedure specifications—design information. (For small tasks or procedures with well-known algorithms we may violate this general principle and provide the complete task or procedure body in the package body.)

This effect, having the package bodies completely coded during the design phase, results from the style of having the tasks shown as stubs, with the bodies being separate. We then use a mix of pseudocode and actual Ada to specify the task bodies, with the final coding details deferred to the coding phase of development.

Note: We choose to mix English-like pseudocode with Ada statements in the bodies. The result is that the separate task bodies are not proper compilable Ada. We take this approach as being most natural for the tutorial style in which we are presenting the material. For the actual design of a large system, it is likely desirable to make the pseudocode into Ada comments (i.e., preceded by --), and add sufficient detail to the code to make the separate task bodies compilable. This allows the compiler to help ensure consistency, between unit specifications and their use, during the detailed design phase.

For large tasks, there might be a third level of refinement: the task bodies may contain stubbed procedures that are later defined with their abstract algorithms.

The "road map" to the detailed design is the structure graph provided as Figure 3-5. It should be your constant reference point as you review the detailed design. You should compare the detailed algorithms described in the tasks below to the more abstract algorithms expressed earlier as part of the top-level design.

This section presents the detailed design for:

- Blue_Keyboard
- Blue_To_Red_Relay
- Blue_Display

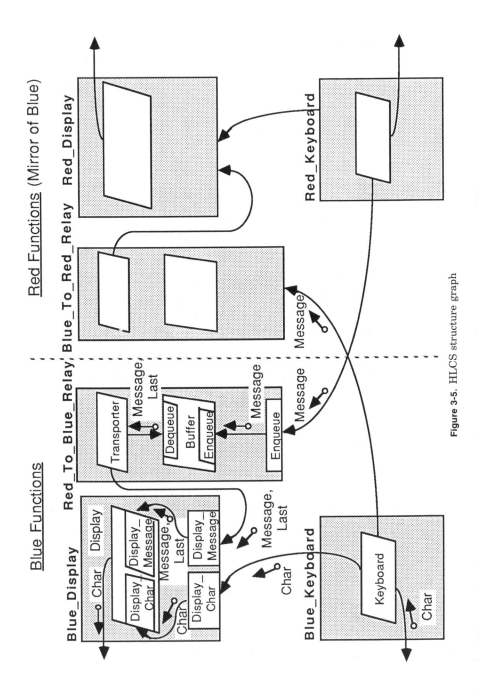

Figure 3-5. HLCS structure graph

3.4.1 Blue__Keyboard

```
package body Blue_Keyboard is
   task Keyboard is
     -- Calls
       -- Blue_Display.Display_Char
       -- Blue_To_Red_Relay.Enqueue
       -- Blue_Devices.Keyboard_Input
   end Keyboard;

   task body Keyboard is separate;
end Blue_Keyboard;

with Definitions; use Definitions;
with Blue_Devices;
with Blue_Display;
with Blue_To_Red_Relay;
separate (Blue_Keyboard)
   task body Keyboard is
   begin
     loop
       Build_Message:
       loop
         get a character from Keyboard_Input;
         add the character to the message;
         send the character to Blue_Display.Display_Char;
         exit Build_Message when the character is ASCII.CR;
       end loop Build_Message;

       send the message to Blue_To_Red_Relay.Enqueue;
     end loop;
   end Keyboard;
```

3.4.2 Blue__To__Red__Relay

```
with Red_Display;
package body Blue_To_Red_Relay is

   -- This buffer allows the overwriting of old messages
   -- in the circular queue. It sets the Boolean parameter
   -- "Last" to True when the buffer is empty
```

```
task Bounded_Buffer is
  entry Enqueue (Message : in  Message_Type);
  entry Dequeue (Message : out Message_Type;
                 Last    : out Boolean);
end Bounded_Buffer;

task body Bounded_Buffer is separate;

task Transporter is
  -- Calls
    -- Bounded_Buffer.Dequeue
    -- Red_Display.Display_Message
end Transporter;

task body Transporter is
  Message : Message_Type;
  Last    : Boolean;
begin
  loop
    Bounded_Buffer.Dequeue       (Message, Last);
    Red_Display.Display_Message (Message, Last);
  end loop;
end Transporter;

  procedure Enqueue (Message : in Message_Type) is
  begin
    Bounded_Buffer.Enqueue (Message);
  end Enqueue;
end Blue_To_Red_Relay;
```

Note: The buffer body will not be presented at the detailed design level; buffer algorithms will be explained in detail in Chapter 7, The Bounded Buffer.

3.4.3   Blue__Display

```
with Definitions; use Definitions;
package body Blue_Display is
  task Display is
    entry Display_Message (Message : in Message_Type;
                           Last    : in Boolean);
    entry Display_Char     (Char    : in Character);
    -- Calls
      -- Blue_Devices.Display
  end Display;

  task body Display is separate;

  procedure Display_Message (Message : in Message_Type;
                             Last    : in Boolean) is
  begin
    Display.Display_Message (Message, Last);
  end Display_Message;

  procedure Display_Char (Char : in Character) is
  begin
    Display.Display_Char (Char);
  end Display_Char;
end Blue_Display;

with Blue_Devices;
separate (Blue_Display)
  task body Display is
  begin
    loop
      select
        accept Display_Message (Message : in Message_Type;
                                Last    : in Boolean) do
          get the message and the Last indicator;
        end Display_Message;
```

```
      Display_All_Messages_Loop:
      loop
        Display_The_Message_Loop:
        loop
          send a character to Display;

          exit Display_The_Message_Loop when the character
          is ASCII.CR;
        end loop Display_The_Message_Loop;
        send Display an ASCII.LF; -- ends display the message

        exit Display_All_Messages_Loop when Last character received;

        accept Display_Message (Message : in Message_Type;
                                Last    : in Boolean) do
          get the message and the Last indicator;
        end Display_Message;
      end loop Display_All_Messages_Loop;
    or
      when Display_Message'Count = 0 =>
        accept Display_Char (Char : in Character) do
          save the character;
        end Display_Char;

        send the character to Display;

        Display_The_Message_Loop_2:
        while the character /= ASCII.CR loop
          accept Display_Char (Char : in Character) do
            save the character;
          end Display_Char;

          send the character to Display;
        end loop Display_The_Message_Loop_2;
        send Display an ASCII.LF; -- ends display the message
    or
        terminate;
      end select;
    end loop;
  end Display;
```

It is worth noting that the algorithm in task Display is already influenced by Ada syntax. The "accept Display_Message" following the select is repeated at the end of the Display_All_Messages loop.

This caters to the Ada syntax requirement that a select statement must consist only of accept alternatives (each of which may be followed by a sequence of statements). If it were not for this requirement, the algorithm would place the "accept Display_Message" at the top of the loop, and dispense with the first "accept Display_Message". We design the algorithm in this manner in order to demonstrate consistency between the pseudocode and the final Ada.

3.5 Code

The coding phase is the completion of the separate task and procedure bodies. It is the filling in of the final details of the data structures and coding details of the algorithms. Since the package specifications and bodies are completely coded during the top-level and detailed design, the coding phase only involves the subunits. You should compare the final code to the detailed algorithms presented as part of the detailed design.

A final step is the provision of the main procedure to activate the system.

This section presents the code for:

- Keyboard
- Bounded_Buffer
- Display
- The main procedure: HLCS

3.5.1 Keyboard

```
with Blue_Devices;
with Blue_Display;
with Blue_To_Red_Relay;
with Definitions; use Definitions;
separate (Blue_Keyboard)
```

```
task body Keyboard is
  Message : Message_Type;
begin
  loop
    Build_Message:
    for I in Message'Range loop
      Blue_Devices.Keyboard_Input (Message (I));
      Blue_Display.Display_Char   (Message (I));
      exit Build_Message when Message (I) = ASCII.CR;
    end loop Build_Message;

    Blue_To_Red_Relay.Enqueue (Message);
  end loop;
end Keyboard;
```

3.5.2 Bounded__Buffer

```
separate (Blue_To_Red_Relay)
  task body Bounded_Buffer is
    Buffer_Size : Positive := Max_Messages - 1;
    -- the task actual buffer is Buffer_Size plus one
    -- message "buffered" in the transporter

    Buffer : array (1 .. Buffer_Size) of Message_Type;

    Remove,
    Insert : Positive range 1 .. Buffer_Size := 1;
    Count  : Natural  range 0 .. Buffer_Size := 0;
  begin
    loop
      select
          accept Enqueue (Message  : in  Message_Type) do
            Buffer (Insert) := Message;
          end Enqueue;

          if Count < Buffer_Size then
            Count := Count + 1;
          else
            Remove := (Remove mod Buffer_Size) + 1;
          end if;

          Insert := (Insert mod Buffer_Size) + 1;
      or
```

```
      when Count > 0 =>
        accept Dequeue (Message : out Message_Type;
                        Last    : out Boolean) do
          Message := Buffer (Remove);
          Last := (Count = 1); -- Last message in the buffer when True
        end Dequeue;

        Remove := (Remove mod Buffer_Size) + 1;
        Count  := Count - 1;
      end select;
    end loop;
end Bounded_Buffer;
```

The size of the buffer is one less than the maximum number of messages stored since the transporter stores a message.

The logic of the condition "if Count < Buffer_Size" is that we must not increment Count when we are overwriting old messages. Further, when we are overwriting old messages (and moving Insert) we must move Remove in order to ensure that the messages are received in the correct order.

The bounded buffer will be discussed in detail in Chapter 7, The Bounded Buffer.

3.5.3 Display

```
separate (Blue_Display)
  task body Display is
    Message : Message_Type;
    Last    : Boolean;
    Char    : Character;
  begin
    loop
      select
        accept Display_Message (Message : in Message_Type;
                                Last    : in Boolean) do
          Display.Message := Message;
          Display.Last := Last;
        end Display_Message;
```

```
        Display_All_Messages_Loop:
        loop
          Display_The_Message_Loop:
          for I in Message'Range loop
            Blue_Devices.Display (Message (I));
            exit Display_The_Message_Loop when Message (I) = ASCII.CR;
          end loop Display_The_Message_Loop;
          Blue_Devices.Display (ASCII.LF); -- ends display the message

          exit Display_All_Messages_Loop when Last;

          accept Display_Message (Message : in Message_Type;
                                  Last    : in Boolean) do
            Display.Message := Message;
            Display.Last := Last;
          end Display_Message;
        end loop Display_All_Messages_Loop;
      or
        when Display_Message'Count = 0 =>
          accept Display_Char (Char : in Character) do
            Display.Char := Char;
          end Display_Char;

          Blue_Devices.Display (Char);

          Display_The_Message_Loop_2:
          while Char /= ASCII.CR loop
            accept Display_Char (Char : in Character) do
              Display.Char := Char;
            end Display_Char;

            Blue_Devices.Display (Char);
          end loop Display_The_Message_Loop_2;
          Blue_Devices.Display (ASCII.LF);
      or
        terminate;
      end select;
    end loop;
  end Display;
```

3.5.4 Main Program

```
with Blue_Keyboard;
with Red_Keyboard;
procedure HLCS is
begin
  null;
end HLCS;
```

3.6 Discussion

The HLCS requirement is typical of a large real-time system, with simplified algorithms and processing in order to allow it to be somewhat easily understood and implemented. One of the important points is that the operators not be restricted to simple exchange of messages, but that the system buffer messages for later delivery. Gehani [GEH84, page 169] addresses this sort of problem without the buffering requirement. It is still an interesting problem.

There is an implicit requirement that the messages be delivered in the order sent—that the queue be first-in first-out. (This is a typical way to order the messages in a buffer in any event, but the design of the buffer had to explicitly take this into account by incrementing the Remove index when an old message was overwritten. Note the code following the Enqueue of the task Buffer.)

However, the most interesting overall requirement is that the display must (1) be prepared (if nothing is ready to be displayed immediately) to accept either a message (one line) or a character, (2) not allow the creation of a message to be interrupted, and (3) empty the buffer of all pending messages when the operator completes an outgoing message.

This latter set of requirements calls for careful design of the system, particularly the display. Since the display needs to interact (in a nondeterministic manner) with either its own color keyboard or the other color keyboard (via the message buffer), it can be implemented most naturally as a called task. This in turn influences the design of the keyboard and, even more so, the design of the intermediary buffering tasks. These issues are discussed at length in Part 2, Task Intercommunication.

The given design arranges the data flow, the calls on entries, the use of a select statement with a guarded entry, and the internal logic of the Display task, to ensure that the requirements are met while at the same time avoiding polling or busy waiting. The exercises below, and the solutions given to some of them, address this issue further.

3.7 Exercises

Exercise 3.1. This problem is a sequence of exercises with generics. First, make the Blue_To_Red_Relay use a generic buffer. Then, make the entire Relay generic (not necessarily using a generic buffer); instantiate instances for Blue_To_Red and Red_To_Blue. Finally, make the display and the keyboard generic. Instantiate instances for each of the Red and Blue communication centers. This exercise emphasizes the essential symmetry of the HLCS solution. (The final part of this problem is solved below.)

Exercise 3.2. Add error checking to the keyboard and display tasks. For example, ensure that no more than 64 characters are input before a carriage return, that no nonprinting characters are input, and so on.

Exercise 3.3. Use data flow diagrams [YOU79] to define the HLCS, and relate the data flow diagrams to the process graph.

Exercise 3.4. Build the HLCS in four packages, rather than six, by breaking up the relay packages and putting the buffers with the keyboards and the transporters with the displays. Try other packaging combinations.

Exercise 3.5. Partition the system differently at the process graph level. For example, consider breaking the display function into two separate tasks. Reimplement the system, thinking about how your earlier tasking decisions affect packaging decisions.

Exercise 3.6. The given solution takes the messages out of the buffer as discrete a stream of characters. (The buffer need not know anything about messages. The display can distinguish individual messages by the carriage return.) Is this more efficient?

Exercise 3.7. The given solution uses the parameter "Last" to indicate when the last message is taken out of the buffer. Try an alternate apprach by providing an array of messages consisting of everything in the buffer.

Exercise 3.8. Another alternative to the use of a "Last" indicator is to provide a "buffer-empty" condition as a function exported by the buffer package. Try this approach. (You will find that there is a race condition that may prevent the final message from being removed from the relay. This message is "trapped" in the transporter, until the next set of messages are read.)

Exercise 3.9. The given solution with the "Last" indicator essentially defines the conclusion of message sending by the fact that the buffer becomes empty. The Red message center may be adding messages to the buffer while they are being displayed at Blue, but once the buffer is empty additional messages will not be displayed until the next set of messages are called for. Modify the solution so that these additional messages are read. (This calls for a combination of the "Last" indicator *and* a buffer-empty condition from the relay.)

Exercise 3.10. The given solution guarantees that messages will be displayed when available. This is because the guard on the entry that displays characters, "when Display_Message'Count = 0 =>", prevents an eager operator from starting another message before the incoming messages are displayed. However, there is nothing to prevent starvation of the operator.

This is fine for the current problem because of the relative slowness of creating messages compared to the short time taken to display them. If we have a slightly different situation, one in which messages are coming in rapidly over a communication channel (or if we simply wish to ensure correct functioning regardless of the speed of the relative processes, generally a good idea), we will need an alternate approach.

Guarantee that the operator is not starved. Ensure that, when both opportunities are continuously available, there is a strict alternation between preparing messages and reading/displaying messages. The system should still allow continuous creation of messages (or continuous display of messages) if only one alternative is available.

Exercise 3.11. Combine the situations of 3.9 and 3.10 (this is solved below.)

3.8 Partial Solutions to Exercises

We do not provide the full approach of top-level and detailed design, but instead provide only the code for the alternate solutions.

Solution 3.1 Generic HLCS. Here is the generic version of the HLCS developed earlier. Since our emphasis is on tasking, not generics, extensive discussion is not provided. However, this does provide an example of the interaction of tasks and generics.

```
----------- GENERIC HOT LINE COMMUNICATION SYSTEM (HLCS) ----
---------- Global definitions ----------
-- same as before

---------- generic Display_Handler ----------

with Definitions; use Definitions;
generic
  with procedure Device_Display (Char : in Character);
package Display_Handler is
  procedure Display_Message (Message : in Message_Type;
                             Last    : in Boolean);
  procedure Display_Char    (Char    : in Character);

  -- Calls Device_Display
end Display_Handler;

---------- generic Relay ----------

generic
  Buffer_Size : Positive;
  type Buffered_Type is private;
  with procedure Consumer_Take_Buffered (Buffered : in Buffered_Type;
                                         Last     : in Boolean);
package Buffer_Relay is
  procedure Enqueue (Buffered : in Buffered_Type);
  -- Calls
    -- Consumer_Take_Buffered
end Buffer_Relay;

---------- generic Keyboard_Handler ----------

with Definitions; use Definitions;
generic
  with procedure Device_Keyboard_Input  (Char    : out Character);
  with procedure Display_Char            (Char    : in  Character);
  with procedure Buffer_Enqueue_Message  (Message : in Message_Type);
```

```
package Keyboard_Handler is
  -- Calls
    -- Device_Keyboard_Input
    -- Display_Char
    -- Buffer_Enqueue_Message
end Keyboard_Handler;


---------- Display_Handler package body ----------

with Definitions; use Definitions;
package body Display_Handler is
  task Display is
    entry Display_Message (Message : in Message_Type;
                           Last    : in Boolean);
    entry Display_Char (Char : in Character);

    -- Calls Device_Display
  end Display;

  task body Display is
    Message : Message_Type;
    Last    : Boolean;
    Char    : Character;
  begin
    loop
      select
        accept Display_Message (Message : in Message_Type;
                                Last    : in Boolean) do
          Display.Message := Message;
          Display.Last := Last;
        end Display_Message;

        Display_All_Messages_Loop:
        loop
          Display_The_Message_Loop:
          for I in Message'Range loop
            Device_Display (Message (I) );

            exit Display_The_Message_Loop when Message (I) = ASCII.CR;
          end loop Display_The_Message_Loop;

          Device_Display (ASCII.LF);

          exit Display_All_Messages_Loop when Last;
```

```
            accept Display_Message (Message : in Message_Type;
                                    Last    : in Boolean) do
             Display.Message := Message;
             Display.Last := Last;
            end Display_Message;
        end loop Display_All_Messages_Loop; -- finish displaying
                                            -- all pending messages
     or
       when Display_Message'Count = 0 =>
         accept Display_Char (Char : in Character) do
            Display.Char := Char;
         end Display_Char;

         Device_Display (Char);

         Display_The_Message_Loop_2:
         while Char /= ASCII.CR loop

            accept Display_Char (Char : in Character) do
               Display.Char := Char;
            end Display_Char;

            Device_Display (Char);
         end loop Display_The_Message_Loop_2;

         Device_Display (ASCII.LF);
       or
         terminate;
       end select;
     end loop;
  end Display;

  procedure Display_Message (Message : in Message_Type;
                             Last    : in Boolean) is
  begin
    Display.Display_Message (Message, Last);
  end Display_Message;

  procedure Display_Char (Char : in Character) is
  begin
    Display.Display_Char (Char);
  end Display_Char;
end Display_Handler;
```

```
---------- Display_Handler instantiations ----------

with Display_Handler;
with Blue_Devices;
package Blue_Display is new Display_Handler
       (Device_Display => Blue_Devices.Display);

with Display_Handler;
with Red_Devices;
package Red_Display is new Display_Handler
       (Device_Display => Red_Devices.Display);

---------- Relay package body ----------

-- Generic relays and buffers are covered in
-- Chapter 7, The Bounded Buffer

---------- Buffer instantiations ----------

with Buffer_Relay;
with Definitions;
with Red_Display;
package Blue_To_Red_Relay is new Buffer_Relay
     (Buffer_Size   => Definitions.Max_Messages,
      Buffered_Type => Definitions.Message_Type,
      Consumer_Take_Buffered => Red_Display.Display_Message);

with Buffer_Relay;
with Definitions;
with Blue_Display;
package Red_To_Blue_Relay is new Buffer_Relay
     (Buffer_Size   => Definitions.Max_Messages,
      Buffered_Type => Definitions.Message_Type,
      Consumer_Take_Buffered => Blue_Display.Display_Message);
```

---------- Keyboard package body ----------

```
with Definitions; use Definitions;
package body Keyboard_Handler is
  task Keyboard is

    -- Calls
      -- Device_Keyboard_Input
      -- Display_Char
      -- Buffer_Enqueue_Message
  end Keyboard;
  task body Keyboard is
    Message : Message_Type;
  begin
    loop
      Build_Message:
      for I in Message'Range loop
        Device_Keyboard_Input (Message (I) );
        Display_Char (Message (I));
        exit Build_Message when Message (I) = ASCII.CR;
      end loop Build_Message;

      Buffer_Enqueue_Message (Message);
    end loop;
  end Keyboard;
end Keyboard_Handler;
```

----------Keyboard instantiations ----------

```
with Keyboard_Handler;
with Blue_Devices;
with Blue_Display;
with Blue_To_Red_Relay;
package Blue_Keyboard is new Keyboard_Handler
    (Device_Keyboard_Input  => Blue_Devices.Keyboard_Input,
     Display_Char           => Blue_Display.Display_Char,
     Buffer_Enqueue_Message => Blue_To_Red_Relay.Enqueue);

with Keyboard_Handler;
with Red_Devices;
with Red_Display;
with Red_To_Blue_Relay;
```

```
package Red_Keyboard is new Keyboard_Handler
   (Device_Keyboard_Input   => Red_Devices.Keyboard_Input,
    Display_Char             => Red_Display.Display_Char,
    Buffer_Enqueue_Message => Red_To_Blue_Relay.Enqueue);


---------- Main Program ----------

with Blue_Keyboard;
with Red_Keyboard;
procedure Generic_HLCS is
begin
   null;
end Generic_HLCS;
```

This problem provides an interesting illustration of the interaction of generics and tasks. Of particular note is the method of using procedures as generic parameters in order to have generic library units that call entrance procedures of other packages.

The order of compilation and instantiation is also important. There is a situation in which units must be instantiated in order to provide the library units to be accessed by later instantiations. For example the displays are instantiated first, then provide actual parameters for the instantiation of the keyboards.

Exercises 3.2–3.10 are not solved.

Solution 3.11   Empty Buffer and Never Starve Writer.

Empty Buffer: We first address the issue of emptying the buffer. The approach is to have the relay task explicitly export a buffer-empty condition. The display then checks to see if any messages have been placed in the buffer while the transporter (thinking it had the last message) was waiting to rendezvous with the display. This needs a change to both the relay and the display task. (We will only show the change to the display.)

Don't Starve Operator: We next address the issue of not starving the operator. We must continue to guarantee that the messages from the other color communication center are not starved. To accomplish this, we will take a state machine approach that eliminates the loops following the accept statements. The changes of state are made explicit, as shown in Figure 3-6.

This method has the advantage of clarifying the system's changes of state, but makes less explicit the idea of looping to finish one function—sending/creating a message or receiving messages—before

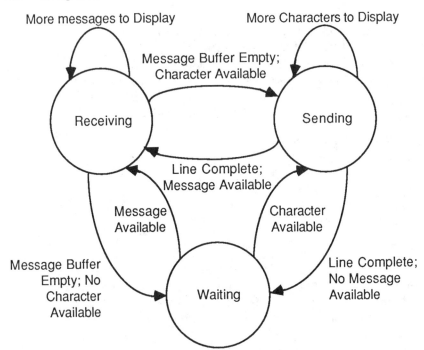

Figure 3-6. Display state diagram

returning to the waiting state. (By waiting state we mean ready to either send/create a message or receive messages). Only the display task must be changed to implement this approach, and it could be implemented independently of the change having to do with emptying the buffer.

Here is the new solution, showing the specification of the modified relay (in this case showing the relay that passes messages from Red to Blue) and the completely coded version of the Blue_Display task.

```
----- Here is the new Red_To_Blue_Relay.

with Definitions; use Definitions;
package Red_To_Blue_Relay is
   function Empty return Boolean;
   procedure Enqueue (Message : in Message_Type);
   -- Calls
   -- Blue_Display.Display_Message
end Red_To_Blue_Relay;
```

(Function Empty just calls an entry in the buffer task to see if it is empty or not. We will not give the code here.)

```
----- Here is the new Display.

separate (Blue_Display)
  task body Display is
    type Display_State is (Sending, Receiving, Waiting);
    State : Display_State := Waiting;

-- STATES:

--  Sending  : the operator is building a message to send

--  Receiving: the display is taking messages from the buffer and
--             displaying them

--  Waiting  : ready to become either Sending or Receiving

    Message : Message_Type;
    Last    : Boolean;
    Char    : Character;
  begin
    loop
      select
        when (State = Receiving or State = Waiting) =>
          accept Display_Message (Message : in Message_Type;
                                  Last    : in Boolean) do
            Display.Message := Message;
            Display.Last := Last;
          end Display_Message;

          Display_The_Message_Loop:
          for I in Message'Range loop
            Blue_Devices.Display (Message (I));
            exit Display_The_Message_Loop when Message (I) = ASCII.CR;
          end loop Display_The_Message_Loop;
          Blue_Devices.Display (ASCII.LF); -- ends display the message
```

```
            if Last and Red_To_Blue_Relay.Empty then
              if Display_Char'Count > 0 then
                State := Sending;
              else
                State := Waiting;
              end if;
            else
              State := Receiving;
            end if;
        or
          when (State = Sending or State = Waiting) =>
            accept Display_Char (Char : in Character) do
              Display.Char := Char;
            end Display_Char;

            Blue_Devices.Display (Char);

            if Char = ASCII.CR then
              Blue_Devices.Display (ASCII.LF); -- ends display the message

              if Display_Message'Count > 0 then
                State := Receiving;
              else
                State := Waiting;
              end if;
            else
              State := Sending;
            end if;
        or
          terminate;
        end select;
      end loop;
    end Display;
```

It is the condition "if Last and Red_To_Blue_Relay.Empty" that
ensures that not only was the buffer completely emptied, it has not
received any additional messages while the presumed "Last" message was being displayed.

Keys to Understanding

- Process abstraction is the primary decomposition principle for the design of concurrent Ada programs.

- The overall structure of a concurrent system involves tasks inside packages. Usually the interfaces between tasks in different packages will be via "entrance" procedures in the package specifications.

- There should be a task for each external device that interacts with a system.

- A task that needs to "simultaneously" interact with several other tasks should be called by the other tasks.

- Intermediary tasks can introduce asynchronous behavior into otherwise highly coupled task interactions.

- Two tasks can combine to provide a buffering relay.

- Generics can be effectively used with tasks.

- A combination of graphical methods and clearly defined step-wise refinement aids in the design and presentation of a concurrent system.

Task Intercommunication

Part 2 deals with the methods of communication between tasks. The foundation for later material is established by explaining the details of the rendezvous and how tasks control the rendezvous. Introduction of the notion of caller and called tasks makes it clear that the direction of rendezvous is an important design decision. Much of the remaining material deals with intermediary tasks, used to uncouple the close interaction of the rendezvous.

Intermediary tasks are discussed at length because they are the mechanism by which the programmer controls the degree of synchronization between tasks accomplishing the functioning of the system. Task communication in Ada is synchronized, or unbuffered. The rendezvous by itself synchronizes what should often be two asynchronous processes. Young [YOU82, page 153] points out there is a "..frequent need to introduce 'third party' processes to decouple asynchronous processes." Buhr [BUH84, page 60ff] also addresses the issue of uncoupling in regard to the direction of rendezvous.

The discussion of use of intermediary tasks (Young's "third party" tasks) revolves around three types of uncoupling processes—buffer, transporter, and relay—and their implementation as Ada tasks and packages.

The case study is quite long and somewhat design oriented. It uses intermediaries, illustrates the importance of the direction of entry calls, and points out several aspects of Ada that influence the design and implementation of large concurrent systems.

Rendezvous

Objective: To fully discuss the methods for controlling establishment of a rendezvous

The rendezvous is the unified mechanism in Ada for synchronization and mutual exclusion. The rendezvous has considerable similarity to a procedure, in regard to its invocation. However, a called task, unlike a called procedure, controls both *when* an entry is called and *where* it is called (and hence controls the execution occurring in response to a call).

The following sections discuss the effect of the call/accept combination, details of the call, details of accepting a call, the effect of the delay statement, details of control over the rendezvous, the effect of task priority, and a mechanism for enforcing a specific rendezvous protocol.

4.1 Call/Accept Combination

The calling task is said to "issue an entry call," to "call an entry," or somewhat colloquially, to "call the other task." The task that has declared the entry is said to "accept the call"; it is the called or accepting task. The call/accept combination creates a situation in which the two tasks intend to "meet." The first task to arrive at the rendezvous waits for the other. When they rendezvous, they are synchronized in terms of their execution. Further, they may exchange information during the rendezvous, with the called task executing instructions on behalf of both tasks.

We may view the caller as a person looking for service—let's say someone wishing to purchase postage stamps. The called task may be viewed as providing the service—let's say a post office clerk who sells stamps, and also has his own independent duties to perform when not selling stamps. This analogy was popularized by Ichbiah [ICH84b]. Although it does not fit all circumstances, it often reflects the flavor of the call/accept combination and we will refer to it frequently. The situation is pictured in Figure 4-1. We will refer to the person looking for stamps as the "Customer" task, and the clerk selling stamps as the "Post_Office" task.

Figure 4-1. Post office analogy

4.2 The Entry Call

When a task wishes to rendezvous with another task that has declared some entries, it calls one of the entries. The usual visibility rules prevail, so that, except in the case of a nested task calling its parent (an enclosing task), the name of the entry is not immediately visible; it must be preceded by the name of the task that declared the entry. The call, therefore, consists of name of the task, "dot," name of the called entry, formal part (parameter list). There is no analogy of the "use" clause for tasks. For example, if the specification of Post_Office is

```
task Post_Office is
  entry Purchase (Payment : in Money;
                  Stamps  : out Postage);
end Post_Office;
```

then a call from the Customer to the Post_Office is:

```
Post_Office.Purchase (Some_Money, Book_Of_Stamps);
```

The Customer provides some money and receives a book of stamps. (The payment will always be just the right amount, and therefore no change is required.)

If the evaluation of an expression is required to determine values for the actual parameters, the evaluation is accomplished as part of the entry call, before the rendezvous takes place. In fact, if the Customer must wait in a queue of tasks that have called the same entry (discussed in the next section), these evaluations take place before the Customer is placed in the queue.

What do we mean by an evaluation to determine the values for the actual parameters? The actual parameter Some_Money corresponds to a formal parameter of mode "in." Therefore, it may be a function or an expression. If Some_Money is a function, the function is executed and the resulting value determined as a part of the entry call, before the rendezvous takes place. Further (assuming that the type of the parameter is a real type), Some_Money could be replaced by an expression such as "1.23 + 0.67". The evaluation of the expression, yielding the value of "1.9", takes place as part of the issuing of the entry call.

If the called task is not waiting at the called entry point (and is, therefore, not prepared to accept the call), the calling task is blocked. It is no longer ready to run, it does not have the resources it requires, and it cannot proceed with execution. It must be suspended. In a single processor system, or one that has more "ready" tasks than available processors, it must give up the processor on which it was executing—i.e., the run-time environment will schedule and dispatch another task.

Figure 4-2 provides a simple illustration of the states of execution in a system having more tasks than processors. It includes the very common case of a single processor with a number of tasks. It is similar to Figure 1-1, but is specific to the interaction of the Ada rendezvous. You can see that there is a state transition from *running*

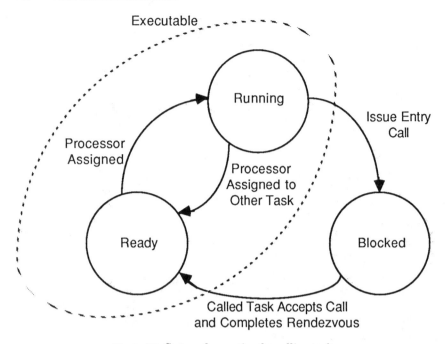

Figure 4-2. States of execution for calling task

(the state in which the task issued the entry call) to *blocked* (the state in which it is suspended while waiting for the called task to reach the accept statement corresponding to the called entry.) When the called task reaches the accept statement and executes the rendezvous, the calling task becomes *ready* and will gain access to the processor at some later time. When the task is blocked, it is under the management of the Ada run-time environment, but otherwise consumes no processor resources.

Once a task has issued an entry call of the sort illustrated, it is completely committed to the rendezvous. It will remain blocked until the rendezvous is complete.

What happens when a number of tasks call an entry before the called task reaches the rendezvous point? They are queued, in a strictly first-in first-out manner. This is discussed further in Section 4.3.2.

4.3 Accepting an Entry Call

This section discusses the basic rules governing the declaration and acceptance of an entry, the characteristics of the rendezvous and the accept statement, and the effect of declaring families of entries.

4.3.1 Entry Declaration and Accept

The task accepting an entry call must first have declared the entry. For example, as we saw earlier,

```
task Post_Office is
  entry Purchase (Payment : in Money;
                  Stamps  : out Postage);
end Post_Office;
```

In the body of the task there is an accept statement corresponding to the entry.

```
accept Purchase (Payment : in Money;
                 Stamps  : out Postage) do
  Cash_Box  := Cash_Box + Payment;

  -- assume a function that provides stamps
  Stamps    := Stamps_For (Payment);
end Purchase;
```

If the entry call has already been issued when the Post_Office reaches this accept statement, the code of the accept statement is immediately executed while the calling Customer task remains suspended. If the entry call has not been issued, then the Post_Ofice task becomes blocked. After the call is issued, the calling task is suspended while Post_Office executes the code of the accept statement. After the rendezvous, the tasks go their separate ways, continuing their execution in parallel.

NOTE

The phrase "the tasks go their separate ways" is used here to emphasize the abstract nature of the concurrent interaction. If there are more tasks than processors, the run-time environment must use some method to schedule the next task to execute. This may depend upon the priority of tasks. (Priorities are discussed at the end of this chapter.)

Second Note: As noted above, the calling task is suspended while the called task executes the code of the rendezvous. In a single processor system, this requires a context switch. In this situation, and in others, it may be possible for the compiler to optimize the code to prevent a context switch. In fact, some of the Ada tasks may not implemented as separate tasks at all. Habermann and Perry [HAB80] and Hilfinger [HIL82] discuss how certain types of task interactions may be replaced (by the Ada compiler/run-time in a manner invisible to the programmer) either by procedure calls or by the use of semaphores—a simpler form of concurrent control.

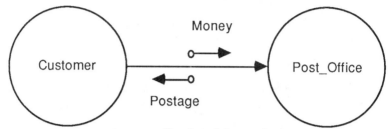

Figure 4-3. Simple task interaction

Figure 4-3 is a process graph illustrating the interaction between the Customer and the Post_Office. The arrowhead touching the Post_Office indicates that it is the called task. The Customer is the calling task. The data flows and direction of data flow are shown with the small arrows. The most important aspect of the names of the data on process graphs is that they communicate the meaning of the task interaction. The names of the data are often, as they are in this case, the names of the types of the data.

4.3.2 Characteristics of the Rendezvous

The rendezvous represents the meeting of two tasks at a point at which they are synchronized and may exchange data. The execution of the sequence of statements of the accept statement constitutes the rendezvous. The execution is done in mutual exclusion—the rendezvous is a critical region for the tasks involved. The call to the entry and the execution of the accept statement is somewhat similar to a procedure call, but it is considered to be executed by the called task, on behalf of both itself and the calling task.

When a task reaches an accept statement, it is committed to a rendezvous with some other task that will call the entry. Notice the difference between this situation and that resulting from a task issuing an entry call. The calling task is committed to a rendezvous with a specific entry of a specific task, while the called task has committed itself only to a specific entry; it is willing to rendezvous with any task calling the entry.

Suppose several tasks have called an entry before the called task is prepared to rendezvous. What is the effect? Let's discuss this in a specific way by considering the Purchase entry in the Post_Office task.

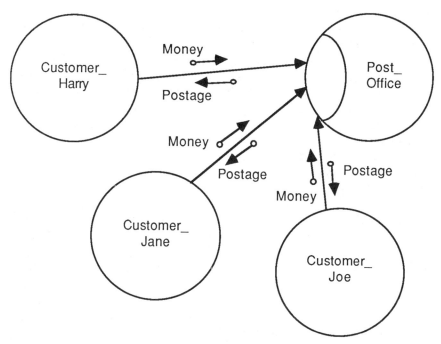

Figure 4-4. Many tasks calling the same entry

Figure 4-4 illustrates a number of tasks calling the same entry in the Post_Office. When several calls have been made to the Purchase entry while the clerk is doing other chores, the calling tasks become queued, waiting for the Post_Office to provide service. It is just as though many Customers are waiting for service. The service protocol is strictly first-in first-out, regardless of task priorities.

When the clerk reaches the accept statement, he services the first Customer in line, then goes about his other duties. Therefore, each execution of the accept statement removes one caller from the queue. If we wish the clerk to serve more than one customer before doing his other duties, we can simply program a loop to repeat the accept statement.

When the rendezvous is complete, the two tasks continue their execution in parallel.

4.3.3 Characteristics of the Accept Statement

The execution of the code of the accept statement is much like that of the procedure call. The formal "in" and "in out" parameters are associated with the actual parameters, the code is executed, and values are provided for parameters of "out" mode. The scope of the parameters is limited to the text of the accept statement. Therefore, the code of the task outside the accept statement cannot access the parameters of the accept statement.

The accept statement inherits declarations exactly as though it were a nested procedure declared in a block at the point of the accept statement. It inherits visibility of the declarations local to the task, as well as anything visible to the task itself.

Although the accept statement cannot have either a declarative part or an "exception" part, it can achieve the effect of having both by way of a nested block. The block may have both a declarative part and exception handlers.

The accept statement must appear in the sequence of statements of the task body. It may not appear in any nested program unit in the declarative part of the task body. For example, it may not appear in a procedure nested within the task body.

The called task may have more than one accept statement for an entry declaration. It may, therefore, accept the rendezvous at different locations in the program text. Furthermore, the actions that it takes during the rendezvous may differ, depending on which of the accept statements handles the entry call. For example, the task may maintain its own internal state; the accept statement that it executes in response to an entry call may well depend upon this state. However, the interface for each accept statement must be the same since it must be that specified in the entry declaration.

Regardless of how many accept statements are associated with each entry, there is still a single queue of tasks waiting for service from the entry. Each entry has an attribute, 'Count, which is the number of tasks on the queue for the entry. For example,

```
Purchase'Count
```

is the number of tasks in the queue for the Purchase entry.

The code that may be executed in an accept statement is very general. It may for example, contain calls to entries of other tasks, and may contain nested accept statements, including an accept for another call to the entry that is being served. That is, the following code is legal.

```
...
   accept An_Entry_Call (...) do
      ...
   Other_Task.Enqueue (...);
   accept Different_Call (...) do ... end Different_Call;
      ...
   accept An_Entry_Call (...) do ... end An_Entry_Call;
      ...
   end An_Entry_Call;
...
```

The task that has first called the entry An_Entry_Call is held in the rendevous while all this activity is going on (including another accept for the entry that has been called to start this rendezvous). This is another example in which the *code* of the accept statement will differ for two different accepts for the same entry.

Buhr [BUH84, page 153ff] feels it is preferable to avoid such a situation, which he calls *nonlinear*. However, such interactions may well be useful. One circumstance might be that a server task requires interaction with other tasks in order to perform its job. Another situation might be that, for timing considerations, the caller must know that a server's job involving interaction with other tasks (including hardware) is complete before the caller continues its own execution.

4.3.4 Family of Entries

There is one queue, with a first-in first-out priority for each entry. Sometimes it may be advantageous to partition this queue into a number of subqueues, to discriminate among the levels of service provided. For example, suppose we wished our post office to have a separate service window based upon the first letter of the last name of the Customer desiring service. Instead of having 26 entries, it is convenient to have a set (a family) of entries indexed by the characters of the alphabet. This works as long as we wish to provide the same actions regardless of the last name of the person whom the post office is serving.

Assume that Windows has been defined as:

```
subtype Windows is Character range 'A' .. 'Z';
```

We then can have a family of 26 entries, one entry for each uppercase letter of the alphabet. The task specification is:

```
task Post_Office is
    entry Purchase (Windows) (Payment : in Money;
                             Stamps  : out Postage);
end Post_Office;
```

An entry is called as:

```
Post_Office.Purchase ('S') (Some_Money, Book_Of_Stamps);
```

In the body of Post_Office, we can do many different kinds of things to provide appropriate service. For example, we might favor certain letters by not accepting calls to other entries while the queues for the favored entries are nonempty. The accept statements are identified by the entry index. For example:

```
for Next in Windows loop
    accept Purchase (Next) (...) do
      ...
```

or in an individual instance as:

```
accept Purchase ('A') (...) do ...
```

The Rationale [ICH79, pages 11-16] contains an extended example of the use of a family of entries as a general scheduling algorithm.

4.4 The Delay Statement

Ada provides a delay statement to allow a task to be suspended for a specified period of time. The time is specified as a number of seconds (or fraction of a second). For example:

```
Minutes         : constant Duration := 60.0;
Milliseconds    : constant Duration :=  0.001;
Update_Periodic : constant Duration := 200.0;
...
delay  0.05;
delay  1.34;
delay  10 * Minutes;
delay  160 * Milliseconds;
delay  Update_Periodic;
```

A simple expression is allowed following the reserved word delay. The result of the expression must be of type Duration. A typical expression is that shown: an Integer times a Duration.

An implementation must allow for representation of durations of at least one day (86,400 seconds). A delay with a negative value is the same as a delay with a zero value.

The length of delay is a *minimum* value. When the delay statement is executed, the state of the task changes from *running* to *blocked*. After the indicated delay period has passed, the task state changes to *ready*, but it is not necessarily *running*.

The delay statement is often used in relation to the predefined package Calendar (see ANS83, page 9–11). Calendar provides the type Time as an abstract (private) type; the function Clock, which returns a value of the current Time; and a number of other functions to allow the manipulation of objects of type Time and Duration. Among these are overloaded addition, subtraction, and comparison operators.

A common use of the delay statement is to arrange for a task to execute periodically. An approriate way to execute periodically with an *average* interval of (the previously defined constant) Update_ Periodic is:

```
use Calendar;
task body Periodic_Timer is
  Next_Time : Time := Clock + Update_Periodic;
begin
  Periodic_Loop: loop
    delay Next_Time - Clock;

    -- do whatever is to be done periodically

    Next_Time := Next_Time + Update_Periodic;
  end loop Periodic_Loop;
end Periodic_Timer;
```

This task executes in a context where the capabilities of Calendar have been made available with the "with" clause. The "use" clause provides immediate visibility to the type Time and the functions Clock, "+", and "-".

Next_Time is always the "next" time that the periodic event is to occur, and hence is always incremented by Update_Periodic. The amount of delay is expressed as the difference between the scheduled next time and the clock in order to compensate for two things:

1. The time taken to "do whatever is to be done periodically."

2. The time taken by other system activities. Remember that the delay is a *minimum* time, not an exact time.

The method above will produce cyclic events repeating on the *average* each Update_Interval seconds. As long as the duration of each interval (including the cyclic function and other system processing) is less than Update_Periodic, there will be no cumulative drift away from the desired average frequency of occurrence.

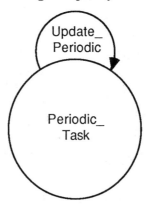

Figure 4-5. Process graph for periodic task

Figure 4-5 illustrates the process graph for a periodic task. The notation is suggestive of the task having a rendezvous with itself, while the periodic interval is shown within the looped arrow.

4.5 Control over the Rendezvous

This section first discusses the control over the rendezvous that may be exercised by the calling task, and then the rather more extensive control available to the called task.

4.5.1 Calling Task

The calling task has two methods of controlling its fate in regard to the rendezvous: the timed and conditional entry calls.

4.5.1.1 Timed Entry Call. The timed entry call allows the calling task to issue an entry call that will be canceled if the rendezvous does not start within a given time period. If the Customer in our previous example were somewhat impatient, willing to wait for stamps only for a limited period of time, he would use a timed entry call. For example:

```
select
   Post_Office.Purchase (Some_Money ...);
   Mail_Letters;
or
   delay 30.0;
   Hand_Deliver_Letters;
end select;
```

The Customer issues an entry call to Post_Office.Purchase. If the call is not accepted immediately, Customer goes on the queue for the entry. If the call is accepted within 30 seconds, the rendezvous takes place and the optional sequence of statements following the call (here it is just the procedure call "Mail_Letters") is executed.

If the call is not accepted within the specified duration of 30 seconds, the call is canceled. The calling task is removed from the queue and the optional sequence of statements following the delay statement is executed. The sequence is just the procedure call "Hand_Deliver_Letters".

The value of the expression following the delay statement may be zero (or negative, with the same result as zero). If so, the rendezvous occurs only if the called task is immediately prepared to accept the call (i.e., it is waiting at an accept statement).

Some care is needed when using the timed entry call, since it affects the 'Count attribute of the entry it is calling. We will see this later when we discuss the guarded selective wait.

4.5.1.2 Conditional Entry Call. The conditional entry call allows the calling task to issue an call that will be canceled if the rendezvous is not immediately available. If the Customer were even more impatient than in the example above, he would use a conditional entry call. For example:

```
select
   Post_Office.Purchase (Some_Money ...);
   Mail_Letters;
else
   Hand_Deliver_Letters;
end select;
```

The Customer issues an entry call to Post_Office.Purchase. If the call is not accepted immediately, the else part (the alternate sequence of statements following the else) is executed. The alter-nate sequence of statements is required, but can be a null state-ment. If the call is accepted immediately, the rendezvous takes place and the optional sequence of statements following the entry call is executed.

There may be a delay statement in the else part, but the effect is very different from that of the timed entry call. For example,

```
select
    Post_Office.Purchase (Some_Money ...);
    Mail_Letters;
else
    delay 30.0;
    Hand_Deliver_Letters;
end select;
```

In this case, if the rendezvous is not available immediately, the customer will delay 30 seconds before hand delivering the letters. The delay has nothing to do with waiting for the rendezvous.

4.5.1.3 Summary of the Controlled Entry Call. The calling task can issue either

- A conditional entry call
- A timed entry call

In the first instance, the rendezvous takes place immediately if the called task is ready to accept the entry. Otherwise it does not take place at all. In the second case, the calling task waits for a limited period of time, in the queue for the called entry. These are the *only* two aspects of control over the rendezvous for the calling task.

4.5.2 Called Task

The called task uses the "selective wait" to control its fate in regard to the rendezvous. The selective wait alone provides considerable control, and it is made more powerful by the use of guards on alter-natives, and timed and conditional capabilities similar to timed and conditional entry calls. Finally, the selective wait may be combined with a "terminate" to allow a group of tasks to cooperatively cease execution.

4.5.2.1 General. The selective wait gives a called task the capability to accept any one of a number of alternatives. The alternatives are accept statements, delay statements, and a terminate statment. A selective wait may also have an "else" part that is executed if no alternative is immediately available. We will first discuss the simplest form of the selective wait.

4.5.2.2 Simple Selective Wait. We will modify our post office, allowing it to provide more forms of service, in order to illustrate the selective wait. Here is the new task specification:

```
task Post_Office is
   entry Purchase (Some_Money ...);
   entry Mail      (...);
   entry Complain (...);
end Post_Office;
```

Based on the above entries, an example of the simple select statement is:

```
select
   accept Purchase (Some_Money ...) do
      ...
   end Purchase;
or
   accept Mail (...) do
      ...
   end Mail;

   ... -- optional sequence of statements
   ...
or
   accept Complain (...) do
      ...
   end Complain;
   ... -- optional sequence of statements
end select;
```

The syntax is helpful in illustrating that one *or* another *or* another will be selected for execution. A sequence of statements may follow the rendezvous. After one of the branches of the select statement is executed, the select statement is satisfied and control passes to the statement following "end select;". There may be more than one accept statement for a single entry.

Which of the rendezvous will be accepted when this task reaches the select statement? Let's look at three situations that may occur before the task reaches the select statement.

1. None of the entries have been called.

2. One of the entries has been called.

3. Two or more of the entries have been called.

In the latter two instances we assume that not only has the entry call been issued but that a task is still waiting for service.

In the first instance the task blocks at the select statement, just as it would block at any "accept", for an entry that had not been called. The rendezvous simply occurs with the first task to call any one of the entries in the select statement.

In the second instance the rendezvous takes place immediately with the task that called the entry, just as if the called task had reached a simple accept statement for that entry.

In the third instance an arbitrary choice is made among the entries that have been called. That is, any one of the entries that have been called may be accepted. How is the selection made? The *Ada Langauge Reference Manual* [ANS83, page 9-13] states that "the language does not define which one." This arbitrary selection introduces a degree of nondeterminism in the called task; it must be prepared to deal with any of the alternative rendezvous.

A vital point is that the correctness of the program must not depend upon any specific method of selection of the alternatives of the select statement. Barnes states [BAR84, page 221], "the implementor is free to choose some efficient mechanism that nevertheless introduces an adequate degree of non-determinism so that the various queues are treated fairly and none gets starved." This is certainly desirable in many instances. However, the usual interpretation of "arbitrary" is that there is no implication of "fairness" in the selection criteria, and an implementation may use a mechanism that allows tasks to starve.

4.5.2.3 Selective Wait with Guards. It is possible to introduce a conditional test in front of a select alternative. The condition is evaluated when the program reaches the select statement. If the condition is true, the select alternative is said to be "open." If the condition is false, the select alternative is said to be "closed." A closed alternative is not eligible for selection. The condition is called a "guard." An alternative without a guard is always open. We can modify our post office to illustrate the use of guards.

```
select
  when Number_Of_Stamps > 0 =>
    accept Purchase (Some_Money ...) do
      ...
    end Purchase;
or
  accept Mail (...) do
    ...
  end Mail;
      ... -- optional sequence of statements
      ...
or
  when Complaint_Department_Open =>
    accept Complain (...) do
      ...
    end Complain;
    ... -- optional sequence of statements
end select;
```

The Purchase and Complain alternatives are guarded; they are available for selection only when the conditions are true. The Mail alternative is always open. The arbitrary choice of alternatives, discussed in the section above on the simple select statement, is made among open alternatives. If no alternatives are open when the select statement is reached, the predefined exception Program_Error is raised.

It is possible to use an attribute of an entry as one of the conditions for a guarded accept. For example, we might prefer to serve customers wishing to mail letters over those wishing to complain. We can do so by:

```
or
  when (Complaint_Department_Open and Mail'Count = 0) =>
    accept Complain ...
```

Only if there are no customers queued for mailing will the post office accept a complaint. We must take care in using the attribute however, since a task may issue a conditional entry call to the Mail entry (or be aborted, as discussed in Chapter 12, Termination). Either circumstance may change the value of the attribute between the time that the guards are evaluated (at the start of the select statement), and the execution of the accept statement. For example, suppose tasks are queued on the Complain entry, and that an impatient customer is waiting to mail a package when the Post_Office task reaches the select statement. The guard on the Complain entry is evaluated as false. If the impatient customer now leaves *before the entry call is accepted* (and there are no other customers in the queue) the post office will wrongly fail to consider serving the Complaint queue, and the complaining customers are improperly delayed.

The example above illustrates that the conditions of the guards are evaluated at the time the task reaches the select statement. The guards are not reevaluated while the task is waiting for a rendezvous. This is true for all guards, not just those dependent upon the 'Count attribute. The example also illustrates that the condition may be more complex than a simple single condition. The boolean expression has no particular limitation; it is just like the boolean expression in an "if" statement. The parentheses in the example are not required, simply added for clarity.

The statement following the guard must be an "accept" (or a delay or terminate, as we will see later); it may not be some other type of statement. For example, it is not permitted to have a guarded alternative of the form:

```
select
  accept ...
or
  when Some_Condition =>
    Iterations := Iterations + 1; -- illegal
or
  ...
end select;
```

The optional else part of the selective wait, discussed in a later section, does allow the execution of any sequence of statements when no rendezvous is available. However, it may not be guarded.

4.5.2.4 Selective Wait with Delay (Timed).

The called task may control the rendezvous in a manner analogous to the timed entry call of a calling task. The selective wait provides for a delay alternative in addition to a selection of rendezvous. If the clerk in the post office has other tasks to do, he may do them after he has waited for customers for 2 minutes. The select statement looks like:

```
select
  when Number_Of_Stamps > 0 =>
    accept Purchase (Some_Money ...) do
      ...
    end Purchase;
or
  accept Mail (...) do
    ...
  end Mail;
  ...
or
  when Complaint_Department_Open =>
    accept Complain (...) do
      ...
    end Complain;
or
  delay 2 * Minutes;
  Go_Sort_Mail;
  ...   -- any sequence of statements
end select;
```

If there are no calls to an open accept statement, the Post_Office task is suspended. If a call is issued within 2 minutes, the rendezvous occurs. If no call is issued within 2 minutes, the procedure Go_Sort_Mail is executed, along with any other tasks the clerk must perform. If the rendezvous occurs, the select statement is satisfied; it is left without the execution of the procedure Go_Sort_Mail.

Any entry calls to alternatives of the select statement during the execution of the sequence of statements following the delay are merely queued. The sequence of statements is optional. When execution of the statements is complete, the select statement is left.

The delay statement may be guarded. There may be more than one delay alternative in the select statement. If more than one delay alternative is open, the shortest delay governs the time the task is willing to wait for a rendezvous. If there are two or more open delay alternatives with the same delay, one of them is arbitrarily selected. The effect of zero delay (or a negative delay) is that, in the absence of an open accept alternative with a pending call, the task will immediately execute the sequence of statements following the delay statement, or leave the select statement in the case in which there are no statements.

The time of the delay is to the *start* of the rendezvous (in a manner similar to the timed entry call). The delay is canceled when a rendezvous occurs. The next time the called task reaches the selective wait with a delay, the delay timing is restarted. That is, the amount of delay is not accumulated from execution to execution of the select statement.

4.5.2.5 Selective Wait with Else (Conditional). The select statement with an else part gives a called task a capability analogous to the calling task's conditional entry call. This form of the select statement allows the execution of any sequence of statements, not just a selection among alternative rendezvous. An example is:

```
select
  when Number_Of_Stamps > 0 =>
    accept Purchase (...) do
      ...
    end Purchase;
or
  accept Mail (...) do
    ...
  end Mail;
    ...
or
  when Complaint_Department_Open =>
    accept Complain (...) do
      ...
    end Complain;
else
  Go_Sort_Mail;
  ...   -- any sequence of statements
end select;
```

The procedure Go_Sort_Mail is executed if no accept alternative can be accepted immediately. This occurs if no tasks have called entries of open alternatives, or if all alternatives are closed. If a rendezvous does occur, the else part of the select statement is not executed. A select statement with an else part will never raise Program_Error as a result of all alternatives being closed.

Notice the different effect of the "else" and the "or." The "else" takes effect immediately if no rendezvous is available, while the "or" implies a more nearly equivalent relationship, with the task waiting for any one of the alternatives to be satisfied.

The select statement with an else part is the called task's analogy to the conditional entry call. An impatient called task can use this mechanism to rendezvous only if it can do so immediately; otherwise it continues about its business. A select statement may not contain both an else part and a delay alternative; they are mutually exclusive.

4.5.2.6 Selective Wait with Terminate. A select statement may contain an alternative that allows the task to terminate when it is no longer needed. It terminates cooperatively with other tasks. For the post office example, we have:

```
select
   when Number_Of_Stamps > 0 =>
      accept Purchase (Some_Money ...) do
         ...
      end Purchase;
or
   accept Mail (...) do
      ...
   end Mail;
   ...
or
   when Complaint_Department_Open =>
      accept Complain (...) do
         ...
      end Complain;
or
   terminate; -- note no optional following statements
end select;
```

When a task is waiting for a rendezvous at such a select statement, it is in a state such that, if it is no longer to be called, it will terminate. This termination occurs in cooperation with a number of "related" tasks. The exact termination condition is somewhat complex, and tied to the rules of task termination. Basically, the termination conditions are that the task will terminate if all the tasks that are eligible to call its entries are in a state such that they will never do so. Since its entries will never be called, it should terminate. This topic will be discussed fully in Chapter 12, Termination.

The syntax is somewhat confusing here, in that the terminate alternative is not an "or" condition with the other alternatives. This sort of select statement is often misunderstood to mean that the task terminates if no rendezvous is available. Not so. The task is willing to wait at this select statement for a rendezvous, as long as other tasks that are potentially able to call the rendezvous are still active.

The terminate alternative may be guarded. If the guard is false, the terminate alternative is closed, and the effect is as though the task were not waiting at a select statement with a terminate alternative.

A terminate alternative may not be in a select statement that has either a delay alternative or an else part; they are mutually exclusive. There may be only one terminate alternative in a select statement. No statements are allowed following the terminate statement.

4.5.2.7 Summary of the Selective Wait. Figure 4-6 summarizes what we've said about the selective wait. The conditions of rendezvous are affected by the use of "delay", "else", or "terminate" in the select statement.

The easiest case is that in which only one open entry has been called; there is an immediate rendezvous. If two or more open entries have been called, an arbitrary selection among them is made; there is still an immediate rendezvous.

If no open entries have been called, we must consider the effect of the else part, and the delay and terminate alternatives. These are mutually exclusive. There may be an else part, *or* one or more delays, *or* a terminate, but no combination of the three options.

The remaining discussion only applies if no immediate rendezvous is available. An available rendezvous is always prefered to other options in the selective wait.

If the else part is present, it is executed immediately when no rendezvous is available.

If there are one or more open delay alternatives, the task waits for either a call to an open entry or the expiration of the shortest delay. If there is a call to an open entry, the rendezvous takes place and the delay is cancelled. If the delay expires, the optional statements following the delay statement are executed.

If there is an open terminate alternative, the task waits for either a call to an open entry or the occurance of the termination conditions. If there is a call to an open entry, the rendezvous takes place and the terminate alternative has no effect. If the termination conditions occur, the task terminates normally. No statements are allowed following the terminate alternative.

If there is no else part and no open delay or open terminate alternative, the task simply waits for an entry call. If none of the entries are open, the exception Program_Error is raised.

```
if < only one open entry has been called > then

    immediate rendezvous;

elsif < two or more open entries have been called > then

    arbitrary selection;

elsif < no open entries have been called > then

    if < else part > then

        execute else part;

    elsif < open delay alternative > then

        wait for first of entry call or expiration of delay;

    elsif < open terminate alternative > then

        wait for first of entry call or terminate conditions;

    else

        wait for entry call;

    end if;

end if;
```

If there are no open alternatives and no else part, the exception
                Program_Error is raised.

Figure 4-6. Summary of selective wait

4.5.3 Summary of Control over the Rendezvous

Figure 4-7 summarizes how both calling and called tasks use the
select statement to control the rendezvous. Both types of tasks have
the ability to conditionally choose to enter into a rendezvous.

4.6 Task Priorities

Tasks may have relative priorities. If an implementation implements a priority mechanism, it does so with the pragma Priority as:

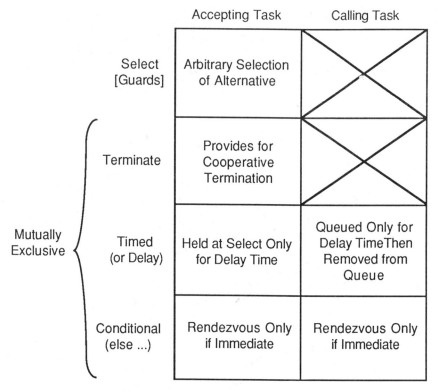

Figure 4-7. Summary of control over the rendezvous

```
pragma Priority (static_expression);
```

The pragma is placed in the task specification. The static_ expression must be determinable at compile time; Ada tasks have static, not dynamic, priorities. The type of the expression is Integer. The range of priorities is implementation-defined, but lower values always mean lower priority, a lower degree of urgency.

The intent of priorities is to relate to an Ada run-time environment the relative degree of urgency of tasks when there are more tasks than processors. This includes the common case of a single processor with multiple tasks. The rule governing allocation of processing resources [ANS83, page 9-16] is:

> If two tasks with different priorities are both eligible for execution and could sensibly be executed using the same physical processors and the same other processing resources, then it cannot be the case that the task with the lower priority is executing while the task with the higher priority is not.

This simply means that the highest priority tasks execute when the resources they require become available. A resource may be a rendezvous with another task. In a system with fewer processors than tasks, the intent is that the scheduling is preemptive, so that when a high priority task changes state from "blocked" to "ready", it immediately changes state to "running".

Priorities are not to be used to ensure mutual exclusion. They simply indicate a relative degree of urgency. We will still make no assumptions about the relative speed of each of the independent processes—Ada tasks. After all, the same code may one day run on a multiprocessor system (with one processor per task)—providing actual concurrency and making the idea of priority meaningless.

A rendezvous executes with the higher priority of the two tasks involved. The queueing of tasks that have called the same entry remains first-in first-out, without regard to priority. Priority similarly does not affect selection of alternatives in a selective wait; the selection remains nondeterministic.

4.7 Enforcing a Rendezvous Protocol

It is frequently desirable for a called task to control the calling protocol used by its callers. For example, we might wish to forbid conditional or timed entry calls, to make the use of the 'Count attribute safer. (Of course a task in an entry queue may still be aborted, thereby asynchronously leaving the queue. However, we expect aborts to be very rare and their use carefully controlled.) Alternatively, we may wish to *require* conditional calls. We can accomplish this by embedding the task in a package body, using what we call *entrance procedures* to enforce the protocol. Entrance procedures were illustrated in Chapter 3, the first case study. For the post office situation, we have:

```
package Mail_Station is
   procedure Purchase (Some_Money ...);
   procedure Mail     (...);
   procedure Complain (...);

   pragma Inline (Purchase, Mail, Complain);
end Mail_Station;
```

```
package body Mail_Station is
  task Post_Office is -- repeating the declaration of 4.5.2
    entry Purchase (Some_Money ...);
    entry Mail    (...);
    entry Complain (...);
  end Post_Office;

  procedure Purchase (Some_Money ...) is
    ...
  end Purchase;

  procedure Mail    (...) is
    ...
  end Mail;

  procedure Complain (...) is
  begin
    select
      Post_Office.Complain (...);
    or
      delay 30.0;
    end select;
  end Complain;
end Mail_Station;
```

We have illustrated the use of the entrance procedure in the instance of the Complain entry. The calling tasks may not call Post_Office.Complain directly, but must call Mail_Station.Complain. The entrance procedure then issues the call to the entry while enforcing the protocol that if the complaint is not serviced within 30.0 seconds, the caller must go away. Typically, some indication (either the use of a parameter or an exception) will be provided to indicate whether service has been completed. This will be illustrated in the Cobbler problems.

The use of an entrance procedure is also useful in the circumstance in which we wish some, but not all, of a task's entries to be available to other processes. This style of interface supports the general concept of information hiding by making the interface between packages as small as possible, and by revealing as little as possible about the workings of the package providing the interface. Burns [BUR84, page 113] recommends that "... this 'procedural interface' should be used for all tasks, especially as the package is a far more useful design structure."

What about the overhead of the extra procedure call? The pragma Inline, illustrated above, is a suggestion to the compiler that the call should be expanded at the point of call (in a manner similar to a macro), rather than actually be a procedure call. (We illustrated the use of Inline in the first case study.) Many compilers are likely to do this without the suggestion, as a routine case of optimization. We will not use pragma Inline in the rest of the book, its use being either unnecessary or understood.

4.8 Exercises

In the exercises at the end of Chapter 2, we saw how a monitor could be used to protect a shared variable. Only one task was allowed access at a time. Now we wish to address a more general case, in which we distinguish between readers and writers. Readers only read the shared data; they do not update it. Writers update the data.

The classic problem is to allow only one writer, but (when there is no writer) to allow multiple readers. There is no conflict when several tasks simultaneously read a shared variable; the conflict only occurs between reading and writing.

Exercise 4.1. First Reader-Writer

Purpose: To introduce the classic readers-writers problem

Problem: Create a package with the following specification.

```
package Access_Shared is
   procedure Read_Shared  (Item :    out Integer);
   procedure Write_Shared (Item : in     Integer);
end Access_Shared;
```

The package contains a shared variable of type Integer. The body of the package is to allow multiple readers, but (when there are no readers) only a single writer. Create a procedure with multiple tasks that read and write the shared variable.

Solution:

```
package body Access_Shared is
  Shared_Item : Integer := 1;

  task Controller is
    entry Start_Write;
    entry Stop_Write;
    entry Start_Read;
    entry Stop_Read;
  end Controller;

  task body Controller is
    Number_Of_Readers : Natural := 0;
    No_Writer         : Boolean := True;
  begin
    loop
      select
        when No_Writer =>
          accept Start_Read;
            Number_Of_Readers := Number_Of_Readers + 1;
      or
        accept Stop_Read;
          Number_Of_Readers := Number_Of_Readers - 1;
      or
        when No_Writer and Number_Of_Readers = 0 =>
          accept Start_Write;
            No_Writer := False;
      or
        accept Stop_Write;
          No_Writer := True;
      or
        terminate;
      end select;
    end loop;
  end Controller;

  procedure Read_Shared (Item :    out Integer) is
  begin
    Controller.Start_Read;
    Item := Shared_Item;
    Controller.Stop_Read;
  end Read_Shared;
```

```
  procedure Write_Shared (Item : in     Integer) is
  begin
    Controller.Start_Write;
    Shared_Item := Item;
    Controller.Stop_Write;
  end Write_Shared;
end Access_Shared;


----- Here is the procedure to use the package -----

with Access_Shared;
with Text_IO;  use Text_IO;
procedure Readers_Writers is

task type Readers;
task type Writers;

Many_Readers : array (1 .. 10) of Readers;
Many_Writers : array (1 .. 10) of Writers;

task body Readers is
  Item : Integer;
begin
  Access_Shared.Read_Shared (Item);
  Put_Line ("Just read " & Integer'Image (Item));
end Readers;

task body Writers is
  Item : Integer := Initialize.An_Integer; -- see discussion
begin
  Access_Shared.Write_Shared (Item);
  Put_Line ("Just wrote");
end Writers;

begin -- main procedure
  null;
end Readers_Writers;
```

Discussion: The entrance procedures enforce the proper protocol (sequence of calls) for read/write and write/write mutual exclusion, but simultaneous reading. Notice the similarity to the use of semaphores in Exercise 2.2: Semaphore_Shared_Record. However, here the use of the protocol is embedded in the package providing the shared resource; a using program cannot forget or misuse a sema-phore.

It is the guards on the Start entries that cause tasks to queue when it is inappropriate for them to access the shared variable.

The package uses *arrays* of tasks. The code

```
task type Readers;
task type Writers;
```

establishes that Readers and Writers are *templetes* for tasks. The code

```
Many_Readers : array (1 .. 10) of Readers;
Many_Writers : array (1 .. 10) of Writers;
```

creates the set of tasks themselves. This will be explained in detail in Chapter 10, Task Types and Objects.

The task body Writer uses a call to a function (presumed to be vis-ible at that point) to assign a unique value to Item in each of the Writer tasks. The function Initialize.An_Integer is

```
package Initialize is
   function An_Integer return Integer;
end Initialize;

package body Initialize is
   Init_Value : Integer := 0;

   function An_Integer return Integer is
   begin
     Init_Value := Init_Value + 1;
     return Init_Value;
   end An_Integer;
end Initialize;
```

This provides each of the Writer tasks a unique initial value. The order in which the values are assigned to the tasks is nondetermi-nate, but we don't care about the order, only about the uniqueness. Note the use of a variable, Init_Value, in the packge body to retain the value from one invocation of the function to the next. This is equivalent to what is called an "own variable" in Algol.

There is a potential problem with the solution given; a steady stream of readers will prevent writers from ever writing, i.e., the writers are starved. This is a particularly serious problem since it is likely that the writing of new information is vital to the operation of the system.

Exercise 4.2. Writers Have Priority

Purpose: To improve the first readers-writers solution

Problem: Modify the first readers-writers solution so that writers are not starved.

Solution: The only change is to the body of the controller, as indicated at the comment "--**" below.

```
task body Controller is
   Number_Of_Readers : Natural := 0;
    No_Writer         : Boolean := True;
begin
   loop
      select                                        -- **
         when No_Writer and Start_Write'Count = 0 =>  -- **
            accept Start_Read;                        -- **
            Number_Of_Readers := Number_Of_Readers + 1;
      or
         accept Stop_Read;
         Number_Of_Readers := Number_Of_Readers - 1;
      ...
      ...
```

Discussion: The only change to the previous example is noted by "--**". All we needed to do in order to give writers priority over readers was to block readers whenever a writer is queued on the Start_Write entry. We have a different potential problem now, since a steady stream of writers will starve readers!

Exercise 4.3. Fair Readers-Writers

Purpose: To finish the introduction of the readers-writers problem

Problem: Make the solution "fair." That is when a writer finishes writing, allow all waiting readers to read before the next writer obtains access. (But newly arriving readers must wait until either the next write has been completed or there are no writers waiting.) If there are no waiting readers, allow writers to write.

Solution: The only additional modification (adding to the solution of Exercise 4.2) is shown below at "--**".

```
   ...
   ...
   or
      when No_Writer and Number_Of_Readers = 0 =>
         accept Start_Write;
         No_Writer := False;
   or
      accept Stop_Write;
      No_Writer := True;

         -- make sure all pending readers get a chance
      for I in 1 .. Start_Read'Count loop            -- **
         accept Start_Read;                          -- **
         Number_Of_Readers := Number_Of_Readers + 1; -- **
      end loop;
   or
      terminate;
   end select;
   end loop;
end Controller;
```

Discussion: The only change to the previous example is noted by "--**". We simply accept a number of calls equal to the number of waiting readers. The number of waiting readers is available as the Count attribute of the entry. Is there a potential danger in doing this? We are guaranteed that there are no timed entry calls (since we are making the calls in the entrance procedure of the package), but there is still the chance that one of the readers could be aborted.

If the task leaves the queue for the Start_Read entry at an inopportune time (and if no other readers have since arrived), the "for loop" (of the newly added code) will not be completed. The system will block waiting for a reader, even though writers are waiting to write.

There is no really clean alternative (another reason for forbidding the use of abort except in extreme and carefully controlled circumstances), but we could modify the loop to include a conditional accept, as in:

```
-- ensure no blocking as a result of a task leaving entry queue
-- by being aborted while readers are being serviced

for I in 1 .. Start_Read'Count loop
  select
    accept Start_Read;
    Number_Of_Readers := Number_Of_Readers + 1;
  else
    null;
  end select;
end loop;
```

This works, but adds to the complexity of the solution, and is costly in terms of execution time of the accept statement.

An alternate solution is to create an agent task in the entrance procedure (this approach uses access types with tasks, as we will discuss in Chapter 13, Pointers to Tasks). The agent continues to exist even if the original calling task is aborted, and hence the rendezvous will occur.

Keys to Understanding

- The called task can use a selective wait to establish a potential rendezvous with tasks calling any of a number of entries. If no task is waiting for a rendezvous, the called task can depart from the select statement immediately or it can delay for a specified time while waiting for a rendezvous. It can also arrange for cooperative termination.

- An alternative of a select statement (including delay and terminate) may be guarded.

- A task may not have a select statement with a mix of delay_alternative, terminate_alternative, and else clause. It may have only one of the three options: delay, terminate, else.

- The calling task can only be in only one entry queue at a time. However, it can use the *conditional* entry call to rendezvous only if the called task is waiting at its accept statement, or it can use the *timed* entry call to delay for only a specified period of time as it waits for the rendezvous.

- The capabilities of the package Calendar and the use of the delay statement provide for task self-suspension and for cyclic processing. The delay establishes a minimum time only.

- Task priorities may be used to control the relative sequence of processing. A rendezvous executes with the priority of the task having the higher priority.

- Packages may be used effectively to control access to tasks by hiding the task in the package body. The package specification provides entrance procedures to control access and enforce a desired protocol for task interaction.

5

Caller and Called Tasks

Objective: To determine the effect on task interaction of making a task a "caller," or of making it "called"

A caller is a task that calls an entry in another task. A called task is one that declares an entry and accepts the entry call. Pyle [PYL85] treats the caller/called subject at considerable length. In fact, he treats caller or "active" tasks in his initial discussion of concurrency, but defers the more difficult discussion of called or "passive" tasks, treating it as an advanced topic. Buhr [BUH84] addresses the caller/called issue at some length in relation to the kinds of delays in a concurrent system. Gehani [GEH84] is concerned with the issue in regard to a possible tendency to use polling when writing active or caller tasks.

The sections below first address general issues, including introducing the process graph notation for calling and called tasks. Understanding the meaning of calling and called lays the foundation for noting the asymmetry of the Ada rendezvous; this has to do with the nature and capability of calling and called tasks. The final topic is some general guidelines for making the caller/called decision.

5.1 General

There are several descriptive names for calling and called tasks. Pyle [PYL85] and Burns [BUR85] use "active" and "passive," while Young [YOU82] and others use "caller" and "server." Buhr [BUH84] uses "caller" and "acceptor" (he also consistently uses "source" and "target" to indicate direction of data flow), while the Rationale [ICH79] uses the most direct phrase "calling task" or "caller," and "called task." We prefer the direct phrasing of the Rationale, but will occasionally use alternate terminology when it is more descriptive. The aliases are:

Task Issuing Call	Task Accepting Call
Caller	Called
Caller	Server
Caller	Acceptor
Caller	Callee
Calling task	Called task
Active task	Passive task
Actor	Server

The process graph notation for the calling and called tasks is shown in Figure 5-1.

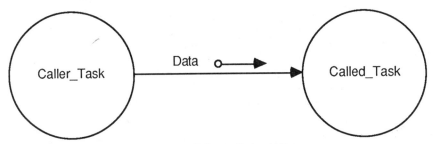

Figure 5-1. Caller/called notation

The called task offers the entry and accepts the call.

```
task Called_Task is
  entry Take_Data (Data : in Data_Type);
end Called_Task;
```

```
task body Called_Task is
begin
   ...
   accept Take_Data ...
   ...
end Called_Task;
```

The caller or calling task issues the entry call.

```
task body Caller_Task is
begin
   ...
   Called_Task.Take_Data ( ... );
   ...
end Caller_Task;
```

The task names make the relationship clear. The task touched by the arrowhead is the called task. The direction of data flow is independent of caller/called relationships. A called task may be called by many callers, including many calls to the same entry. Caller/called tasks may have several lines connecting them, and a called task may also call other tasks, including a task by which it is called. These relationships are shown in the Figures 5-2 through 5-6.

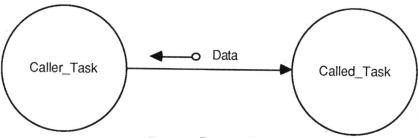

Figure 5-2. Data to caller

Figure 5-5 shows calls to *different* entries of Called_Task. A caller may issue several entry calls to the same entry (at different times and different places in the source text), but such calls are shown on the process graph only once. Similarly, a called task may have accept statements in different textual locations, but only one entry is shown on the process graph. (Despite the fact that the called task may perform very different actions depending upon when it accepts a call, the interface is always the same and there is a single queue of callers for each entry). These conventions are analogous to the traditional structure chart conventions for calling procedures.

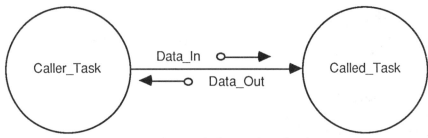

Figure 5-3. Data both ways (transform)

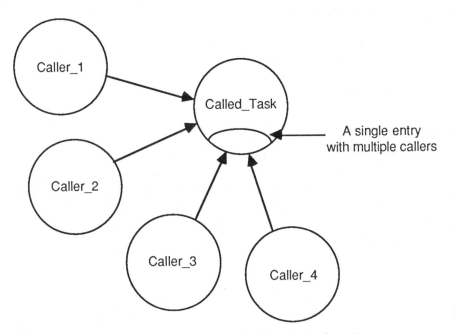

Figure 5-4. Many callers (data flow direction irrelevant)

Figure 5-6 illustrates that a task need not be exclusively caller or called, but rather plays one role or another at any one time. Or, as we prefer to think of it, a task plays one role or another *with respect to a data flow*. Burns, however, makes the point that tasks should not do this; they should be either active or passive [BUR85, page 204]. This is likely a good guideline, but too rigid when stated as a rule.

We may also usually think of a task as being a caller or a called task *with respect to another task*. However, it is possible for two tasks to have a mutual caller/called relationship. This is dangerous, however, since cyclic calling relationships can lead to deadlock (a situation in which two (or more) tasks is blocked since they are

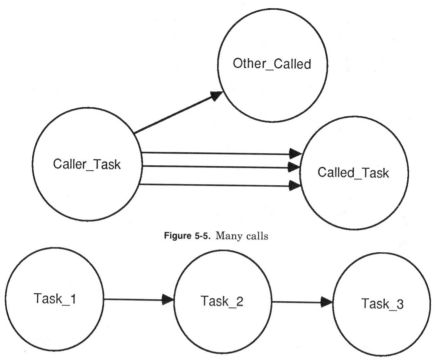

Figure 5-5. Many calls

Figure 5-6. Both caller and called

each waiting for the other to perform some action). This mutual caller/called relationship should almost always be avoided.

The caller/called role is not restricted to *tasks*, but is instead applicable to processes in general. When a process is represented as a package, the method we typically use to access the internals of the package is by a call to a subprogram. Once again, the direction of data flow is irrelevant. The fact that a process calls a procedure implies that it is a "caller," while declaring the procedure and accepting the procedure call implies the process is called. The process graph for called process is shown in Figure 5-7. The lines crossing the package boundary, with arrowheads touching called tasks, indicate procedure calls to the called package.

The code corresponding to the externally visible part of the package of Figure 5-7 is:

```
package Called is
   procedure Provide_Data_Out (Data_Out : out Data_Type);
   procedure Take_Data_In     (Data_In  : in  Data_Type);
end Called;
```

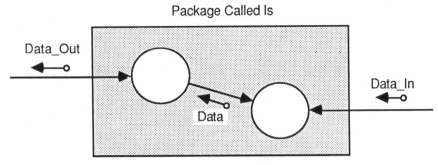

Figure 5-7. Package as called process

The callers of this package contain code to invoke the procedures Called.Provide_Data_Out and Called.Take_Data_In.

Consistent use of the graphics shown in the previous figures will make concurrent programs easier to understand and will allow the designer to think clearly about the problem at hand.

5.2 Asymmetry

There is considerable asymmetry between the capabilities of calling and called tasks. Some of the asymmetry is a natural consequence of the relationship between a calling process and its general purpose server. Some of the asymmetry is a feature of the Ada language. There are four aspects to the asymmetry: identity, declaration, modularity, and nondeterminism. They are addressed below.

5.2.1 Identity

The calling task must know the name of the called task, but not vice versa.

The calling task calls an entry by using both the name of the called task and the name of the entry. (A task nested within another task may call an entry without the use of the task name, but that is a special case.) The called task must be prepared to provide service to any task. It is, therefore, easy to create general-purpose library units with exclusively passive tasks—they do not to know the names of their callers.

5.2.2 Declaration

The called task must declare its entries, but the calling task cannot declare its calls.

A *called* task must provide a declaration of its intent or ability to be called (as part of the interface specification), but a *caller* provides no such information. For design purposes, such information is valuable. To provide this information we may place comments (in the declarative part) that name each called task (or package) and specific entry (or procedure) called. The declaration of an entry by a called task is (as required by Ada):

```
task Called_Task is
   entry Take_Data (Data : in Data_Type);
end Called_Task;
```

A commented declaration of an entry call by a caller task might be:

```
task Caller_Task is
   -- Calls
      -- Called_Task.Take_Data
end Caller_Task;
```

5.2.3 Modularity

A call to an entry of another task may be issued from within a procedure, either subordinate to a task or in any other context (such as a procedure in a package body). However, a call may be accepted only within the sequence of statements of a task body (and not within a procedure in the declarative part of the task body).

For example, in an algorithmically complicated task, or one with many entries, we might wish to have something like:

```
task Do_It is
   entry Take ...
   entry Provide ...
end Do_It;

task body Do_It is -- ***** not legal Ada *****
   procedure Take_It is
   begin
      ...
      accept Take ... -- illegal
      -- complicated processing
      -- maybe another Take ...
      ...
   end Take_It;
```

```
procedure Provide_It is
-- similar to Take_It processing
  -- accepting Provide
end Provide_It;

begin -- Do_It
  loop -- this loop is easy to understand
    Take_It;
    Provide_It;
    -- of course this could be much more complex
  end loop;
end Do_It;
```

However, Ada does not allow such modularization. The task must be rewritten to allow all the accept statements to reside in the sequence of statements of the task body. This is usually not a problem, since the program can be designed in such a way as to avoid the situation. For example, the complex processing may be relegated to some library package that provides its services to this task. The task then becomes short, and the confinement of the task interfaces to one spot (the sequence of statements) becomes natural and convenient. However, as Habermann points out [HAB83, page 438],

> This represents a great loss in the power of computational abstraction within tasks.

The inability to place an accept statement in a procedure is also inconvenient when a task wishes to interact with any of several tasks, whichever is ready first. As we will see below, this can be elegantly accomplished only by a called task, using a selective wait and accept statement. This desirable sort of interaction cannot be encapsulated within a procedure.

5.2.4 Nondeterminism

A called task can wait for many callers, but a caller can be in only one queue at a time.

This is the most important of the aspects of the asymmetry between caller and called tasks. The control mechanisms that Ada provides for a calling task, the conditional and timed entry calls, are relevant only to the single task and entry being called. Specifically, Ada does not allow a caller to issue two or more calls, being prepared to rendezvous with whichever task is first ready. Anything like this:

```
either -- ***** not Ada!! *****
  One_Task.Provide_Work (...);
or
  Other_Task.Provide_Job (...);
end either;
```

is not allowed. Of course for a passive or called task, this sort of code:

```
select -- good Ada
  accept Take_Work (...) do ... end;
or
  accept Take_Job (...) do ... end;
end select;
```

is perfectly appropriate and widely useful.

Our example of the customer and the clerk in the post office (in Chapter 4) can be used to illustrate how this is useful for the called task, and why the caller is disadvantaged by not having a corresponding capability.

The customer is the caller, while the post office is the called task. Suppose that the post office not only had an entry called Purchase, but also one called Mail. A single clerk could handle both windows by use of the selective wait.

```
select
  accept Purchase (...) do ... end;
or
  accept Mail (...) do ... end;
end select;
```

This is pictured in Figure 5-8. The clerk can wait for a customer to arrive at either window. Whichever function is required first will receive service. If there are customers waiting at both windows, the clerk services them in some nondeterministic manner—not defined by Ada.

An alternate solution would involve two clerks (two tasks in a post office package) to provide service. The use of the selective wait only requires a single task. This is the advantage gained by being a called task.

On the other hand, suppose the customer wanted to get stamps, but also wanted to pick up some envelopes to mail his letters. (This is why he wanted the stamps in the first place.) A frequent situation will be that there are queues both at the post office and the

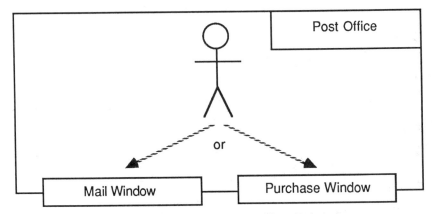

Figure 5-8. The clerk can go to either window

stationery store. He would like to be able to wait in *both* locations at the same time. This is pictured in Figure 5-9.

He cannot do this, however, (that's why he's frowning) since Ada does not give such a privilege to a calling task. The only solution is to use more than one task. Either there must be two tasks (which must then later decide how to coordinate their efforts to mail the letters), or the customer may have two helpers, one to wait in each queue. The helpers later return the stamps and the envelopes to the customer. This requirement of having two or more tasks in such situations is a disadvantage to the calling process.

An alternative to having more than one task is for the caller to use the conditional or timed entry calls to poll the post office and the stationery store. (Polling is the checking for service at the two locations alternately, leaving if not served, and returning later.) Polling is almost always undesirable in situations such as that illustrated.

Gehani [GEH84, page 155] points out that the lack of ability to issue an entry call in a selective wait (such as we did in the bogus "either" statement above) can lead to polling. He also points out [page 156] that an intervening buffer task can be used to prevent polling and overcome the restriction on callers. This issue is treated at length in Chapter 8, Buffer-Transporter Model of Task Interaction.

Much of the discussion of intermediary tasks in later chapters has to do with this aspect of the caller/called asymmetry.

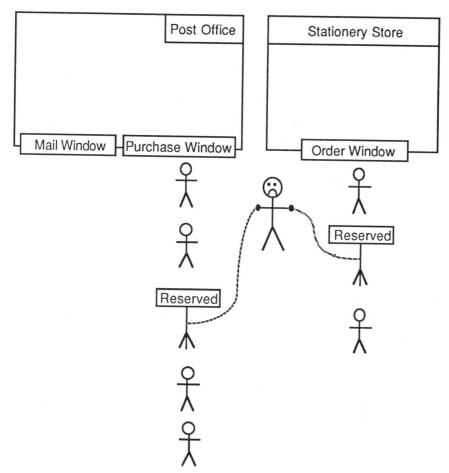

Figure 5-9. The customer cannot wait in two lines at the same time

5.3 Complexity

Called tasks are more complex than callers. There are three reasons for this. First, the called task must deal with the nondeterminism mentioned in the discussion of asymmetry. Second, the called task has greater control over the rendezvous. Third, the called task has more information available. The three topics are discussed below.

5.3.1 Nondeterminism

A called task deals with nondeterminism.

A called task using a selective wait, as is frequently the case, must cope with the nondeterminacy of not knowing which entry will be called, which entry will be accepted if several are called, or at what time (relative to other activity in the system) any entry will be accepted.

It is this nondeterminism, however, that makes a called task particularly useful. It can wait for many potential callers. The calls may be to any of several locations (the accepts in the select statement). It is this notion of waiting for a call that leads to the phrase "passive" for such tasks. After waiting, it can then provide service to the appropriate caller.

Pyle [PYL85, page 210] indicates that an important form of service has to do with intertask communication. He discusses the desirability of using passive tasks to

... provide communication media between sibling active tasks.

Pyle also indicates that these tasks are more difficult to create than active tasks. He goes even further in stating that most programmers will primarily use active tasks (using the service of previously written passive tasks) to create their programs. Burns [BUR85] adopts a similar philosophy.

It is not clear that this will be the best approach to concurrency. There is a place for active tasks as intermediaries, and it may be important to have application tasks be "passive" in order to allow interaction with any of many possible callers.

5.3.2 Control

A called task has greater control.

The only control over the rendezvous held by a calling task is the ability to rendezvous only if the opportunity is immediately available, or to wait only for a limited time for the rendezvous. The called task, on the other hand, has these control mechanisms plus the ability to wait for one of many tasks (as we discussed above), the ability to guard entries, the ability to nest rendezvous, control over the execution of the code of the rendezvous itself, and greater control over what occurs in the event of an exception.

5.3.3 Information

A called task has access to more information than a calling task.

Consistent with the greater flexibility and control of the called task is its greater knowledge. Most of this knowledge is maintained internally and coded by the programmer. This includes information such as receipts or "passes" that allow special access, number of active readers of a data structure, and so on. However, one important item of information is maintained by the run-time environment only for the called task. This is the 'Count attribute, which tells the called task how many callers are queued on an entry. This may be used to control the called task's interaction with its callers. A simple example is:

```
select
  accept High_Priority ... do ... end;
or
  when High_Priority'Count = 0 =>
    accept Low_Priority ... do ... end;
end select;
```

The 'Count attribute is used with a guarded accept to control task interaction in a desirable way. However, the attribute must be used with caution, since timed entry callers and aborted callers leave the queue at arbitrary times.

5.4 Guidelines

Some general guidelines form making caller/called decisions are:

1. Busy tasks should be called.

   "Busy" is used here in the sense of interacting with several other tasks. Since a caller can only wait for a single rendezvous, it risks being held up by the task it is calling. A called task can wait for any of many rendezvous. Buhr [BUH84, page 62] establishes the same principle—that a busy task prefers to be called.

2. Algorithmically complex tasks should be callers.

   The call is more concise (textually shorter) than the accept and the rendezvous. Further, the called task usually provides a service by executing some code in the rendezvous. It is important to simplify an algorithmically complex task as much as possible (in terms of its task interactions) in order to make the algorithm clear.

3. Some tasks are like operating systems—calls to them are like Executive Service Requests.

   This is consistent with the role of tasks in providing intertask communication. For example, passive tasks used as buffers and pools of data provide the facilities that would otherwise be provided by an operating system. These are the intermediary tasks we discuss in the following chapters.

4. Called tasks usually provide service.

    This is consistent with the called task's ability to be a library routine, to serve any of many callers, and to execute code in the rendezvous on behalf of itself and the caller.

5. Be careful of polling—use appropriate buffers.

    The asymmetry of Ada may encourage polling. Event-driven mechanisms are typically more efficient than polling. Certainly mutual polling between two tasks is always bad, since the two tasks may continuously "miss" each other by seeking a rendezvous while the other task is doing its other work.

5.5 Exercises

The exercises for Chapter 5 are related to what we will call the *squasher* problem.

The problem has been discussed by many authors. We will use the example to address several aspects of Ada design and along the way will amplify on the solution provided by Dahl [DAH72, page 188].

Problem Statement

The problem is to read text from cards (80 characters per card) and print the text on a line printer (125 characters on each line). Pack as many characters as possible on each line (ignoring word boundaries), marking the transition from one card to the next card only by inserting an extra space. In the text, any consecutive pair of asterisks ("**") is to be replaced by the up_arrow ("^"). The end of text on the final card is marked by ASCII.ETX. On ETX, blank fill the current line, and prepare to receive and squash another set of cards.

Exercise 5.1. Approaches to the Squasher Problem

Purpose: To point out alternate methods of attack for the design of a Squasher program

Problem: Analyse the Squasher problem, considering how concurrent processes can be effectively used. Address various alternatives for caller/called decisions.

Solution: *Initial Analysis.* This can be considered to be a sequential problem with the following steps:

1. Get a card.
2. Disassemble the card into a character stream, including an extra space at the end of each card.
3. Squash the character stream (replace "**" by "^").
4. Assemble the character stream into lines.
5. Print the lines.

Although this requirement *can* be met with a sequential program, it is not easy to do so. The fact that cards and lines differ in length, and that the squashing changes the effective length of a card, causes considerable attention to have to be paid to how many characters have been input, squashed, and assembled for output.

It is easier to consider the process as a *continuous* one in which all five steps are, at least conceptually, occuring concurrently. At this level of consideration of the problem, we are not concerned with how or when the individual operations are performed, only with their effect on the input and output streams. This is an interesting application of concurrency to a problem that does not deal with external parallel activities.

(This approach is philosophically close to attempts to implement data flow diagrams directly in the programming language, rather than going through traditional structured design steps to transform the data flow diagrams into structure charts for sequential processing.)

Caller/Called Alternatives. There are a number of ways to view the problem, particularly in relation to caller/called decisions. Some of them are shown in Figure 5-10. In Figure 5-10, as in the code examples to follow, we assume the existance of tasks to perform the functions of (1) reading and providing cards and (2) taking and printing lines. The remaining tasks are:

- Disassembler (D): Takes cards and provides characters, inserting a space between cards
- Squasher (S): Takes characters, "squashes," and provides characters
- Assembler (A): Takes characters and provides lines

Figure 5-10a shows the simplest approach of left to right calls as cards, characters, and lines become available. Figure 5-10b shows the same flow implemented with calls in the opposite direction.

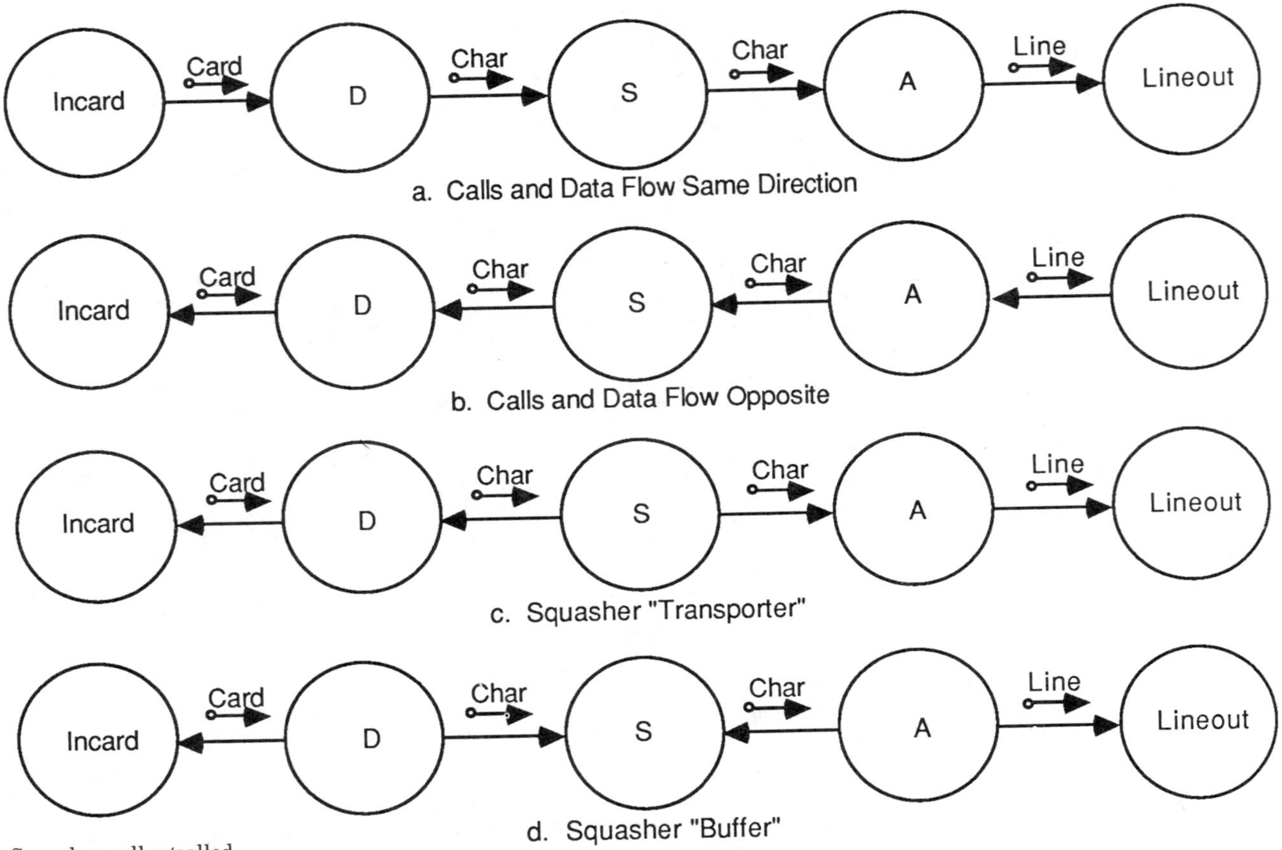

Figure 5-10. Squasher caller/called

a. Calls and Data Flow Same Direction

b. Calls and Data Flow Opposite

c. Squasher "Transporter"

d. Squasher "Buffer"

Figure 5-10c treats the Squasher as a buffer that does some additional work (squashing), while Figure 5-10d treats it as a transporter that does some extra work. There are additional alternatives.

Exercise 5.2. Active Squasher

Purpose: To illustrate an active squasher

Problem: Solve the Squasher problem, using a Squasher task that is strictly a caller.

Solution: We will present two solutions. The first is of historical interest, while the latter takes better advantage of Ada's features.

First Solution. The problem is posed and solved in [DAH72, page 188ff]. It is solved there using coroutines, but we can adapt the solution to an Ada style, using an active squasher. The caller/called relationships are as in Figure 5-10c.
The solution is:

```
task Disassembler is
  entry Provide_Char (Char : out Character);
  -- Calls Incard.Provide_Card
end Disassembler;

task body Disassembler is
  Card : String (1 .. 80);
begin
  loop
    Incard.Provide_Card (Card);

    -- provide the characters
    for I in Card'Range loop
      accept Provide_Char (Char : out Character) do
        Char := Card (I);
      end Provide_Char;
    end loop;

    -- insert a space between cards
    accept Provide_Char (Char : out Character) do
      Char := ' ';
    end Provide_Char;
  end loop;
end Disassembler;
```

```
task Squasher is
  -- Calls
     -- Disassembler.Provide_Char
     -- Assembler.Take_Char
end Squasher;

task body Squasher is
  C1, C2 : Character;
begin
  loop
    Disassembler.Provide_Char (C1);

    if C1 = '*' then
       Disassembler.Provide_Char (C1);

       if C1 = '*' then -- two * in a row
         C2 := '^'
       else -- not two in a row

         Assembler.Take_Char ('*');
         C2 := C1;
       end if;
    else
       C2 := C1;
    end if;

    Assembler.Take_Char (C2);
  end loop;
end Squasher;
```

The algorithm makes a distinction between C1 and C2 since the original use of coroutines in the solution by Dahl made use of different common variables (C1 and C2) to communicate between the Squasher/Disassembler (using C1) and Squasher/Assembler (using C2). We will look at additional algorithms later.

```
task Assembler is
  accept Take_Char (Char : in Character);
  -- Calls Lineout.Take_Line
end Assembler;
```

```
task body Assembler is
  Line : String (1 .. 125);
begin
  loop
    Get_line:
    for I in Line'Range loop
      accept Take_Char (Char : in Character) do
        Line (I) := Char;
      end Take_Char;

      if Line (I) = ASCII.ETX then -- blank fill
        for J in I .. Line'Last loop
          Line (J) := ' ';
        end loop;
        exit Get_Line;
      end if;
    end loop Get_Line;

    Lineout.Take_Line (Line);
  end loop;
end Assembler;
```

Second Solution. The interesting algorithm is that of squasher. We will do away with the use of C1 and C2, and use a single local character, Ch. The algorithm continues to take the approach of Figure 5-10c in that it makes the Squasher active with respect to transfer of data—it is exclusively a caller.

```
task Squasher is
  -- Calls
    -- Disassembler.Provide_Char
    -- Assembler.Take_Char
end Squasher;

task body Squasher is
  Ch : Character;
```

```
    begin
    loop
      Disassembler.Provide_Char (Ch);

      if Ch = '*' then
        Disassembler.Provide_Char (Ch);

        if Ch = '*' then -- two * in a row
          Assembler.Take_Char ('^');
        else -- not two in a row
          Assembler.Take_Char ('*');
          Assembler.Take_Char (Ch);
        end if;
      else
        Assembler.Take_Char (Ch);
      end if;
    end loop;
  end Squasher;
```

Exercise 5.3. Passive Squasher

Purpose: To illustrate a passive squasher

Problem: Solve the Squasher problem, using a Squasher task that is strictly a called task.

Solution: This problem has been solved by Welsh [WEL81]. We follow his algorithm while introducing changes in presentation/coding style. The algorithm is based on an approach with the Squasher represented as in Figure 5-10d. It is passive with respect to transfer of data, essentially acting as a server. The algorithm for Squasher is:

```
    task Squasher is
      accept Take_Char    (Char : in  Character);
      accept Provide_Char (Char : out Character);
    end Squasher;
```

```
task body Squasher is
  Ch : Character;
begin
  loop
    accept Take_Char      (Char : in  Character) do
        Ch := Char;
    end Take_Char;

    if Ch /= '*' then
      accept Provide_Char (Char : out Character) do
          Char := Ch;
      end Provide_Char;
    else
      accept Take_Char (Char : in  Character) do
          Ch := Char;
      end Take_Char;

      if Ch /= '*' then -- not two * in a row
        accept Provide_Char (Char : out Character) do
          Char := '*';
        end Provide_Char;

        accept Provide_Char (Char : out Character) do
          Char := Ch;
        end Provide_Char;
      else -- two * in a row
        accept Provide_Char (Char : out Character) do
          Char := '^';
        end Provide_Char;
      end if;
    end if;
  end loop;
end Squasher;
```

The algorithm shown is faithful to Welch. For comparison to the
earlier algorithm, we can reverse the logic of the central "if" statement as:

```
if Ch = '*' then
  accept Take_Char (Char : in  Character) do
    Ch := Char;
  end Take_Char;

  if Ch = '*' then -- two * in a row
    accept Provide_Char (Char : out Character) do
      Char := '^';
    end Provide_Char;
  else -- not two in a row
    accept Provide_Char (Char : out Character) do
      Char := '*';
    end Provide_Char;

    accept Provide_Char (Char : out Character) do
      Char := Ch;
    end Provide_Char;
  end if;
else -- not a *
  accept Provide_Char (Char : out Character) do
    Char := Ch;
  end Provide_Char;
end if;
```

Comparing the algorithms of Exercises 5.2 and 5.3, we note that the active task is textually shorter and easier to read. This supports the heuristic we established in this chapter that, in the absence of other criteria, a task with a complex algorithm should be active.

Keys to Understanding

- A task is a "caller" (or active task) if it issues an entry call, including a call to a procedure in another process. A task is "called" (or a server, or a passive task) if it offers an entry call and corresponding accept. A task may be a caller with respect to one data flow and a server with respect to another data flow.

- Use of consistent notation on a process graph helps clarify the caller/called relationships early in the design phase.

- The caller/called relationship is not a characteristic of a pair of tasks, but is in relationship to each signal or flow of data. However, it is probably unwise for two tasks (or any of a number of tasks) to establish a cycle of calls. Such a situation could easily lead to deadlock.

- The asymmetric nature of the rendezvous causes the distinction between the two types of tasks.

- The caller/called decision has an important impact on task interactions and program design.

6

Producer-Consumer Model
of Task Interaction

> Objective: To illustrate the producer-consumer
> model of task interaction

The producer-consumer model of task interaction is one in which one task, the producer, produces information to be used by another task, the consumer. This sort of task interaction is common in concurrent systems, and we will see it frequently throughout the remainder of the book. The sections below define producer and consumer tasks, describe how intermediary tasks influence caller/called relationships, allow partial asynchronous operation of the producer and consumer, and discuss the issue of synchronous and asynchronous communication in relation to the use of intermediary tasks.

6.1 Producer-Consumer

A very common sort of task interaction is that in which one task passes information to another task. We consider the task that is the source of the information to be the producer, while the task that receives the information (or is the target of the information) is the consumer.

The producer produces some item of information (perhaps by calculation, by receiving input from some device, or other means), while the consumer consumes the information (perhaps putting it into a database, providing output to some device, or using it to calculate new information, hence also becoming a producer). We will use "producer" and "consumer" in the broadest sense, including the case in which the consumer also becomes a producer with regard to some other task, or when the consumer sends a reply to the producer in response to the data item provided.

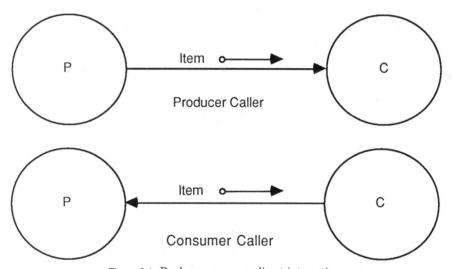

Figure 6-1. Producer-consumer direct interaction

The two basic producer-consumer interactions are shown graphically in Figure 6-1. Note that the producer may be the caller in the interaction or may be the called task. The code for each situation is shown below.

First, the producer as caller:

```
task Producer is
   -- Calls Consumer.Take_Item
end Producer;

task Consumer is
   entry Take_Item (Item : in Item_Type);
end Consumer;
```

```
task body Producer is
  Item : Item_Type;
begin
  -- initial code to produce the item

Consumer.Take_Item (Item);

  -- more code
end Producer;

task body Consumer is
  Item : Item_Type;
begin
  -- initial code

  accept Take_Item (Item : in Item_Type) do
    Consumer.Item := Item;
  end Take_Item;

  -- more code, consuming the item
  -- alternatively, could have consumed the item during
  -- the rendezvous
end Consumer;
```

Here is the equivalent code for consumer caller.

```
task Producer is
  entry Provide_Item (Item : out Item_Type);
end Producer;

task Consumer is
  -- Calls Producer.Provide_Item
end Consumer;
```

```
task body Producer is
  Item : Item_Type;
begin
  -- initial code to produce the item

  accept Provide_Item (Item : out Item_Type) do
      Item:= Producer.Item;
  end Provide_Item;

  -- more code
end Producer;

task body Consumer is
  Item : Item_Type;
begin
  -- initial code

  Producer.Provide_Item (Item);

  -- more code, consuming the item
end Consumer;
```

Whether the producer is the caller or the called task, there may also be a reply, as shown in Figure 6-2.

Here is the code for producer-consumer with reply.

```
task Producer is
  -- Calls Consumer.Take_Item
end Producer;

task Consumer is
  entry Take_Item (Item  : in Item_Type;
                   Reply : out Reply_Type);
end Consumer;
```

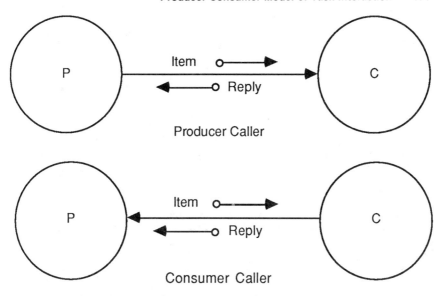

Figure 6-2. Direct interaction with reply

```
task body Producer is
  Item  : Item_Type;
  Reply : Reply_Type;
begin
  -- initial code to produce the item

  Consumer.Take_Item (Item, Reply);

  -- more code, using the reply
end Producer;

task body Consumer is
  Item  : Item_Type;
begin
  -- initial code

  accept Take_Item (Item  : in Item_Type;
                    Reply : out Reply_Type) do
    Consumer.Item := Item;
    Reply := A_Function_of (Item);
  end Take_Item;

  -- more code, consuming the item
end Consumer;
```

The case for the consumer being the caller is similar to the above.

6.2 Use of Intermediary Tasks

An important characteristic of the task interaction of Figures 6-1 and 6-2 is that it limits the amount of asynchronous action of the two tasks; they are tightly coupled by the rendezvous. The direct producer-consumer interaction also forces a specific caller/called relationship on the interacting tasks; one must be a caller, while the other is called.

This section shows how intermediary tasks can be used to uncouple the task communication of the producer and consumer; they will no longer directly interact in a rendezvous. The effect of the use of intermediary tasks is twofold:

- The tasks have greater opportunity for concurrent operation.

- The programmer has greater control over the caller/called characteristics of the producer and consumer.

There are three styles of intermediaries:

- Buffer

- Transporter

- Relay

They are shown graphically in Figure 6-3.

The characteristic that distiguishes the three forms of interaction is the caller/called nature of the producer and consumer, and hence their caller/called relationship to the intermediary.

The task interaction shown in Figure 6-3a uses a *buffer* as an intermediary. The important characteristic of this interaction is that both the producer and consumer are callers. (We will use *buffer* in this special way—to mean an intermediary that is a strictly called task. There should be no confusion with the more general use of buffer as any sort of temporary storage area.)

The interaction of Figure 6-3b uses a *transporter*. The important characteristic of this interaction is that both the producer and consumer are called. The term transporter has been introduced by Buhr [BUH84, page 63] for this sort of task.

Figures 6-3c and 6-3d show the two different calling directions for producer-consumer interaction with an intervening task we call a *relay*. The important characteristic of this interaction is that the relay is *called* by one of the interacting tasks, but the relay *calls* the

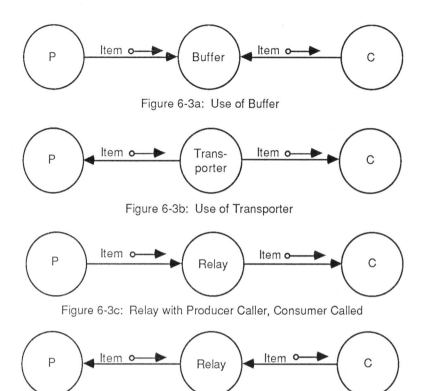

Figure 6-3a: Use of Buffer

Figure 6-3b: Use of Transporter

Figure 6-3c: Relay with Producer Caller, Consumer Called

Figure 6-3d: Relay with Producer Called, Consumer Caller

Figure 6-3. Producer-consumer with intermediaries

other interacting task. Burns [BUR84, page 128] refers to this sort of task as a *messenger*.

The material below provides coded examples for each of the three sorts of interaction: buffer, transporter, relay.

Here is the code for Figure 6-3a: buffer.

```
-- Producer and Consumer are caller

task Producer is
  -- Calls Buffer.Enqueue
end Producer;

task Consumer is
  -- Calls Buffer.Dequeue
end Consumer;
```

```
task Buffer is
  entry Dequeue (Item : out Item_Type);
  entry Enqueue (Item : in  Item_Type);
end Buffer;

task body Producer is
  Item : Item_Type;
begin
  -- initial code to produce the item
  Buffer.Enqueue (Item);
  -- more code
end Producer;

task body Consumer is
  Item : Item_Type;
begin
  -- initial code
  Buffer.Dequeue (Item);
  -- more code, consuming the item
end Consumer;

task body Buffer is
  Item : Item_Type;
begin
  loop
    accept Enqueue  (Item : in  Item_Type) do
      Buffer.Item := Item;
    end Enqueue;
    accept Dequeue (Item : out Item_Type) do
      Item := Buffer.Item;
    end Dequeue;
  end loop;
end Buffer;
```

Here is the code for Figure 6-3b: transporter.

```
-- Producer and Consumer are called

task Producer is
  entry Provide_Item (Item : out Item_Type);
end Producer;
```

```
task Consumer is
  entry Take_Item (Item : in Item_Type);
end Consumer;

task Transporter is
  -- Calls
    -- Producer.Provide_Item
    -- Consumer.Take_Item
end Transporter;

task body Producer is
  Item : Item_Type;
begin
  -- initial code to produce the item
  accept Provide_Item (Item : out Item_Type) do
    Item := Producer.Item;
  end Provide_Item;
  -- more code
end Producer;

task body Consumer is
  Item : Item_Type;
begin
  -- initial code
  accept Take_Item (Item : in Item_Type) do
    Consumer.Item := Item;
  end Take_Item;
  -- more code, consuming the item
end Consumer;

task body Transporter is
  Item : Item_Type;
begin
  loop
    Producer.Provide_Item (Item);
    Consumer.Take_Item (Item);
  end loop;
end Transporter;
```

Here is the code for Figure 6-3c: relay.

```
-- only shows the intermediary

task Relay is
  entry Take_Item (Item : in Item_Type);
  -- Calls Consumer.Take_Item
end Relay;

task body Relay is
  Item : Item_Type;
begin
  loop
    accept Take_Item (Item : in Item_Type) do
      Relay.Item:= Item;
    end Take_Item;
    Consumer.Take_Item (Item);
  end loop;
end Relay;
```

Here is the code for 6-3d: relay in the other direction.

```
-- only shows the intermediary

task Relay is
  entry Provide_Item (Item : out Item_Type);
  -- Calls Producer.Provide_Item
end Relay;

task body Relay is
  Item : Item_Type;
begin
  loop
    Producer.Provide_Item (Item);
    accept Provide_Item (Item : out Item_Type) do
      Item := Relay.Item;
    end Provide_Item;
  end loop;
end Relay;
```

You can see from Figure 6-3 and the code above that the intermediaries can be used to effect any desired caller/called relationship for the producer and consumer. If they both wish to be callers, a buffer will accomplish the job. If they both wish to be called, a transporter is necessary. The relay uncouples the producer-consumer direct interaction while retaining the characteristic of one a caller, the other called. Buhr [BUH84, page 60ff] places considerable emphasis on the use of intermediary tasks to influence whether a task should be a caller or a called task.

6.3 Synchronous/Asynchronous Communication

Another reason for the importance of intermediary tasks is that they influence the degree of asynchronous behavior possible for two tasks.

An important feature of the Ada model of concurrency is that it combines notions of synchronization and communication. The rendezvous requires that the two tasks "meet." If one task is early, it must wait for the other task before communication may take place.

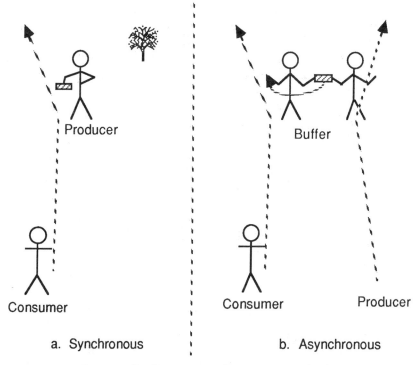

Figure 6-4. Synchronous/asynchronous communication

This is illustrated in Figure 6-4a. The producer, in this case, arrives early, having prepared something for the consumer. The producer waits at the agreed meeting place until the consumer arrives. This means that the producer, even if he had his own processor, cannot be simultaneously producing another item; an opportunity for concurrent operation is lost. We say that the tasks are relatively synchronized; the producer can only produce one item before waiting for the consumer. The situation is symmetric with regard to the consumer; he can only consume one item before he is forced to wait for the producer.

It is often desirable that the tasks not be so closely synchronized. If we uncouple the task interaction, the tasks have greater independence and potential for concurrent operation. This consideration is of particular importance when considering tasks that are handling interactions with external devices via an interrupt mechanism, or for systems in which there is actual concurrency as a result of multiple processing elements.

Uncoupling of task communication is illustrated in Figure 6-4b. The producer hands his output to the buffer and goes his own way, beginning the production of another item. He does not have to wait for the consumer. The consumer comes along later to pick up the item.

This situation is not completely symmetric with regard to the consumer; if he arrives first he must wait unless the buffer contains an item. Furthermore, not all the producer's problems are solved; if the producer produces a second item before the first is consumed, he must wait for the buffer to empty. What is needed is a buffer that can contain more than one item; we will return to this issue later.

The Ada model of using tasks to implement buffers for unsynchronized communication is quite different from traditional models of concurrency; for example, waiting on a semaphore before accessing some region of memory used as a buffer. It is consistent with modern thought as exemplified by Hoare in *Communicating Sequential Processes*. He says [HOA85, page 238], "For many years now, I have chosen to take unbuffered (synchronized) communication as basic." Among other reasons for this, he notes, "When buffering is wanted, it can be implemented simply as a process; and the degree of buffering can be precisely controlled by the programmer."

This method of allowing asynchronous behavior (in Ada) is also alluded to by Young [YOU82, page 153]: he notes, "... the frequent need to introduce 'third party' processes to decouple asynchronous processes." Burns [BUR84, page 131] notes that the use of intermediary tasks "... helps to enforce the concurrent nature of the domain and reduces the tendency to tie task executions too closely together." Burns and Pyle [PYL85] rely a great deal on *passive* (called) processes to provide the buffering and task communication methods for application-oriented *active* (or calling) tasks.

The intermediary tasks shown in Section 6.2 do not meet all the requirements for intermediaries. There are two shortfalls:

- They contain only one item.

- The transporter and relay force strictly alternating communication.

The intermediaries provide only a slight degree of asynchronous operation. When the single item buffer (or transporter or relay) is full, the producer must wait; when it is empty, the consumer must wait (presuming we neither overwrite data nor reread old data). What is required is internal storage of a number of items so that typically the intermediary is neither empty nor full, but in-between. This would allow both the producer and consumer to always interact with the intermediary without blocking (except for the brief time the intermediary may be serving the other task). The topic of buffering multiple items is discussed in Chapter 7, The Bounded Buffer.

The transporter and relay force strictly alternating communication since they must alternately serve first one task and then the other. They do not have as much flexibility as the buffer. The buffer can use the selective wait construct to serve either the producer or the consumer. The transporter and relay cannot do this since they issue calls to other tasks. This difference between the intermediaries relates to the issue of asymmetry of the rendezvous—discussed in Chapter 5. The forced alternation of service is a severe deficiency in the transporter and relay as discussed thus far.

Another deficiency of the transporter and relay is that they store only a single item. We mentioned the same deficiency for the buffer, but (as Chapter 7 will show) it is easy to construct a buffer that stores multiple items. This deficiency is not as easy to fix for the transporter and relay. Since they make calls, they cannot use the selective wait.

It is possible to contruct a task with the characteristic of the transporter and relay that *does* provide service without the forced alternation discussed above. However, it turns out that the task must poll (alternatly checking for rendezvous with each of the producer and consumer) in order to do so. Similar methods also allow a transporter or relay to store more than one item. Improved methods of constructing transporters and relays are discussed in Chapter 8, Buffer-Transporter Model of Task Interaction.

6.4 Exercises for Chapter 6

Exercise 6.1. Create a buffer that stores two items.

Exercise 6.2. Create a transporter that stores two items.

Exercise 6.3. Create a relay that stores two items.

Exercise 6.4. Discuss the desirability of your solutions.

These problems will be solved as part of the general discussion in Chapters 7 and 8. We will not provide separate solutions.

Keys to Understanding

- Producers are sources of data, often generating the data by computation or by interaction with an input device.

- Consumers are targets of data, often passing the data to an ouput device or using it in some calculation. The consumer may become a producer with respect to a different data flow and interaction with another task.

- In order to uncouple task interaction, intermediaries are often used between the producer and consumer.

- Intermediary tasks support three caller/called relationships for the producer and consumer: both caller, both called, one caller/other called. The respective intermediary tasks are called buffer, transporter, and relay.

- The Ada tasking model provides for combined synchronization and communication, leading to tightly coupled communication. A programmer can use intermediary tasks to introduce and control asynchronous communication.

- The single-item buffer only provides minimal capability to introduce asynchronous behavior; the multiple item buffer will be shown in Chapter 7.

- The transporter and relay suffer two deficiencies: they force strictly alternate service and they buffer only a single item. Furthermore, it is difficult to have them store more than one item. The deficiencies, and methods of correction of the deficiencies, will be addressed in Chapter 8.

The Bounded Buffer

> Objective: To present a variety of different buffers, including basic buffers, tasks, monitors, and a useful unprotected buffer shared by two tasks

Buffers are very important to the construction of concurrent systems in Ada. As temporary repositories of data that are flowing through them, they serve to uncouple the tasks producing and consuming the data. As "passive" or strictly called units, they can modify the caller/called relationship between tasks communicating information through the buffers.

We will look at buffers in detail, concentrating on the single model of the bounded buffer implemented as a circular queue: a first-in-first-out (FIFO) discipline. Other sorts of buffering schemes, last-in-first-out (or stack), priority ordered, double buffer, and so on, follow the same general pattern as those given below.

The point of the bounded buffer is to provide a temporary storage location for items being passed from a producer to a consumer. It allows the two interacting tasks to operate asynchronously as long as the buffer is not empty (consumer must wait when the buffer is empty) or the buffer is not full (producer must wait when the buffer is full).

These waiting conditions are only one of many possible design alternatives and decisions. Other decisions are possible. For example, the producer may be allowed to overwrite old information, or the consumer may be allowed to take a default action when the buffer is empty.

The sections below first address buffers as a general concept, applicable to both sequential and concurrent systems. They then discuss how tasks are used to ensure mutually exclusive access (i.e., the mutual exclusion concept of Chapter 2), and how tasks are appropriately encapsulated in packages to provide monitors. The chapter concludes with the presentation of a buffer that is not accessed in mutual exclusion, but can safely be used by a single producer-consumer pair. Throughout the chapter, generics are introduced to illustrate the general nature of the buffering paradigm.

7.1 Buffers Without Concurrency

Buffers are important components of Ada systems. This section introduces the basic idea of the bounded buffer, illustrating several buffer approaches with different levels of abstraction. It then addresses an alternate algorithm, and ends with generic buffers.

7.1.1 Basic Algorithm

This section introduces the basic ideas of the buffer, shows methods of accessing the buffer, addresses the concept of a buffer that is never full (since it overwrites old data), and presents some important ideas of how to encapsulate buffers.

7.1.1.1 Introduction.
Figure 7-1 illustrates the basic points of the bounded buffer. The declarations establish the definition and storage for the buffer. For illustration, we will use a buffer of characters. "Buffer" is the array in which information will be stored. We will consider it to be a circular array, as though the last position (8, in this example) is immediately followed by the first position (1). We use Insert as the index of where we will insert items in the buffer, and Remove as the index to remove items from the Buffer.

In_Char is the value to be placed in the buffer; it might be a local value or the formal "in" parameter of a procedure or an accept statement. The example shows how something is placed in the Buffer, and the proper method of incrementing the index. The index is

BUFFER ALGORITHM WITH USE OF BUFFER-COUNT

Buffer_Size : constant := 8;

Buffer : array (1 .. Buffer_Size) of Character;
Remove, Insert : Positive range 1 .. Buffer_Size := 1;
Count   : Natural range 0 .. Buffer_Size := 0;

The Buffer is full when Count + Buffer_Size;
(insert in Buffer when Count < Buffer_Size)

    Buffer (Insert) := In_Char; -- input Character
    Insert   := (Insert mod Buffer_Size) + 1;
    Count   := Count + 1;

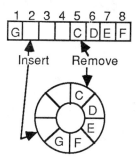

SAMPLE BUFFER

1 2 3 4 5 6 7 8

A B C D

Remove   Insert

The Buffer is empty when Count = 0;
(remove from Buffer when Count > 0)

    Out_Char := Buffer (Remove); -- output Character
    Remove   := (Remove mod Buffer_Size) + 1;
    Count   := Count - 1;

BUFFER AFTER 2 REMOVALS, 3 INSERTIONS

1 2 3 4 5 6 7 8

G   C D E F

Insert   Remove

Figure 7-1. Bounded buffer concepts (using Buffer-Count).

incremented modulo the buffer size in order to provide for proper wraparound in the circular buffer.

The example also shows how to take something out of the buffer and how to increment the Remove index and decrement the count. Both the insert and remove are conditional; you can't take something out of an empty buffer or put something in a full one.

It is important to note at this point how the modulo operation makes the array into a circular buffer; when an index has a value of 8, an increment operation gives it a value of 1, thereby providing the circular effect. Figure 7-1, illustrating the effect of insertions and removals, also shows how the insert and remove indexes move around the array in a circular fashion.

7.1.1.2 Access to the Bounded Buffer. This section shows some complete examples of bounded buffers; the focus is on how to access them. The simplest way is to directly manipulate the indexes and the array. However, there are advantages to using procedures to access the buffer.

Here is the simplest way to access the buffer. We assume this procedure has visibility to some type, called "Item_Type". The structure of Item_Type is not important to the nature of the buffer algorithm; it could be a character, a record, an array, and so on.

```
procedure No_Abstraction is
   My_Item : Item_Type;
   Buffer_Size : constant := 100;
   Buffer : array (1 .. Buffer_Size) of Item_Type;

   Remove,
   Insert : Positive range 1 .. Buffer_Size := 1;

   Count  : Natural  range 0 .. Buffer_Size := 0;
   In_Item,
   Out_Item : Item_Type;
begin
-- the main body of the proceedure (or its nested procedures)
-- uses code like the following to insert and extract items

   -- create an item and place it in the buffer
   ...

   if Count < Buffer_Size then
     Buffer (Insert) := My_Item;
     Insert := (Insert mod Buffer_Size) + 1;
     Count  := Count + 1;
   end if;

   -- take something from the buffer, and use it
```

```
    if Count > 0 then
      My_Item := Buffer (Remove);
      Remove   := (Remove mod Buffer_Size) + 1;
      Count    := Count - 1;
    end if;
    ...
end No_Abstraction;
```

The code to access the buffer must be repeated each time the buffer is accessed. Perhaps a comment is added each time to explain what the block of code is doing. Further, it is altogether too easy to erroneously omit the check on buffer-full/buffer-empty conditions. Removing from an empty buffer or storing into a full buffer causes the buffer to be corrupted; later use will be erroneous, and the data removed from the "empty" buffer will also be erroneous. A failure to check the condition of the buffer is particulary harmful in the common case in which several programmers are writing code that shares the buffer.

In short, accessing the buffer in this direct way is clumsy and error-prone. A better approach is shown below.

```
procedure Procedure_Abstraction is
   My_Item : Item_Type;
   Buffer_Size : constant := 100;
   Buffer : array (1 .. Buffer_Size) of Item_Type;

   Buffer_Empty,
   Buffer_Full   : exception;

   Remove,
   Insert : Positive range 1 .. Buffer_Size := 1;

   Count  : Natural  range 0 .. Buffer_Size := 0;

   function Empty return Boolean is
   begin
      return Count = 0;
   end Empty;

   function Full  return Boolean is
   begin
      return Count = Buffer_Size;
   end Full;
```

```ada
procedure Enqueue (In_Item : in Item_Type) is
begin
  if Full then
    raise Buffer_Full;
  end if;

  Buffer (Insert) := In_Item;
  Insert := (Insert mod Buffer_Size) + 1;
  Count  := Count + 1;
end Enqueue;

procedure Dequeue (Out_Item : out Item_Type) is
begin
  if Empty  then
    raise Buffer_Empty;
  end if;

  Out_Item := Buffer (Remove);
  Remove   := (Remove mod Buffer_Size) + 1;
  Count    := Count - 1;
end Dequeue;

begin
  -- create an item and place it in the buffer
  ...
  if not Full then
    Enqueue (My_Item);
  end if;

  -- take something from the buffer, and use it

  if not Empty then
    Dequeue (My_Item);
  end if;
  ...
-- uses the capability of the procedures, but could still
-- access the buffer directly.
-- A good abstraction, but not secure.

exception
  -- handle exceptions here
  ...
end Procedure_Abstraction;
```

This is a much better way to access the buffer; it is easier to read, easier to code, and less error-prone. If there is an attempt to add to a buffer that is full or remove from a buffer that is empty, an exception is raised rather than allowing the erroneous access.

We may wish an alternate action if the buffer is empty (or full); so we may write code such as:

```
if not Empty then
  Dequeue (My_Item);
else
  ...  -- the alternate action
end if;
```

The following is also appropriate:

```
begin
  Dequeue (My_Item);
exception
  when Buffer_Empty =>
    ...  -- the alternate action
end;
```

The use of the call to Empty is best if the buffer is often empty, while the latter form is preferred if the buffer is usually nonempty, i.e., it is "exceptional" for the buffer to be empty.

The issues of when and how to use exceptions is complex and even controversial; there is a good discussion by Nielsen [NIE88, Chapter 18].

We can still improve our access to the buffer. As the previous example pointed out:

```
-- uses the capability of the procedures, but could still
-- access the buffer directly.
-- A good abstraction, but not secure.
```

Although encapsulating the buffer access in proceedures is much improved over repeated direct access, the buffer can still be misused and is therefore potentially error-prone. For example, a programmer may write code that takes something from an empty buffer by failing to use the Dequeue procedure, or access the middle of the buffer by avoiding the Enqueue/Dequeue procedures entirely.

A better, and secure, formulation is to place the buffer in the body of a package. Access to the buffer is provided by the procedures, exactly as in the example above. However, correct use of the buffer is now enforced. We consider the buffer to be an "object." The package in some sense "manages" the object. Hence we call it an object manager.

```
package Queue_Object_Manager is
   procedure Enqueue (In_Item  : in  Item_Type);
   procedure Dequeue (Out_Item : out Item_Type);
   function Empty return Boolean;
   function Full  return Boolean;

   Buffer_Empty,
   Buffer_Full   : exception;
end Queue_Object_Manager;

package body Queue_Object_Manager is
   Buffer_Size : constant := 100;
   Buffer : array (1 .. Buffer_Size) of Item_Type;

   Remove,
   Insert : Positive range 1 .. Buffer_Size := 1;

   Count  : Natural  range 0 .. Buffer_Size := 0;

   function Empty return Boolean is ...
   function Full  return Boolean is ...
   procedure Enqueue (In_Item : in Item_Type) is ...
   procedure Dequeue (Out_Item : out Item_Type) is ...
end Queue_Object_Manager;
```

The ellipses "..." in the example above indicate that the code is unchanged from the procedures in the previous example.

The procedures are used as before, but encapsulating them in a package provides a secure formulation of the buffer. It ensures that the buffer cannot be polluted by incorrect use (such as entering an item in the middle of the buffer), and is guaranteed to alert an erroneous attempt to add to a full buffer or take from an empty one.

Let's look at some important characteristics of the buffer we have developed. In the next section we will extend some of the ideas discussed to introduce the concept of the abstract data type.

We called the package that encapsulated the buffer an "object manager." It "manages" a single object, the buffer. By manage the buffer, we mean that the package defines the buffer (implicitly) and provides operations on the buffer; it puts items in the buffer, takes them out, and checks to see if the buffer is empty or full. All operations on the buffer are, therefore, centralized in this package. This is an important concept; it illustrates the principle of information hiding [PAR72].

What is the information that is hidden? It is the structure of the buffer and the methods of operating upon it. Hiding the structure of the buffer is advantageous since we know that "customers" of the buffer package (the units that use it) contain no code that depends upon the structure of the buffer or the exact access mechanisms. This gives us the flexibility to change the way we manipulate the buffer without affecting the users.

For example, we could change the buffer from an array to a linked list, with associated algorithm changes. If we did this, the user of the package would not have to change. This has important implications for ease of development and change of programs, including maintenance of large software systems.

The encapsulation of a buffer in this manner retains the high level of abstraction that we first gained from introducing procedures to access the buffer. The user of the package adds an item to the buffer with the statement,

```
Enqueue (An_Item);
```

or checks to see if the buffer is empty with the statement,

```
if Empty then ...
```

These statements are simpler, clearer, and more abstract than actually performing the related operations on the buffer itself, using and upadating the associated idexes.

7.1.1.3 Type Manager Buffer. It is frequently useful to go beyond the concept of an object manager and develop a package that provides similar services on objects that are created by users. Although the objects are created by the users, they are defined by the package. That is, the package specifies the type of the object. It provides the type definition in the package specification, thereby *exporting* the type definition. We call such a package a *type manager*. It provides services similar to those of the object manager, but can operate on multiple instances of the type. The type that is exported is called an *abstract data type*. This is in constrast to the earlier buffer, which we sometimes call a *resource*.

Here is an example that illustrates a type manager and a buffer as an abstract data type.

```
package Queue_Type_Manager is
   type Queue_Buffer is limited private;

   procedure Enqueue (Buffer  : in out Queue_Buffer;
                      In_Item : in  Item_Type);
   procedure Dequeue (Buffer   : in out Queue_Buffer;
                      Out_Item : out Item_Type);

   function Empty (Buffer : in Queue_Buffer) return Boolean;
   function Full  (Buffer : in Queue_Buffer) return Boolean;

   Buffer_Empty,
   Buffer_Full   : exception;
private
   Buffer_Size : constant := 100;
   type Table is array (1 .. Buffer_Size) of Item_Type;

   type Queue_Buffer is
      record
        Remove,
        Insert  : Positive range 1 .. Buffer_Size := 1;
        Count   : Natural  range 0 .. Buffer_Size := 0;
        Storage : Table;
      end record;
end Queue_Type_Manager;

package body Queue_Type_Manager is
   function Empty (Buffer : in Queue_Buffer) return Boolean is
   begin
      return Buffer.Count = 0;
   end Empty;

   function Full  (Buffer : in Queue_Buffer) return Boolean is
   begin
      return Buffer.Count = Buffer_Size;
   end Full;

   procedure Enqueue  (Buffer  : in out Queue_Buffer;
                       In_Item : in Item_Type) is
   begin
      if Full (Buffer) then
        raise Buffer_Full;
      end if;
```

```
    Buffer.Storage (Buffer.Insert) := In_Item;
    Buffer.Insert := (Buffer.Insert mod Buffer_Size) + 1;
    Buffer.Count  := Buffer.Count + 1;
  end Enqueue;

  procedure Dequeue (Buffer   : in out Queue_Buffer;
                     Out_Item : out Item_Type) is
  begin
    if Empty (Buffer) then
      raise Buffer_Empty;
    end if;

    Out_Item      := Buffer.Storage (Buffer.Remove);
    Buffer.Remove := (Buffer.Remove mod Buffer_Size) + 1;
    Buffer.Count  := Buffer.Count - 1;
  end Dequeue;
end Queue_Type_Manager;
```

Now the procedures (Full, Enqueue, and so on) operate not on a local buffer, but rather on the buffer that is passed to the procedure as a parameter. What is the significant difference between a type manager and an object manager? The object manager operates on its *local buffer*, while the type manager operates on a buffer belonging to the *user* of the buffer package.

There are several interesting aspects of the package Queue_Type_Manager.

- The package exports a type, Queue_Buffer. Users of the package are free to create objects of the type.

- The package exports a series of operations. These operations all take, as a parameter, an object of the exported type.

- The type of the object is limited private. The user of the package can do nothing with objects of the type except perform the operations exported by the package.

The effect of the manner in which the package defines the type and operates on objects of the type is that it allow for a very concise representation of an abstract queueing mechanism.

What are the relative advantages of object managers and type managers?

The object manager is somewhat simpler. First, it is conceptually easier to understand. Further, it presents a narrower interface than the type manager. This is represented by the package specification, and procedure specifications and calls. The procedure interface does not need the extra parameter—the buffer itself that has been created by the user. In addition, the code is textually shorter. For all these reasons, the object manager is preferred when there is in fact only a single object.

The type manager is somewhat more general. It meets the needs for both single and multiple objects. When multiple objects are needed, it is both clearer and more efficient in terms of code size than the creation of multiple object managers. This will be so even if the multiple object managers are created as instantiations of a generic object manager. Therefore, when multiple objects of the same type are created, the type manager is preferred. Chapter 16, Case Four: Multiple Keyboard Handler (MKH), provides a good example of the use of a type manager.

Our primary interest here in object managers and type managers—and in the notion of abstract data type—is related to the use of intermediaries. The subject is much broader, however, and is important to how large systems are designed. The larger issue is beyond the scope of this book. We will, however, continue to occasionally mention abstract data types as we proceed.

7.1.1.4 Overwriting Buffer. An overwriting buffer is one that is essentially never full. When a new item is presented, the oldest item in the buffer is discarded (overwritten). The indexes must be updated to retain proper sequencing of removals from the buffer. For an encapsulated buffer, there is no longer any need to export the function Full or the exception Buffer_Full. Other than that specification change, the only change is to the package body in the procedure Enqueue. The new version is:

```
procedure Enqueue (In_Item : in Item_Type) is
begin
   Buffer (Insert) := In_Item;
   Insert := (Insert mod Buffer_Size) + 1;

   if Count = Buffer_Size then
     Remove := (Remove mod Buffer_Size) + 1;
   else
     Count := Count + 1;
   end if;
end Enqueue;
```

If the buffer is not full, the procedure operates normally.

When the buffer is full, the Insert and Remove indexes point to the same item (i.e., the oldest item in the buffer).

There are three issues to address in this instance:

1. The new item is inserted to overwrite the old item, and the Insert index is incremented to point to what has become the oldest item in the buffer.

2. To properly remove the oldest item on the next call to Dequeue (rather than the new item just inserted in the buffer), the Remove index is also incremented.

3. Count must not be updated if the buffer is already full.

7.1.2 Alternate Algorithm

The algorithm we have seen so far for the simple bounded buffer makes explicit use of the count of the number of items in the buffer. The alternate algorithm we are about to consider does not explicitly count the number of items in the buffer, but rather determines the buffer-empty and buffer-full conditions by comparing the Insert and Remove indexes into the buffer. The indexes are manipulated in such a way that the buffer is considered to be empty when Insert is equal to Remove, and the buffer to be full when Insert is one "behind" Remove. Remember that if Remove is at the first location of the buffer and Insert is at the last location of the buffer, then (in a circular buffer sense) Insert is one "behind" Remove.

These ideas are expressed in Figure 7-2 in a general way. You can see that the approach is very similar to the original algorithm by comparing Figure 7-2 with Figure 7-1.

Appropriate modifications to the buffer are shown below.

```
function Empty return Boolean is
begin
   return Insert = Remove;
end Empty;

function Full  return Boolean is
begin
   return (((Insert mod Buffer_Size) + 1) = Remove);
end Full;
```

BUFFER ALGORITHM WITHOUT USE OF BUFFER-COUNT

True_Buffer_Size : constant := 8;   <u>SAMPLE BUFFER</u>
Buffer_Size : constant := True_Buffer_Size + 1;

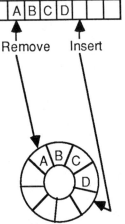

Buffer : array (1 .. Buffer_Size) of Character;
Remove, Insert :
        Positive range 1 .. Buffer_Size := 1;

Buffer is full when
    (Insert mod Buffer_Size + 1) = Remove;
(insert in Buffer when
    ((Insert mode Buffer_Size) + 1) /= Remove)

    Buffer (Insert) := In_Char; -- input Character
    Insert   := (Insert mod Buffer_Size) + 1;

Buffer is empty when Insert = Remove;
(remove from Buffer when Insert /= Remove)

    Out_Char := Buffer (Remove); -- output Character
    Remove   := (Remove mod Buffer_Size) + 1;

<u>BUFFER AFTER 2 REMOVALS, 4 INSERTIONS</u>

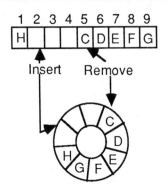

Figure 7-2. Bounded buffer concepts (without Buffer-count)

```
procedure Enqueue (In_Item : in Item_Type) is
begin
  if Full then
    raise Buffer_Full;
  end if;

  Buffer (Insert) := In_Item;
  Insert := (Insert mod Buffer_Size) + 1;
end Enqueue;

procedure Dequeue (Out_Item : out Item_Type) is
begin
  if Empty  then
    raise Buffer_Empty;
  end if;

  Out_Item := Buffer (Remove);
  Remove   := (Remove mod Buffer_Size) + 1;
end Dequeue;
```

Some extra details about the buffer-empty and buffer-full conditions are shown in Figure 7-3.

Notice that the algorithm requires that one of the elements of the buffer remain unused, even when the buffer is full. Therefore, the true size of the buffer is one less than the number of elements in the array used to create the buffer.

The first algorithm described does not suffer from this characteristic, and is also a little easier to understand. The alternate algorithm does not need to store and manipulate Count. It is particularly applicable to the sharing of an unprotected buffer by two tasks, the topic of the final part of this chapter.

7.1.3 Generic Buffers

In a concurrent system, there are likely to be many buffers, differing only in their length and the type of the object that they store. The natural way to handle such a situation is to create a generic buffer and instantiate instances of it for specific needs.

7.1.3.1 Object Manager. Here is a generic buffer in the object-manager style.

Buffer Empty

Remove = Insert

Hence remove from Buffer:

when Remove /= Insert

accept ....

Buffer Full

Insert is one less than Remove, or:

(Insert + 1) = Remove

Wrap-around requires:

(Insert mod Buffer_Size + 1) = Remove

Hence add to Buffer:

when (Insert mod Buffer_Size + 1)/= Remove
accept ....

Note: One buffer location always goes unused.

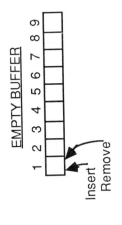

Figure 7-3. Buffer-empty/buffer-full conditions

```
generic
   Buffer_Size : Positive := 100;
   type Buffered_Type is private;
package Queue_Object_Manager is
   procedure Enqueue (In_Item  : in  Buffered_Type);
   procedure Dequeue (Out_Item : out Buffered_Type);
   function Empty return Boolean;
   function Full  return Boolean;

   Buffer_Empty,
   Buffer_Full   : exception;
end Queue_Object_Manager;

package body Queue_Object_Manager is
   Buffer : array (1 .. Buffer_Size) of Buffered_Type;

   Remove,
   Insert  : Positive range 1 .. Buffer_Size := 1;
   Count   : Natural  range 0 .. Buffer_Size := 0;

   function Empty return Boolean is ...
   function Full  return Boolean is ...
   procedure Enqueue (In_Item : in Buffered_Type) is ...
   procedure Dequeue (Out_Item : out Buffered_Type) is ...
end Queue_Object_Manager;
```

The major change to the nongeneric buffer to make it generic is the addition of the generic clause and parameters.

The generic parameters are the size of the buffer and the type of the item to be buffered. The package body no longer has the constant Buffer_Size, and the type Item_Type is replaced by the type Buffered_Type. The procedures that accomplish the operations of the buffer are unchanged. Alternatively, the procedures could use the alternate algorithm without use of Count. The users of the package are unaffected by the choice of algorithm.

An alternate generic approach is to use an *index* of a buffer as a generic parameter, rather than the size of the buffer. This is slightly more general, since we can use *any discrete type* (for example, an enumeration type) as the actual index. In this case it is natural to use the algorithm without Count since we are no longer explicitly concerned with the size of the buffer (only whether it is full or empty).

Here is a generic buffer of style object manager, using the *index* as the generic parameter. First, the specification:

```
generic
  type Index is (<>);
  type Buffered_Type is private;
package Index_Queue_Object_Manager is
...
end Index_Queue_Object_Manager;
```

The rest of the specification is unchanged, as shown by "...". The package body is:

```
package body Index_Queue_Object_Manager is

  Buffer : array (Index) of Buffered_Type;

  Remove,
  Insert  : Index := Index'First;

  function Next (Discrete : in Index) return Index is
  begin
    if Discrete = Index'Last then
      return Index'First;
    else
      return Index'Succ (Discrete);
    end if;
  end Next;

  function Empty return Boolean is
  begin
    return Insert = Remove;
  end Empty;

  function Full  return Boolean is
  begin
    return (Next (Insert) = Remove);
  end Full;
```

```
procedure Enqueue (In_Item : in Buffered_Type) is
begin
   if Full then
     raise Buffer_Full;
   end if;

   Buffer (Insert) := In_Item;
   Insert := Next (Insert);
end Enqueue;

procedure Dequeue (Out_Item : out Buffered_Type) is
begin
   if Empty  then
     raise Buffer_Empty;
   end if;

   Out_Item := Buffer (Remove);
   Remove := Next (Remove);
end Dequeue;
end Index_Queue_Object_Manager;
```

The buffer is now declared using the Index type. Insert and Remove are declared using Index, and initialized with the attribute First. The count is no longer required.

The local *helping* function Next uses a check on Index'Last, and the successor and First attributes, to replace the modulo operation. The Full and Empty procedures are similar to those shown earlier. The Enqueue and Dequeue procedures are modified to use the attributes of Index, rather than the constant value Buffer_Size.

This general style can also be used for buffers that are not generic. That is, an index for the buffer would be explicitly declared; the remainder of the buffer's code would use the attributes of the index.

7.1.3.2 Type Manager. Here is a generic buffer in the type-manager style.

```
generic
   Buffer_Size : Positive := 100;
   type Buffered_Type is private;
package Queue_Type_Manager is
   type Queue_Buffer is limited private;
```

```
      procedure Enqueue (Buffer  : in out Queue_Buffer;
                         In_Item : in  Buffered_Type);
      procedure Dequeue (Buffer   : in out Queue_Buffer;
                         Out_Item : out Buffered_Type);

      function Empty (Buffer : in Queue_Buffer) return Boolean;
      function Full  (Buffer : in Queue_Buffer) return Boolean;

      Buffer_Empty,
      Buffer_Full   : exception;
   private
      type Table is array (1 .. Buffer_Size) of Buffered_Type;

      type Queue_Buffer is
        record
          Remove,
          Insert  : Positive range 1 .. Buffer_Size := 1;
          Count   : Natural  range 0 .. Buffer_Size := 0;
          Storage : Table;
        end record;
   end Queue_Type_Manager;
```

Recalling the type manager of Section 7.1.1.3., we see that Buffer_Size is now a generic parameter rather than a constant in the private part of the specification. The type is Buffered_Type rather than Item_Type. The body of the package is unchanged.

The type-manager style may also be used to construct a generic buffer that has a generic parameter that is the *type* of the index to the buffer. The resulting buffer combines the various styles we have seen in previous sections. Here is the specification for such a buffer.

```
   generic
      type Index is (<>);
      type Buffered_Type is private;
   package Queue_Type_Manager is
      type Queue_Buffer is limited private;

      procedure Enqueue (Buffer  : in out Queue_Buffer;
                         In_Item : in  Buffered_Type);
      procedure Dequeue (Buffer   : in out Queue_Buffer;
                         Out_Item : out Buffered_Type);
```

```
function Empty (Buffer : in Queue_Buffer) return Boolean;
function Full  (Buffer : in Queue_Buffer) return Boolean;

Buffer_Empty,
Buffer_Full   : exception;
private
   type Table is array (Index) of Buffered_Type;

   type Queue_Buffer is
     record
       Remove,
       Insert  : Index := Index'First;
       Storage : Table;
     end record;
end Queue_Type_Manager;
```

The only differences in the specification are to the generic parameter, replacing "Buffer_Size" with "Index", and to the private part. The changes to the body are similar to those shown in Section 7.1.3.1, but written in the style of a type manager.

7.2 Tasks Ensure Mutual Exclusion

In this book we are interested in buffers primarily because of their use in concurrent systems. We saw in Chapter 2 that unprotected sharing of data can lead to erroneous programs; we need to treat access to shared data as a critical section and ensure that it is executed in mutual exclusion. It is natural to use tasks to provide that mutual exclusion, allowing access to the buffer only by calls to entries in the task.

The producer and consumer call the appropriate entries of the buffering task. They will typically receive immediate service, being held up (blocked) only on buffer-full or buffer-empty conditions. (They may also be temporarily blocked while being queued for access to entry to the buffer.)

7.2.1 Bounded Buffer

This section addresses basic issues of the bounded buffer encapsulated in a task, and shows how earlier versions of unprotected buffers may be used to easily construct protected buffers.

7.2.1.1 Basic Algorithm. The basic algorithm is still that illustrated in Figure 7-1. Here it is adapted for a task. (We will continue to illustrate the approach using the abstract type Item_Type.)

```
task Bounded_Buffer is
  entry Enqueue (In_Item  : in  Item_Type);
  entry Dequeue (Out_Item : out Item_Type);
end Bounded_Buffer;

task body Bounded_Buffer is
  Buffer_Size : constant := 100;
  Buffer : array (1 .. Buffer_Size) of Item_Type;

  Remove,
  Insert : Positive range 1 .. Buffer_Size := 1;
  Count  : Natural  range 0 .. Buffer_Size := 0;
begin
  loop
    select
      when Count < Buffer_Size =>
        accept Enqueue (In_Item  : in  Item_Type) do
          Buffer (Insert) := In_Item;
        end Enqueue;

        Insert := (Insert mod Buffer_Size) + 1;
        Count  := Count + 1;
    or
      when Count > 0 =>
        accept Dequeue (Out_Item : out Item_Type) do
          Out_Item := Buffer (Remove);
        end Dequeue;

        Remove := (Remove mod Buffer_Size) + 1;
        Count  := Count - 1;
    end select;
  end loop;
end Bounded_Buffer;
```

The important difference between this solution and the earlier use of buffers is that access to the buffer is in a critical section: the accept statements for Enqueue and Dequeue. The way to prevent an insert to a full buffer or a removal from an empty buffer is to use of guards on the accept statements. For example:

```
when Count < Buffer_Size => -- prevents adding to a full buffer
```

```
when Count > 0 => -- prevents removal from an empty buffer
```

The housekeeping work of incrementing the indexes and modifying the count is accomplished outside the rendezvous. This is done to maximize concurrency; the calling task is allowed to go on its own way as soon as possible.

(It is worth noting, however, that certain optimization techniques that can transform tasks into procedure calls protected by semaphores may require that all the code of a task be contained inside the task's accept statements. These are commonly referred to as the Habermann–Nassi optimizations [HAB80].)

7.2.1.2 Using Existing Buffer Package. This section shows how to use an existing buffer package to make it easier to construct a task that guarantees mutually exclusive access to a buffer. We assume the existence of a library package called "Buffer" that has the same specification and effect as our earlier package Queue_Object_ Manager of Section 7.1.1.2.

Both Buffer and task Bounded_Buffer are in a context in which the type definition Item_Type is visible.

```
task Bounded_Buffer is
  entry Enqueue (In_Item  : in  Item_Type);
  entry Dequeue (Out_Item : out Item_Type);
end Bounded_Buffer;

with Buffer; -- assume a package called Buffer
task body Bounded_Buffer is
begin
  loop
    select
      when not Buffer.Full =>
        accept Enqueue (In_Item  : in  Item_Type) do
          Buffer.Enqueue (In_Item);
        end Enqueue;
    or
```

```
      when not Buffer.Empty  =>
        accept Dequeue (Out_Item : out Item_Type) do
          Buffer.Dequeue (Out_Item);
        end Dequeue;
    end select;
  end loop;
end Bounded_Buffer;
```

This code is even simpler than our earlier task Bounded_Buffer—as long as we first understand how the Buffer package works. The effect of the two different Bounded_Buffer tasks is not quite identical. In the earlier task, the housekeeping needed to update the Count and the indexes was done external to the accept statement. Here, it is done during the call to the Enqueue and Dequeue procedures and hence in the accept statement. The calling task is, therefore, still blocked during this process.

This task uses the functions Empty and Full exported by the Buffer package. This is an illustration of why general-purpose buffer packages should provide these *observing* functions as well as the *modifying* procedures to Enqueue and Dequeue.

Note that this task must be the *only task using the Buffer*. Otherwise we would be back in a situation where we had uncontrolled concurrent access to an unprotected data structure.

The next section shows a better way to accomplish the use of an existing buffer to create a task that provides mutually exclusive access; it uses generics.

7.2.1.3 Using Generic Buffer Package. An even more common use of the approach above is to combine the abstraction of the buffer and the abstraction provided by generic units. This allows us to take advantage of a library of reusable software components constructed as generic packages. If we have a generic version of Queue_Object_Manager in our library, we could instantiate our own buffer within the body of the task Bounded_Buffer. The use of the generic version is:

```
task Bounded_Buffer is
  entry Enqueue (In_Item  : in  Item_Type);
  entry Dequeue (Out_Item : out Item_Type);
end Bounded_Buffer;
```

```
with Queue_Object_Manager; -- generic version from 7.1.3.1
task body Bounded_Buffer is

    package Buffer is new Queue_Object_Manager
                         (Buffer_Size   => 100;
                          Buffered_Type => Item_Type);

begin
    ...
end Bounded_Buffer;
```

This buffer, like the nongeneric version, is easy to understand—
given we understand the original buffer abstraction, the generic
buffer, and the way in which the instantiation works to provide the
task with the services it uses.

There are two important advantages of such a use of a buffer:

1. Since the Buffer is contained within the instantiating task, we
    are guaranteed that no other task has access to it.

2. The generic buffer need not have visibility of the type definition
    Item_Type. The actual Buffer gains the knowledge it needs
    (about the structure of objects of type Item_Type) through the
    generic parameter during instantiation.

7.2.2   Overwriting Buffer

Here is a task version of the overwriting buffer (presented in Section
7.1.1.4.). The only change to the task buffer discussed immediately
above is to the accept statement for Enqueue. It is no longer
guarded, and uses the algorithm for overwriting the oldest item in
the buffer.

```
accept Enqueue (In_Item : in Item_Type) do
    Buffer (Insert) := In_Item;
    Insert := (Insert mod Buffer_Size) + 1;

    if Count = Buffer_Size then
        Remove := (Remove mod Buffer_Size) + 1;
    else
        Count := Count + 1;
    end if;
end Enqueue;
```

We could also have used the capabilities of an unprotected over-writing buffer package.

7.2.3 Alternate Algorithm

Here is the code for the simple Bounded_Buffer without explicitly keeping track of the count of number of items in the buffer.

```
task Bounded_Buffer is
  entry Enqueue (In_Char  : in  Character);
  entry Dequeue (Out_Char : out Character);
end Bounded_Buffer;

task body Bounded_Buffer is
  True_Buffer_Size : constant := 100;
  Buffer_Size      : constant := True_Buffer_Size + 1;
  Buffer : array (1 .. Buffer_Size) of Character;

  Remove,
  Insert : Positive range 1 .. Buffer_Size := 1;
begin
  loop
    select
      when ((Insert mod Buffer_Size) + 1) /= Remove =>
        accept Enqueue (In_Char : in Character) do
          Buffer (Insert) := In_Char; -- input character
        end Enqueue;

        Insert := (Insert mod Buffer_Size) + 1;
    or
      when Insert /= Remove =>
        accept Dequeue (Out_Char : out Character) do
          Out_Char := Buffer (Remove); -- output character
        end Dequeue;

        Remove := (Remove mod Buffer_Size) + 1;
    end select;
  end loop;
end Bounded_Buffer;
```

7.2.4   Buffer as Parameter

Tasks can also take a buffer as parameter, similar to the way a package can be used as a type manager.

Compared to the Bounded_Buffer task that illustrated the basic buffering algorithm (in Section 7.2.1.1), the changes to the entry declarations are:

```
entry Enqueue  (Buffer  : in out Queue_Buffer;
                In_Item : in Item_Type);

entry Dequeue (Buffer   : in out Queue_Buffer;
               Out_Item : out Item_Type);
```

And the changes to the accept statements are:

```
accept Enqueue  (Buffer  : in out Queue_Buffer;
                 In_Item : in Item_Type) do
  Buffer.Storage (Buffer.Insert) := In_Item;
  Buffer.Insert := (Buffer.Insert mod Buffer_Size) + 1;
  Buffer.Count  := Buffer.Count + 1;
end Enqueue;

accept Dequeue (Buffer   : in out Queue_Buffer;
                Out_Item : out Item_Type) do
  Out_Item      := Buffer.Storage (Buffer.Remove);
  Buffer.Remove := (Buffer.Remove mod Buffer_Size) + 1;
  Buffer.Count  := Buffer.Count - 1;
end Dequeue;
```

As we saw in comparing the object and type managers, the difference bewteen the two styles of buffering tasks is in the fact that we have an extra parameter—the actual buffer.

In this style, the code of the buffering algorithm operates on the actual buffer passed as a parameter. There is no longer any local buffer in the task body. The housekeeping (updating the Count and indexes) must necessarily be accomplished during the execution of the accept statement.

7.3   Monitors

The variations on the Bounded_Buffer task have illustrated different approaches and algorithms for buffering. The preferred use of such tasks is to encapsulate them in a package. The package will provide a procedural interface to the protected data structure, even hiding the fact that a task is used to implement the critical section. Such a package is called a monitor.

The specification of a monitor package looks a great deal like the nonconcurrent buffers we saw in the first part of the chapter. Actually, they provide an even simpler interface, since there is no need to provide special consideration for buffer-full and buffer-empty conditions. The task in the package will simply block callers until space (or an item) is available.

7.3.1 Object Manager

Here is a monitor package analogous to the very first buffer package we looked at.

```
package Monitor_Queue is
  procedure Enqueue (In_Item  : in  Item_Type);
  procedure Dequeue (Out_Item : out Item_Type);
end Monitor_Queue;

package body Monitor_Queue is

  task Bounded_Buffer is
    entry Enqueue (In_Item  : in  Item_Type);
    entry Dequeue (Out_Item : out Item_Type);
  end Bounded_Buffer;

  task body Bounded_Buffer is
    ...
  end Bounded_Buffer;

  procedure Enqueue (In_Item  : in  Item_Type) is
  begin
    Bounded_Buffer.Enqueue (In_Item);
  end Enqueue;

  procedure Dequeue (Out_Item : out Item_Type) is
  begin
    Bounded_Buffer.Dequeue (Out_Item);
  end Dequeue;
end Monitor_Queue;
```

Here we again show the style of providing a procedural interface with an entrance procedure. The Bounded_Buffer task is the same task we developed in the previous section.

7.3.2 Type Manager

Here is a monitor analogous to the type-manager buffer package.

```
package Type_Monitor_Queue is
   type Queue_Buffer is limited private;

   procedure Enqueue (Buffer  : in out Queue_Buffer;
                      In_Item : in  Item_Type);
   procedure Dequeue (Buffer   : in out Queue_Buffer;
                      Out_Item : out Item_Type);
private
   Buffer_Size : constant := 100;
   type Table is array (1 .. Buffer_Size) of Item_Type;

   type Queue_Buffer is
     record
       Remove,
       Insert  : Positive range 1 .. Buffer_Size := 1;
       Count   : Natural  range 0 .. Buffer_Size := 0;
       Storage : Table;
     end record;
end Type_Monitor_Queue;
```

The entrance procedures then make calls on a Bounded_Buffer task (in the package body) of the style illustrated in Section 7.2.3, using the Buffer as a parameter.

7.3.3 Generic Monitors

We can also provide generic monitors. In fact, since tasks cannot be generic, we must use an enclosing package to encapsulate the buffering task if we wish for the flexibility of a generic approach to provide for parameterization.

7.3.3.1 Object Manager. A generic monitor is:

```
generic
   Buffer_Size : Positive := 100;
   type Buffered_Type is private;
package Monitor_Queue is
   procedure Enqueue (In_Item  : in  Buffered_Type);
   procedure Dequeue (Out_Item : out Buffered_Type);
end Monitor_Queue;
```

```
package body Monitor_Queue is
  task Bounded_Buffer is
    entry Enqueue (In_Item  : in  Buffered_Type);
    entry Dequeue (Out_Item : out Buffered_Type);
  end Bounded_Buffer;

  task body Bounded_Buffer is

    ...
  end Bounded_Buffer;

  procedure Enqueue (In_Item  : in  Buffered_Type) is ...
  procedure Dequeue (Out_Item : out Buffered_Type) is ...
end Monitor_Queue;
```

The major change to the nongeneric buffer to make it generic is the addition of the generic clause and parameters. The body of the task no longer will contain the constant Buffer_Size. A typical instantiation of the monitor is:

```
package Character_Buffer is new Monitor_Queue
                (Buffer_Size   => 8;
                 Buffered_Type => Character);
```

7.3.3.2 Type Manager. Similarly, we can have a generic type-manager monitor. For example:

```
generic
  Buffer_Size : Positive := 100;
  type Buffered_Type is private;
package Type_Monitor_Queue is
  type Queue_Buffer is limited private;

  procedure Enqueue (Buffer   : in out Queue_Buffer;
                      In_Item  : in  Buffered_Type);
  procedure Dequeue (Buffer   : in out Queue_Buffer;
                      Out_Item : out Buffered_Type);
```

```
private
  type Table is array (1 .. Buffer_Size) of Buffered_Type;

  type Queue_Buffer is ...

  ...
end Type_Monitor_Queue;
```

The changes to the body are similar to those we saw earlier.

7.4 Safe Unprotected Shared Buffer

It is occasionally useful for two tasks to share a buffer that is not accessed in a critical section. We will see an example in Chapter 16, Case Four: Multiple Keyboard Handler (MKH). We call such a buffer an unprotected buffer.

This section demonstrates that two (but only two) tasks may safely access such a properly constructed buffer. The algorithm used to access the buffer must be of the style that determines buffer-full/buffer-empty by comparison of the Remove and Insert indexes; it must not use a count variable.

7.4.1 Two Tasks Share Buffer

Here is an abstract algorithm for two tasks sharing an unprotected data structure.

```
procedure Main is
  True_Buffer_Size : constant := 8;
  Buffer_Size      : constant := True_Buffer_Size + 1;
  Buffer : array (1 .. Buffer_Size) of Character;

  Remove,
  Insert : Positive range 1 .. Buffer_Size := 1;
```

```
task Producer;
task body Producer is
begin
  compares Insert and Remove;

  if the buffer is not full
    inserts Characters into the buffer;
  end if;

  increments Insert index;
end Producer;

task Consumer;
task body Consumer is
begin
  compares Insert and Remove;

  if the buffer is not empty
    removes Characters from the buffer;
  end if;

  increments Remove index;
end Consumer;
begin -- main
  null;
end Main;
```

Here we have a situation in which two concurrent processes access a common data structure. This is usually a prescription for trouble; specifically, inconsistent data. It works in this case, however, since Producer and Consumer have different roles in regard to the Remove and Insert indexes. Although each task reads both indexes, only the Consumer task modifies Remove and only the Producer task modifies Insert.

Figure 7-4 provides a pictorial description of the abstract code shown above. Consumer can see, but does not modify, the Insert index. Similarly, Producer can see, but does not modify, the Remove index.

One topic we have not yet considered: what does Producer do when the buffer is full (or Consumer do when the buffer is empty)? If the tasks cannot interact with the buffer, they must either go do other work and check the buffer later, or delay and wait to check the buffer again at the end of the delay. Either of these situations leads to polling the buffer. This is in contrast to the use of a buffer

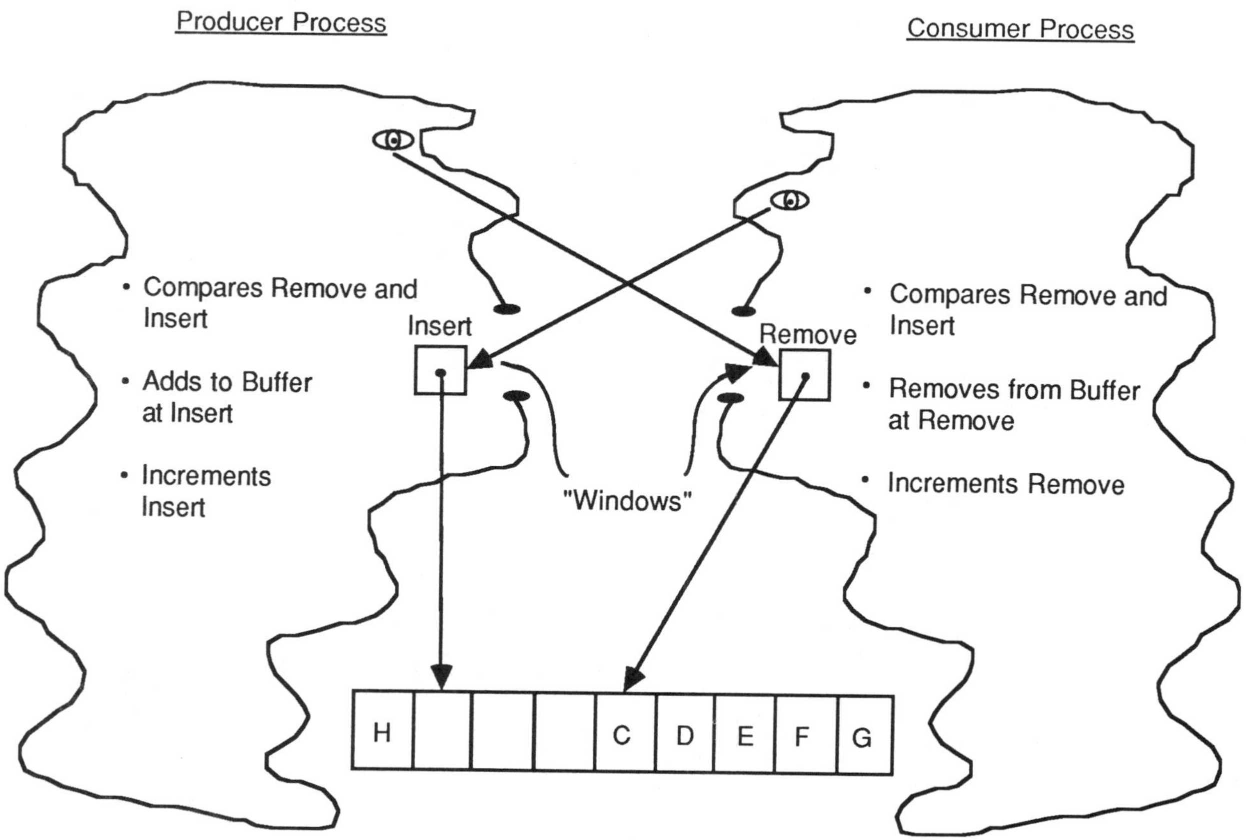

Consumer Process

- Compares Remove and Insert
- Removes from Buffer at Remove
- Increments Remove

Remove

"Windows"

Producer Process

- Compares Remove and Insert
- Adds to Buffer at Insert
- Increments Insert

Insert

| H | | | | C | D | E | F | G |

Figure 7-4. Visibility/use of unprotected share buffer

protected by a task, in which the calling task is blocked when it cannot access the buffer.

Let's return to the issue of determining buffer-full and buffer-empty conditions. Remember that we still have simultaneous actions by the two tasks; while Consumer is reading *Insert*, Producer may be concurrently incrementing it. Similarly, Consumer may be concurrently incrementing *Remove* while while Producer is reading it. Therefore, there can still be an incorrect determination of the buffer-full or buffer-empty conditions.

Let's first look at the situation from the standpoint of the Consumer. The Consumer may decide the buffer is full (i.e., that Remove = Insert), when actually an item has been added and Insert incremented. But—the wrongful determination is "safe" in that it only creates an extra delay, not an inconsistent data access.

Figure 7-5 restates the situation, comparing the Producer and Consumer processes. Let's look at the situation now from the point of view of Producer.

Producer may incorrectly conclude that the buffer is full (and therefore wait an unnecessary cycle if the Consumer has removed an item), but can never incorrectly conclude that the buffer is not full. Why can't it reach an incorrect conclusion that the buffer is not full? Because Producer itself is the only process that can change the state from not full to full! (Note that we do assume the tasks are coded correctly; it would be fatal if the tasks *decremented* rather than *incremented* the indexes.)

We see then that the Producer can make a mistake that is relatively harmless (making it poll one additional and unnecessary time), but cannot make the mistake that would lead to an erroneous program (putting something into a full buffer).

Similarly, the Consumer can make the relatively harmless mistake, but cannot make the mistake that would lead to an erroneous program (taking something from an empty buffer).

The procedure below brings the information together in a complete code fragment modifying the shared buffer.

```
procedure Main is
  True_Buffer_Size : constant := 8;
  Buffer_Size      : constant := True_Buffer_Size + 1;

  -- Here is the buffer being accessed by the two tasks
```

Safety of Concurrent Access

Producer Process

- Compares Remove and Insert

- May determine that buffer is full
  if full then
      delay ...;
  else
      add item to buffer;
  end if;

- Writes only to Insert

- The buffer-full determination may be wrong:
  - Dequeue may have "simultaneously" removed an item from the buffer
  - and incremented Remove

- but that's ok!
  - an extra delay
  - not-full determination is always correct

Consumer Process

- Compares Remove and Insert

- May determine that buffer is empty
  if empty then
      delay ...;
  else
      remove item from buffer;
  end if;

- Writes only to Remove

- The buffer-empty determination may be wrong:
  - Enqueue may have "simultaneously" added an item to the buffer
  - and incremented Insert

- but that's ok!
  - an extra delay
  - not-empty determination is always correct

Figure 7-5. Enqueue/dequeue share unprotected buffer

```
-------------------------------------------------------------------
    Buffer : array (1 .. Buffer_Size) of Character;
-------------------------------------------------------------------


Remove,
Insert : Positive range 1 .. Buffer_Size := 1;

task Producer;
task body Producer is
  In_Char : Character;
begin
  loop
    -- get something (In_Char) to put into the buffer

    -- and now insert the something into the buffer
    Insert_Loop:
    loop
      if ((Insert mod Buffer_Size) + 1) /= Remove then
        Buffer (Insert) := In_Char;
        Insert := (Insert mod Buffer_Size) + 1;
        exit Insert_Loop;
      else
        delay Appropriate_Delay_Interval;
      end if;
    end loop Insert_Loop;
  end loop;
end Producer;


task Consumer;
task body Consumer is
  Out_Char : Character;
begin
  loop
    -- get something (Out_Char) from the buffer
    Remove_Loop:
```

```
loop
  if Insert /= Remove then
    Out_Char := Buffer (Remove);
    Remove := (Remove mod Buffer_Size) + 1;
    exit Remove_Loop;
  else
    delay Appropriate_Delay_Interval;
  end if;
end loop Remove_Loop;

-- put the something where it is supposed to go
end loop;
end Consumer;
begin -- main
  null;
end Main;
```

7.4.2 Encapsulated Buffer

The tasks above accessed the buffer directly; they checked the indexes, accessed the buffer, and incremented the indexes. In earlier sections we noted that it is desirable to use an encapsulating package to achieve a higher degree of abstraction. We can do so in this case of two tasks sharing an unprotected buffer by using a buffer of the form Queue_Object_Manager previously discussed in Section 7.1.2.

The Producer and Consumer would then interact as:

```
with Buffer;
-- We assume that this Buffer uses the algorithm
-- without ''Count'', and that it buffers characters.
procedure Main is
  task Producer;
  task body Producer is
    In_Char : Character;
```

```
    begin
      loop
        Insert_Loop:
        loop
          if not Buffer.Full then
            Buffer.Enqueue (In_Char);
            exit Insert_Loop;
          else
            delay Appropriate_Delay_Interval;
          end if;
        end loop Insert_Loop;
      end loop;
    end Producer;

    task Consumer;
    task body Consumer is
      Out_Char : Character;
    begin
      loop
        Remove_Loop:
        loop
          if not Buffer.Empty then
            Buffer.Dequeue (Out_Char);
            exit Remove_Loop;
          else
            delay Appropriate_Delay_Interval;
          end if;
        end loop Remove_Loop;
      end loop;
    end Consumer;
  begin -- main
    null;
  end Main;
```

This approach follows our usual method of providing abstract references to data structures rather than accessing the data structure directly. As we have seen in other examples, a properly constructed generic buffer (using the algorithms previously discussed) could be instantiated, rather than using an existing buffer in the library. This offers the advantage that the size and type would be introduced as generic parameters, and that access to the buffer would be strictly limited to the instantiating unit.

7.5   Exercises

There is only one exercise for this chapter; it is quite long.

An important characteristic of a buffer is that data *flows through* it; it does not hold the data. Related to this is the fact that once an item is read, it is gone from the buffer and is not available to be read again. In addition, the data in the buffer are never modified while they pass through the buffer. An alternate mechanism for task communication is a *pool* of continuously available data—data that can be read, modified, and so on. This is often considered to be a *database*. The problem below revolves around developing a pool or database package. Do not be overly concerned with all the details of how the database manages data. The main point is that it is an alternate sort of intermediary to those we have seen earlier.

Databases are important in real-time systems. However, they are generally available as off-the-shelf components or constructed by small teams specializing in database issues. Therefore, this is the only place that we address the general notion of database. [Although the case study in Chapter 9, Air Track Display System (ATDS) uses a simplistic database to maintain a track file.]

Exercise 7.1.   A Database or Pool

Purpose: To illustrate an intermediary that is a permanent, rather than temporary, repository of data

Problem: Develop a simple generic database handler to provide mutually exclusive concurrent access to an indexed dataset for a group of tasks. The type of data stored is Item_Type, a generic parameter of a private type. The data are indexed by values of type Key. The type Key is also to be a generic parameter. The type Key specifies the number of items to be stored as part of the type definition.

Provide the capability to:

- Write to the pool (entering a new item for the given key)
- Read from the pool (based on a key)
- Update an item (new value goes in, old value comes out)
- Delete an item
- Ask if an item exists

Raise exceptions for all impossible or inappropriate operations, for example:

- Nothing_To_Read
- Nothing_To_Update
- Old_Item_Overwritten

Here is a general purpose outline and some hints (although you may solve the problem in a number of different ways).

```
generic
  type Key is (<>);
  type Item_Type is private;
package Pool is
-- subprogram declarations to access the pool

-- Parameters of type key to be of mode in, and
-- of type Item_Type to be in or out in accordance with operation.

  Nothing_To_Read : exception; -- etc.
end Pool;

package body Pool is
-- must use a task to encapsulate the data
-- set to ensure mutual exclusion

task ...
  -- entries to accomplish the database access
end ...;

-- Subprograms to satisfy the specification.
-- The subprogram bodies make calls on the task entries.

-- Database status can be captured in the subprogram body,
-- and exceptions returned when appropriate.

-- For example:

  procedure Read ( ... ) is
    Is_There : Boolean;
```

```
    begin
       -- Call the database access task, with a parameter Is_There.
       -- (Of course other parameters get the data and pass it back
       -- to the calling program through the procedure.)
       if not Is_There then
          raise Nothing_To_Read;
       end if;
    end Read;


-- There are other ways to handle the exception situation.


-- And so on for the other procedures


    task body ..
       -- Here is where the work gets done.
       -- You must declare storage for the data of type Item_Type, using
       -- the generic type Key both as an index and definition of size
       -- of the store.

       -- You may also wish to have an array indicating the existance
       -- of an item in the database.

       -- The general structure of the task is:

       loop
         select
           accept ..
         or
           accept ..

         or ...
         or
           terminate;
         end select;
       end loop;
    end ...
end Pool;


-- The instantiation of the Pool is as:
...
type Index is range 1 .. 100;
type Data is ... -- likely a record of some sort
```

```
package Database is new Pool
                (Key       => Index,
                 Item_Type => Data);

-- then later access by:

I : Index;
D : Data;
...
Database.Read (I, D);
```

You need not instantiate and use the pool (unless you wish to test it) as part of this assignment.

Solution:

```
-- Example of a Pool: a database, indexed dataset, etc.

-- See the excellent example in [PYL85, 13.5.2]. This is an
-- adaptation of Pyle's sample MASCOT pool.

generic
  type Key is (<>);
  type Item_Type is private;
package Pool is
  procedure Add_Item    (K : out Key; Item : in  Item_Type);
  procedure Read_Item   (K : in  Key; Item : out Item_Type);
  procedure Write_Item  (K : in  Key; Item : in  Item_Type);

  procedure Update_Item (K : in  Key; New_Item : in  Item_Type;
                                      Old_Item : out Item_Type);

  procedure Delete_Item (K : in  Key);

  function Item_Exists  (K : Key) return Boolean;

  Storage_Full,
  Nothing_To_Read,
  Nothing_To_Update,
  Nothing_To_Delete,
  Old_Item_Overwritten : exception;
end Pool;
```

```
package body Pool is
  task Data is
    entry Add     (K      : out Key;
                   Item  : in  Item_Type;
                   Added : out Boolean);
    entry Read    (K      : in  Key;
                   Item  : out Item_Type;
                   Stored : out Boolean);
    entry Write   (K      : in  Key;
                   Item  : in  Item_Type;
                   Stored : out Boolean);
    entry Update (K        : in  Key;
                   New_Item : in  Item_Type;
                   Old_Item : out Item_Type;
                   Stored   : out Boolean);
    entry Delete (K       : in  Key;
                   Stored : out Boolean);
    entry Query  (K       : in  Key;
                   Stored : out Boolean);
  end Data;

  procedure Add_Item (K    : out Key;
                      Item : in  Item_Type) is
    Added_To_Store : Boolean;
  begin
    Data.Add (K, Item, Added_To_Store);

    if not Added_To_Store then
      raise Storage_Full;
    end if;
  end Add_Item;

  procedure Read_Item (K    : in  Key;
                       Item : out Item_Type) is
    There : Boolean;
  begin
    Data.Read (K, Item, There);

    if not There then
      raise Nothing_To_Read;
    end if;
  end Read_Item;
```

```
procedure Write_Item (K    : in Key;
                      Item : in Item_Type) is
  Was_There : Boolean;
begin
  Data.Write (K, Item, Was_There);

  if Was_There then
    raise Old_Item_Overwritten;
  end if;
end Write_Item;

procedure Update_Item (K        : in  Key;
                       New_Item : in  Item_Type;
                       Old_Item : out Item_Type) is
  There : Boolean;
begin
  Data.Update (K, New_Item, Old_Item, There);

  if not There then
    raise Nothing_To_Update;
  end if;
end Update_Item;

procedure Delete_Item (K : in Key) is
  There : Boolean;
begin
  Data.Delete (K, There);

  if not There then
    raise Nothing_To_Delete;
  end if;
end Delete_Item;

function Item_Exists (K : in Key) return Boolean is
  There : Boolean;
begin
  Data.Query (K, There);
  return There;
end Item_Exists;
```

```
task body Data is
  type Database  is array (Key) of Item_Type;
  type Existence is array (Key) of Boolean;
  Store  : Database;
  Exists : Existence := (Key => False);
begin
  loop
    select
      accept Add (K     : out Key;
                  Item  : in  Item_Type;
                  Added : out Boolean) do
        declare
          Storage_Index : Key;
        begin
          Added := True;
          Storage_Index := Key'First;

          while Exists (Storage_Index) loop
            Storage_Index := Key'Succ (Storage_Index);
          end loop;

          Store (Storage_Index) := Item;
          K := Storage_Index;

        exception
          when Constraint_Error =>
            Added := False;
        end;
      end Add;
    or
      accept Read (K      : in  Key;
                   Item   : out Item_Type;
                   Stored : out Boolean) do

        if Exists (K) then
          Item := Store (K);
        end if;

        Stored := Exists (K);
      end Read;
    or
```

```
          accept Write (K       : in  Key;
                        Item    : in  Item_Type;
                        Stored : out Boolean) do
        Stored     := Exists (K);
        Store (K)  := Item;
        Exists (K) := True;
      end Write;
    or
      accept Update (K        : in  Key;
                     New_Item : in  Item_Type;
                     Old_Item : out Item_Type;
                     Stored   : out Boolean) do

        if Exists (K) then
          Old_Item  := Store (K);
          Store (K) := New_Item;
        end if;

        Stored := Exists (K);
      end Update;
    or
      accept Delete (K       : in  Key;
                     Stored : out Boolean) do
        Stored     := Exists (K);
        Exists (K) := False;
      end Delete;
    or
      accept Query (K       : in  Key;
                    Stored : out Boolean) do
        Stored := Exists (K);
      end Query;
    or
      terminate;
    end select;
  end loop;
    end Data;
end Pool;
```

Keys to Understanding

- We have used an array to implement a circular bounded buffer, by using modulo operations on indexes to the array. The basic algorithm keeps explicit count of the number of items in the buffer.

- An alternate algorithm does not explicitly count the number of items in the buffer; an additional storage location is then required in the buffer.

- Buffers should be encapsulated in packages, rather than having producers and consumers access the buffer directly.

- Object and type managers are two paradigms for buffering.

- It is easy to construct a buffer that overwrites the oldest item; it therefore always accepts data.

- Tasks are used to ensure mutually exclusive access to buffers by inserting and removing only in a critical section: the rendezvous.

- Unprotected buffers in packages can be used as components inside tasks to build protected buffers. This is particularly useful if the buffer packages are generic.

- Tasks protecting buffers should be encapsulated in packages to provide monitors. It is useful to make monitors generic.

- Two tasks can safely and effectively access a properly constructed unprotected data structure.

- Object managers and type managers, and abstract data types, are important to the creation of concurrent systems.

- The buffers illustrated in this chapter will be used as standards for style, and will be referenced throughout the remainder of the book.

8

Buffer-Transporter Model of Task Interaction

> Objective: To illustrate the buffer-transporter model of task interaction

Chapters 6 and 7 introduced the notion of the intermediary and showed how the simple buffer can be effectively used to store multiple items and hence uncouple producer-consumer interaction. Chapter 6 left some open questions about deficiencies in the intermediaries called transporter and relay. This chapter completes the discussion of transporter and relay, as Chapter 7 completed the discussion of the buffer.

The sections to follow show why the buffer (as a strictly called intermediary) is not always satisfactory, illustrate some difficulties with storing multiple items in a transporter or relay, and present a method of building transporters and relays that have desirable characteristics—at the cost of an additional task.

8.1   Attempting a Flexible Consumer

A task may frequently wish to have the flexibility to interact with any of several other tasks—whichever first desires interaction. This section addresses a specific instance of that situation, a consumer that wishes to interact with two buffers. This is only a single instance of a more general case; alternatively, the producer might wish to place things in either of two buffers, or either (or both of the producer and consumer) might wish to interact with a buffer and also some other task.

A consumer may well wish to be able to take items from either of two buffers. In the usual situation of using an unconditional entry call, the consumer must commit to a rendezvous with a *single* buffer. This leads to three problems:

1.   Once the consumer has committed to a call on one buffer (i.e., on the dequeue entry of the buffer), it can be blocked by a buffer-empty condition—even if the other buffer has items to consume.

2.   If other consumers have placed prior calls to the buffer, the consumer will be placed in a queue awaiting service even if the other buffer has items and is not busy.

3.   When both of the buffers are empty, the consumer wishes to obtain the first item available—irrespective of the buffer in which it is placed; this cannot be accomplished if it is blocked on only one of the buffers.

We will discuss the situation using the third situation as an example, keeping in mind that there are really three problems. The first attempt below is incorrect, shown to illustrate what *not* to do.

8.1.1   Wrong Approach

Since the consumer is a calling task (assuming we continue to use the standard simple buffer), the mechanism for control over the rendezvous is the conditional entry call. Let's see if we can circumvent the problems above using this approach. Here is the code to interact with either of two buffers without being held up by one of them.

```
loop
  select
    Buffer1.Dequeue (Item);
    exit;
  else
    null;
  end select;

  select
    Buffer2.Dequeue (Item);
    exit;
  else
    null;
  end select;
end loop;
```

This solution allows the consumer to take from either buffer, whichever first becomes nonempty. However, the consumer must poll (alternatively interogate) the two buffers. This is usually undesirable (at least in a system with more tasks than processors) since it uses processor resources. It is also clumsy if several consumers are calling several buffers.

8.1.2 Right Approach

The way to obtain the desired effect is to make the consumer a *called* task, rather than a caller. It then can simply wait at an accept statement, allowing either of the buffers to call its entry when they have an item to be consumed.

The consumer offers an entry such as:

```
task Consumer is
  accept Take_Item (Item : in Item_Type);
end Consumer;
```

In the body of the consuming task, there is an accept statment.

```
accept Take_Item (Item : in Item_Type) do
  ...
end Take_Item;
```

The consumer may wish to interact, not only with two buffers, but with other tasks as well, offering an entry for the other interaction.

The proper (and easy) approach is to place the two accepts in a selective wait.

```
select
  accept Take_Item (Item : in Item_Type) do ... end;
or
  accept Other_Interaction do ... end;
end select;
```

In the earlier (polling) example, this circumstance would have required yet another conditional call in the polling sequence. We conclude that in order to accommodate the consumer's desire to interact with several tasks, it is necessary that it be a called task, rather than a caller.

If the consumer is to be called, the intermediary task must be a caller. That is, it must be a transporter or relay, as discussed in Chapter 6.

The next section provides a first attempt at creating an intermediary that allows the consumer to be a called task. Section 8.3 will provide a better approach.

8.2 A Polling Relay

In order to allow the consumer to be a called task, the buffering intermediary must issue the call. Therefore it must be a relay or a transporter. We will only address the case of the relay. The situation is similar for the case of the transporter.

The relay we saw in Chapter 6 only buffered a single item, and forced a strict alternation in service between the producer and consumer. If we are to store multiple items (and be able to provide multiple items without an intervening store), we must provide service to the producer and consumer in some order other than strict alternation. We must allow repeated producer interactions (storing items) and also allow repeated consumer interactions (obtaining items from the buffer). We must also account for proper operation when the buffer is empty or full.

Since the relay issues a call to an entry of the consumer, the mechanism to allow it the flexibility of repeated interactions with the consumer (without blocking on an entry of a busy task) is the conditional entry call. Since the relay is called by the producer, the mechanism to allow repeated interaction with the producer without blocking at the accept statement is the selective wait with an else part. Here is the code:

```
task Polling_Buffering_Relay  is
  entry Store (Item : in Item_Type);
  -- Calls Consumer.Take_Item
end Polling_Buffering_Relay;

with Queue_Object_Manager; -- a generic buffer
task body Polling_Buffering_Relay is
  Item : Item_Type;

  package Buffer is new Queue_Object_Manager
                    (Buffer_Size   => 100;
                     Buffered_Type => Item_Type);
begin
  loop
    if not Buffer.Full then
      select
        accept Store (Item : in Item_Type) do
         Buffer.Enqueue (Item);
       end Store;
      else
        null;
      end select;
    end if;

    if not Buffer.Empty then
      Buffer.Dequeue (Item);

      select
       Consumer.Take_Item (Item);
      else
        null;
      end select;
    end if;
  end loop;
end Polling_Buffering_Relay;
```

This is a very unattractive solution. It requires repeated checks on conditions, polling continuously. Even worse, the solution above is incorrect since it does not account for intermediate storing of the item taken out of the buffer, in the event that there is no successful rendezvous with the consumer. We will not bother to fix it up (it gets even messier), since, in any event, it is the wrong approach.

8.3 Buffer-Transporter

The way to achieve the effect of the buffering relay without polling is to use a buffer and a transporter in sequence. This will uncouple the interacting tasks while allowing the consumer to be a called task, rather than a caller. We call the general approach the "buffer-transporter" model for intermediary tasks. This model of task interaction has also been referred to in the literature as the "agent" model [HIL82] or "buffer with transport" [BUH84, page 68].

There are two variations of the buffer-transporter model: the buffering relay and the buffering transporter.

8.3.1 Buffering Relay

We will first solve the problem posed earlier, of a consumer needing to take from either of two buffers, whichever first becomes non-empty. This will require transporters for the consumer: the buffering relay model. It uses two tasks to implement the relay function. If there is no chance for ambiguity, we will simply use the term relay. Since the chain of tasks is producer-buffer-transporter-consumer, we sometimes call this the PBTC model.

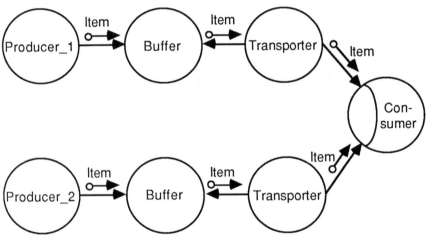

Figure 8-1. Relay model

Figure 8-1 shows two producers placing items into buffers. The consumer is willing to interact with either buffer. Of course, there could be many producers and many consumers involved in these interactions. The code below illustrates how the effect of the graphics is obtained without polling or unnecessary waiting.

Code for 8-1: Relay__Buffer:

```
task Producer_1 is
  -- Calls Relay_Buffer_1.Enqueue
end Producer_1;

task Producer_2 is
  -- Calls Relay_Buffer_2.Enqueue
end Producer_2;

task Consumer is
  entry Take_Item (Item : in Item_Type);
end Consumer;

package Relay_Buffer_1 is
  procedure Enqueue (Item : in Item_Type);
  -- Calls Consumer.Take_Item
end Relay_Buffer_1;

package Relay_Buffer_2 is
  procedure Enqueue (Item : in Item_Type);
  -- Calls Consumer.Take_Item
end Relay_Buffer_2;
```

The task bodies for the producers simply produce the information and call their respective buffers. They are unchanged from the calling producers that we saw in Chapter 6.

The task body for the consumer simply waits at its accept statement for a call from either of the Relay_Buffer tasks. We saw this in Section 8.1.2.

The interesting part of the example is the Relay_Buffers themselves. We will show only Relay_Buffer_1. Relay_Buffer_2 is exactly the same.

```
package body Relay_Buffer_1 is
  task Buffer is
    entry Dequeue (Item : out  Item_Type);
    entry Enqueue (Item : in   Item_Type);
  end Buffer;
```

```
task Transporter is
  -- Calls
    -- Buffer.Dequeue
    -- Consumer.Take_Item
end Transporter;

task body Buffer is separate; -- a typical simple bounded buffer

task body Transporter is
  Item : Item_Type;
begin
  loop
    Buffer.Dequeue        (Item);
    Consumer.Take_Item    (Item);
  end loop;
end Transporter;

procedure Enqueue (Item : in Item_Type) is
begin
  Buffer.Enqueue (Item);
  end Enqueue;
end Relay_Buffer_1;
```

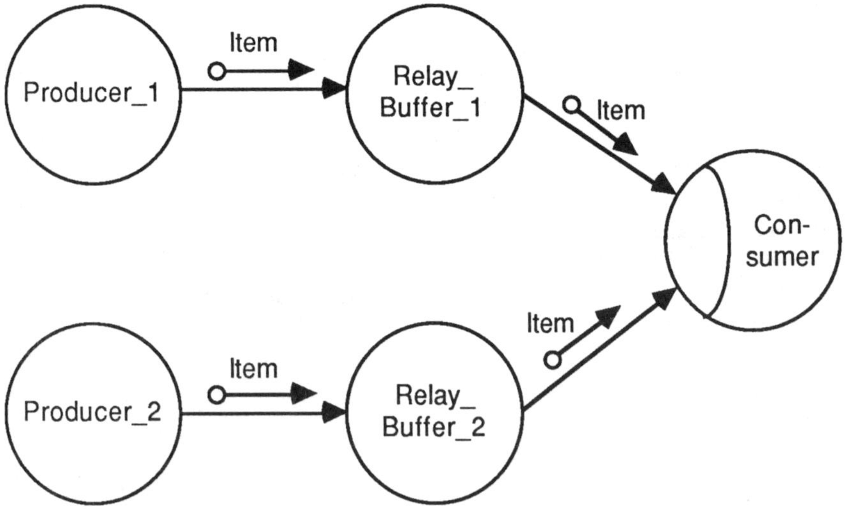

Figure 8-2. Relay_Buffer as a process

The code above uses a package to encapsulate the buffer and transporter to achieve an integrated effect. We may draw the process graph either as in Figure 8-2 or Figure 8-3 (explictly showing the

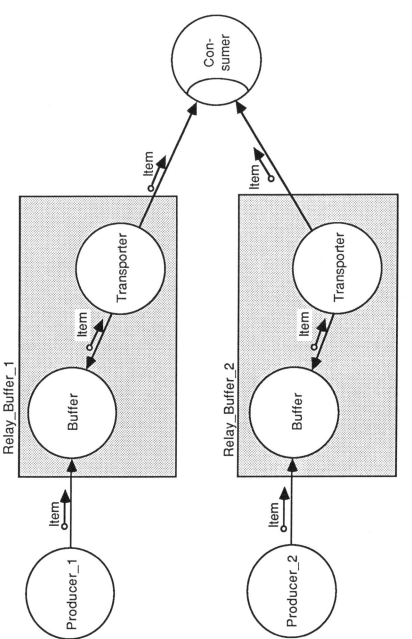

Figure 8-3. Relay_Buffer as a package

packaging). A buffer and transporter will often be grouped in this manner. The resulting construct is called a Relay_Buffer package. It is by no means the only method, however, and many other appropriate designs are possible—for example, the transporter might be packaged with the consumer. This would be especially appropriate for the situation in which many consumers were using transporters to be called tasks with respect to the data from the buffers.

We can also have a buffering relay with consumer caller and a producer that is called. This is a producer-transporter-buffer-consumer (PTBC) model and is an adaptation of the PBTC model. It is shown as Figure 8-4.

The code is a simple adaptation of the earlier example and will not be shown here.

8.3.2 Buffering Transporter

This section provides a solution to the problem of *both* the producer and consumer needing to be callers. This will require transporters for both the producer and consumer: the buffering transporter model. It uses three tasks to implement the transporter function. If there is no chance for ambiguity, we will simply use the term transporter. Since the chain of tasks is producer-transporter-buffer-transporter-consumer, we sometimes call this the PTBTC model. It is shown as Figure 8-5.

This approach may be necessary when both the producer and consumer have a requirement to have alternate interactions with other tasks. This is the advantage of the buffering transporter over the buffering relay, but it costs yet another task to accomplish the interaction.

Code for 8-5: Buffering Transporter:

```
task Producer is
  entry Provide_Item (Item : out Item_Type);
end Producer;

task Consumer is
  entry Take_Item (Item : in Item_Type);
end Consumer;
```

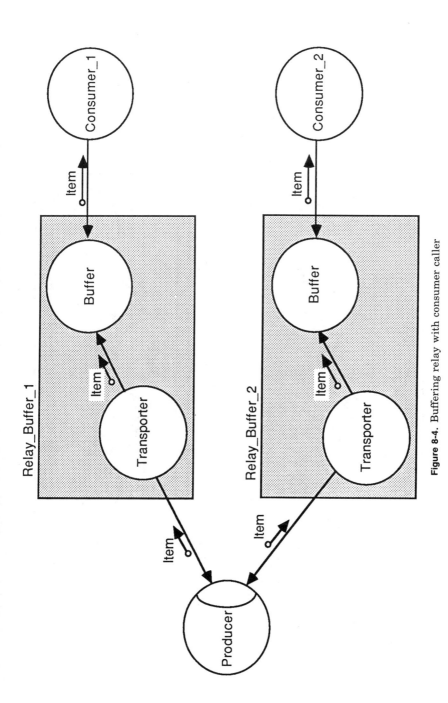

Figure 8-4. Buffering relay with consumer caller

239

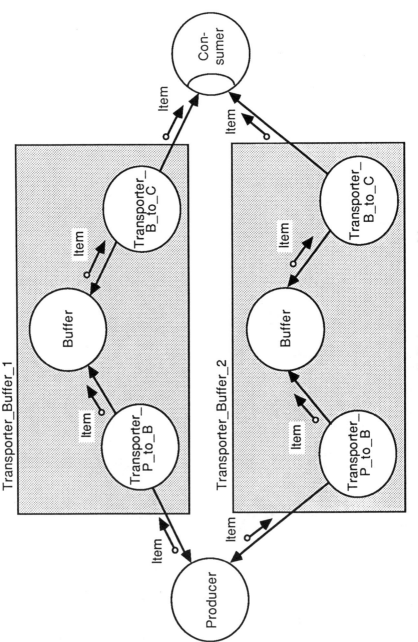

Figure 8-5. Buffering transporter model

```
package Transporter_Buffer_1 is
  -- Calls
    -- Producer.Provide_Item
    -- Consumer.Take_Item
end Transporter_Buffer_1;

package Transporter_Buffer_2 is
  -- Calls
    -- Producer.Provide_Item
    -- Consumer.Take_Item
end Transporter_Buffer_2;
```

The task body for the producer simply produces the information and waits for calls from the buffers.

The task body for the consumer simply waits for calls from the buffers and consumes the items when available.

The interesting part of the example is the Transporter_Buffers themselves. We will show only Transporter_Buffer_1. Transporter_Buffer_2 is exactly the same.

```
package body Transporter_Buffer_1 is
  task Buffer is
    entry Dequeue (Item : out Item_Type);
    entry Enqueue (Item : in  Item_Type);
  end Buffer;

  task Transporter_P_to_B is
    -- Calls
      -- Producer.Provide_Item
      -- Buffer.Enqueue
  end Transporter_P_to_B;

  task Transporter_B_to_C is
  -- Calls
    -- Buffer.Dequeue
    -- Consumer.Take_Item
  end Transporter_B_to_C;

  task body Buffer is separate; -- a typical simple bounded buffer
```

```
task body Transporter_P_to_B is
  Item : Item_Type;
begin
  loop
    Producer.Provide_Item (Item);
    Buffer.Dequeue        (Item);
  end loop;
end Transporter_P_to_B;

task body Transporter_B_to_C is
  Item : Item_Type;
begin
  loop
    Buffer.Enqueue     (Item);
    Consumer.Take_Item (Item);
  end loop;
end Transporter_B_to_C;
end Transporter_Buffer_1;
```

8.4 Polling

In the previous sections and chapters, we mentioned the issue of
polling. Now that we have covered the topics of caller/called, intermediary tasks, the clumsy and correct methods of buffering relays,
and the equivalent methods for transporters, it is appropriate to
address the issue of polling at length.

Polling is the repeated test of some condition to determine if it is
true. If no useful work is accomplished in the interval between one
check and the next, the polling is called "busy waiting."

The reason that polling, particularly busy waiting, is generally
undesirable is that it uses processor resources for the checking of the
condition. There are also potential context switches to and from the
polling task. (We are addressing the situation in which there are
more tasks than processors.)

A task that is blocked waiting for a rendezvous (rather than polling) uses little in the way of processor resources. In fact, it is generally true that waiting for some event to occur is more efficient than
continuous checking to see if the event has occured. It is also likely
to result in a simpler algorithm.

Gehani addresses the issue at length, referring to "the polling bias
in Ada" [GEH84, page 149]. He states that Ada has "... inadequa-
cies in its task interaction facilities; they encourage the design of
programs that poll." The features of Ada that allow polling are the
conditional entry call and the selective wait with the else part.

Of course polling is not *always* undesirable. It is certainly acceptable if each task has its own processor, it is useful where work must be done between tests of the condition, and it is vital in interacting with certain sorts of hardware (illustrated in Chapter 16, Case Study Four: Multiple Keyboard Handler). In fact, short duration polling may even be more efficient, in some circumstances, than a context switch from task to task.

The fact that Ada *allows* polling does not necessarily mean that it *encourages* it. However, it is an aspect of task interaction that must be kept in mind during the development of concurrent systems. Polling is frequently undesirable, and to be avoided unless one has a specific reason.

8.5 Characteristics

The variations of the buffer-transporter model of task interaction share three important general characteristics:

1. Either the producer and consumer, or both, are called tasks.
2. There is a buffering capability that allows the interacting tasks to operate asynchronously, i.e., to be only loosely coupled.
3. There is no polling.

The only drawback to this model of task interaction is that it introduces an extra task, since two tasks are necessary to accomplish buffering. (For the buffering transporter, three tasks are necessary.)

Let's review how we got to the point where we found it necessary to use multiple tasks to implement an intermediary.

The reason we introduced the incorrect approach for the consumer to interact with two buffers was to make it clear that the consumer *must be a called task*, rather than a caller. Therefore the intermediary must call the consumer—must be a relay. The reason we introduced the incorrect approach for the buffering relay was to make it clear that the effect we desire to achieve *cannot be done with a single task*. Therefore, we need two tasks to accomplish the desired interaction of a buffering relay (three tasks for the buffering transporter). The Chapter 5 explanation of caller/called issues and the asymmetry of the rendezvous established the foundation for this discussion.

The use of multiple tasks to implement communication functions will take longer than direct task interactions (since there are more rendezvous). Whether or not this gives rise to problems for system throughput and response time depends upon the performance characteristics and requirements of the specific system being built, and upon the quality of the Ada implementation. It is likely that some highly optimized compilers will reduce, or even eliminate, the time needed for a context switch for certain sorts of Ada tasks, particularly simple buffers and transporters.

Optimizations of this sort are discussed by Habermann [HAB80] and Hilfinger [HIL82]. For example, a task (such as a buffer) may not actually be implemented as a separate thread of control with its own context. Alternatively, the execution of the code of an accept statement may occur as a procedure call, rather than as a rendezvous needing a full context switch.

8.6   Summary of Buffer, Transporter, and Relay

This section summarizes a number of issues dealing with task interaction, based on the ideas of Chapters 5 through 8.

A situation in which one task passes information to another is called a producer-consumer relationship. The task that is the source of the information is called the producer and the task that is the recipient of the information is called the consumer. One or more rendezvous are used to pass the information from the producer to the consumer.

The rendezvous is a synchronous communication mechanism and therefore may limit the amount of asynchronous action taken by two tasks. (Nielsen [NIE86] discusses this at length in relating concepts of task coupling to the structured design concepts of module coupling.) It is often desirable to uncouple the task interactions to some extent in order to allow more independence and increase the amount of concurrency. Intermediary tasks are often used to accomplish the uncoupling.

Intermediary tasks are classified as buffer, transporter, or relay, depending upon the caller/called relationships between the tasks.

A buffer is a pure server task. It provides one entry for storing of items, and another for providing items.

A transporter is a pure caller. It obtains an item by calling a producer (or intermediary task), and "transports" that item by calling a consumer (or intermediary task).

A relay is a mixture of a caller and server. It provides one entry for providing items. It obtains an item by calling a producer (or intermediary task) and "relays" that item when it is called by a consumer (or intermediary task).

Alternatively, a relay may provide one entry for storing items. It then obtains an item by being called by a producer and relays the item by calling a consumer.

In addition to providing more independence between tasks, intermediary tasks can also be used to alter caller/called relationships. Sometimes it is more advantageous to be a calling task and other times it is more advantangeous to be called task. A buffer allows two *calling* tasks to communicate, while a transporter allows two *called* tasks to communicate. A relay preserves the caller/called relationships while providing a degree of uncoupling.

A buffer is properly implemented as a single task. Implementing a single-task transporter or relay that stores more than one item leads to polling. They can be effectively implemented with extra tasks.

A producer may want to communicate with a consumer via a buffer, but the consumer may want to be a called task in order to allow it to accept a variety of different requests. This can be accomplished by having a transporter task take information from the buffer and pass it onto the consumer, i.e., there is a chain of tasks: producer-buffer-transporter-consumer. This is called a buffering relay. There are two intermediary tasks used between the producer and consumer. Each time an item is passed from the producer to the consumer, three rendezvous occur—the producer with the buffer, the transporter with the buffer, and the transporter with the consumer. The situation is similar, but reversed, if the producer is to be a called task while the consumer is a caller.

If the producer and consumer both wish to be called tasks, it is necessary to use a transporter on each side of the buffer. This results in a chain of tasks: producer-transporter-buffer-transporter-consumer. This use of three intermediaries is called a buffering transporter. Each time an item is passed from the producer to the consumer, four rendezvous must take place.

The buffering relay and buffering transporter effectively avoid polling but introduce extra tasks. This may be important for certain applications (depending on how compute-bound the selected processor is). Advanced compiler optimization methods may eliminate some potential performance problems.

Exercises

Work the exercises Cobbler_1 through Cobbler_4. The Cobbler exercises are presented in Appendix A and solved in Appendix B. Remember that the exercises are an integral part of the text of the book. They are placed in an appendix not to place them out of the mainstream of the book, but in order to group them together to be also read one after the other.

Keys to Understanding

- Simple intermediaries, implemented as single tasks, may not do a complete job of uncoupling task interaction. Further, the intermediary may have to poll.

- A combination of a buffer and a transporter allows the producer and the consumer to be called tasks rather than calling tasks. We call this the buffer-transporter model of task interaction.

- The buffer-transporter model allows effective, loosely coupled task interaction without polling.

- If one or the other (of the producer and consumer) is to be called, the approriate intermediary is the buffering relay.

- If both the producer and consumer are to be called, the appropriate intermediary is the buffering transporter.

- The buffering relay and buffering transporter introduce extra tasks as intermediaries. This may or may not be important, depending on the application and the environment.

Case Two: Air Track Display System (ATDS)

> Objective: To provide a model of a large real-time system that illustrates caller/called decisions, use of intermediaries, and the overall architecture of a large system

This case study introduces additional new material, including issues related to the design of larger systems. It is a very long case study, the longest in the book. It is important to introduce, at at an early stage, the sort of complexity for which we need the tools provided by Ada.

The following sections present a software requirements specification, the environment for the ATDS software development, a top-level and detailed design, code, discussion, and additional exercises.

9.1   Software Requirements Specification

The Air Track Display System (ATDS) displays aircraft tracks obtained from radar sites. It accepts radar data inputs about track location, and operator inputs to establish tracks or change the location of a specified track. It outputs aircraft location to a display. Figure 9-1 illustrates the situation, showing the ATDS interaction with the radar, operator, and display.

It periodically extrapolates all aircraft locations and (independently) also periodically updates the display. The ATDS level of resolution is the meter, and the system provides for tracking on a two-dimensional grid of 100,000 meters in each direction.

There are three methods of updating an aircraft location in ATDS:

- Operator initiation or change of a track
- Radar inputs that correlate with an established track
- ATDS extrapolation at periodic intervals

The remainder of the specification uses Ada-style names for certain system parameters, such as the frequency of periodic update or number of aircraft tracks. Such parameters are called *adaptation data*. They are to be prominantly located and easy to find in the coded solution, and changes to such parameters are to require nothing more than a single change to a literal value and a recompilation. We saw use of such parameters in the HLCS case study, for example, Message_Length.

The literal values for the adaptation data will be given at the end of the software requirements.

The operator initiates tracks by providing a location as a set of (X, Y) coordinates and a track number of zero. The ATDS assigns track numbers. It may have as many as Maximum_Number_Of_Tracks tracks. After assignment of a track number, the track is recorded in the track file and is said to be established. For simplicity in this case study the ATDS does not immediately inform the operator of the track number. The number is displayed when the ATDS periodically displays the aircraft locations. The operator may change the location of an aircraft by providing the track number (other than zero) and a new set of coordinates. For simplicity in this example, tracks are never dropped.

The radar provides input as a set of coordinates. The data are provided from a number of different radars with varying acquisition rates; hence, the data are presented to ATDS asynchronously.

The ATDS is concerned only with the tracks that have been initiated (i.e., established) by the operator. It attempts to correlate each

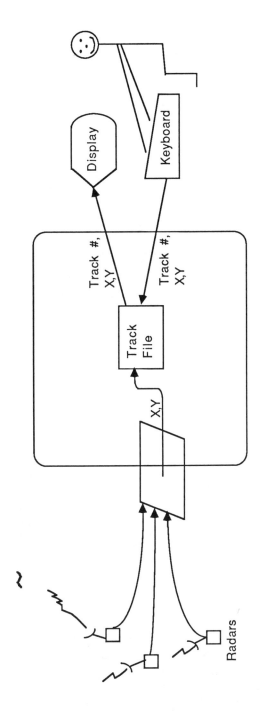

Figure 9-1. ATDS overview

radar input (X, Y) with an established track. If the input coordinates are within Proximity meters of an established track, the input is then said to be successfully correlated with the track. This new input is considered to be the new valid location of the established track and the track file is updated with the new location. If the radar input does not successfully correlate with any of the established tracks, it is ignored. For simplicity, do not be concerned with "best" correlation. Assume that the first correlation found is correct.

The (X, Y) pair and the time of last update are kept in the track file. The (X, Y) are updated (extrapolated) by the system on a periodic basis, i.e., at Update_Periodic intervals. For simplicity, assume all aircraft are moving at the same Velocity_Of_Aircraft [i.e., at the same speed and in the same direction (northeast)].

All tracks in the track file are displayed at Display_Periodic intervals. The display consists of the track number and some symbol (the ATDS is not concerned with the details of the display) placed at the coordinates provided by ATDS.

Adaptation Data:

1. Update_Periodic—1 second

2. Display_Periodic—5 seconds

3. Maximum_Number_Of_Tracks—200

4. Proximity—1000 meters

5. Velocity_Of_Aircraft—1000 kilometers per hour to the northeast
    Simplification of Aircraft Extrapolation. A velocity of 1000 kilometers per hour to the northeast is about 280 meters per second to the northeast, or 200 meters per second in each of the X and Y directions. Therefore the extrapolation consists of adding 200 to each of the X and Y coordinates for each second (or fraction of a second) since the last update. The resulting adaptation data is the Speed in the X and Y directions.

6. Speed—200 meters per second in each of X and Y directions

9.2 ATDS Environment

Figure 9-2a is a context diagram for the ATDS. Since it interfaces with three external devices, there should be a task in the ATDS for each of the devices. However, part of the ATDS software has already been designed by the company that is building the hardware interfaces to the external devices. This software is the ATDS Executive services, and hides the details of the hardware interaction from the ATDS application software that we are going to design as part of this case study.

Figure 9-2b shows the context for the ATDS application software; the display and console handlers, and the radar handler/raw data buffer combination, pass the data back and forth from the application software and the external devices.

These executive services are provided in the form of packages. The external devices package provides the interfaces to the operator and display as shown below. The radar handler is also in that package, but we don't see it since the radar handler is a calling task—it puts the X, Y coordinates from the radars into the raw data buffer. The executive services include the raw data buffer, as shown below, which the application software will call in order to receive a set of coordinates.

The executive services packages are dependent upon an application-defined package called "Definitions", which must contain the type definitions for "Coordinates" and "Track_ID" as integer subtypes.

Executive Services Packages

```
with Definitions; use Definitions;
package External_Devices is
   procedure Get_Data_From_Operator (X, Y : out Coordinates;
                                     Track_ID : out Track_Number);
   -- Holds caller in rendezvous until operator inputs data.

   procedure Display_A_Track (X, Y : in Coordinates;
                              Track_ID : in Track_Number);
   -- Holds caller in rendezvous until track is displayed.

   -- Calls
     -- Raw_Data_Buffer.Enqueue
end External_Devices;
```

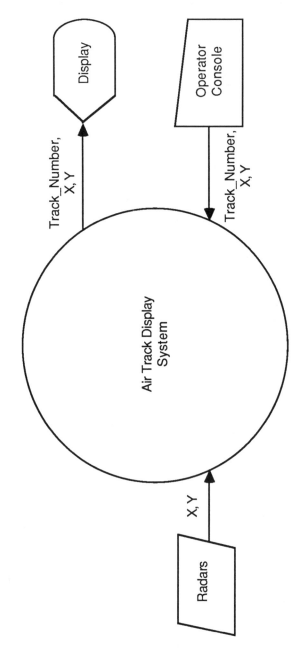

Figure 9-2a. ATDS context diagram

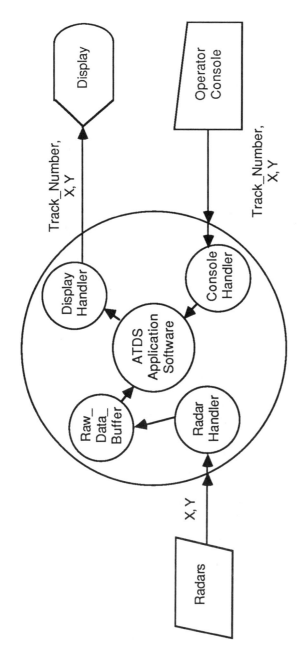

Figure 9-2b. ATDS context diagram + executive services

```
with Definitions; use Definitions;
package Raw_Data_Buffer is
   procedure Enqueue (X, Y :  in Coordinates);
   -- Enqueue overwrites old information when the buffer is full

   procedure Dequeue (X, Y : out Coordinates);
   -- Dequeue causes the calling task to block when the buffer is empty
end Raw_Data_Buffer;
```

The ATDS application program takes data from the buffer and uses the procedures in the External_Devices package to display data and communicate with the operator.

9.3   Top-Level Design

This section presents the graphical design and the Ada package specifications.

9.3.1   Graphical Design

The first step we will take to develop a solution to the problem stated by the ATDS requirement is to identify the major elements of concurrency. Figure 9-3a is a process graph establishing a process for each external interface and one process for Track_FIle_Monitor. Even though the ATDS Executive is providing handlers for the hardware, we will establish a separate process for each of the the display and operator interactions. This is important since the operator and display interfaces provided by the ATDS Executive cause the calling process to block if no interaction is immediately available. If we did not have a separate thread of control for the operator interaction, for example, the entire ATDS application program could be suspended waiting for an operator action. (If we were writing the hardware handlers, we might choose to perform these ATDS functions in the same tasks as the hardware handlers.)

In order to document the processing to be accomplished in Figure 9-3a, we now write, as we did in case study number one, "minimal" specifications ("minispecs") for each of the processes. The minispecs assume that the reader understands the software requirements. The minispecs allocate the requirements to distinct processes. We show the External_Devices package, and the Radar_Handler, as "clouds" to illustrate that we do not need to understand their internal details. (We will show the Raw_Data_Buffer as a process since we know more about its likely implementation.) However, we will still write   brief   minispecs   for   External_Devices,   as   well   as   the

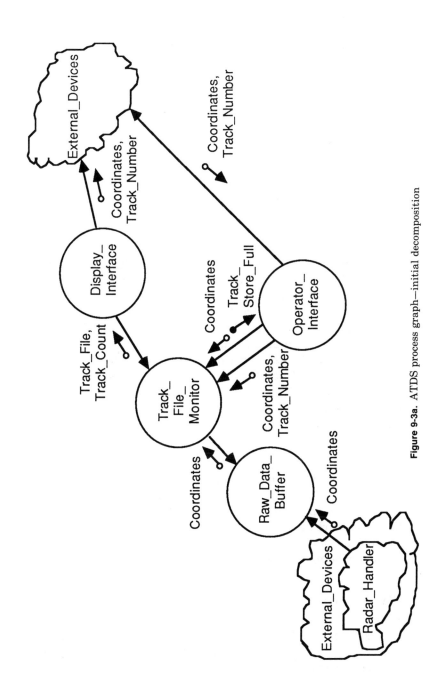

Figure 9-3a. ATDS process graph—initial decomposition

Raw_Data_Buffer, in order to describe their interaction with the Track_File_Monitor.

This section presents minispecifications for:

- Operator_Interface
- Display_Interface
- Track_File_Monitor
- Raw_Data_Buffer
- External_Devices

Minispecifications for the ATDS

Operator_Interface

The Operator_Interface uses the capability of External_Devices to obtain a track number and set of coordinates from the operator. If the track number is zero, the coordinates are sent to Track_File_Monitor to initiate a track. Otherwise, the track number and coordinates are sent to Track_File_Monitor to change the location of an aircraft established as an existing track. If the track file is full, Track_File_Monitor raises an exception in response to the attempt to initiate a track. Operator_Interface handles the exception. (For simplicity in this problem, the only response to the exception is the output of a message.) If the operator has not input any information, this process is blocked.

NOTE

The exception is shown on the process graph as an arrow with a solid base. This notation (the solid or filled in base) is used to show control information, in a manner similar to the usual structure chart notation of structured design [YOU79]. The control information is usually an exception, but could also be a parameter being used as control information.

Display_Interface

The Display_Interface periodically obtains the complete set of tracks (the track file) from Track_File_Monitor and displays the track number and coordinates of each track. Track_Count is the number of established tracks.

Track_File_Monitor

The Track_File_Monitor takes sets of coordinates from the buffer and attempts to correlate them with established tracks. If the coordinates successfully correlate, they are used as the new location of the track. New tracks are established and track coordinates are changed, based on input from Operator_Interface. If the track file is full, an exception is raised on the attempt to establish a track. Periodically, track coordinates are extrapolated. When requested, the track file is provided to Display_Interface.

Raw_Data_Buffer

The Raw_Data_Buffer enqueues sets of coordinates from the radar and stores them. When the buffer is full, old information is overwritten. Dequeues a set of coordinates upon request.

External_Devices

External_Devices interacts with the operator and the display. Holds the calling task in a rendezvous until the interaction is complete.

The process graph of Figure 9-3a essentially has a process for each external device and one process for "everything else." It is often the situation that the process for everything else, in this case the Track_File_Monitor, is a concurrent program. Buhr [BUH84] and Nielsen [NIE88] formalize this approach, always assigning "edge" processes and then decomposing what they call the "middle part." They call this an "edges-in" design strategy. (We will see an alternate strategy in Chapter 18, Remote Temperature Sensor.) This is an application of process abstraction. The next step in the design is to determine the concurrent portions of Track_File_Monitor.

Additional Minispecifications for Decompostion of Track_File_Monitor

The Track_File_Monitor is quite complicated. In fact, it contains more than a single concurrent function; it must simultaneously do three things: (1) Be prepared to take a track from the Raw_Data_Buffer. This involves a call to the Dequeue entry and a possible wait for data. (2) Be prepared to accept a call, asynchronously, from either the operator or display interfaces. (3) Keep track of time until the next extrapolation of tracks.

The second function involves interation with two tasks, and is actually three subfunctions (since the operator interface may nondeterministically call either of two entries). However, since the operator and display interfaces are callers, with Track_File_Monitor being called, the three subfunctions can be accommodated with one thread of control, a single task.

The other functions, however, must involve separate tasks. We therefore decompose the Track_File_Monitor process into three separate tasks as shown in Figure 9-3b. We will now write the mini-specs for the three separate components of the Track_File_Monitor:

- Monitor
- Extrapolation_Timer
- Transport_Coordinates

Monitor

The Monitor accomplishes all functions of the Track_File_Monitor, with the assistance of the following two tasks. It uses the capability of a *helper* package, Track_Services, that provides a set of subprograms to help the Monitor task perform its job. The helper package will be shown and discussed in the next part of the top-level design.

Extrapolation_Timer

The Extrapolation_Timer tells the Monitor when it is time to extrapolate all tracks.

Transport_Coordinates

Transport_Coordinates transports coordinates from the Raw_Data_Buffer to the Monitor. Note that this allows the Monitor to be strictly a called task; the transporter waits in place of the Monitor.

NOTE

The notation shown for the Extrapolation_Timer process indicates a process that has a periodic aspect; the period is indicated within the loop, as in the example, Update_Periodic.

9.3.2 Package Specifications

With the understanding described above of what the processes must accomplish, we are ready to design the interfaces between major components. At this point we also make some packaging decisions—literally the establishment of Ada packages.

Although we formally postpone the discussion of the internals of the task bodies until the detailed design phase, we now must have some understanding of how the tasks will interact.

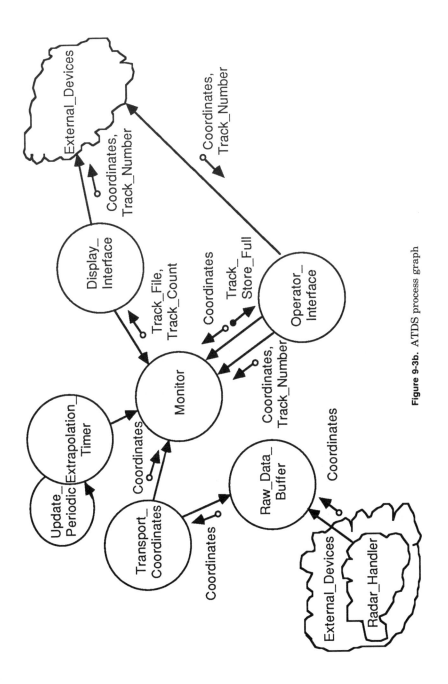

Figure 9-3b. ATDS process graph

259

We will express our abstract high-level understanding of the internal functioning of the processes through the use of "abstract algorithms." We will postpone as many decisions as possible, focusing primarily on the aspects of the algorithms that have to do with task interactions. However, these abstract algorithms will be written using Ada constructs, taking advantage of the Ada control structures when appropriate. We will present the abstract algorithms along with the package specifications developed for the top-level design.

This section presents the specifications for:

- Definitions
- ATDS Executive (Raw_Data_Buffer and External_Devices)
- Track_File_Monitor
- Track_Services
- Operator_Interface
- Display_Interface

Their relationship is shown in Figure 9-4.

9.3.2.1 Definitions. We first establish the basic set of definitions to be used throughout the ATDS. This includes the major type definitions as well as constants representing adaptation data. The package is:

```
with Calendar; use Calendar;
package Definitions is

   type Coordinates  is range -100_000 .. 100_000; -- Needed for Proximit

-- Adaptation data

   Update_Periodic           : constant Duration := 1.0;
   Display_Periodic          : constant Duration := 5.0;
   Maximum_Number_Of_Tracks  : constant := 200;
   Proximity                 : constant Coordinates := 1000;
   Speed                     : constant := 200;

-- Type definitions

   type Track_Count    is              range 0 .. Maximum_Number_Of_Track
   subtype Track_Number is Track_Count range 1 .. Track_Count'Last;
```

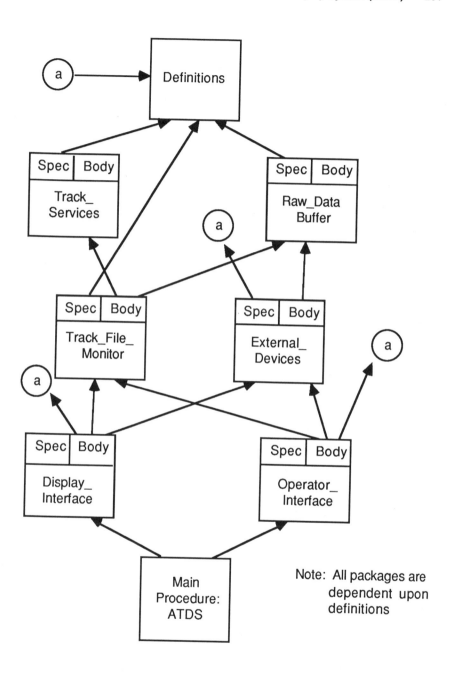

Figure 9-4. ATDS dependency graph

```
type Track_Record is
  record
    X, Y   : Coordinates;
    Update : Time;
  end record;


type Track_File is array (Track_Number range <>) of Track_Record;
end Definitions;
```

The definitions are fairly straightforward. We have constants established for each of the adaptation parameters. The maximum number of tracks in the system is also embedded in the definition of the type "Track_Count". If we wish to refer to the number later, it is always available as the attribute Track_Count'Last.

We defined new types for Coordinates and Track_Count in order to take advantage of Ada's strong type checking. Track_Number is a subtype of Track_Count since objects of the two types must be compatible—they both refer to the tracks in the system.

Next we specify the Raw_Data_Buffer and the package External_Devices, as part of the ATDS Executive.

9.3.2.2 ATDS Executive.

```
----- Raw_Data_Buffer package -----

with Definitions; use Definitions;
package Raw_Data_Buffer is
  procedure Enqueue (X, Y :  in Coordinates);
  procedure Dequeue (X, Y : out Coordinates);
end Raw_Data_Buffer;
```

```
----- External_Devices package -----

with Definitions; use Definitions;
with Raw_Data_Buffer;
package External_Devices is
  procedure Get_Data_From_Operator (X, Y : out Coordinates;
                                    Track_ID : out Track_Number);
  procedure Display_A_Track (X, Y : in Coordinates;
                             Track_ID : in Track_Number);

  -- Calls
    -- Raw_Data_Buffer.Enqueue
end External_Devices;
```

We will not consider the External_Devices or Raw_Data_Buffer packages any further. The general topic of buffering to provide for mutual exclusion and asynchronous behaviour was addressed in detail in Chapters 5 through 8.

9.3.2.3 Track_File_Monitor.

Abstract Algorithm:

The Track File Monitor consists of three tasks: Monitor, Extrapolation_Timer, and Transport_Coordinates. We will present brief algorithms for each task.

```
----- Monitor -----

loop
  select
    provide the latest track file to the caller;
  or
    add a track to a non-full track file, or return
    indication of full track file;
    update coordinates and time of an existing track;
  or
    take a track for correlation;
    if the track successfully correlates then
      update the coordinates and time for the track;
    end if;
```

```
or
   extrapolate all tracks;
 end select;
end loop;


----- Extrapolation_Timer -----

loop
  delay appropriate time interval;
  alert monitor that it is time to extrapolate;
end loop;


----- Transport_Coordinates -----

loop
  get a track from the Raw_Data_Buffer;
  deliver the track to Monitor;
end loop;
```

Specification:

```
with Definitions; use Definitions;
package Track_File_Monitor is

    procedure Latest_Track_File (Tracks : out Track_File;
                                 Number_Of_Tracks : out Track_Count);
    procedure Add_Track    (X, Y : in Coordinates);
    procedure Update_Track (X, Y : in Coordinates;
                            Track_ID : in Track_Number);

    Track_Store_Full : exception; -- raised by Add_Track

    -- Calls
      -- Raw_Data_Buffer.Dequeue
      -- Track_Services.Update
      -- Track_Services.Correlate
      -- Track_Services.Extrapolate
end Track_File_Monitor;
```

At this point it is useful to compare the package specifications to the process graphs of Figures 9-3a and 9-3b. We see that we have implemented the Track_FIle_Monitor process as a package, with nested tasks being those shown in Figure 9-3b. This need not have been the case; we could have packaged in an altogether different manner. For example, if we were responsible for the implementation of the Raw_Data_Buffer, we might well have packaged the transporter (Transport_Coordinates) with the buffer in order to provide a relay as discussed in Chapter 8. However, it will frequently be the case that the decomposition of the process graphs will also give us guidance for creation of packages. The PAMELA [CHE86] design method uses this packaging method as its primary structuring mechanism.

The process Track_File_Monitor is implemented as a package, with each of its entries represented by a procedure. (We will call these "entrance procedures" to distinguish them from entries to tasks.) Each interface shown in the process graph of Figure 9-3a is represented in the package specification.

The specification of entrance procedures to hide the task entry is a useful mechanism. It is an aspect of information hiding in that the calling processes do not really have to know (and are better off not knowing) the implementation details of the functionality represented by the procedure call. It also prevents any external process from aborting the tasks internal to a package, and prevents them from making condtional or timed entry calls. Alternatively, an entrance procedure could be used to force a conditional or timed entry call.

The data flows shown on the diagram are the parameters to the entrance procedures. It is important that the names of the data flows be meaningful. They are usually the names of the types of the parameters of the entries or entrance procedures, but may alternatively be the names of the formal or actual parameters (if those names provide more information to the reviewer). In this way, we can easily relate the process graph (later the structure graph) to the detailed design and code.

The control item is represented by an exception. The comment on the exception declaration in the package specification is not strictly necessary, since Figure 9-3b shows in which process (but not in which procedure) the exception is raised, but it does no harm and helps communicate and relate the Ada design to the graphical design.

9.3.2.4 Track_Services. The package Track_Services was not identified as a result of the decomposition into concurrent processes. Rather, it resulted from a realization that a number of functions that were required by the Monitor task could be appropriately grouped together as a package of services. This is an important point; it illustrates that not all top-level design components are identifiable as a result of the analysis of concurrency and the mapping of concurrency from the problem space into the solution space. This sort of package is likely to be even more important in very large systems.

An acceptable alternative to grouping the procedures together in a services package would be to nest them in the body of task Monitor. They would be established as stubs during the refinement of the task body, and would then have their algorithms expanded later, as the final step of the detailed design.

The advantage of the approach we have chosen is that the package is potentially reusable by other programs and projects. It is also visible at the top-level design stage, which may help the reader/reviewer better understand the ATDS functioning.

Track_Services does not have any embedded tasks. It is called only by the Monitor task in Track_File_Monitor. The algorithms presented are those of the three procedures.

Abstract Algorithm:

```
----- Update -----

update the track file (for the given track number), with the
given coordinates and the current time;

----- Correlate -----

for each track in the track file, loop
   determine distance from track in the file to
   the track being correlated;

   if the distance is less than or equal to Proximity,
   update the track and exit the loop;
end loop;

----- Extrapolate -----

for each track in the track file, loop
   determine the distance the track has
   moved since last update;

   update the track location and update time;
end loop;
```

Specification:

```
with Definitions; use Definitions;
package Track_Services is
   procedure Update (Tracks       : in out Track_File;
                     X, Y         : in Coordinates;
                     Track_Number : in Track_Count);
   procedure Correlate  (Tracks : in out Track_File;
                         X, Y   : in Coordinates);
   procedure Extrapolate (Tracks : in out Track_File);
end Track_Services;
```

9.3.2.5 Operator__Interface.

Abstract Algorithm:

```
loop
   get data from operator; -- wait as long as necessary

   if this is a new track then
     add track to track file,
       using Track_File_Monitor; -- may raise exception ***
   else
     update track file, using Track_File_Monitor;
   end if;

   *** handle the exception here, by printing message for operator;
end loop;
```

Specification:

```
package Operator_Interface is
   -- Calls
     -- External_Devices.Get_Data_From_Operator
     -- Track_File_Monitor.Add_Track
     -- Track_File_Monitor.Update_Track
end Operator_Interface;
```

Our package specification has no entrance procedures since this package contains only calling tasks. We now have a "Calls" section of the specification to define, as comments, the active or calling interfaces of this package. These comments are not strictly necessary since some of the relationships with other processes are shown in the process graph, and will also be provided in the context clause preceeding the package body—which we will see later. However, the "Calls" comments help in communicating the design and relating the specification to the graphical design. When meaningful names are chosen for packages and entrance procedures, the comments give a reviewer additional insight into how the design will work.

9.3.2.6 Display__Interface.

Abstract Algorithm:

```
loop
   calculate delay until next periodic display;
   delay appropriate time;
   get all established tracks from Track_File_Monitor;

   loop for all established tracks
     display a track, using External_Devices;
   end loop;
end loop;
```

Specification:

```
package Display_Interface is
   -- Calls
     -- Track_File_Monitor.Latest_Track_File
     -- External_Devices.Display_A_Track
end Display_Interface;
```

The operator and display interfaces could have just as well been in a single package, but separating them (particularly with the use of the "Calls" comments) makes the Ada design follow more closely the graphical representation, and helps reviewers more quickly and accurately understand the design.

9.3.2.7 Summary of Top-Level Design. At this point, we have completed a significant amount of the design of the ATDS. Figure 9-4 summarizes the relationship of the packages in terms of relative dependency based on the "withing" (the context clauses) of each package. Figure 9-4 also defines a partial order of compilation and, during execution, of elaboration. The addition of a main procedure (in this case with no declarative part and a null body) that "withs" the two interface packages completes the design and will provide a starting point for the eventual execution of the ATDS.

We consider the top-level design to be complete at this point, being represented by the graphical design (both the process graphs and the minispecs) and the Ada package specifications, including the abstract algorithms.

We continue to the detailed design phase by first defining the package bodies, and then by refining the task and procedure bodies to describe the algorithmic functioning of the processes.

9.4 Detailed Design

The detailed design consists of the development of the package bodies to the point where the internal tasks are well defined, i.e., their specifications are established and a detailed algorithm of the task body is described. The difference between the abstract algorithms in the top-level design and the algorithms of the task bodies is in level of detail. The pseudocode defining the task bodies is a complete definition of the processing of the task; the only factor omitted is coding details such as definition of loop variables, some data items, and precise expression of mathematical formulas.

The task specifications are provided immediately in the package bodies, while the task bodies are typically indicated as stubs (i.e., separate). The task bodies are then completely provided (as separate compilation units) in terms of interfaces, with algorithms presented by pseudocode as discussed above. The entrance procedures and their interaction with the corresponding task entries are completely defined.

The top-level design was heavily dependent upon a graphical representation of concurrency. The detailed design is primarily dependent upon the use of pseudocode to express the process interfaces and algorithms. In order to communicate the design to another reader/reviewer, it is useful (indeed, virtually necessary for nontrivial designs) to provide a picture as a *road map* to the complete detailed design. An effective method for providing a graphic illustration of a detailed design is the structure graph discussed in Chapter 1 and illustrated in Chapter 3.

It is important to introduce the structure graph early, in order to provide a road map to the pseudocode to follow. A structure graph of the ATDS is provided as Figure 9-5.

As you read the detailed design below, and as you read the code in the next section, compare the Ada-defined interfaces to the graphic picture. You will see how close the correspondence is, and how very much information is clearly summarized in the structure graph.

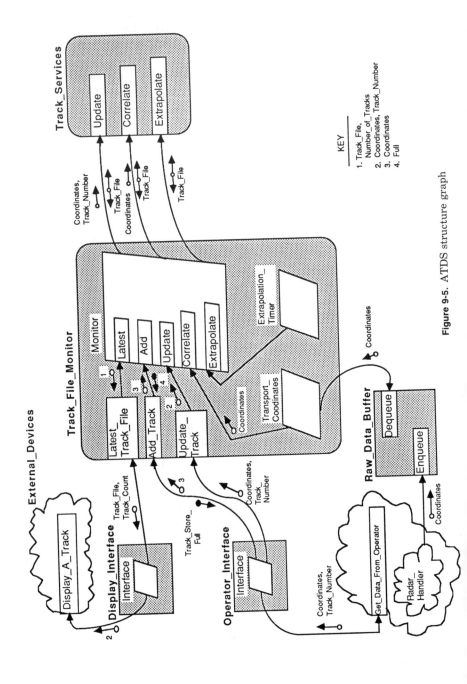

Figure 9-5. ATDS structure graph

270

We will discuss the detailed design of the ATDS in the same order as the presentation of the package specifications, beginning with the package body for the Track_File_Monitor.

This section presents the detailed design for:

- Track_File_Monitor (tasks Monitor, Extrapolation_Timer, and Transport_Coordinates)
- Track_Services (procedures Update, Correlate, and Extrapolate)
- Operator_Interface (task Interface)
- Display_Interface (task Interface)

9.4.1 Track__File__Monitor

package body Track_File_Monitor is

```
----- Monitor  -----

  task Monitor is
    entry Latest (Tracks            : out Track_File;
                  Number_Of_Tracks : out Track_Count);

    entry Add    (X, Y : in Coordinates;
                  Full : out Boolean);

    entry Update (X, Y     : in Coordinates;
                  Track_ID : in Track_Number);

    entry Correlate (X, Y : in Coordinates);

    entry Extrapolate;

    -- Calls
      -- Track_Services.Update
      -- Track_Services.Correlate
      -- Track_Services.Extrapolate
  end Monitor;
```

Here we see the specification of the five functions performed by the Monitor. The direction of data flow is apparent from the mode of the parameters and is consistent with the abstract algorithm.

```
----- Extrapolation_Timer  -----
task Extrapolation_Timer is
  -- Calls
    -- Monitor.Extrapolate

  -- Delays for appropriate extrapolation interval and tells
  -- Monitor that it is time to extrapolate
end Extrapolation_Timer;
```

This is the task that performs the function of keeping track of time until extrapolation is required.

```
----- Transport_Coordinates  -----

  task Transport_Coordinates is
    -- Calls
      -- Raw_Data_Buffer.Dequeue
      -- Monitor.Correlate

    -- Transports a set of coordinates from the
    -- buffer to the track file Monitor
  end Transport_Coordinates;
```

Transport_Coordinates does the waiting for new tracks from the buffer.

```
  task body Monitor              is separate;
  task body Extrapolation_Timer  is separate;
  task body Transport_Coordinates is separate;
```

```
----- Entrance Procedures -----
```

The use of entrance procedures hides the interaction with the actual Monitor task.

```
  procedure Latest_Track_File (Tracks           : out Track_File;
                               Number_Of_Tracks : out Track_Count) is
  begin
    Monitor.Latest (Tracks, Number_Of_Tracks);
  end Latest_Track_File;
```

```
procedure Add_Track (X, Y : in Coordinates) is
  Full : Boolean;
begin
  Monitor.Add (X, Y, Full);
  if Full then
    raise Track_Store_Full;
  end if;
end Add_Track;
```

In Add_Track, the exception is conveniently raised in the entrance procedure, hiding the implementation (using the Boolean parameter) from the calling task The exception is shown on the structure graph in the same manner as we showed it on the process graph—an arrow with a filled in base.

NOTE

Buhr describes and uses a special notation for exceptions that graphically illustrates that an exception causes a return to a different location than a normal return Although it is important to remember that this is so, we will use the simpler notation shown in Figure 9-5.

```
procedure Update_Track (X, Y      : in Coordinates;
                        Track_ID : in Track_Number) is
begin
  Monitor.Update (X, Y, Track_ID);
end Update_Track;
end Track_File_Monitor;
```

You should compare the algorithms given below with the abstract algorithms given in the top-level design.

```
----- Monitor -----

with Track_Services; use Track_Services;
separate (Track_File_Monitor)
  task body Monitor is
```

```
begin
  loop
    select
      accept Latest (Tracks            : out Track_File;
                     Number_Of_Tracks : out Track_Count) do
        provide the part of the track file corresponding
        to existing tracks;

        indicate the number of tracks being provided;
      end Latest;
    or
      accept Add (X, Y : in Coordinates;
                  Full : out Boolean) do
        if the track store is full then
          set Full to True;
        else
          set Full to False;
          increment number of tracks in the track store;
          use Track_Services.Update to add the track to the track st
        end if;
      end Add;
    or
      accept Update (X, Y     : in Coordinates;
                     Track_ID : in Track_Number) do
        use Track_Services.Update to update the track;
      end Update;
    or
      accept Correlate (X, Y : in Coordinates) do
        use Track_Services to correlate all tracks;
      end Correlate;
    or
      accept Extrapolate do
        use Track_Services to extrapolate all tracks;
      end Extrapolate;
    end select;
  end loop;
end Monitor;
```

The specification for the entry/accept called Add shows the use of
a Boolean parameter to pass information back to the entrance procedure (which uses the information to raise an exception). An alternate style is to raise the exception directly during the rendezvous.
However, we then must handle the exception at the end of the select
statement. The changes to Monitor are:

----- An Alternate Monitor -----

```
task body Monitor is
begin
  loop
    Handle_Track_Store_Full:
    begin
      select
        accept Latest ...
        end Latest;
      or
        accept Add (X, Y : in Coordinates) do
          if the track store is full then
            raise Track_Store_Full;
          end if;

          increment number of tracks in the track store;
          use Track_Services.Update to add the track to the track store;
        end Add;
      or
        accept Update ...
        end Update;
      or
        accept Correlate ...
        end Correlate;
      or
        accept Extrapolate ...
        end Extrapolate;
      end select;
    exception
      when Track_Store_Full =>
        null;
    end Handle_Track_Store_Full;
  end loop;
end Monitor;
```

The trade-off is between the advantage of not having the extra parameter, Full, but having to have a block to handle the exception. While we will consistently use exceptions to handle interpackage communication, we will often use parameter passing for intrapackage communication.

The style of pseudocode, while detailed, is quite abstract from coding issues. For example, in the first accept statement, we say "provide the number of tracks in the slice;". We might have chosen to define a variable, Track_Count, in the declarative part of the task body. Then we could have said, "Number_Of_Tracks := Track_Count;" as an alternative to the more abstract phrase. We would also replace "increment number of tracks in the track store;" (in the second accept statement) with "Track_Count := Track_Count + 1;". Some other changes would also occur naturally.

Another example of the abstract style of pseudocode is, in the third accept, "use Track_Services.Update to update the track;". If we had defined the necessary local data structure for the Track_Storage, we might have said "Track_Services.Update (Track_Storage, X, Y, Track_ID);"

The more detailed style (in the sense of coding detail) is illustrated later in the detailed design of the interface tasks. Either style can be used, depending upon level of knowledge at the detailed design phase, and upon individual or team programming style.

```
----- Extrapolation_Timer -----

with Calendar; use Calendar;
separate (Track_File_Monitor)
  task body Extrapolation_Timer is
  begin
    initialize the next scheduled extrapolation;

    Periodic_Loop:
    loop
      calculate the appropriate delay time until extrapolation as:
        (next scheduled extrapolation) - current time;

      delay the appropriate time;

      alert monitor that it is time to extrapolate;

      calculate the next scheduled extrapolation as:
        (previous extrapolation time) + Update_Periodic;
    end loop Periodic_Loop;
  end Extrapolation_Timer;
```

```
----- Transport_Coordinates -----

with Raw_Data_Buffer;
separate (Track_File_Monitor)
  task body Transport_Coordinates is
  begin
    loop
      get the coordinates from the Raw_Data_Buffer;
      send the coordinates to Monitor;
    end loop;
  end Transport_Coordinates;
```

We see that Track_File_Monitor is a "passive" process; it does not make any calls. This is consistent with the top-level design in which there were no comments in the specification to indicate calls. The main functioning is accomplished by the task Monitor, which is prepared to rendezvous with calls to its five primary functions. The actual calls are accomplished by the entrance procedures.

Before we proceed further, let's stop and look at the detailed design process as it is developing for this case study.

The design of the package bodies is the first step of the detailed design. It just provides the task specifications and interactions. It adds additional detail and specificity to the abstract algorithm provided in the top-level design. At this level of understanding, we are also relying on the minispecs (and the graphical illustrations) created as part of the top-level design. We will gain our detailed understanding of how the tasks are implemented (as opposed to what they are required to do) by looking at the detailed design of the task bodies—the next step of the detailed design.

There are two important observations to be made on the style of the detailed design.

The first is that we continue to rely on the fact that the reader or reviewer of the design understands the top-level design. (In the short run this reader is the co-worker, supervisor, and technical director of the programmer; in the long run it is the maintenance programmer who has only the code and the written documentation available to understand what is going on.) That is, the reader understands what this task is doing and is looking to the detailed design for an explanation of how it is to be accomplished.

The second is that we rely upon the reader having a detailed understanding of the programming language Ada. We assume that the reader (ultimately the maintenance programmer) can follow the logic of the design based on an understanding of the semantics of the Ada constructs. For example, the logic of the monitor largely

depends upon the fact that the selective wait allows the task to wait
upon any one of a number of calls.

9.4.2 Track__Services

```
package body Track_Services is
    procedure Update      (Tracks         : in out Track_File;
                           X, Y           : in Coordinates;
                           Track_Number : in Track_Count) is separate;

    procedure Correlate   (Tracks : in out Track_File;
                           X, Y   : in Coordinates)        is separate;

    procedure Extrapolate (Tracks : in out Track_File)     is separate;
end Track_Services;
```

```
----- Update -----
```

```
with Calendar; use Calendar;
separate (Track_Services)
    procedure Update (Tracks : in out Track_File; X, Y : in Coordinates;
                      Track_Number : in Track_Count) is
    begin
      update the indicated track, based on Track_Number, with the
      input X, Y, and the current time;
    end Update;
```

```
----- Correlate -----
```

```
with Coordinates_Math;
use  Coordinates_Math; -- contains Coordinates_Square_Root
separate (Track_Services)
    procedure Correlate   (Tracks : in out Track_File;
                           X, Y   : in Coordinates) is

      -- Attempts to correlate the input X,Y with a track in the track t
      -- If the coordinates correlate, they are used to update the locat
      -- of the track The time of Last update is set to current time.

      Distance : Coordinates;
```

```
begin
  -- correlate with current tracks (simple, not best, algorithm)
  Correlation_Loop:
  for Track_Index in Tracks'Range loop
    calculate the Distance from the track to the input X and Y;

    if Distance <= Proximity then
      update the track with the input X, Y, and the current time;
      exit Correlation_Loop;
    end if;
  end loop Correlation_Loop;
end Correlate;
```

----- Extrapolate -----

```
with Calendar; use Calendar;
separate (Track_Services)
  procedure Extrapolate (Tracks : in out Track_File) is

    -- Extrapolates all tracks to current Time.
    -- All aircraft travel the same speed
    -- and in northeast direction.

    Time_Of_This_Update : Time := Clock;
    Delta_Time       : Duration;
    Delta_Distance : Coordinates;

  begin
    -- update all tracks
    for Track_Index in Tracks'Range loop
      calculate time since last update;
      calculate distance traveled in time since last update;
      add the distance to each of the X and Y coordinates for the track;
      update the time that the track was last updated;
    end loop;
  end Extrapolate;
```

9.4.3 Operator__Interface

```
package body Operator_Interface is
   task Interface is
     -- Calls
       -- External_Devices.Get_Data_From_Operator
       -- Track_File_Monitor.Add_Track
       -- Track_File_Monitor.Update_Track
   end Interface;

   task body Interface is separate;
end Operator_Interface;


with Track_File_Monitor;
with External_Devices;
with Definitions; use Definitions;
separate (Operator_Interface)
   task body Interface is
     X, Y : Coordinates;
     Track_ID : Track_Number;
     Add_Track_Indicator : constant Track_Count := 0;
   begin
     Interface_With_Operator:
     loop
       Handle_Track_Store_Full:
       begin
         External_Devices.Get_Data_From_Operator (X, Y, Track_ID);

         if Track_ID = Add_Track_Indicator then
           call Track_File_Monitor.Add_Track to initiate a track;

           Track_File_Monitor.Add_Track may raise Track_Store_Full
           exception, transferring control to the exception handler;
         else
           call Track_File_Monitor.Update_Track to update
           an established track;
         end if;
```

```
    exception
      when Track_File_Monitor.Track_Store_Full =>
        provide a message to the operator
      end Handle_Track_Store_Full;
    end loop Interface_With_Operator;
  end Interface;
```

In this design we have an example of a rather complete refinement; the internal data structures are well defined and the call to
get the data from the operator is a completely specified entry call.
The degree of refinement also holds for the algorithm. For example,
we use the phrase "if Track_ID = Add_Track_Indicator then ..."
rather than the more abstract "if the track is a new track then ...".
Either style is appropriate.

9.4.4 Display_Interface

```
package body Display_Interface is
  task Interface is
    -- Calls
      -- Track_File_Monitor.Latest_Track_File
      -- External_Devices.Display_A_Track
  end Interface;

  task body Interface is separate;
end Display_Interface;

with Track_File_Monitor;
with External_Devices;
with Calendar; use Calendar;
with Definitions; use Definitions;
separate (Display_Interface)
  task body Interface is
    Tracks : Track_File (Track_Number);
    Number_Of_Tracks : Track_Count;
    Next_Time : Time;

  begin
--    Note: The calculation of the delay must provide for an average
--          delay of Display_Periodic. It must account for the variable
--          time taken to execute other processes in order to not allow
--          the periodic interval to drift away from its specified value.
```

```
   initialize Next_Time as current time plus Display_Periodic;

Periodic_Display:
loop
  delay an interval until time for next display (Next_Time - Clock)

  call Track_File_Monitor.Latest_Track_File to obtain
  all established tracks;

  for all established tracks, loop
    call External_Devices.Display_A_Track, providing the X and Y
    coordinates and the track number;
  end loop;

  calculate the time for next display by
  adding Display_Periodic to Next_Time;
  end loop Periodic_Display;
end Interface;
```

In this example we see an illustration of the use of the names of the internal data items to further amplify the algorithm, e.g., the specification of the delay interval as "(Next_Time - Clock);".

9.4.5 Summary of Detailed Design

We have now reached a point in the design where both the interfaces and the internal logic of the processes is well defined. All that remains is the filling in of final data structure and completion of coding detail to inplement the algorithms defined in pseudocode.

The next incremental step is to change any abstract procedure calls to actual procedure calls and to complete the details of the algorithms in the procedures and task bodies.

9.5 Code

Since the code is a continuing refinement of the detailed design, we present the refinement of the task and procedure bodies, in the same order as in the detailed design. Since the package specifications and bodies were actually complete Ada code, we do not repeat them here.

Since the emphasis of this book is on tasking, and since the most interesting aspects of tasking are the task interactions that have already been discussed, we will have relatively few comments on the code. This section presents the code for:

- Track_File_Monitor: (task bodies for Monitor, Extrapolation_ Timer, and Transport_Coordinates)
- Track_Services (procedures Update, Correlate, and Extrapolate)
- Operator_Interface (task body Interface)
- Display_Interface (task body Interface)
- The main procedure: ATDS

9.5.1 Track_File_Monitor

The body of Track_File_Monitor was completely coded during detailed design. The only additional refinement is the bodies of the tasks Monitor, Extrapolation_Timer, and Transport_Coordinates.

```
----- Monitor -----
with Track_Services; use Track_Services;
separate (Track_File_Monitor)
  task body Monitor is
    Track_Storage : Track_File (Track_Number);
    Last_Track : Track_Count := 0;
  begin
    loop
      select
        accept Latest (Tracks : out Track_File;
                       Number_Of_Tracks : out Track_Count) do
        Tracks := Track_Storage (1 .. Last_Track);
        Number_Of_Tracks := Last_Track;
        end Latest;
      or
        accept Add (X, Y : in Coordinates; Full : out Boolean) do
          Full := Last_Track = Track_Count'Last;
          if Last_Track < Track_Count'Last then
            Last_Track := Last_Track + 1;
            Track_Services.Update (Track_Storage, X, Y, Last_Track);
          end if;
        end Add;
      or
        accept Update (X, Y : in Coordinates;
                       Track_ID : in Track_Number) do
          Track_Services.Update (Track_Storage, X, Y, Track_ID);
        end Update;
      or
```

```
        accept Correlate (X, Y : in Coordinates) do
          Track_Services.Correlate (Track_Storage, X, Y);
        end Correlate;
      or
        accept Extrapolate do
          Track_Services.Extrapolate (Track_Storage);
        end Extrapolate;
      end select;
    end loop;
  end Monitor;
```

We have completed the data definitions and the full call to the entrance procedures of Track_Services. The Latest entry makes use of a slice to return only those tracks that are established, rather than the entire track file.

----- Extrapolation_Timer -----

```
with Calendar; use Calendar;
separate (Track_File_Monitor)
  task body Extrapolation_Timer is
    Next_Time : Time := Clock + Update_Periodic;
  begin
    Periodic_Loop:
    loop
      delay Next_Time - Clock;

      Monitor.Extrapolate;

      Next_Time := Next_Time + Update_Periodic;
    end loop Periodic_Loop;
  end Extrapolation_Timer;
```

The data structures are added, and the coding details are added to the delay algorithm to ensure there is no cumulative drift. This is the algorithm that was presented in Chapter 4.

----- Transport_Coordinates -----

```
with Raw_Data_Buffer;
separate (Track_File_Monitor)
  task body Transport_Coordinates is
    X, Y : Coordinates;
```

```
begin
  loop
    Raw_Data_Buffer.Dequeue (X, Y);
    Monitor.Correlate (X, Y);
  end loop;
end Transport_Coordinates;
```

9.5.2 Track__Services

Here is the code for the three procedures of the service package.

```
----- Update -----

with Calendar; use Calendar;
separate (Track_Services)
  procedure Update (Tracks       : in out Track_File;
                    X, Y         : in Coordinates;
                    Track_Number : in Track_Count) is
  begin
    Tracks (Track_Number) := (X, Y, Update => Clock);
  end Update;

----- Correlate -----

with Coordinates_Math; use Coordinates_Math;
-- Coordinates_Math contains Coordinates_Square_Root

separate (Track_Services)
  procedure Correlate  (Tracks : in out Track_File;
                        X, Y   : in Coordinates) is

    -- Attempts to correlate the input X,Y
    -- with a track in the track file.
    -- If the coordinates correlate, they
    -- are used to update the location
    -- of the track. The time of last update
    -- is set to current time.

    Delta_X, Delta_Y, Distance : Coordinates;
```

```
begin
  -- correlate with current tracks (simple, not best, algorithm)
  Correlation_Loop:
  for Track_Index in Tracks'Range loop
    Delta_X := Tracks (Track_Index).X - X;
    Delta_Y := Tracks (Track_Index).Y - Y;

    -- Distance is square root of sum of squares of delta X and Y
    Distance := Coordinates_Square_Root
                       (Delta_X ** 2 + Delta_Y ** 2);

    if Distance <= Proximity then
      Tracks (Track_Index) := (X, Y, Update => Clock);
      exit Correlation_Loop;
    end if;
  end loop Correlation_Loop;
end Correlate;
```

The correlation algorithm is overly simple, but satisfactory for our
purposes. We assume that the package Coordinates_Math (likely an
instantiation of a generic math package) provides the procedure for
taking the square root of a coordinate.

----- Extrapolate -----

```
with Calendar; use Calendar;
separate (Track_Services)
  procedure Extrapolate (Tracks : in out Track_File) is

    -- Extrapolates all tracks to current Time.
    -- All aircraft travel the same speed
    -- and in northeast direction.

    Time_Of_This_Update : Time := Clock;
    Delta_Time       : Duration;
    Delta_Distance : Coordinates;
  begin
    -- update all tracks
    for Track_Index in Tracks'Range loop
      Delta_Time := Time_Of_This_Update
                          - Tracks (Track_Index).Update;

      Delta_Distance := Coordinates (Delta_Time * Speed);
```

```
        Tracks (Track_Index).X := Tracks (Track_Index).X
                                        + Delta_Distance;

        Tracks (Track_Index).Y := Tracks (Track_Index).Y
                                        + Delta_Distance;

        Tracks (Track_Index).Update := Time_Of_This_Update;
      end loop;
   end Extrapolate;
```

9.5.3   Operator__Interface Body

```
with Track_File_Monitor;
with External_Devices;
with Definitions; use Definitions;
with Text_IO; use Text_IO;
separate (Operator_Interface)
   task body Interface is
     X, Y : Coordinates;
     Track_ID : Track_Number;
     Add_Track_Indicator : constant Track_Count := 0;
   begin
     Interface_With_Operator:
     loop
       Handle_Track_Store_Full:
       begin
         External_Devices.Get_Data_From_Operator (X, Y, Track_ID);

         if Track_ID = Add_Track_Indicator then
           Track_File_Monitor.Add_Track (X, Y);
         else
           Track_File_Monitor.Update_Track (X, Y, Track_ID);
         end if;
       exception
         when Track_File_Monitor.Track_Store_Full =>
         Put_Line ("Track store full.");
       end Handle_Track_Store_Full;
     end loop Interface_With_Operator;
   end Interface;
```

9.5.4 Display__Interface Body

```
with Track_File_Monitor;
with External_Devices;
with Calendar; use Calendar;
with Definitions; use Definitions;

separate (Display_Interface)
  task body Interface is
    Tracks : Track_File (Track_Number);
    Number_Of_Tracks : Track_Count;
    Next_Time : Time := Clock + Display_Periodic;
  begin
  Periodic_Display:
  loop
    delay Next_Time - Clock;

    Track_File_Monitor.Latest_Track_File (Tracks,
                                    Number_Of_Tracks);

    for Track_Index in 1 .. Number_Of_Tracks loop
      External_Devices.Display_A_Track (Tracks (Track_Index).X,
                               Tracks (Track_Index).Y,
                               Track_Index);

    end loop;

    Next_Time := Next_Time + Display_Periodic;
  end loop Periodic_Display;
end Interface;
```

9.5.5 Main Procedure

Execution of the program starts with the main procedure. Prior to execution, packages "withed" by the main procedure must be elaborated. The chain of elaboration causes the execution of all parts of the program. The main procedure itself is simply a null statement.

```
with Operator_Interface;
with Display_Interface;
procedure ATDS is
begin
  null;
end ATDS;
```

9.6 Discussion

It is useful to observe that the program units we have seen in this case study are in one of three categories:

- *Application*: An application-oriented package (Track_File_ Monitor, Operator_Interface, Display_Interface) is one that contains the subprograms and tasks that accomplish the main processing to satisfy the software requirements posed by the problem statement.

- *Communication*: A communication-oriented package is one whose primary purpose is to provide for data transfers between the application packages. They also affect the caller/called relationships of the major components of the application packages. Such packages, and their components, were the main topic of Chapters 6 to 8.

- *Helper*: A helper package is one that provides a set of services to "help" an application package accomplish its function.

Application-oriented packages can be thought of as processes. We used process abstraction to model the natural concurrency of the ATDS, and arrived at the initial decomposition of Figure 9-3a. Further consideration of concurrency requirements dictated the decomposition of the Track_File_Monitor into several lower-level processes. The Track_File_Monitor was later implemented as a package with several tasks (capturing the nature of the Track_File_Monitor process as a concurrent program).

We have been using the phrase "process abstraction" as a *method* of design. It can also be considered to be a *mechanism*. Wegner defines a *process abstraction* as a data abstraction with "... an independently executing thread of control ..." [WEG84]. The package Track_File_Monitor is also a process abstraction in this regard. Its internal state is maintained by the track file; operations that modify the internal state are illustrated by the procedure Add_Track; and it has independent threads of control that cause tracks to be extrapolated and updated based on radar data.

The Helper category includes previously developed software such as the Executive Services, and also includes packages that provide needed information, such as the Definitions package. However, the most important use of such a package is to provide a set of services that allow us to defer detail.

When we are designing the main processing to satisfy the software requirements, we should not have to pause (either logically or literally) to address minor details of how to accomplish major processes. Rather, we should assume whatever capabilities necessary to easily accomplish the high-level functions we require. We document our assumptions in a package specification. Later, we will implement the helper package when we code the package body.

This use of helpers is illustrated in this problem by the Track_Services package. The Monitor task has a set of quite complex functions to perform. However, if we assume a package that can perform functions such as correlation and extrapolation in single logical steps (from the viewpoint of the user of the package), then Monitor is easy to design.

A thorough explanation of the use of packages to defer detail, and the related topics of process abstraction, abstract data types, and object-oriented design, is beyond the scope of this book; it is a major issue of system design. Dijkstra [DAH72, especially page 50ff] addresses this issue in a particularly insightful way. Other useful references are CHE86, LIS86, and BOO87. The topic is addressed in detail in NIE88. You may also wish to review our short discussion of data abstraction in Chapter 7.

An approach to the Track_Services based on use of an abstract data type is shown in the solution to exercise 9.6 below.

9.7 Exercises

Exercise 9.1. Instead of having a package of Track_Services, use nested procedures in the task body Track_File_Monitor. Note how this changes the level of decomposition during top-level and detailed design.

Exercise 9.2. Do your own implementation of Raw_Data_Buffer. Package the buffer with the transporter, Transport_Coordinates. Note how this changes the interface to Track_File_Monitor.

Exercise 9.3. Put the task specification of Monitor in the package specification rather than the package body. You will no longer need entrance procedures, but the entry Extrapolate is now public, rather than private as it was before.

Exercise 9.4. Place the actual storage for the track file in Track_Services rather than Track_File_Monitor. This changes the interface, particularly since the parameter of type Track_File is no longer needed. The latest track file must now be provided by Track_Services.

Exercise 9.5. The current solution has two copies of the track file (in order to cater to potential concurrency of input and output); one in Track_File_Monitor and one in Display_Interface. Build on problem 9.4 to only have a single copy of the track file, with Track_Services now providing a display service in addition to its other functions. Think about how this affects real and apparent concurrency. (Whether this is a good solution depends upon detailed architecture and timing issues—how many processors there are, how long the display takes to operate, and the time taken for a context switch if the system has only one processor.)

Exercise 9.6. Group the Track_File related defintions together in the Track_Services package, and have the package export Track_File as a limited private type. This will call for some restructuring of the solution, including more services to be provided by Track_Services. (There must also be some way to accommodate processes other than Track_File_Monitor.) This can be done by building on the solution presented, or by building on Exercise 9.5.

Note: This problem illustrates a *closed* abstract data type. This is sometimes called a *type manager* since it "manages" or provides the definition and operations for a type of some object.

We may also have an *open* abstract data type. The open abstract data type is similar to the original Track_Services package, except that the type definitions for the track file would be combined with the operations in the Track_Services package, rather than in the package Definitions.

Exercise 9.5 is also an illustration of a form of abstraction. In fact, its encapsulation of the track file is even more complete than in a closed abstract data type; even the type definition is hidden in the package body. Such an approach is sometimes called a *resource* or an *object manager*, the track file being the "object." The important difference between the resource approach and the closed abstract data type approach is that the resource only provides a single copy of the object. (Actually, one could have multiple objects, with an additional operation to select an object; but this complicates the interface.)

Exercise 9.7. Build simulators for the radar and the operator. Examine the timing and effeciency aspects of each of the alternate designs above.

9.8 Partial Solutions to Exercises

Exercises 9.1–9.5 are not solved.

Solution 9.6 Track_Services as Abstract Data Type. We will focus on the changes needed to the specification of Track_Services, and on the changes to the user of this helper pacakge— the Monitor task. We will not develop the body of Track_Services. In many instances, it will change little from its current form.

Here is the specification for Track_Services exporting the Track_FIle as an abstract data type. You can compare it to the old version in paragraph 9.3.2.4.

```
with Definitions; use Definitions;
package Track_Services is
   type Track_File is private;

   procedure Add (Tracks : in out Track_File;
               X, Y   : in Coordinates);

   -- raise exception, rather than Full as parameter
   Track_File_Full : exception;

   procedure Update (Tracks        : in out Track_File;
                  X, Y           : in Coordinates;
                  Track_Number : in Track_Count);
   procedure Correlate   (Tracks : in out Track_File;
                  X, Y   : in Coordinates);
   procedure Extrapolate (Tracks : in out Track_File);
private
   -- track file is defined here,
   -- rather than in the Definitions package
end Track_Services;
```

Note: The body would have to be modified to provide extra procedures, e.g., additional services would have to be provided to the display interface task. We will not do so for this example.

The changes from the original version (Section 9.3.2.4) are:

- The private type definition for Track_File
- The procedure to Add to the track file
- The Track_File definition in the private part

Users of this package will use the type Track_Services.Track_File to define their own instances of an actual track file. Then Track_Services will perform operations on objects of the type. Track_File is an *abstract data type*.

The package is actually very similar in nature to the old version, especially in the sense that it is still a *helper* package. An important difference is that since the users no longer have visibility into the structure of the track file, the package encapsulating the abstract data type must now provide *all* operations on objects of the type. This is the reason for the inclusion of the "Add" procedure; the user used to do the "add" function, but now needs the operation to be performed by the helper.

Why do we do this? The basic reason is to simplify the using packages, and make them easier to change, by *hiding* the design decision of the structure of the track file. The seminal paper behind the notion of "information-hiding" is by Parnas [PAR72].

We retain knowledge of the structure of Track_File in the Track_Services package; the full type definition is in its private part.

The last point is to note the use of an exception to communicate the fact that the track file is full and cannot be added to. We do not use a "Full" parameter to make the indication. Our usual method of communicating exceptional conditions across package boundries is the use of an exception.

Here is the new detailed design of the Monitor. You can compare it with the old version in Section 9.4.1.

```
with Track_Services; use Track_Services;
separate (Track_File_Monitor)
  task body Monitor is
  begin
    loop
      select
        accept Latest (Tracks : out Track_File) do
          provide the track file;
        end Latest;
      or
```

```
      accept Add (X, Y : in Coordinates;
                  Full : out Boolean) do
        use Track_Services.Add to add the track to the track store;
        set Full to False;

        (Handle the Track_Services.Track_Store_Full exception by
         setting Full to True);
      end Add;
   or
      accept Update (X, Y    : in Coordinates;
                     Track_ID : in Track_Number) do
        use Track_Services.Update to update the track;
      end Update;
   or
      accept Correlate (X, Y : in Coordinates) do
        use Track_Services to correlate all tracks;
      end Correlate;
   or
      accept Extrapolate do
        use Track_Services to extrapolate all tracks;
      end Extrapolate;
    end select;
  end loop;
end Monitor;
```

Update, Correlate, and Extrapolate are similar to the original version since they used the services of Track_Services in any event. Add, however, is quite different. In the old version, it accessed the data structure directly. In this approach, we remove the dependency on the data structure. We do this by using Track_Services. (We could have used Track_Services in the old approach, but did not do so since the function to be performed was so simple that it was clearer to do it immediately rather than add the level of abstraction of the extra call. This is a close decision however, and we might have used an Add procedure from Track_Services anyway.)

What have we gained by not accessing the data structure, instead using Track_Services? First, we do not have to be concerned about the structure of the track file at all. Since the structure of the track file is not visible, the use of the Add procedure from Track_Services does not add any conceptual overhead. Second, the implementor of the Track_Services package is free to change the representation of and access methods to the track file. In real systems, the track file is a major data structure that is difficult to design, and is likely to undergo change.

The second point is important during system maintenance, and is an example of the sort of use of Ada that will lead to more maintainable systems.

However, it is also important during program development. The two separate teams developing the Track_File_Monitor and Track_Services *do not have to agree on a data structure before beginning their separate development.* Further, the Track_Services team is free to change the representation without consultation with the other team (at least to the degree that timing issues are not involved). This is a vitally important issue for how a system should be decomposed and work assigned; it is another aspect of the previously discussed information hiding [PAR72]. This topic is worthy of further discussion, but is beyond the scope of this book on concurrency.

Here is the code for the new version of the Monitor. You can compare it to Section 9.5.1.

```
with Track_Services; use Track_Services;
separate (Track_File_Monitor)
  task body Monitor is
    Track_Storage : Track_Services.Track_File;
  begin
    loop
      select
        accept Latest (Tracks : out Track_File) do
          Tracks := Track_Storage;
        end Latest;
      or
        accept Add (X, Y : in Coordinates;
                    Full : out Boolean) do

          Handle_Track_Store_Full:
          begin
            Track_Services.Add (Track_Storage, X, Y);
            Full := False;
          exception
            when Track_Services.Track_Store_Full =>
              Full := True;
          end Handle_Track_Store_Full;
        end Add;
      or
```

```
         accept Update (X, Y : in Coordinates;
                        Track_ID : in Track_Number) do
           Track_Services.Update (Track_Storage, X, Y, Track_ID);
         end Update;
      or
         accept Correlate (X, Y : in Coordinates) do
           Track_Services.Correlate (Track_Storage, X, Y);
         end Correlate;
      or
         accept Extrapolate do
           Track_Services.Extrapolate (Track_Storage);
         end Extrapolate;
      end select;
    end loop;
  end Monitor;
```

Keys to Understanding

- It is good practice to establish a separate process for each external device.

- The Raw_Data_Buffer and the Transporter were important in the design to provide for intermediate storage and to uncouple the interactions of the tasks in the system.

- After the initial concurrent processes are identified, continue to decompose into more detailed concurrent processes when a process has more than one (simultaneous) function to perform. This method, using process abstraction, will help the solution model the natural concurrency of the problem.

- The top-level decomposition need not be only into tasks. Packages providing services can make the tasks easier to define and design.

- The design process involves several successive levels of refinement. This refinement involves increasing detail of interface specifications, data structures, and algorithms.

- Abstract data types are not a concurrency issue per se, but are a key aspect of the design of large systems.

Task Manipulation

Part 3 is largely concerned with the details of the Ada tasking model. It explains the general nature of tasks as objects, similar to any other object in the language. The objects must have a type, and then can be delared individually or as components of composite objects, can be passed as parameters to subprograms, and can be declared as "private" in package declarations. We then provide considerable detail regarding the activation, process of execution, completion, and termination of tasks.

The first chapters of Part 3 avoid the topic of having pointers (objects of an access type) to tasks, and the associated creation of tasks by the evaluation of allocators. We do this in order to concentrate on the basic issues of activation and termination of tasks. Creating tasks by the evaluation of allocators affects their declaration, activation, and termination in special ways; all such information, as well as a useful paradigm for the use of such tasks, is centralized in Chapter 13, Pointers to Task Objects.

The case study illustrates the use of arrays of tasks in the context of a problem that uncouples a client-server interaction through the use of a "receipt" for an item that belongs to the client but is processed by the server. A solved exercise of the case study illustrates an effective alternate interaction using an agent task created through the evaluation of an allocator.

Task Types and Objects

Objective: To introduce the notion of a task type and to demonstrate the characteristics of objects created through use of task types

Until now, we have created tasks by the description of their interface with the outside world, and their processing. Ada however, lets us describe the interface and the processing in a general way (almost in a "generic" way, but not in the sense of an Ada generic). We can then use this general description to create multiple objects with the same characteristics.

10.1 Type Declarations

A task type is a template for the creation of task objects. This is the same as any other type declaration; for example, a record type declaration defines the name and type of the components of objects of the type. A task type defines the task's interface, its internal data structure, and the execution of objects of the type. Let's look at an example.

```
task type Producers is
  entry Get_Started;
end Producers;

task body Producers is
  Item : Item_Type;
begin
  accept Get_Started;
  loop
    -- produce an item
    Buffer.Enqueue (Item);
  end loop;
end Producers;
```

The task specification contains the word "type." If the specification had simply been "task Producers", we would have created a single task, called Producers, that would produce items and put them into the Buffer (assumed to be visible at the point of use). However, since we have added the word "type", we have not created a task at all, but only a template for a task.

10.2 Simple Object Declarations

When we wish to create the actual tasks, we declare them as objects of the given type as:

```
T1, T2, T3 : Producers;
```

The three tasks are now identical, in specification, in internal data structure, and in action (execution). They each have entries and can be called as:

```
T1.Get_Started;
T2.Get_Started;
T3.Get_Started;
```

Then they each will produce items and put them in the same buffer. The tasks are not only identical from the outside, they cannot distinguish among themselves! That is, the tasks are not aware of their own identity. If we wish them to have self-awareness, and the ability to identify themselves to other tasks, we must expicitly provide the identification. This can be done by a modification of the task type and the explicit use of an entry call for identification.

```
task type Producers is
  entry Task_ID (ID : in Integer);
end Producers;

task body Producers is
  My_ID : Integer;
  Item  : Item_Type;
begin
  accept Task_ID (ID : in Integer) do
    My_ID := ID:
  end Task_ID;

  loop
    -- produce an item
    Buffer.Enqueue_With_Producer_ID (Item, My_ID);
  end loop;
end Producers;
```

Then we use the calls:

```
T1.Task_ID (1);
T2.Task_ID (2);
T3.Task_ID (3);
```

Each of the three tasks go about their business of producing items and providing them to the buffer, identifying themselves as they do so.

The tasks T1, T2, and T3 are objects, but they are not variables; in some ways they act as constants. However, they cannot be assigned to and, therefore, cannot be initialized.

Although we speak casually of "the tasks T1, T2, and T3 ...", it is strictly more correct to state that the three task objects T1, T2, and T3 *designate* tasks. (We use the more casual phrase because it is simply easier to say "The task T1 ..." rather than "The task designated by task object T1 ...".)

What is the task "object" that we are talking about? In an abstract sense, we don't really care. Furthermore, it may vary from implementation to implementation. However, if it helps you to think about the object, you may think of the object as a pointer to a task control block that *designates* the task itself, represented by the task control block.

The tasks designated by the object are permanently bound to the object. The task objects are essentially objects of limited private type. They share the characteristics of all limited objects in terms of assignment and as parameters to subprograms or generic units. A task type may also appear in the private part of a package as the actual type corresponding to a visible type declaration such as "type T is limited private;".

10.3 Task Objects as Parameters to Subprograms

Suppose there were some complicated processing associated with the call to an entry of a task; in the example above this might have to do with the calculation of the identification of the task. We wish to abstract the processing into a procedure, with the task as the parameter. We can do so as:

```
procedure Initialize_Task (T : in Producers) is
  ID : Integer;
begin
  -- calculate the new ID
  T.Task_ID (ID);
end Initialize_Task;
```

The procedure simply has a parameter of the appropriate type, just as any other procedure call, and then performs operations on the formal parameter. The call is always effectively by reference. The procedure has knowledge of the entries of the task since it "sees" the type definition Producers. The mode of the formal parameter could also be "in out" since the association is by reference in any event. It makes no sense, however, to have "out" mode since the task object always acts as a constant. No assignments may be made to a task object. Mode "out" is illegal.

Passing a task as a parameter is also important when using a task type as the actual type corresponding to a limited private type in a package declaration. Problem Cobbler_7 will illustrate this point.

10.4 Task Objects as Returned Value of a Function

Suppose we had a series of tasks of type "Loan_Officer" that provided different levels of service based on different initial states and on their different "experience" gained during functioning of the system. We might wish to select one of the loan officers based on some complex function involving, for example, the size of the loan and the customer's credit rating. It could be useful to encapsulate the selection criteria in a function that returns the appropriate loan officer.

An entry in the returned task can then be called through use of the function name. A partial specification of the loan officers is:

```
task type Loan_Officer is
  entry Loan_Request (Loan_Size : in  Money;
                      Customer  : in  Customer_Number;
                      Approved  : out Boolean);
  entry ...
end Loan_Officer;

Vice_Presidents : array (...) of Loan_Officer;
Assigned_Officer : Loan_Officer;
```

The function specification is:

```
function Appropriate_Loan_Officer
             (Loan_Size     : Money;
              Credit_Rating : Credit_Catagory)
                             return Loan_Officer;
```

Hidden in the function body is the complex selection process of choosing the task to service the loan request. The function call and associated entry call are shown below.

The function is called and returns an object of the task type. That is the code:

```
Assigned_Officer := Appropriate_Loan_Officer
       (Loan_Amount, Rating); -- returns a task as a value
```

The entry of the designated task is, in turn, called. That is the code:

```
Assigned_Officer.Loan_Request (Loan_Amount, Client_Num, Approval);
```

The rendezvous then takes place, with the result being the determination of whether or not the loan is approved.

```
if Approval ... -- whatever is to be done
```

10.5 Composite Object Declarations

Since task types can be used to create task objects, it is natural that
we should be able to create arrays of such objects and to have such
objects as components of records. We create an array of task objects
as:

```
Many_Producers : array (Integer range 1 .. 10) of Producers;
```

We access the tasks by using an index into the array in the usual
way. To provide an identification for each task, we can:

```
for ID in Many_Producers'Range loop
  Many_Producers (ID).Task_ID (ID);
end loop;
```

We index into the array with the loop parameter "ID" and call the
initializing entry with an actual value. We then have 10 tasks,
each with its own identification.

We can also have records containing tasks, such as:

```
type Task_Record is
  record
    The_Producer : Producers;
      ...
  end record;

A_Record : Task_Record;
```

We access the entries to the task by using the name of the task
object in the record as:

```
A_Record.The_Producer.Task_ID (...);
```

Tasks in records might be used to associate a task with data that
it operated on, or to create a complex data structure (linked list,
binary tree, etc.) containing tasks that are dynamically created as
required.

Exercises

Work the exercises Cobbler_5 through Cobbler_11.

Keys to Understanding

- A task type is a template that can be used for the creation of many tasks with the same entries.

- The body of the task type defines the execution of all task objects of the type.

- Named objects may be created through the use of the task type. They are true objects, of a limited private type, with characteristics similar to other objects of limited private type.

- The different task objects of the same type may be explicitly given unique identifications.

- Task objects may be passed as parameters to subprograms or to generic program units, and may be returned as the value of a function.

- Arrays of tasks allow for easy specification of a large number of similar tasks.

11

Activation

Objective: To describe the mechanism for initiating the execution of tasks

There is no explicit initiation mechanism for Ada tasks. Tasks are implicitly activated immediately following the elaboration of the declarative part of the construct (program unit or block statement) in which they are declared. This leads to a structured "fork-join" approach (similar to the use of cobegin-coend in other languages) in which the lifetime of a task is closely tied to the normal scope rules of the language.

The sections below first discuss the basic rules of task activation and provide a detailed discussion of elaboration (since understanding elaboration is vital to understanding task activation). They then address task types, introduce the effect of exceptions, and point out some additional aspects of task and package interaction. Discussion of the activation rules for tasks created by the evaluation of an allocator is deferred to Chapter 13, Pointers to Task Objects, in order to focus on the basic issues of activation.

11.1   Basic Rules

Each task has a *master*, also called the *parent*. The master of a task is the construct—subprogram, block, task, or library package—that declares the task. A task is *dependent* upon its master. It is called the *child* of the master.

A task is activated (begins execution) after the elaboration of the declarative part of its master. The activation starts immediately following the begin of the master, but before the execution of the master's sequence of statements. (Actually, a task can also be activated by a nested package that is not the master of the task. The effect of nested packages is deferred until Section 11.5, Activation by Packages.)

Task execution is a two-stage process.

- The first stage is *activation*, which is the elaboration of the declarative part of the task body.

- The second stage is *execution*, the execution of the sequence of statements following the begin of the task body.

If several tasks are declared by a master, their activation occurs in parallel. These are called *sibling* tasks. All the sibling tasks must complete activation before the master begins to execute its sequence of statements.

When a task completes activation, it may begin its execution stage without regard to the stage of its sibling tasks. Hence task activation and execution of sequence of statements can proceed in parallel. This does not affect the requirement that all tasks must complete activation prior to execution of the master's sequence of statements.

For the following code skeleton,

```
Master:
declare
    ... -- some declarations

    task T1 ... end T1;
    task body T1 is ... end T1;

    task T2 ... end T2;
    task body T2 is ... end T2;

    ... -- more declarations
```

```
task T3 ... end T3;
task body T3 is ... end T3;

... -- additional declarations
begin
... -- sequence of statements
end Master;
```

the time lines of Figure 11-1 show start of existence, activation, execution of sequence of statements, and termination.

For Figure 11-1, the lines are defined as:

The solid line _____ indicates elaboration of a declarative part. For the tasks T1, T2, and T3 this is the activation stage.

The dashed line ------ indicates that a task exists (has been elaborated), but is not yet activated, is blocked, or has terminated (i.e., it is not actually executing).

The dotted line .... indicates that a task is executing (or at least ready to execute).

Notes—keyed to Figure 11-1:

1. The block comes into existence and begins elaboration of the declarative part. This includes elaboration of the task specifications and the task bodies of tasks T1, T2, and T3.

2. Although all three tasks are elaborated at this point, the block still has additional declarations (perhaps some subprograms) to elaborate.

3. At the *begin* (the completion of elaboration of the block), the three tasks commence activation, the elaboration of the declarative part of the task bodies.

4. Task T2 completes activation and may commence execution. It does not have to wait for the completion of activation of its siblings.

5. All tasks have completed activation. Note that T3 has also completed execution and has terminated. The Master can now commence execution.

6. The Master completes execution of its sequence of statements, but is not left while it still has active dependent tasks (children). It is considered to be "waiting" at the end statement.

7. The last child completes execution, terminates, and the Master exits.

The elaboration of the declarative part of the Master includes the elaboration of the task specifications and task bodies.

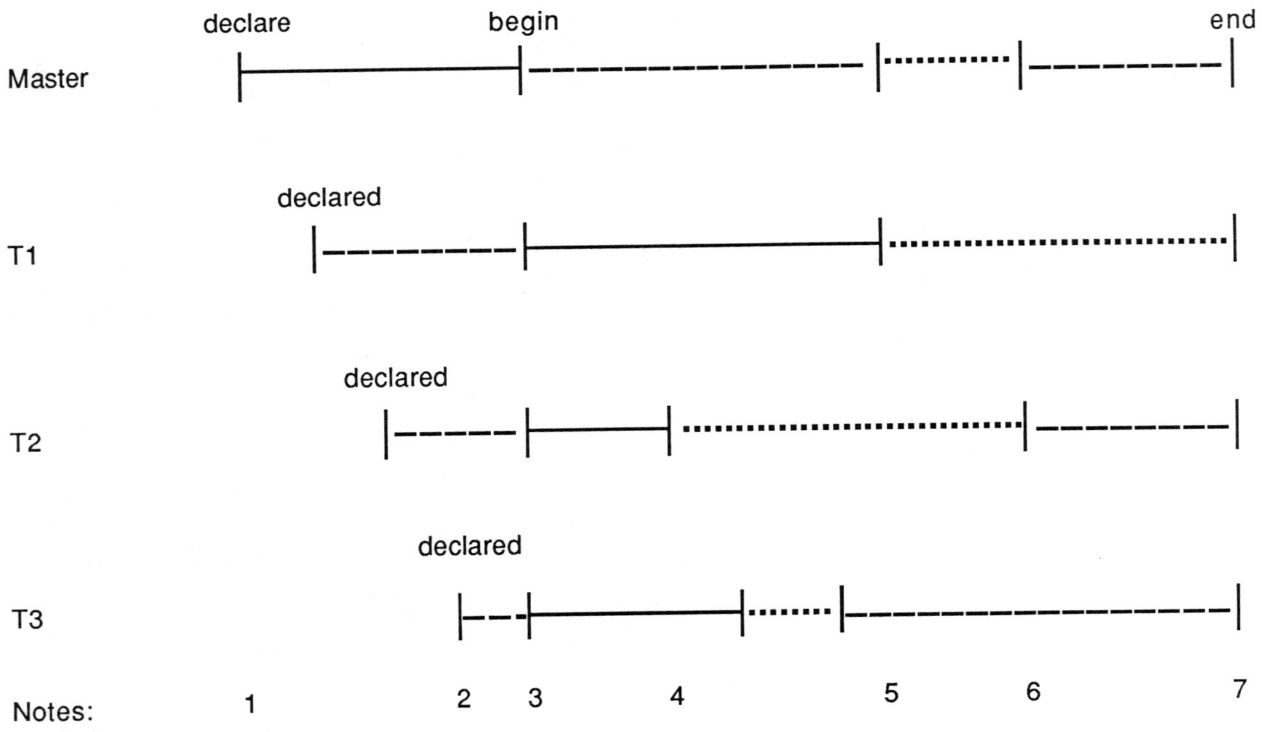

Figure 11-1. Task activation and execution

We think of the task specification as defining the relationship of the task to the outside world. After it is elaborated, the task's entries may be called, with the caller blocked waiting for a rendez-vous in the usual manner. This is also true of a task designated by a task object of some previously defined task type; as soon as the task object is elaborated, its entries may be called.

The task body defines the execution of the task, including the elaboration of the declarative part and the execution of the sequence of statements. Notice that the *task body* is elaborated by the Master, while the *declarative part of the task body* is elaborated as the first phase (activation) of execution of the task.

Figure 11-2 shows the possible states of a task, relative to its activation, that we have thus far discussed. We will add to this Figure throughout Chapters 11 and 12 in order to summarize the states of a task.

11.2   Elaboration

We say that a declaration *introduces* an entity. The process by which a declaration achieves its effect is called *elaboration*. Elaboration occurs at execution time. We say that a declarative part is *elaborated* prior to the *execution* of the sequence of statements (between the begin and end). A simple example of elaboration is:

```
procedure Elaborate_I is
   I : Integer := A + B; -- A and B visible here
begin
   ...
end Elaborate_I;
```

An invocation of Elaborate_I causes it to execute. The first part of the execution is the elaboration of the declarative part. This involves evaluation of the expression A + B, allocation of storage for I, and the initialization of the memory location with the value of the expression.

Note: The process described implies that there is run-time allocation of storage. Upon entry to a block or subprogram storage is allocated in an *activation record*. This storage is allocated on the system stack and is sometimes called a *stack frame*. Storage is also allocated dynamically for packages and tasks.

The initialization can be quite complex, even involving a function call to determine the initial value. For example,

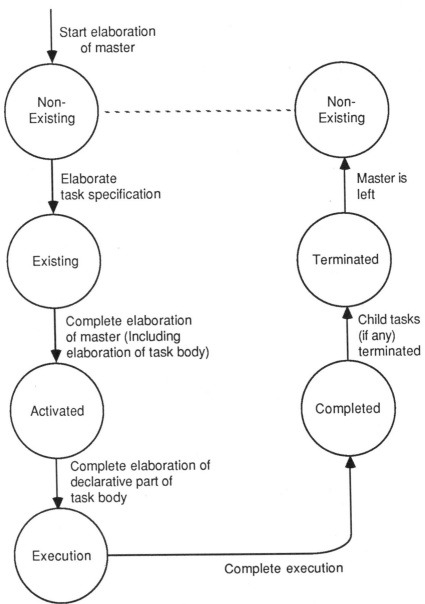

Figure 11-2. Basic states and transitions

```
I : Integer := Init_Function;
```

During elaboration of the declarative part of Elaborate_I (assuming the above declarations), Init_Function executes and returns the initial value for I. Init_Function is a normal function and hence can do things such as invoke other subprograms, cause tasks to execute, write messages to output devices, and so on. (Except in special cases, the function should not have unusual side effects, but it is legal to do so.) The elaboration of a task specification may be similarly complex, for example, involving the execution of functions to establish the discrete range for a family of entries.

Some forms of elaboration do not have any particular effect on storage allocation or other aspects of the run-time environment; they simply make declarations known to the unit being elaborated. Therefore, the entities elaborated may be referenced by the unit. This is true, for example, of type definitions.

Remember that the execution of any construct always entails two steps: first, the elaboration of the declarative part and second, the execution of the sequence of statements between the begin and the end.

A task is elaborated in the declarative part of its master, along with all other declarations. After the declarative part of the master is elaborated, the task begins execution. The first part of execution is activation, being the elaboration of the declarative part of the task body.

Notice the distinction between the *elaboration of the task* and the *elaboration of the declarative part of the task body*.

11.3 Use of Task Types

Task types may be defined in some external unit, for example a package, or defined in the same declarative part containing task object definitions. Suppose that the package Task_Definitions contains the task type T. Then we may have:

```
with Task_Definitions;
procedure P is
   task type Local_T is ... end Local_T;

   T1 : Task_Definitions.T;
   T2 : Local_T;
   T3 : Local_T;

   task body Local_T is ... end Local_T;
begin
   ...     -- statements of P
end P;
```

The order of events is:

1. The context clause, with Task_Definitions, causes the elaboration of the package Task_Definitions. This, in turn, causes the elaboration of the task specification and body of the task type T.

    Note: The elaboration of the task specification of a task type may involve the evaluation of expressions to define the discrete range of entry families. Once the specification is elaborated, objects of the type may be declared. There is no major effect of the elaboration of the body of the task type; the elaboration simply establishes that tasks of the type may be executed. (As we pointed out in Chapter 10, remember that the formal phrase is that tasks *designated* by objects of the task type may be executed.)

2. The declarative part of procedure P is elaborated, causing the elaboration, in order, of:

    - The task specification of Local_T
    - The task objects T1, T2, and T3
    - The task body of Local_T

3. The three tasks begin execution (activation first) in parallel. The activation involves the elaboration of the declarative parts of all three tasks.

    Notice that T2 and T3 both require elaboration of the declarative parts, even though they are of the same type. This must be so since the elaboration may well involve some actions to make them distinct and identifiable entities.

    (For example, there might be an initializing function call, as we saw in the exercises to Chapter 2, that assigns a value to a local variable called My_ID. The function returns unique values, thereby making the tasks unique. This could be an alternative to the use of an initializing entry to identify a task.)

    Further, T1 is an object of a type that may be used by many other program units; it must have its own, unique, elaboration.

4. After the three tasks have completed activation, the sequence of statements of P executes in parallel with the task execution.

5. The procedure P may not be left until all three tasks complete execution. This is discussed further in Chapter 12, Termination.

11.4   Effect of Exceptions

There are two circumstances in which exceptions affect the activation of tasks:

- Exception during elaboration of the declarative part of the master
- Exception during task activation

   In the first circumstance, all tasks in the declarative part become terminated. In the second, the task with the exception is completed, but the other tasks in the declarative part continue to execute. This is discussed further in Chapter 12, Termination.

11.5   Activation by Packages

Packages can be the enclosing construct that causes activation of tasks. A library unit is also the *master* of the task. A nested package cannot be a master since it is dependent for its own existence on the construct in which it is declared. It is this construct (the one that declares the nested package) that is the master of tasks declared in the package.

11.5.1   Basic Rules

A package is elaborated either by being named in some other library unit's context clause, or by being nested in the declarative part of some other construct. In either event, the elaboration of the package causes the corresponding elaboration and execution of tasks declared within the package.

   Whether a task is declared in the package specification or body, it is not activated until after the elaboration of the package body. If there is no body (for example task objects declared in a package specification using some externally visible task types), an implicit body with a begin and a single null statement is assumed.

11.5.2   Nested Packages

Remember that a nested package is elaborated during the elaboration of the declarative part in which it is contained. The package declaration is first elaborated; this consists of the elaboration of the basic declarative items of the specification. Next, the package body is elaborated. This consists of:

1.   The elaboration of the declarative part of the package body, followed by

2. The execution of the body's sequence of statements

Although a nested package cannot be the master of a task, it does affect the tasks's activation. If a task is inside a nested package, it is activated immediately following the elaboration of the declarative part of the package body. (Then the sequence of statements of the package body is executed, completing the package elaboration in parallel with the execution of the task.)

The package elaboration occurs during, and completes before the end of, the elaboration of the master. Therefore, the task begins activation before the completion of elaboration of the master. This is different than if the task were declared immediately in the declarative part of the master.

Figure 11-3 shows the state changes of a task in a nested package.

11.5.3 Effect of Exceptions

The effect of exceptions is similar to that previously discussed. There are the same two cases to consider, exceptions either during elaboration of the package, or during task activation.

If an exception is raised during the elaboration of the package specification or package body declarative part, the tasks created by the elaboration are terminated, and hence never activated. The remaining effect of the exception depends upon whether the package is a declarative item (nested in some other construct), or a library unit.

- For a nested package, the exception is raised immediately after the declarative item.

- For a library unit, the execution of the main program is abandoned.

If an exception is raised in one of the tasks during its activation, it becomes completed, its sibling tasks are not affected, and Tasking_Error is raised following the begin of the package body. If the package body contains an exception handler for Tasking_Error, then the elaboration of the package is complete upon execution of the exception handler. If the package body does not contain an exception handler, the effect again depends upon whether the package is a declarative item or a library package.

- For a nested package, the exception is propagated to the enclosing construct with the same effect as that described in Section 11.4 for an exception during the elaboration of the master.

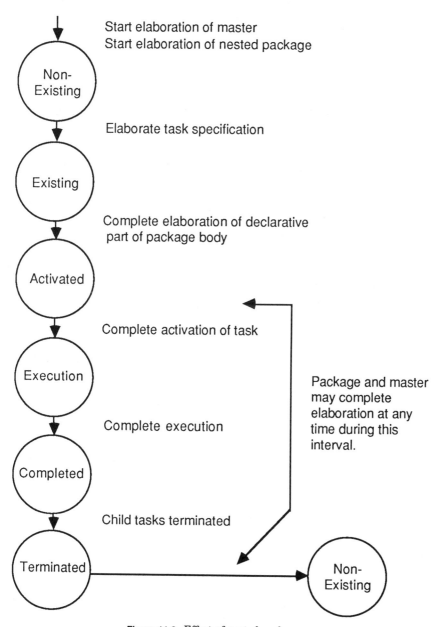

Figure 11-3. Effect of nested package

- For a library unit, the execution of the main program is abandoned.

Keys to Understanding

- Tasks are implicitly activated following the elaboration of the declarative part of the enclosing construct, in a manner consistent with the scope rules of the language.

- There are two steps to the execution of tasks: activation (the elaboration of the declarative part of the task body) and execution of the task's sequence of statements.

- Multiple task objects of the same type have independent elaboration, activation, and execution.

- If an exception occurs during the elaboration of the enclosing construct, the tasks created by the construct are never activated. If an exception occurs during the activation of a task, its siblings are unaffected, but Tasking_Error is raised following the begin of the enclosing construct.

- A library package may be a master of a task. A nested task is not a master, but will cause activation of the tasks it elaborates.

12

Termination

Objective: To describe the circumstances and effect of task termination

A task reaches the end of its active existence by terminating. A terminated task cannot be reactivated. There are four reasons why a task may terminate:

1. The task may complete execution of its sequence of statements.

2. An exception may be raised (special case of completion of execution).

3. The task may be aborted.

4. A number of tasks may cooperatively terminate.

After detailed discussion of the idea of the master of a task and some related discussion of termination issues, each of the four reasons for termination are explained. The final section provides an integrated discussion of the effect of the predefined exception Tasking_Error and the circumstances under which it is raised.

12.1 Master of a Task

In Chapter 11, we introduced the idea of the master of a task. Although the enclosing construct that initiates task execution is usually the master, the more important aspect of the master/task relationship has to do with termination of tasks. The termination of tasks is defined in terms of the masters of the tasks. We will now define *master*, and the effect of task execution on the master, in greater detail.

The master of a task is the construct whose execution creates the task object that designates the task. That is, the master is the construct that declares and elaborates the task object. (Remember that we are defering discussion of tasks created by evaluation of allocators until Chapter 13, Pointers to Task Objects.) A master may be a:

- Subprogram
- Block
- Task
- Library package

It is important to recognize that *each activation* (i.e., each instance, or each execution) of a subprogram or block establishes a new master, and a new set of subordinate tasks. Each time a subprogram is called, or each time a block is executed in some thread of control, its declarative part is elaborated, thereby creating new subordinate tasks and a new parent-child relationship. We refer to all the tasks created by a single master as *siblings*.

The vital guideline for the termination of tasks is that a task may not terminate until its dependent tasks have terminated. A similar guideline is that a block or subprogram may not be left (i.e., it may not exit its current scope or current activation) until all dependent tasks have terminated. (*Note:* A task may be dependent upon a hierarchy of *indirect* masters. For example, a task inside a block that is itself in a procedure is *directly* dependent upon the block, but also dependent upon the procedure, the caller of the procedure, and so on.) The general rule combining the guidelines above is:

Rule: Execution may not *leave* a master (we say that the master may not *exit*) until all its dependent tasks (children) have terminated.

The consequences of not leaving a master in accordance with this rule are:

- For a subprogram activation—control may not return to the caller.

- For the execution of a block statement—control may not leave the block statement (i.e., the statement logically following the block statement may not execute).

- For a task—the task may not terminate.

- For a library package—not applicable, as termination and the concept of "leaving" is not defined for library packages.

The subprogram activation, block activation, or task may *complete execution*, then wait for the termination of dependent tasks. Completion of execution for each construct is:

- Procedure—completion of execution of its sequence of statements or reaching a return statement

- Function—completion of evaluation of the result expression of a return statement

- Block—completion of execution of its sequence of statements or reaching

    exit

    return

    goto transferring control out of the block

- Task—completion of execution of its sequence of statements
- All the constructs above—raising of an exception and either

    No handler exists

    Handler completes execution

Completion of execution for packages is undefined. (Further, there is no language-defined mechanism for the completion of tasks in library packages.)

The above rules are applicable to masters in general. Let's return our focus specifically to the termination of tasks. The principle of not terminating until dependent tasks have terminated implies that a task may be in an intermediate state in which it is not terminated, but is no longer executing statements and is unable to enter a rendezvous. This state is called "completed." (We will later see that there is another intermediate state, called "abnormal," in which a task is not terminated but cannot enter a rendezvous. The abnormal state occurs when a task or its master is aborted. Don't confuse the two states "completed" and "abnormal.") A task may be in a completed state for an extended period of time while waiting for its dependent tasks to terminate.

Examples:

```
task T;
task body T is
  task Y;
  task body Y is ... end Y;
begin
  null;
end T;
```

Activation of T causes initiation of Y, dependent on T. After Y completes activation, Y and the sequence of statements of T execute in parallel. T can become "completed" and must then wait for Y to terminate before it can terminate. Similarly,

```
declare
  type Small is range 1 .. 2;
  A : Small := 1;

  task T; -- same T as previous example
  task body T is ... end T;
begin
  A := 2;
end;
```

After the activation of T (and hence after the activation of Y), T, Y, and the executable part of the block execute in parallel. The block cannot exit until T is terminated. The order of events for activation and termination is:

- The elaboration of the declarative part of the block (including the elaboration of the specification and body of T)
- The activation of T, which is the elaboration of the declarative part of the body of T (including the elaboration of the specification and body of Y)
- The activation of Y, which is the elaboration of the declarative part of the body of Y
- The parallel execution of:

The sequence of statements of Y

The sequence of statements of T

The sequence of statements of the enclosing block

- Y, T, and the block may *complete* in any order
- Termination of Y
- Termination of T
- Leave the block

Be careful to distinguish between the *elaboration of the body of a task* and the activation, which is *the elaboration of the declarative part of the body of a task*. The body of a task must be elaborated before the task is executed, while the first part of that execution is the task activation. Figure 11-1 in the chapter on activation is worth reviewing—it reinforces that the block may not be left until the child tasks have completed execution.

These rules regarding the master and its dependent tasks are logical. They ensure that declarations and objects required by dependent tasks are available throughout the lifetime of the task. For example, the task Y may declare objects of type "Small", and may use the object "A". Remember that although a block or subprogram may complete execution, it cannot *exit* until its dependent tasks have terminated.

It is possible to test the status of another task using the attributes Terminated and Callable. If "T" is an object designating a task, for example, our earlier use of "T",

T'Terminated

is True if the task has terminated, False otherwise. Similarly,

T'Callable

is True if the entries of the task may be called, but False if the task has terminated, completed, or is in an abnormal state following an abort. Care must be taken in the use of these attributes since a task may change state (from Callable to not Callable, òr not Terminated to Terminated) between the time its state is checked and the issue of an entry call.

12.2   Termination Conditions for Tasks

There are four reasons that a task may complete execution and terminate. They are:

1. Complete execution

2. Exceptions

3. Abort

4. Cooperative termination

The next four sections discuss the four reasons.

12.2.1   Complete Execution

The most straightforward way for a task to end its active existence is to complete execution of its sequence of statements. If the task has no dependent tasks, it terminates. Otherwise, it waits at the end until dependent tasks have terminated, and then it terminates.

The task still exists in some sense however, for as long as it is visible to other tasks. For example, other tasks may still call the terminated tasks entries (which causes Tasking_Error to be raised), and may query the task's attributes, Terminated and Callable. We cannot say that a task's existance is truly ended until its master is terminated (for a task) or left (for an activation of a block or subprogram).

A special case of termination as a result of completion of execution is that of termination being precipatated by an exception.

12.2.2   Exceptions

The sections below discuss (1) exceptions during elaboration of a master or task declarative part, (2) exceptions during task execution, and (3) the special case of an exception during rendezvous.

12.2.2.1   Exceptions During Elaboration.   There are two circumstances in which exceptions occur during elaboration:

- Exception during elaboration of the declarative part of the master
- Exception during task activation

The first situation is illustrated by:

```
Master:
declare
    task T1;
    task T2;

    I : Small_Int := Returns_Big_Integer; -- causes exception

    task body T1 ... end T1;
    task body T2 ... end T2;
begin
...
end Master;
```

Since the exception is raised during the elaboration of the declarative part of Master, the block is abandoned.

The exception is propagated to the point immediately following the block statement. (The exception during the elaboration of the declarative part of the block cannot be handled by an exception handler in the block.) The tasks become terminated and are, therefore, never activated.

The second situation is illustrated by:

```
Master:
declare
    task T1;
    task T2;

    I : Small_Int := Returns_Small_Integer; -- no exception

    task body T1 ... end T1; -- exception is raised
                             -- during activation
    task body T2 ... end T2;
begin
...
end Master;
```

In this situation, the elaboration of the declarative part of Master is successfully completed.

Both T1 and T2 are activated, but T1 is completed by an exception during elaboration of its declarative part. This causes the predefined exception, Tasking_Error, to be raised in the Master immediately following the begin. (This makes sense—T1 cannot handle the exception raised in its declarative part, so it must be handled by the Master.)

The exception is not raised until all other dependent tasks (i.e., T2) have completed activation. Since the exception is raised at the begin, the sequence of statements of the Master is not executed.

The Master is still not left until all other dependent tasks (i.e., T2) have terminated. If there is an exception handler for Tasking_ Error, the handler is executed (in parallel with execution of T2). After execution of the handler, Master still waits for termination of T2. Notice that T2 will continue to execute; it is not affected by the exception in T1 or the raising of the exception Tasking_Error in the Master.

Figure 12-1 shows the effect of exceptions during the elaboration of the master or the task itself.

In summary: An exception may be raised during the elaboration of the master, or may be raised during the activation (elaboration of the declarative part of the body) of one of the dependent tasks.

During Elaboration of Master: An exception raised during the elaboration of the master will cause the dependent tasks never to be activated, and hence terminated. The state change is from existing to terminated. None of the tasks declared in the master will be activated.

During Activation of Task: An exception raised during the activation of a task causes that task to become completed. The state change is from activated to completed. Other tasks in the same declarative part are not affected. The master is affected since Tasking_Error is raised immediately following the begin of the master.

12.2.2.2 Exception During Task Execution. Any unhandled exception during execution of the task will cause it to become completed. The exception is *not* propagated to the enclosing unit. (Remember that propagation is the reraising of an unhandled exception at some point other than the original occurence of the exception. That does not occur in this circumstance.)

Exceptions that are handled in inner frames of the task have no effect on termination of the task. This situation occurs when there is a block that contains an exception handler in the body of the task. If an exception is raised and handled locally, there is no effect on the task.

If an exception is handled by an exception handler at the outermost level of the task, the task becomes complete at the conclusion of execution of the handler.

Here is an example illustrating the last two points.

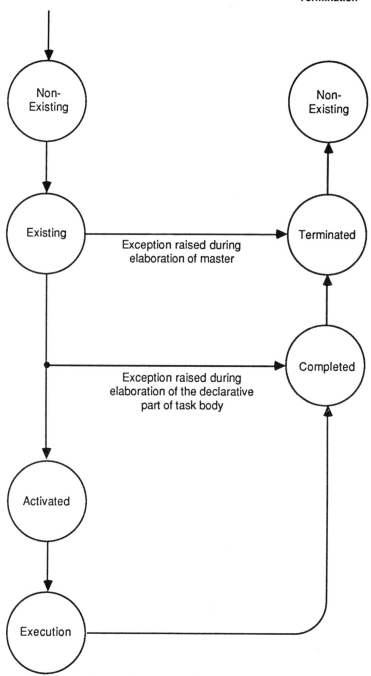

Figure 12-1. Effect of exceptions

```
task body T is
begin
  ...
  Exception_Handler_Block:
  begin
    ...
    -- exception Program_Error raised here
  exception
    when Program_Error =>
      ...
  end Exception_Handler_Block;
  ...  -- execution continues normally here
  -- exception Constraint_Error raised here
  ...
  ...
exception
  when Constraint_Error =>   -- handler at outermost
                             -- level of task
  ...
end T;
```

The exception Program_Error is handled within an inner frame and has no effect on task execution.

The exception Constraint_Error is handled by the task, but the task becomes complete upon completion of execution of the handler. If there had been no handler, the task would have become complete immediately.

12.2.2.3 Exception in a Rendezvous. Since a rendezvous is considered to be executed (by the called task) on behalf of both the calling and called task, it is sensible that both tasks should be alerted of an exception during the rendezvous. Therefore, an unhandled exception during the rendezvous is propagated to the calling task at the point of call, and within the called task at the end of the accept statement. If the accept statement is within a select statement, the exception is propagated to the end of the select statement.

The exception may be handled within an inner frame of the accept statement, in which case the accept statement completes normally. The called task is never aware that there was an exception. We will begin our examples with the exception being handled in an inner frame, then illustrate the propagation of an unhandled exception.

An accept statement may not have an exception handler. However, it may handle an exception in an inner frame within the accept statement by using a block with an exception handler. For example,

```
accept Take_Item (Item : in Item_Type) do
  Exception_Handler_Block:
  begin
    if Some_Condition then
      raise My_Error;
    end if;
    ... -- whatever is to be done
  exception
    when My_Error =>
      ... -- whatever appropriate
  end Exception_Handler_Block;

  ... -- may be other code here
end Take_Item;
```

Whether the exception is raised or not, the rendezvous ends normally and the caller and called task each proceed in the usual manner.

If the exception is not handled in an inner frame, the exception is propagated to both the calling and called tasks. Consider the following situation.

```
task Called is
  entry Take_Item (Item : in Item_Type);
end Called;

task body Called is
begin
  accept Take_Item (Item : in Item_Type) do
    if Some_Condition then
      raise My_Error;
    end if;

    -- whatever is to be done when there
    -- is no exception
  end Take_Item;

  -- the exception is propagated here,
  -- after the accept statement
  ...
end Called;
```

```
task Caller;
task body Caller is
  My_Item : Item_Type;
begin
  Called.Take_Item (My_Item);

  -- and the exception is propagated here,
  -- in the calling task
  ...
end Caller;
```

A rendezvous is the execution of code by the called task on behalf of both the called *and* calling tasks. Therefore it makes sense that an unhandled exception during the rendezvous has an effect on both tasks.

An exception during a rendezvous that is not handled in an inner frame causes abandonment of the rendezvous and propagation of the exception both to the calling task (at the point of call) and in the called task (immediately following the accept statement). If the accept statement is an alternative in a select statement, the exception is propagated to the end of the select statement.

In this case the exception is propagated to two different locations. Once the exception is propagated, it is handled like any other exception not occurring during a rendezvous.

12.2.3 Abort

Any task may abort (cause the unconditional termination) any other task that is visible. A task may abort itself. The abort statement consists of the reserved word abort followed by a list of task names. For example,

```
abort T1, T2, T3;
```

When a task is aborted, the abort also applies to any dependent tasks. This includes the tasks in a currently executing block statement, and tasks dependent upon a subprogram currently called by the aborted task. You can see that the effect of an abort statement is quite far-reaching and generally unpredictable—it depends upon the dynamic nature of the execution of a system.

The immediate effect of the abort statement is to cause the aborted tasks to become *abnormal*. If a task is already terminated, it does not become abnormal—the abort statement has no effect on the terminated task. The order in which the tasks become abnormal (e.g., T1, T2, or T3 first) is not defined by the language—it is implementation dependent. The completion of an abnormal task depends upon its current status.

Certain tasks will be completed immediately, that is, as part of the execution of the abort statement. They are:

- Tasks suspended (blocked) at an accept, select, or delay statement—any delay is canceled

- Tasks suspended at an entry call (and not yet in a rendezvous)—the task is removed from the entry queue

- Tasks that have not yet started activation (become terminated as well as completed)

Other tasks will be completed later, *no later than* one of the following synchronization points:

- The end of its activation

- A point at which it would activate some other task

- An entry call

- The start or end of an accept statement (We will discuss this further under the topic of tasks aborted while in rendezvous.)

- Reaching a select or delay statement

- An exception handler

- An abort statement

The rule is that the abnormal task may not communicate with, or have certain sorts of effect upon, other tasks. Note that an abnormal task is not forbidden from modifying unprotected shared variables. If fact, the task may become completed *while the task is updating the variable*. The value of the variable is then undefined. This aspect, as well as the uncertainty of when the task will become completed, adds to the high degree of disruption caused by an abort. It is also likely that "... executing an abort statement may wreak havoc with the execution timing of other tasks on the same processor" [BAK85].

The effect of the abort statement on tasks in a rendezvous depends on whether the caller or called task becomes abnormal.

If the caller in a rendezvous becomes abnormal, it does not become completed before the completion of the rendezvous. Therefore, the rendezvous completes normally and the called task is completely unaffected.

On the other hand, if the called task in a rendezvous is aborted, the exception Tasking_Error is raised in the calling task (at the point of entry call). The exception Tasking_Error is also raised at the point of call in any task that is queued for any entry of an aborted task. Finally, Tasking_Error is raised in any task that calls an entry of an abnormal task. (This includes conditional and timed entry calls.) For all three cases, the exception is raised no later than the completion of the aborted called task.

The value of the attribute Callable is False for any task that is either abnormal or completed.

The abort statement should be used under only the most extreme circumstances. A prefered method is to use a *shutdown* entry in cooperating tasks that are called. One alternative of a select statement could be the notification that the task's job is complete and it should terminate. This would look like:

```
...

select
  accept ...
or
  accept ...
or
  accept Shutdown;
  ... -- "last wishes"
end select;
```

The "last wishes" could also be completed while holding the caller in a rendezvous. It might even be reasonable to have a task that was otherwise a calling task to occasionally poll a shutdown entry as in:

```
...

select
  accept Shutdown;
  ... -- last wishes
else
  null;
end select;
```

A task that knows it is time to finish the job of some set of tasks could then call shutdown entries, perhaps enforcing the shutdown with a later abort of the tasks that have not terminated. For example:

```
...

select
  T1.Shutdown;
or
  delay 100.0;
  abort T1;
end select;
```

This provides T1 with an opportunity for a normal closedown, but enforces the shutdown in any event. The abort of a task that has already terminated has no effect. This use of abort, like any other use of abort, should be considered to be a major design decision, made only with approval of the lead designer on a team programming project.

12.2.4 Cooperative Termination

Cooperative termination of a number of tasks can be brought about through the use of the terminate alternative of the select statement. We have seen a number of examples of the use of the terminate alternative. Its general form is:

```
select
  accept ...
or
  accept ...
or
  terminate;
end select;
```

As we briefly discussed in previous chapters, one important thing to understand is what it *does not* mean. It does not mean that if there are no open alternatives in the select statement, or if there are no pending calls to open alternatives, then the task terminates. What the statement *does mean* is that a set of related tasks will cooperatively terminate under certain conditions.

If a task has reached a select statement with an open terminate alternative, it will terminate under the following conditions:

- The direct master of the task has completed its execution (hence is not a library package).

- All the task's children (its dependent tasks) have terminated or are waiting at a select statement with an open terminate alternative.

- All the task's siblings (the other tasks dependent upon the same master) have terminated or are waiting at a select statement with an open terminate alternative.

All the conditions must be satisfied. The second and third conditions can be summarized as the condition that all tasks dependent upon the same master are terminated or waiting at a select statement with an open terminate alternative. We state it as above in order to stress that both children and siblings are involved in the set of tasks.

Except for tasks in library packages, the effect of the definition of the above conditions is that all the tasks that are able to call each other's entries are dormant (terminated or waiting to be called) and hence can take no action—they are all blocked with no way to unblock. A consequence of this situation is that there are no current calls on entries of any of the related tasks, specifically including any alternatives of the select statement.

The "dormant" effect noted above is not true for tasks in library packages since they may (and typically will) be called by tasks dependent upon masters other than the library package itself. The language does not define termination of tasks in library packages, including whether they must terminate when the main program that caused the elaboration of the enclosing package has been left. Any implementation, however, may make use of the terminate alternative in tasks in such packages to make decisions regarding termination. Burns [BUR85, page 209] recommends; "These tasks should be coded to have terminate alternatives in their select statements ..." This is generally good advice and should be followed for *any* service task in a system that is expected to complete execution.

(Many real-time systems may have no need for a provision for termination. Further, although we have not usually been concerned with execution times for tasking constructs, we note that there is an execution time penalty paid for using terminate alternative in select statements [BAK85, BUR86].)

12.3 The Predefined Exception Tasking_Error

The purpose of this section is to describe the predefined exception Tasking_Error. It unifies the previous discussion of situations that cause this exception to be raised. Although there are some special circumstances under which the exception Tasking_Error is raised, the response of a program to Tasking_Error is the same as for any other exception.

Exceptions are errors or other abnormal (exceptional) situations that arise during program execution. The predefined exception Tasking_Error is raised in several circumstances, often related to calls made to tasks that are no longer able to service entries.

Tasking_Error is raised when exceptions arise during task creation or intertask communication. The possible situations are:

1. Tasking_Error is raised in a calling task (at the point of call) if the called task is:

    ▪ Completed, terminated, or abnormal at the time of call

    ▪ Becomes completed, terminated, or abnormal before accepting the entry call (and therefore the calling task is waiting in an entry queue)

    ▪ Becomes abnormal during the rendezvous

2. Tasking_Error is raised (immediately after the *begin* of the declarative part elaborating a task) if the task becomes completed during its activation as the result of an exception.

    The exception is not raised until all tasks being elaborated by this program unit have completed activation. If several tasks so become completed, Tasking_Error is raised only once. (Tasking_Error is *not* raised if the task being activated becomes completed as a result of being aborted.)

    Note: Cases 3 and 4 below deal with the use of pointers and the evaluation of allocators to create tasks. The topics are addressed here in order to unify the discussion of Tasking_Error. You may wish to refer to this material after reading Chapter 13.

3. Tasking_Error is raised at the point of evaluation of an allocator if the task object created by the allocator becomes completed during its activation as the result of an exception.

4. The final situation is an extension of Case 3 for the case in which the object created by the evaluation of the allocator is a record containing more than one task object and (perhaps) a non-task object with initialization. (This situation is very complex, but many of the subtleties will not be important in a practical

sense. They are detailed in the *Reference Manual for the Ada Programming Language* [ANS83] in order to provide a complete language definition.)

If an exception is raised during the initialization of the (one or more) nontask objects, the tasks designated by the task object components of the record become terminated (and hence never activated).

Otherwise (no exception during initialization), all tasks become activated. If one or more of these tasks are terminated during activation as the result of an exception, Tasking_Error is raised at the point of evaluation of the allocator. Tasks of the record that are not terminated during activation are not affected. However, their entries cannot be called since Tasking_ Error will have been raised prior to assignment of a value to the access object.

Note that these tasks cannot be *aborted* during activation since they do not have a name until after assignment is made to the pointer.

Keys to Understanding

- Termination of tasks is defined in terms of the master of a task. A master is the task that creates a task, called a dependent task.

- A master may not leave until its dependent tasks have terminated. Particularly, a task may not terminate until its dependent tasks have terminated.

- A task may terminate as a result of completion of execution (including after an exception), being aborted, or cooperative termination with a terminate alternative. Once terminated, a task is never reactivated.

- Unhandled exceptions during a rendezvous are propagated both to the calling task and the body of the called task after the end of the accept statement.

- Other unhandled exceptions (not in a rendezvous) have no effect other than causing the task to become completed. The exception is not propagated.

- The consequences of the abort statement are quite severe; it should be used only in the most exceptional circumstances.

- The terminate alternative in a select statement is useful; it should often be used to provide for termination of serivce tasks.

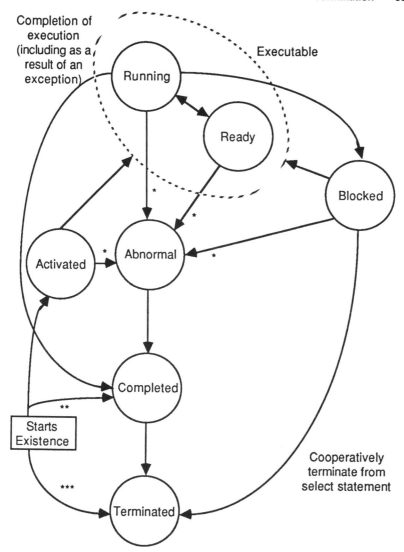

* Aborted
** Exception during elaboration of declarative part of task body
*** Exception during elaboration of master

Figure 12-2. States and transitions from activated to terminated

- The predefined exception Tasking_Error is raised in several different contexts related to intertask communication.
- Figure 12-2 summarizes states and transitions from "activated" to "terminated." It makes use of information (but does not repeat details of) Figures 1-1 and 12-1.

Pointers to Task Objects

> Objective: To describe the effect of creating an
> object that is a pointer to a task

We can create a task by using an allocator to provide an access
value to an appropriate pointer. The pointer, or access object, references or points to the created task. This method of creating a task
has important implications for activation/execution, termination,
and task interaction. The sections below describe the idea of using a
pointer to a task, and then provide a simple example of an "agent
task."

13.1 Pointers to Tasks

The basic idea of creating a task object with an allocator and then
referencing it through a pointer is the same as using a pointer to
reference any other object. The steps are:

1. Define a task type.
2. Define an access type.

3. Define an access object (the pointer).

4. Use an allocator to:

-   Create the task object.

-   Assign an access value (a reference or pointer) to the access object.

5. Call an entry in the task (if applicable).

6. Be sure to distinguish between the task object and the pointer to the task object.

A simple example of the six steps is:

1. Define a task type:

```
task type Mailbox is
    entry Store    (Message : in  Message_Form);
    entry Retrieve (Message : out Message_Form);
end Mailbox;
```

2. Define an access type:

```
type Reference_Mailbox is access Mailbox;
```

3. Define an access object (the pointer):

```
Clerk : Reference_Mailbox;
```

4. Use an allocator:

```
Clerk := new Mailbox;
```

5. Call an entry in the task:

```
Clerk.Store (Letter);
```

6. Distinguish between the task object and the pointer (see Figure 13-1).

If we again execute

```
Clerk := new Mailbox;
```

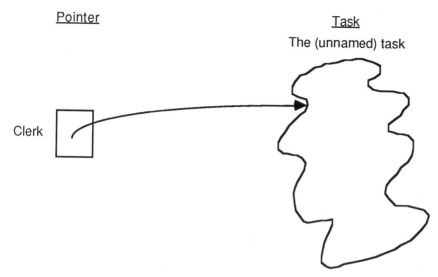

Figure 13-1. Pointer to a task

then Clerk points to a new and different task, as shown in Figure 13-2.

The original task continues to execute even though its entries can no longer be called. The task is still considered to be accessible until it terminates. It could, for example, obtain or deliver data by calls to entries in other tasks.

The attributes 'Callable and 'Terminated are available for tasks created through the use of allocators. We must use the designator ".all" to establish the task object to which the attribute applies. For example,

```
if Clerk.all'Callable then  ... end if;
```

is true if the task Clerk is callable. We must, however, be careful with this attribute. Between the time we query the attribute and the time we make the call, Clerk may reach a state where it is no longer callable. This was discussed in Chapter 12, Termination.

We have been saying that the pointer (such as Clerk) points to the task. If we wish to be completely precise, we should say that Clerk designates a task object (unnamed), while the task object designates the task. For convenience, we will continue to use the shorter phrase that Clerk points to the task.

Now we can put the above code fragments into a complete program to illustrate the master of the task, and to discuss important activation and termination issues.

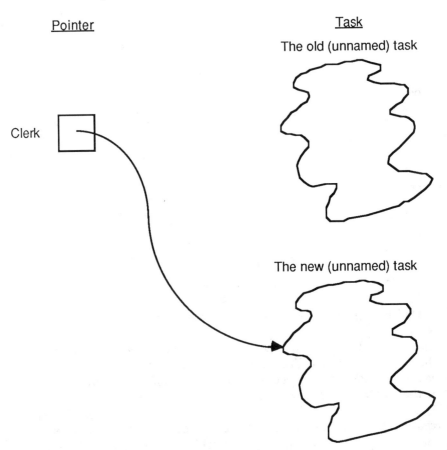

Pointer   Task

The old (unnamed) task

Clerk

The new (unnamed) task

Figure 13-2. Pointing to a new task

```
procedure Master is
   task type Mailbox is
      entry Store    (Message : in  Message_Form);
      entry Retrieve (Message : out Message_Form);
   end Mailbox;                  ------------------------------------- 1

   type Reference_Mailbox is access Mailbox;   ----------- 2
   Clerk : Reference_Mailbox;                  ------------- 3

   Non_Pointer_Task : Mailboox;                ------------- 4

   task body Mailbox is
      ...
   end Mailbox;                  ------------------------------------- 5
```

```
begin -- Master
   Clerk := new Mailbox;                        -------------- 6

   Inner_Block:
   declare
      Another_Clerk : Reference_Mailbox;        -------------- 7

      type Inner_Reference_Mailbox is access Mailbox;   ------ 8
      Inner_Clerk_1 : Inner_Reference_Mailbox;          ------ 9
      Inner_Clerk_2 : Inner_Reference_Mailbox := new Mailbox; -- 10
   begin -- Inner_Block
      Another_Clerk := new Mailbox;             -------------- 11
      Inner_Clerk_1 := new Mailbox;             -------------- 12
   end Inner_Block;                             -------------- 13
   -- other statements ...
end Master;                                     ---------------------- 14
```

The basic rule for determining the master of a task is:

Master of a Task: The master of a task created by the evaluation of an allocator (as at points 6, 10, 11, and 12) is the program unit that elaborates the definition of the access type (as at 2 and 8) for the task. Notice that it is not the creation of the task itself that causes a program unit to be a master. Neither is it the elaboration of the task type (as at 1), nor the elaboration of the pointer (as at 3, 7, 9, and 10) that causes a program unit to be a master. It is the elaboration of the access type that causes a program unit to be a master. This occurs at points 2 and 8.

The important fact to remember about activation of tasks created by allocators is:

Activation Rule: Tasks created through access types begin activation immediately upon evaluation of the allocator. This is so even if the evaluation occurs as part of an initial value (as at point 10). The activation of the task does not wait for the "begin" of the enclosing program unit, but commences immediately.

The usual rules prevail for masters; a block or subprogram body is not left until all its dependent tasks have terminated, and a task may not terminate until all its dependent tasks have terminated. Let's look at the procedure Master in order to investigate the effect of the termination rules. We will have to determine the master of each of the tasks that have been created.

The master of the tasks referenced by Clerk and Another_Clerk is the procedure Master. The master of the tasks referenced by Inner_Clerk_1 and Inner_Clerk_2 is Inner_Block. Therefore, the

Inner_Block must wait (at point 13) until the tasks referenced by Inner_Clerk_1 and Inner_Clerk_2 terminate.

However, despite the fact that Another_Clerk is declared within Inner_Block (and despite the fact that the task referenced by Another_Clerk is activated within the sequence of statements of Inner_Block), Inner_Block does not have to wait for the termination of the task referenced by Another_Clerk. This is true even though the pointer, Another_Clerk, will no longer be visible (in fact, will no longer exist) after the block is left, and there is, therefore, no way to call the task's entries. We say that the referenced task is "anonymous." This is usually bad practice.

Colloquialism: Remember that we are being a bit colloquial in saying "the task referenced by Another_Clerk." To be completely precise we should say "the task designated by the task object referenced by Another_Clerk." This seems unduly clumsy and we will therefore use the shorter phrase.

As expected, the procedure Master waits at point 14 for the termination of Clerk and Another_Clerk. Now let's look at each of the 14 points in the example above to discuss what is happening in relation to task activation and termination.

1. The task type definition is elaborated.

2. The first access type definition is elaborated.

3. A pointer is defined with the access type definition elaborated in Master [at (2)]. Tasks initially referenced by this pointer depend upon the procedure Master.

    This pointer may not have an initial value other than null. If we were to attempt to evaluate an allocator here, we would expect the task to begin execution (in accordance with the activation rule dicussed earlier). However, a task cannot activate until after the elaboration of the body of the task.

4. Non_Pointer_Task is of type Mailbox. It is included here to show that we can mix tasks of this type with tasks created by the use of allocators. It will begin execution after the elaboration of the declarative part of Master in the manner explained in Chapter 11.

5. Now the body of the task type Mailbox is elaborated. Tasks of the type, including those referenced by pointers, are now eligible for activation.

    The definition of the task body was required to follow the pointer and object definitions at (3) and (4). This is in accordance with the usual Ada rules for order of declarations in a declarative part. The implication of this is that pointers to tasks [such as at (3)] that are declared in the same declarative part may not be used to activate tasks as part of their initialization.

6. A task is created and immediately begins execution. It depends upon Master.

7. A second pointer is defined with the access type definition elaborated in Master. Tasks initially referenced by this pointer depend upon the procedure Master.

8. A second access type definition is elaborated. This is a different type than Reference_Mailbox.

9. A pointer is defined with the access type definition elaborated in Inner_Block [at (8)]. Tasks initially referenced by this pointer depend upon the Inner_Block.

10. Same as (9), plus a task is created as part of the initialization of the pointer. The task immediately begins execution.

11. The task begins execution. It does not depend upon Inner_Block.

12. The task begins execution. It depends upon Inner_Block.

13. Inner_Block waits only for the Inner Clerks, not for Another_Clerk. When the block is left, the task referenced by Another_Clerk is anonymous (bad practice).

14. The procedure waits for termination of Clerk and Another_Clerk (and the Non_Pointer_Task).

13.2 An Agent Task

We refer to a task created by the evaluation of an allocator and intended to act on behalf of the creating task as an "agent." This section uses the task Mailbox to uncouple a serving task from a user task. We will make the example specific by illustrating the server task as a "code room" that encrypts (or encodes) a message, while the user task is a "message center" that uses the code room to encrypt a message that is later to be transmitted.

We first complete the definition of the mailbox by providing its task body.

```
task type Mailbox is
   entry Store    (Message : in  Message_Form);
   entry Retrieve (Message : out Message_Form);
end Mailbox;
```

```
task body Mailbox is
  Box : Message_Form
begin
  accept Store    (Message : in  Message_Form) do
    Box := Message;
  end Store;

  accept Retrieve (Message : out Message_Form) do
    Message := Box;
  end Retrieve;
end Mailbox;
```

Now we need an access type for the definition of pointers to a Mailbox task.

```
type Mailbox_Access is access Mailbox;
```

The task that will encrypt the message (the serving task) accepts a message for encryption and also a pointer to a mailbox where the encrypted message will be left.

```
task Code_Room is
  entry Encrypt (Message      : in Message_Form;
                 Message_Slot : in Mailbox_Access);
  -- Calls
    -- Message_Slot.Store
end Code_Room;

task body Code_Room is
  Message      : Message_Form;
  Message_Slot : Mailbox_Access;
begin
  loop
    accept Encrypt (Message      : in Messge_Form;
                    Message_Slot : in Mailbox_Access) do
      Code_Room.Message      := Encrypt.Message;
      Code_Room.Message_Slot := Encrypt.Message_Slot;
    end Encrypt;

    -- encrypt the message, leaving it in
    -- the same format, then ...
```

```
      Message_Slot.Store (Message);
    end loop;
  end Code_Room;
```

The code room takes a message and the address of a mailbox to be used for the return of the encrypted message. When it is done with its work, it places the message in the user's mailbox and prepares to service the next client. There are several advantages to this approach. They are:

1. The user and server are only loosely coupled. They can operate concurrently during the encryption of the message, and do not need to rendezvous again for the return of the message. An alternate approach might be for the server to return the encrypted message by calling an entry in the user, but then the user would have to be known to the server—a very limiting arrangement in terms of reusability. Even if the user only passed a pointer to itself (this can be done), the users would be limited to tasks of a specific type. This would severely limit the generality and reusability of the code room. The approach illustrated above allows the server to be used by a wide variety of different types of user tasks, including those that have no entries at all.

2. The user does not have to wait for service. An alternate approach would be to hold the user in the rendezvous while the message was encrypted. The message would then be an "in out" parameter to the entry call, the tasks would be tightly coupled together, and the opportunities for concurrent execution would be reduced.

3. The server does not have to give a receipt to the user. An alternate approach is to have the server provide a receipt to the user, to be presented when calling for the return of the encrypted message. (The receipt is necessary to ensure that the correct user receives the encrypted message.) This is an alternative approach that uncouples the task interaction, but is somewhat more complicated in terms of ensuring that the receipt is secure, determining what to do if a faulty receipt is presented, and other factors.

The three approaches, hold in rendezvous, give receipt, and take address of agent task, are explored further as part of the series of Cobbler problems.

We have indicated that many different kinds of users may take advantage of the service of the code room. Let's look at a typical sort of interaction. The message center uses the capability of the code room by:

```
task Message_Center is
  -- Calls
    -- Code_Room.Encrypt
    -- Message_Slot.Retrieve
end Message_Center;

task body Message_Center is
  Message      : Message_Form;
  Message_Slot : Reference_Mailbox;
begin
  -- create the message, then ...

  Message_Slot := new Mail_Box; -- point to a new mailbox
  Code_Room.Encrypt (Message, Message_Slot); -- start the
                                             -- encryption
  -- do other work, then ...
  Message_Slot.Retrieve (Message); -- retrieve the encrypted
                                   -- message
  -- send the message
end Message_Center;
```

The message center creates a message by any appropriate method, creates its "agent" task (pointing to the task with Message_Slot), and calls the code room with the message and the address of its agent. While the message is being encrypted and placed in the mailbox, the message center does other work. It then calls the appropriate entry in its agent to obtain the encrypted message. As shown, it waits unconditionally for the message. An alternative is to:

```
loop
  select
    Message_Slot.Retrieve (Message);
  else
    -- do other work
  end select;
end loop;
```

Although we always want to be careful of polling solutions, it is reasonable here if there is a significant amount of "other work" to be accomplished. At least we can be certain that the agent is not doing something else while we are trying to call it; once it stores the encrypted message it does nothing but wait for a call from the message center.

Cobbler_12 presents a complete program using the model of task interaction using an agent, described above.

The agent described so far is of the form "buffer." The message center must call an entry in its agent. Another alternative, if the message center needs to wait for interaction with other tasks at the same time that it waits for its agent, is to make the message center a called task while the agent is the caller. If this is done with a single task (making the agent a single task relay), the agent becomes specific to Message_Center and therefore limits the generality of the code room. As is so often the case, we can gain more generality by the introduction of another intermediary. The use of two agents, one a buffer and the other a transporter (effectively making a relay), gives the ability for the message center to be a called task while maintaining the generality of the original solution. This alternative is explored in Cobbler_15.

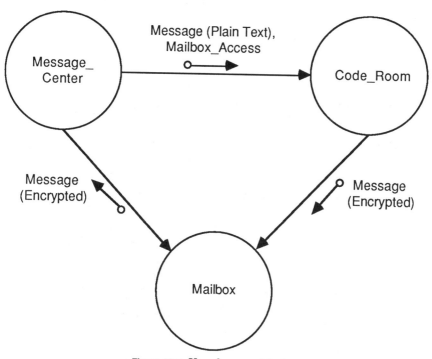

Figure 13-3. Use of an agent task

The process graph for the task interaction is shown in Figure 13-3. Note that when using an agent task we use the name of the task type on the process graph. Although we have used the name "Message_Slot" consistently in the example, an agent task might well have different names in each of the tasks using its services.

Exercises

Work the exercises Cobbler_12 through Cobbler_15.

Keys to Understanding

- Ada provides for dynamically created tasks.
- Dynamically created tasks are dependent upon the program unit that elaborates the access type definition and are activated immediately upon evaluation of the allocator.
- Agent tasks can be used to provide service for their creators, and can support a method of loosely coupled task communication.

14

Case Three: Message Transmission System (MTS)

Objective: To illustrate an important model of client-server task interaction in the context of a message processing environment

This case study illustrates the use of a receipt to ensure that a client requesting service is the only process that is able to later obtain the product of that service. The general model of task interaction that has been illustrated by the cobbler problems should help you begin the formulation of a solution to this problem.

14.1 Software Requirements Specification

The Message Transmission System (MTS) consists of a communication center and a facility for transmission of messages. Figure 14-1 illustrates the MTS situation.

The communication center accepts messages from customers (providing a receipt for each message that may be transmitted), stores

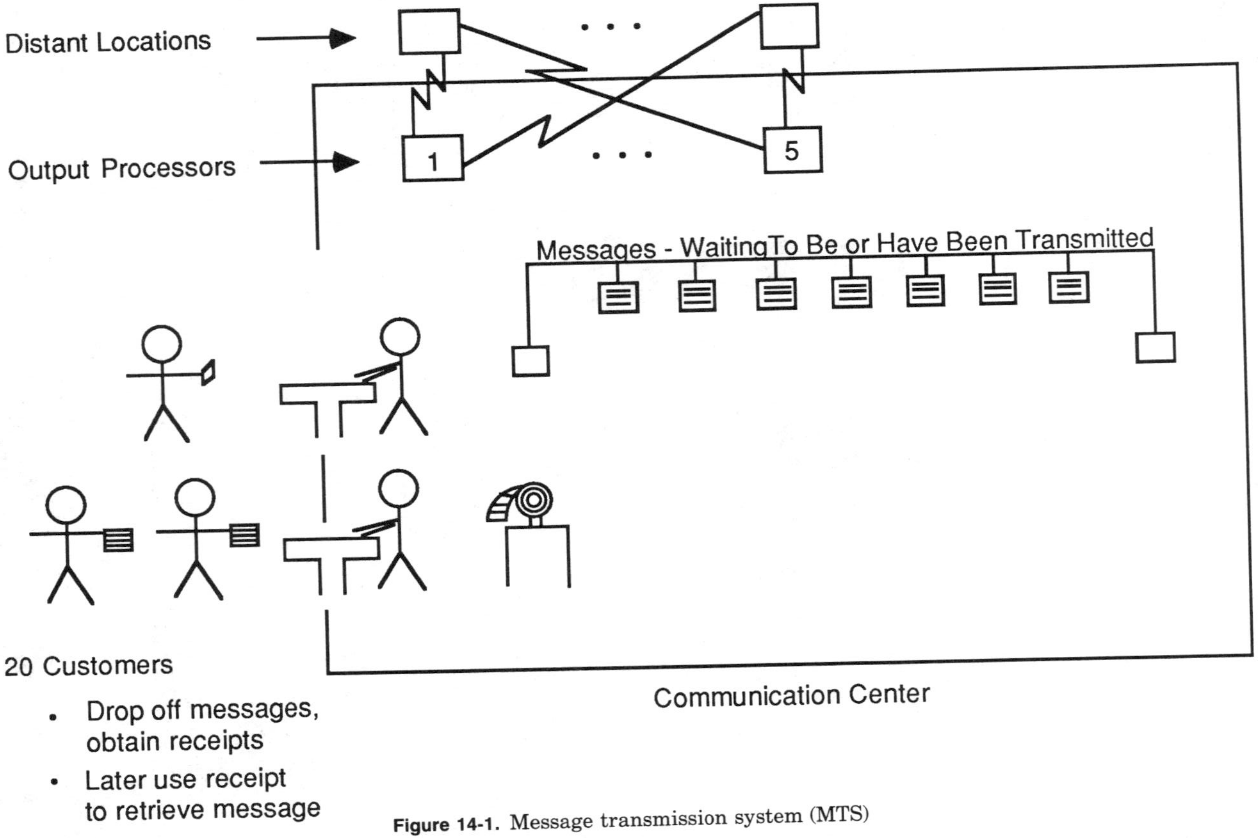

Figure 14-1. Message transmission system (MTS)

Distant Locations

Output Processors

Messages - Waiting To Be or Have Been Transmitted

Communication Center

20 Customers

- Drop off messages, obtain receipts
- Later use receipt to retrieve message

the messages until ready for transmission, and uses the separate facility for transmitting the message text. A copy of the message text is returned to the customer when he calls back (with the proper receipt) to retrieve it.

This case study does not include design of the customers or the transmission facility. The MTS environment will include a package specification for the transmission facility. You should create a skeleton customer to interact with the MTS itself. It should at least issue calls to the interfaces provided by the communication center. Additional detail of the MTS-customer interaction is provided below.

The customers create the messages, provide them to the communication center, and later return to retrieve the message. The customer is not to be kept waiting, either when delivering a message to the communication center or when retrieving a message.

When the customer arrives to deliver a message, he may be informed that the communication center is full (no additional room to store messages). When the customer arrives to pick up a message, he may be informed that the message is not ready, i.e., there has not yet been any attempt to transmit the message. In these two cases, the customer goes away and presumably tries again later.

Some messages will fail in transmission (i.e., not arrive at their destination) as a result of failure of the communication lines in the separate transmission facility. The transmission facility makes several attempts to transmit the message, then gives up. Such a message is considered undeliverable by the communication center and ios to be assigned the status *unable to deliver*.

If the message is successfully transmitted, the *has been sent* version is returned to the customer. The *has been sent* version is a copy of the text of the message exactly as transmitted. (Sometimes this differs in minor detail from the original text as a result of processing in the communication center.)

The transmission facility informs the communication center whether or not the message was successfully transmitted.

In accordance with the various possibilities for messages described above, a message may have one of three classifications of status: *new message*, *has been sent*, or *unable to deliver*. A message is considered by the communication center to consist of two elements: the message text and a status as just described.

For simplicity, we will use messages containing text of a fixed length of 10 characters. The text of the message specifies the location to which the message is to be transmitted.

The customer receives a receipt from the message center when he or she drops off a message, and uses the receipt to later pick up the message, either the original text (if the communication center was unable to deliver the message) or the has *been sent version* (if it was successfully transmitted). The message status tells the customer which type of message text he or she is given.

The communication center does not want to transmit duplicate messages, and refuses service to the customer if the status is other than *new message*.

The communication center has a number of identical output processes (presumably assigned to separate output processors), taking and returning messages through interaction with a buffer of messages. When the buffer is full, the communication center refuses service. There are 5 output processors, 20 customers, and a buffer of size 1000 for the messages.

14.2   MTS Environment

Figure 14-2a is a context diagram for the MTS. The communication center accomplishes the actual transmission of the message through use of the following package:

```
package Transmission_Facility is
   procedure Send (Message : in out String);
   Not_Transmitted : exception;
end Transmission_Facility;
```

The procedure Send accomplishes all necessary processing, including determining where to send the message. The exception indicates whether or not the message was successfully transmitted. If the exception is not raised, the first parameter returns the *has been* sent version of the message.

Figure 14-2b shows the context of the MTS including the services of the Transmission_Facility.

14.3   Top-Level Design

As usual, we first present the graphical design, followed by the package specifications.

14.3.1   Graphical Design

The next level of decomposition after the context diagram is fairly straightforward, with the Ada design closely following the natural concurrency of the problem statement. The process graph is shown in Figure 14-3. There is necessarily a task for each of the transmitters and each of the customers, and we introduce a *clerk* task to

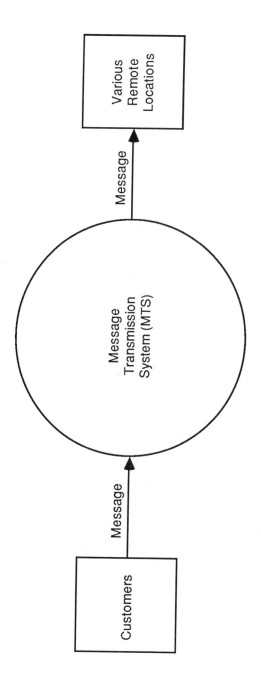

Figure 14-2a. MTS context diagram

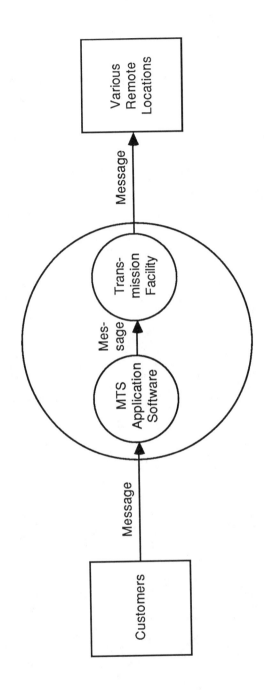

Figure 14-2b. MTS context diagram + transmission facility

serve as an intermediary between the customers and the transmitters. The clerk is a called (passive, or server) task, while the customers and transmitters are callers (active tasks). The design of the clerk is by far the largest part of the case study.

We don't know how Transmission_Facility is implemented, but we will show it as a task in order to discuss its functioning in a minispec.

This section presents minispecifications for:

- Clerk
- Transmitter
- Transmission_Facility
- Customer

Minispecifications for the MTS

Although there are multiple customers and transmitters, they are all identical in terms of functions performed. The discussions below present the functions for each (i.e., an individual) customer and transmitter.

Clerk

The clerk takes messages from customers and passes jobs (each job containing one message) to a transmitter for transmission.

The clerk provides the customer a receipt for the message. (Actually, the customer always has the receipt. He provides a receipt, presumably unmarked, to the clerk. The clerk marks it in a secret manner, that the clerk can read but the customer cannot.) The receipt is a message number that provides a reference so that the clerk can associate the receipt with a message.

The clerk stores messages, in first-in–first-out priority, until a transmitter calls for a message. The message is given (as part of a job) to a transmitter. The job is later accepted and stored when returned by the transmitter. (The other part of the job is the message number.)

The clerk returns the message when a customer calls with a proper receipt.

The following exceptions may be raised when a customer delivers a message:

- Receipt_Is_In_Use: Raised when the receipt has already been marked by the clerk, i.e., it was not unmarked (as it should be)

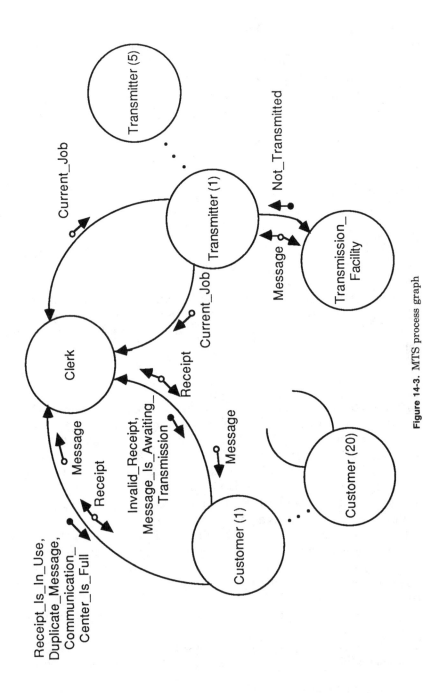

Figure 14-3. MTS process graph

- Duplicate_Message: Raised when the status of the message is other than *new message*

- Communication_Center_Is_Full: Raised when the communication center has no room to store additional messages prior to their transmission

The following exceptions may be raised when a customer picks up a message:

- Invalid_Receipt: Raised when the receipt is invalid, i.e., it has not been marked by the clerk and, therefore, does not correspond to any message

- Message_Is_Awaiting_Transmission: Raised when the clerk is still storing the message before it has been picked up by a transmitter

Transmitter

The transmitter picks up a job from the clerk and passes the associated message to Transmission_Facility. The transmitter waits (blocks) while the message is being sent. Upon completion of action of Transmission_Facility, transmitter sets the message status to *has been sent*. However, if the Not_Transmitted exception is raised, the normal processing (of setting the message status to *has been sent*) is not accomplished and instead the exception handler is executed. The handler sets the status to *unable to deliver*. The transmitter returns the competed job to the clerk. The transmitter blocks on calls to the clerk when there is no work to be done, or when the clerk is busy with other processing.

Transmission_Facility

We are not concerned with the internals of this process, except that it either successfully sends (transmits) the message or not. If it cannot send the message, it raises the exception Not_Transmitted. The transmission facility attempts to send the message a number of times before it concludes that it is unable to transmit.

Customer

The customer creates messages and delivers them to the clerk for transmission, obtaining a receipt to be used for later pickup of the message. For this case study, we are not much concerned with the internal processing of the customer.

14.3.2 Package Specifications

We will choose to package the Clerk and the Transmitters together as a package of services for the Customer. The resulting package will be called the Communication_Center. The Customers will be placed in the package Customers, while the Transmission_Facility package will be as discussed in the MTS environment.

This section presents the specifications for:

- Communication_Center
- Transmission_Facility
- Customer

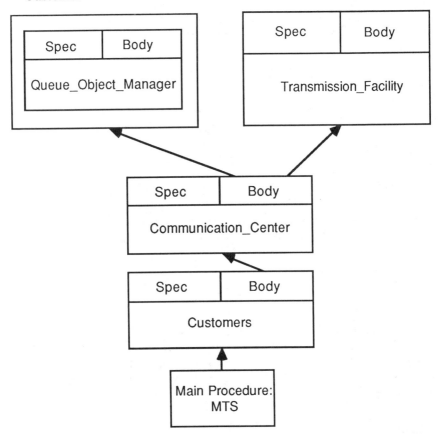

Figure 14-4. MTS dependency graph

Their relationship is shown in Figure 14-4. The Figure also shows the generic Queue_Object_Manager. The extra line around the border indicates that it is a generic package.

14.3.2.1 Communication_Center .

Abstract Algorithm:

```
----- Clerk -----

loop
  select
    accept delivery of a message
      raise an exception if:
        (1) the receipt is in use, or
        (2) the message status is not new message, or
        (3) the storage area for messages is full;
      provide a receipt, based on a message number;
      store the message, using the message number;
  or
    accept pick up a message by a customer
      raise an exception if:
        (1) the receipt is invalid, or
        (2) the message is still awaiting transmission;
      take the message out of storage,
              based on the message/receipt number;
      make the receipt invalid;
      return the message to the customer;
  or
    when there are jobs to be processed  =>
      accept get a job
        determine what message is next to be transmitted;
        take the message out of storage;
        build the job (message and message number);
        give the job to the calling transmitter;
  or
    accept return finished job
      return the message to storage, based on the message number;
  end select;
end loop;


----- Transmitter -----

loop
  get a job from the clerk;
  send the message text (in the job) to Transmission_Facility.Send;
```

```
  if Transmitted then
    change message status to has been sent;
  else
    change message status to unable to deliver;
  end if; -- (implemented by handling exception)

  return finished job to clerk;
end loop;
```

Specification:

```
package Communication_Center is
  Length_Of_Message : constant := 10;
  type Message_Status is (New_Message,
                          Has_Been_Sent,
                          Unable_To_Deliver);

  type Message_Form is
    record
      Text   : String (1 .. Length_Of_Message);
      Status : Message_Status;
    end record;

  type Receipt_Type is limited private;

  procedure Deliver_Message (Message : in Message_Form;
                             Receipt : in out Receipt_Type);
  procedure Pick_Up_Message (Receipt : in out Receipt_Type;
                             Message : out Message_Form);

  Receipt_Is_In_Use,
  Duplicate_Message,
  Invalid_Receipt,
  Communication_Center_Is_Full,
  Message_Is_Awaiting_Transmission : exception;

private
  Max_Number_of_Messages : constant := 1000;
  type Message_ID is range 1 .. Max_Number_of_Messages;
```

```
type Receipt_Type is
   record
      Number   : Message_ID;
      Assigned : Boolean := False;
   end record;
end Communication_Center;
```

14.3.2.2 Transmission_Facility.

Abstract Algorithm: Not needed.

Specification:

```
package Transmission_Facility is
   procedure Send (Message : in out String);
   Not_Transmitted : exception;
end Transmission_Facility;
```

14.3.2.3 Customers.

Abstract Algorithm:

```
loop
   create a message;
   deliver a message to the communication center;
   do other chores;
   pick up message from communication center;
end loop;
```

Note: At some point in the loop, either at the end or at the point of call to the entries of the communication center, handle the exceptions. It also looks at the message text (for *has been sent* messages) and decides whether or not to send them again.

For those messages that the communication center was unable to deliver, the customer must decide if they will be sent by other means or if the communication center should be tried again. If he wishes to attempt to send the message again, he must change the status back to *new message*.

We will not fully complete the design and code of the customer task in this case study, leaving it as an exercise. We will develop only a partial solution in order to demonstrate the interface with the Communication_Center.

Specification:

```
package Customers is
  -- Calls
    -- Communication_Center.Deliver_Message
    -- Communication_Center.Pick_Up_Message
end Customers;
```

14.4   Detailed Design

The emphasis continues to be on the design of the Communication_Center, especially the Clerk task. Figure 14-5 shows the overall structure of the MTS.

This section presents the detailed design for:

- Communication_Center (with tasks Clerk and Transmitter)

- Customers

14.4.1   Communication__Center

```
package body Communication_Center is
  Number_Of_Processors : constant := 5;

  type Job_Ticket is
    record
      Number  : Message_ID;
      Message : Message_Form;
    end record;

  task Clerk is
    entry Deliver_Message (Message : in Message_Form;
                           Receipt : in out Receipt_Type);
    entry Pick_Up_Message (Receipt : in out Receipt_Type;
                           Message :     out Message_Form);
    entry Get_A_Job          (Current_Job : out Job_Ticket);
    entry Return_Finished_Job (Current_Job :  in Job_Ticket);
  end Clerk;
```

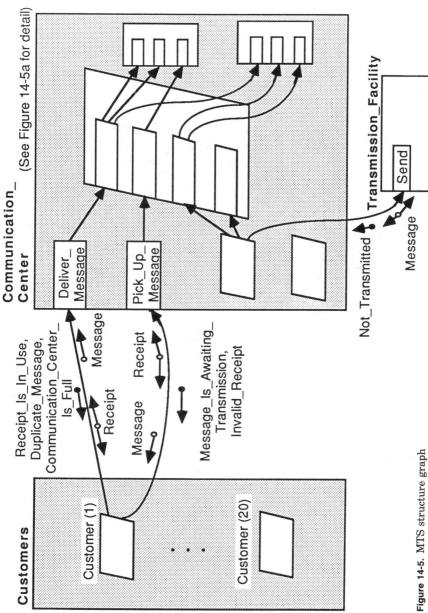

Figure 14-5. MTS structure graph

365

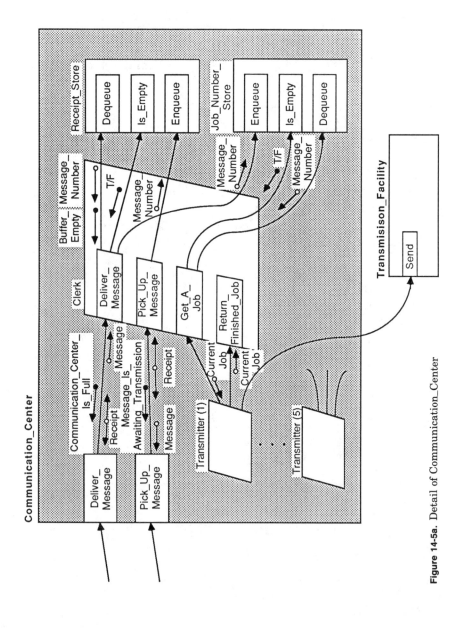

Figure 14-5a. Detail of Communication_Center

```
task type Transmitter_Type is
  -- Calls
    -- Clerk.Get_A_Job
    -- Transmission_Facility.Send
    -- Clerk.Return_Finished_Job
end Transmitter_Type;

Transmitter : array (1 .. Number_Of_Processors) of Transmitter_Type;

task body Clerk            is separate;
task body Transmitter_Type is separate;

procedure Deliver_Message (Message : in Message_Form;
                           Receipt : in out Receipt_Type) is
begin
  if Receipt.Assigned then
    raise Receipt_Is_In_Use;
  elsif Message.Status /= New_Message then
    raise Duplicate_Message;
  end if;

  Clerk.Deliver_Message (Message, Receipt);
  -- may raise Communication_Center_Is_Full
end Deliver_Message;

procedure Pick_Up_Message (Receipt : in out Receipt_Type;
                           Message :    out Message_Form) is
begin
  if not Receipt.Assigned then
    raise Invalid_Receipt;
  end if;

  Clerk.Pick_Up_Message (Receipt, Message); -- may raise
                               -- Message_Is_Awaiting_Transmission
  end Pick_Up_Message;
end Communication_Center;
```

We have chosen to raise three of the exceptions in the entrance procedures, rather than in the body of the Clerk task. This is a very close decision; we could well have raised the exceptions in the body of Clerk.

Let's look at the advantages of each of the alternatives.

The advantage to raising them in the body of Clerk is that the exceptions are raised all in the same place. (And the actual algorithm looks more like the abstract algorithm—which did not concern itself with detail such as an entrance procedure.)

On the other hand, the advantage to raising the exceptions in the entrance procedures is that we take action as soon as the information is available, rather than defering action for the sake of centralization. It seems that this decision is the more simple approach of the two; we choose the simple decision.

The general principle is that it is most simple to take action immediately when the information is available, rather than defer action until some later time.

Now that we have made that decision, we provide complete code in the entrance procedures so that the package bodies will be complete Ada.

Before we give the detailed design for the Clerk, it is useful to provide some explanation of the use of certain storage areas. The data structures for the storage areas themselves will not be defined until we present the code.

Message Storage: The task body contains a message storage area that holds the messages, both those awaiting transmission and those that have been transmitted.

The message storage area is accessed via indexes called message number, receipt number, and job ticket number. These are all equivalent names for messages, and are of type Message_ID

Receipt and Job Number Stores: The task body contains two additional storage areas: the receipt store and the job number store.

The receipt store is a FIFO buffer that contains objects of type Message_ID. These are message numbers, used as receipts. The receipt store holds the set of receipts that are ready for use. When it is empty, the communication center is full.

The job number store is a FIFO buffer that contains objects of type Message_ID. These are job numbers, used as message numbers. The job number store holds the set of jobs that are yet to be transmitted. (A job number is an index to where the message is stored in the message store.) When it is empty, the communication center has no work to do.

Use of the Receipt and Job Number Stores:

- When a message is delivered (in the entry Deliver_Message), a number is taken out of the receipt store, used to store the message, given to the customer as a receipt, and stored in the job number store.

- When a message is taken by a transmitter (in the entry Get_A_Job), the clerk takes the job number out of the job number store. The job number is used to determine which message is next to be transmitted. A *job* is built out of the message and the message number, and is given to the transmitter.

- When jobs are returned (in the entry Return_Finished_Job), the message is returned to the message storage.

- When a message is later picked up by a customer (in the entry Pick_Up_Message), the receipt number is returned to the receipt store.

```
----- separate Clerk -----

with Queue_Object_Manager; -- defined in chapter 7
separate (Communication_Center)
  task body Clerk is

    instantiate a package Receipt_Store
      as a new Queue_Object_Manager:
        the type of object to be queued is Message_ID
        the size of the buffer is Max_Number_of_Messages


    instantiate a package Job_Number_Store
      as a new Queue_Object_Manager:
        the type of object to be queued is Message_ID
        the size of the buffer is Max_Number_of_Messages
```

Note: Since the receipt and job number stores are internal to the task Clerk, they need not be of the monitor style; they do not need any protection against simultaneous access.

```
  begin
    initialize the receipt store;
    loop
      Handle_Exceptions_For_Select:
      begin
        select
          accept Deliver_Message (Message : in Message_Form;
                                  Receipt : in out Receipt_Type) do
```

```
        if receipt store is empty then
          raise Communication_Center_Is_Full;
        end if;

        get a message number from the receipt store;
        assign the number to the customer's receipt;
        store the message, using the number of the receipt;
      end Deliver_Message;
      store the receipt number in the job number store;
    or
      accept Pick_Up_Message (Receipt : in out Receipt_Type;
                              Message :    out Message_Form) do
        if the message is not ready then
          raise Message_Is_Awaiting_Transmission;
        end if;

        get the message from the message store,
                              using the receipt number;
        return the receipt number to the receipt store;
        invalidate the customer's receipt;
      end Pick_Up_Message;
    or
      when the job number store is not empty =>
        accept Get_A_Job (Current_Job : out Job_Ticket) do
          get the next message number from the job number store;
          get the next message from message storage,
                              using the message number;
          build a job from the message number and associated messag
        end Get_A_Job;
    or
      accept Return_Finished_Job (Current_Job : in Job_Ticket) do

        return the message to message storage, using the job number
      end Return_Finished_Job;
    end select;
```

```
        exception
          when either of the two locally raised exceptions =>
            do nothing;
          end Handle_Exceptions_For_Select;
      end loop;
  end Clerk;


----- separate Transmitter_Type -----

with Transmission_Facility;
separate (Communication_Center)
  task body Transmitter_Type is
    Current_Job : Job_Ticket;
  begin
    loop
      get a Current_Job from the clerk;

      Handle_Not_Transmitted:
      begin
        Transmission_Facility.Send (Current_Job.Message.Text);
        Current_Job.Message.Status := Has_Been_Sent;
      exception
        when Transmission_Facility.Not_Transmitted =>
          Current_Job.Message.Status := Unable_To_Deliver;
      end Handle_Not_Transmitted;

      return the Current_Job to the clerk;
    end loop;
  end Transmitter_Type;
```

Here we choose to write complete code for the call to Transmission_Facility and the logic to set the message status of the current job; it is clearer and more concise than a verbalization of the same information.

14.4.2 Customers

```
package body Customers is
  Number_Of_Customers : constant := 20;

  task type Customer_Type is
    -- Calls
      -- Communication_Center.Deliver_Message
      -- Communication_Center.Pick_Up_Message
  end Customer_Type;

  Customer : array (1 .. Number_Of_Customers) of Customer_Type;

  task body Customer_Type is separate;
end Customers;

with Communication_Center; use Communication_Center;
separate (Customers)
  task body Customer_Type is
  begin
    loop
      Handle_Exceptions:
      begin
        create a message;
        deliver the message to the communication center,
                                              obtaining a receipt;
        pick up the message from the communication center,
                                              using the receipt;
      exception
        when
          any of the exceptions raised by the communication center =>
            do whatever is necessary in each case;
      end Handle_Exceptions;
    end loop;
  end Customer_Type;
```

14.5 Code

This section presents the code for:

- Clerk
- Transmitter_Type

■ Customer_Type

14.5.1 Clerk

```
with Queue_Object_Manager;
separate (Communication_Center)
  task body Clerk is

    Message_Storage : array (Message_ID) of Message_Form;
    Message_Number  : Message_ID;

    -- Message_Storage contains the messages, both
    -- those awaiting transmission and those that have
    -- been transmitted.

    -- Message_Number, Receipt.Number, and Job_Ticket.Number are all
    -- equivalent names for messages, and are of type Message_ID

    package Receipt_Store is new Queue_Object_Manager
                      (Buffered_Type => Message_ID,
                       Buffer_Size   => Max_Number_of_Messages);

    -- Receipt_Store holds the set of receipts that are
    -- ready for use. When it is empty, the communication
    -- center is full.

    package Job_Number_Store is new Queue_Object_Manager
                      (Buffered_Type => Message_ID,
                       Buffer_Size   => Max_Number_of_Messages);

    -- Job_Number_Store holds the set of jobs that are yet to be
    -- transmitted. (A job is an index to where the message is
    -- stored in the message store.)  When it is empty, the
    -- communication center has no work to do.

    -- USE OF THE RECEIPT AND JOB NUMBER STORES:

    -- (1) When a message is delivered (entry Deliver_Message), a
    -- number is taken out of the
    -- receipt store, used to store the message, given to the customer
    -- as a receipt, and stored in the job number store.
```

```
-- (2) Transmitters take messages (entry Get_A_Job)
-- and transmit them. The clerk takes the job number
-- out of the job number store.

-- (3) Transmitted messages are returned by the
-- transmitters (entry Return_Finished_Job). The clerk returns the
-- message to the message storage.

-- (4) After a customer picks up the message,
-- (entry Pick_Up_Message), the number is returned to the
-- receipt store.

function Awaiting_Transmission (Message : Message_Form)
                                            return Boolean is
begin
   return Message.Status = New_Message;
end Awaiting_Transmission;
begin -- Clerk
  Initialize_The_Receipt_Store:
  for I in Message_ID loop
    Receipt_Store.Enqueue (I);
  end loop Initialize_The_Receipt_Store;

  loop
    Handle_Exceptions_For_Select:
    begin
      select
        accept Deliver_Message (Message : in Message_Form;
                                Receipt : in out Receipt_Type) do

          Handle_Empty_Receipt_Store:
          begin
            Receipt_Store.Dequeue (Message_Number);

            Message_Storage (Message_Number) := Message;

            Receipt := (Number   => Message_Number,
                        Assigned => True);
```

```
              exception
                when Receipt_Store.Buffer_Empty =>
                  raise Communication_Center_Is_Full;
                end Handle_Empty_Receipt_Store;
              end Deliver_Message;

          Job_Number_Store.Enqueue (Message_Number);
        or
          accept Pick_Up_Message (Receipt : in out Receipt_Type;
                                  Message :     out Message_Form) do

              if Awaiting_Transmission
                          (Message_Storage (Receipt.Number)) then
                raise Message_Is_Awaiting_Transmission;
              end if;

              Message := Message_Storage (Receipt.Number);
              Receipt_Store.Enqueue (Receipt.Number);
              Receipt.Assigned := False;
            end Pick_Up_Message;
        or
          when not Job_Number_Store.Empty =>
            accept Get_A_Job (Current_Job : out Job_Ticket) do

              Job_Number_Store.Dequeue (Message_Number);

              Current_Job := (Number  => Message_Number,
                              Message => Message_Storage
                                         (Message_Number));
            end Get_A_Job;
        or
          accept Return_Finished_Job (Current_Job : in Job_Ticket) do

              Message_Storage (Current_Job.Number) := Current_Job.Message;
            end Return_Finished_Job;
          end select;
        exception
          when Communication_Center_Is_Full |
               Message_Is_Awaiting_Transmission   => null;
        end Handle_Exceptions_For_Select;
      end loop;
  end Clerk;
```

The Queue_Object_Manager is the same generic procedure that we saw earlier in Chapter 7. Once we understand such abstractions, we can freely use them as though they are part of the language—without constantly repeating the explanation of the abstraction.

In the accept Deliver_Message, we take advantage of the fact that the Receipt_Store abstraction raises an exception when it is empty. We handle the exception by raising the proper exception for the specific case of the communication center. An alternate approach is to explicitly check for the empty condition in the receipt store. That is,

```
accept ... do
  if Receipt_Store.Empty then
    raise Communication_Center_Is_Full;
  end if;

  Receipt_Store.Dequeue (Message_Number);
  Message_Storage (Message_Number) := Message;
  Receipt := (Number   => Message_Number,
              Assigned => True);
end ...
```

Either method is good practice. What *is important* is that the task does something explicit that results in the raising of the exception exported by the Communication_Center. What *must not* be done is to simply propagate the exception Receipt_Store.Buffer_Empty to the customer. This exception is not visible there and could only be handled by an exception handler with an "others" alternative.

14.5.2 Transmitter_Type

```
with Transmission_Facility;
separate (Communication_Center)
  task body Transmitter_Type is
    Current_Job : Job_Ticket;
  begin
   loop
     Clerk.Get_A_Job (Current_Job);

     Handle_Not_Transmitted:
     begin
       Transmission_Facility.Send (Current_Job.Message.Text);

       Current_Job.Message.Status := Has_Been_Sent;
```

```
    exception
      when Transmission_Facility.Not_Transmitted =>
        Current_Job.Message.Status := Unable_To_Deliver;
      end Handle_Not_Transmitted;

    Clerk.Return_Finished_Job (Current_Job);
  end loop;
end Transmitter_Type;
```

14.5.3 Customer__Type

```
with Communication_Center; use Communication_Center;
separate (Customers)
  task body Customer_Type is
    Message : Message_Form;
    Receipt : Receipt_Type;

    procedure Create_A_Message (Message : out Message_Form)
                                            is separate;
  begin
    loop
      Handle_Exceptions:
      begin
        Create_A_Message (Message);
        Communication_Center.Deliver_Message (Message, Receipt);
        Communication_Center.Pick_Up_Message (Receipt, Message);
      exception
        when
          Receipt_Is_In_Use             |
          Duplicate_Message             |
          Invalid_Receipt               |
          Communication_Center_Is_Full  |
          Message_Is_Awaiting_Transmission =>
            null; -- or do whatever is necessary
                  -- in each case
      end Handle_Exceptions;
    end loop;
  end Customer_Type;
```

14.6 Discussion

Basically, this is not a very complex problem. The factors that make it interesting, and add to its complexity, are the use of the receipt and the fact that there are multiple transmitters being used. The former issue raises questions of security of the receipt. The latter issue, in conjunction with the use of the receipt to allow a drop-off/pick-up type of service, calls for careful design of the clerk.

We have made the type of the receipts to be limited private. This gives the communication center complete control over the receipts. Since they cannot be modified, a receipt that is assigned is known to be valid and associated with a message. Since a receipt cannot be copied, there is no danger of a wayward customer keeping a copy of the receipt, presenting it at some later time to obtain some other customer's message.

Most of the complexity of the problem is embodied in the Clerk task. Let's review its processing by looking at what is accomplished by each of the entries.

- Deliver_Message: Raises an exception (and does nothing else) if there is no storage room left in the communication center; gets the number of a storage slot and marks it on the customer's receipt; stores the message for later use.

- Pick_Up_Messages: Raises an exception (and does nothing else) if the message is not ready; returns the message to the customer; invalidates the receipt and indicates that the storage location is empty (i.e., the receipt number is available for reuse).

- Get_A_Job: Gives the caller a job to do, based on the next message due to be transmitted (a job consisting of a message and a message number).

- Return_Finished_Job: Uses the message number in the job to return the processed message to the message storage.

The key factor that makes the task interaction complex is the fact that we wish to allow the customer to leave something, go away (and process asynchronously), and return later for a result—a result that is related to what is dropped off. We certainly would not want to return messages to different customers than delivered them to the communication center.

An alternative to the receipt (but involving an extra task for each message) is shown in the exercises.

14.7 Exercises

Exercise 14.1. Complete the design and code of the customer task.

Exercise 14.2. Change the protocol for the communication center/customer interaction so that the customer waits when the communication center is full, blocking until the message can be taken. Similarly, have the customer wait for a message that is not yet ready. Do not raise exception on duplicate message— just transmit again. This simplifies the interface; the only remaining exceptions are related to the use of the receipt.

Exercise 14.3. Give the customer the alternative of waiting or not, i.e., combine the original problem with the previous exercise.

Exercise 14.4. Use task types, task access types, and agents as discussed in Chapter 13 in order to provide for the customer-clerk interaction. This involves the use of an agent task as a mailbox. Start from the base solution of Exercise 14.2 rather than the original problem. This is solved below. (You might also use this approach with the original problem as the base solution.)

Exercise 14.5. Have the customer wait (not operate asynchronously) while the message is transmitted.

Exercise 14.6. Give the customer some significant alternative work to do that could be done concurrently with the message being transmitted.

Exercise 14.7. Simulate the Transmission Facility. Use the simulation and the customer from the previous problem to do timing studies on the alternative task interactions of the original problem, and on Exercises 14.4 and 14.5. Which is most efficient on your compiler/processor? Which task interaction is clearest?

Exercise 14.8. Work the remaining cobbler problem, Cobbler_16. Also think about the four additional problems posed at the end of Appendix B.

14.8 Partial Solutions to Exercises

Exercises 14.1–14.3 are not solved.

Solution 14.4 Use An Agent/Mailbox Task. This is essentially the approach of Cobbler_12. We will not provide much discussion. Here is the code for the Communication_Center.

The package body contains the definition of the access type to be used as a mailman. Much of the other interface information is no longer needed. The issue of raising exceptions related to checking receipts is avoided.

```
package Communication_Center is
   Length_Of_Message : constant := 10;

   type Message_Status is (New_Message,
                           Has_Been_Sent,
                           Unable_To_Deliver);

   type Message_Form is
      record
         Text   : String (1 .. Length_Of_Message);
         Status : Message_Status;
      end record;

   task type Mailbox is
      entry Store    (Message : in  Message_Form);
      entry Retrieve (Message : out Message_Form);
   end Mailbox;

   type Mailbox_Access is access Mailbox;

   procedure Deliver_Message (Message : in Message_Form;
                              Mailman : in Mailbox_Access);

   -- Calls
      -- Mailman.Store
end Communication_Center;
```

```
with Monitor_Queue; -- this must be of the monitor style
package body Communication_Center is

  -- the next declaration used to be in the private part
  Max_Number_of_Messages : constant := 1000;

  Number_Of_Processors : constant := 5;

  type Job_Type is
    record
      Message : Message_Form;
      Mailman : Mailbox_Access;
    end record;


    package Job_Store is new Monitor_Queue
                      (Buffered_Type => Job_Type,
                       Buffer_Size   => Max_Number_of_Messages);


  task type Transmitter_Type is
    -- Calls
    -- Job_Store.Dequeue
    -- Transmission_Facility.Send
    -- Mailman.Store
  end Transmitter_Type;

  Transmitter : array (1 .. Number_Of_Processors) of Transmitter_Type;

  task body Mailbox          is separate;
  task body Transmitter_Type is separate;

  procedure Deliver_Message (Message : in Message_Form;
                             Mailman : in Mailbox_Access) is
  begin
    Job_Store.Enqueue ((Message, Mailman));
  end Deliver_Message;
end Communication_Center;
```

The package body is considerably simpler than the earlier approaches since there is no need for the clerk. We put the storage in the package body so that it is available to all the transmitters. The generic buffer, Monitor_Queue, must now be of the style monitor in order to guard against simultaneous access.

Here is the type definition for the transmitters.

```
with Transmission_Facility;
separate (Communication_Center)
  task body Transmitter_Type is
    Current_Job : Job_Type;
  begin
    loop
      Job_Store.Dequeue (Current_Job);

      Handle_Not_Transmitted:
      begin
        Transmission_Facility.Send (Current_Job.Message.Text);

        Current_Job.Message.Status := Has_Been_Sent;

      exception
        when Transmission_Facility.Not_Transmitted =>
          Current_Job.Message.Status := Unable_To_Deliver;
      end Handle_Not_Transmitted;

      Current_Job.Mailman.Store (Current_Job.Message);
    end loop;
  end Transmitter_Type;
```

Here is the change to the customers. The only change required is to the body of the Customer task.

```
with Communication_Center; use Communication_Center;
separate (Customers)
  task body Customer_Type is
    Message : Message_Form;
    Mailman : Mailbox_Access; -- here is the mailman

    procedure Create_A_Message (Message : out Message_Form)
                                                is separate;
```

```
begin
  loop
      Create_A_Message (Message);

      Mailman := new Mailbox; -- now he points to a mailbox

      Communication_Center.Deliver_Message (Message, Mailman);

      Mailman.Retrieve (Message); -- gets the message
  end loop;
end Customer_Type;
```

The customers must wait (block) if the communication center is full, but can make their own decision about whether to wait for return of the message. The solution shown has the customer block on the agent until the message is ready, but the customer could just as well choose to poll the agent. You can review Cobbler_12 for additional discussion about this method of client-server task interaction.

Keys to Understanding

- The MTS case study illustrates that the task interactions discussed in the cobbler problems are applicable to typical situations that arise in the design and implementation of real-time systems.

- A key design decision was to have the clerk as the focal point to handle the interaction between customers and transmitters. It provided a single storage area for messages.

- Task types and arrays of tasks can be used conveniently to provide for multiple, nearly identical, processes.

- Pointers can be useful (Solution 14.4) to uncouple task interaction without the need for a receipt. The solution is less complex, but it requires an additional task.

Tasks in Real-Time Systems

Part 4 deals with low-level issues that are important for the construction of real-time systems. Although the book in general deals with concurrency in real-time systems, it is this part that addresses the specific features in Ada that allow implementation from the viewpoint of the systems programmer.

Chapter 15 introduces low-level issues in general, dealing with all aspects except interrupts. The case study in Chapter 16 uses some of the concepts, integrating buffer and generic topics from earlier chapters. Chapter 17 focuses exclusively on interrupts. It includes tutorial material, a presentation of interrupts in Ada, and some information about possible implementations. It is vital for the real-time programmer to understand how interrupts are implemented in Ada—both in general and how they are handled in the specific compiler being used to implement a real-time system. Chapter 18 is the final case study of the book. It uses aspects of the interrupt mechanism just introduced, but is also a "graduation exercise" in that it is somewhat more complex in its interaction with external devices and general task communication than are the earlier case studies.

Much of the material in this part is highly implementation-dependent, even more so than other aspects of tasking. It is of critical importance that you be well-versed in all details of the compiler that you are using for the implementation of real-time systems.

Notwithstanding the fact that you must be aware of the specifics of an implementation, an attractive feature of Ada is that almost all of the real-time programming can be done at a high level of abstraction, relative to machine-level issues. Certain parts of the Ada program will deal with machine addresses, interrupt structure, buffers at specific memory locations, and so on. However, most of the program need not be concerned with such detail. The Chapter 17 exercise to revise case study three to deal directly with the hardware illlustrates this point. Little need be changed to avoid the need for the "Executive Services" provided in the original case study.

15

Machine Level Issues

> Objective: To describe Ada features for interact-
> ing at a low level with the system
> hardware

Real-time systems require that the software interact with the external world through low-level interfaces with the system hardware.
Ada provides features for doing so, while retaining as much as possible the idea of a high-level, abstract interface.

The sections below describe the rationale for machine level or
low-level representations, methods of representing hardware features in Ada language constructs, unchecked programming,
implementation-dependent issues, and how the features described
are used for low-level input-output. The discussion is not meant to
be exhaustive; it introduces all the concepts in a general way, but
only provides detail for those aspects of low-level programming
required for later case studies.

Many of the details of machine level programming are implementation-defined. Information for such details is provided as appendix
F of the Ada language Reference Manual [ANS83] for a specific
compiler/processor.

15.1 Rationale for Machine Level Representations

Ada encourages an abstract view of objects; the important feature of an object is its type. The type defines:

- Allowable values for the object
- Allowable operations on the object

Development of real-time systems, and systems programming in general, requires the capability to stay close to the machine in terms of representation of the hardware. The abstract objects must map, on a bit-by-bit basis, to the representation specified by the hardware.

The resolution of the inherent imbalance between the abstract representation and the need to specify physical representations is the *separation principle* [ICH79, page 14-1].

The separation principle requires that type definitions be made in two steps:

1. *Logical properties* specify those aspects of a type needed by the programmer. All algorithms are written based on the logical properties.

2. *Representation properties* map data to physical implementations. The mapping may be by the compiler, or be controlled by the programmer.

The advantage of this distinction is that, to a very high degree, the program may be written only in terms of the abstract views of objects. In addition, the implementation-dependent aspects of the program are clearly specified—leading to improved portability.

The Rationale [ICH79, Chapter 14] amplifies on these concepts.

15.2 Representation Clauses

There are four classes of representation clauses:

- Length
- Enumeration
- Record
- Address

They are addressed below.

15.2.1 Length Clause

Purpose: To specify the amount of storage allocated for some entity

Example:

```
type Medium_Integer is range 0 .. 255;
for Medium_Integer'Size use 8;  -- bits
```

Example:

```
type Register_Type is array (0 .. 15) of Boolean;
for Register_Type'Size use 16;
```

The identifier following the "for" must be a type or subtype. The number following the "use" is the number of bits of storage allocated. The second example assumes a 1-bit representation of Boolean.

The length clause is more general than the simple example illustrates. Its general form is:

```
for representation_attribute use simple_expression;
```

For objects of:	The length clause specifies:
Task types	Upper bound for storage needed
Access types	Storage for all dynamically allocated objects of the type
Fixed point types	The representation of the smallest representable value

15.2.2 Enumeration Clause

Purpose: To specify the mapping of the value of the type to the internal codes used to represent the elements

Example:

```
type Week_Day is (Mon, Tue, Wed, Thu, Fri);
for  Week_Day use (Mon => 2, Tue => 3, Wed => 4,
                   Thu => 5, Fri => 6);
```

Example:

```
type Mix_Code is (ADD, SUB, MUL, LDA, STA, STZ);
for Mix_Code use (ADD => 1, SUB => 2,  MUL => 3,
                  LDA => 8, STA => 24, STZ => 33);
```

The second example is from the Ada Language Reference Manual [ANS83]. It illustrates that the representation of the enumeration values need not be contiguous. The attributes Succ, Pred, and Pos are defined for such types; they operate on the *logical* properties of the enumeration, independent of the enumeration representation clause. For example, Mix_Code'Succ (MUL) is LDA, and Mix_Code'Pos (STA) is 4, not 24.

15.2.3 Record Clause

Purpose: To specify the layout of components of a record type by providing their order, position, and size

Example: (Assume On_Off and Status_Level are defined as needing 1-bit.)

```
type Modes is range 0 .. 63;
for Modes'Size use 6;
type Control_Register is
  record
    Enable : On_Off;
    Mode   : Modes;
    Status : Status_Level;
  end record;

for Control_Register use
  record
    Enable at 0 range 0 .. 0;
    Mode   at 0 range 1 .. 6;
    Status at 0 range 7 .. 7;
  end record;
```

The "for ... use record ... end record" indicates the record representation. The value following the "at" clause is the location of a component in terms of *storage units*. A storage unit is the implementation-dependent unit of storage; for example, storage measured as 8-bit bytes or 16-bit words. Positions of components are first given as a numbered storage unit. Within the storage unit, the precise location is given as a bit range. Storage unit is given by each implementation as the named number System.Storage_Unit. Bit ordering within a storage unit is implementation-defined.

If it is important that a record be aligned on some multiple of storage units (for example, that the record start on even numbered storage units), you can give an *alignment clause* as "at mod 2" or "at mod 4" following the word "record." We will see an example of this later.

15.2.4 Address Clause

Purpose: To specify a required address in storage for an entity (or to associate an entry with an interrupt—see Chapter 17, Tasks as Interrupt Handlers)

Example:

```
Keyboard_Register : Control_Register;
for Keyboard_Register use at 8#177560#;
```

The Keyboard_Register will be located at the given octal address in memory. The location can be given as binary, hexidecimal, or any other base in the range 2 .. 16. The base is given before the "*#*".

The general form of the address clause is:

```
for simple_name use at simple_expression;
```

The simple name may be an object (variable or constant) as shown, or may be the name of a subprogram, package, or task unit. The address is that required for the placement of the machine code for the body of the unit.

The type of the simple_expression must be that of the implementation-defined System.Address.

15.3 Unchecked Programming

Ada provides for an "escape" from the strong typing mechanism to allow any variable to be interpreted as being of any type. This allows, for example, characters or access values to be interpreted as integers. This feature may be used to retain memory locations in an array for later access.

The generic procedure for accomplishing the unchecked conversion is:

```
generic
   type Source is limited private;
   type Target is limited private;
function Unchecked_Conversion (S : Source) return Target;
```

The function can be instantiated as:

```
function Character_To_Integer is new Unchecked_Conversion
                        (Source => Character;
                         Target => Integer);
```

Then for the following definitions,

```
I : Integer;
C : Character := Constant_Character;
```

the function is used as:

```
I := Character_To_Integer (C);
```

The bit pattern that is used to represent the character is interpreted as an integer. This is quite different from the use of the attribute Pos.

```
I := Character'Pos (C);
```

The assignment above gives the *position* of the character within its enumeration. It does not involve any unchecked conversion.

Ada also allows for unchecked deallocation of objects designated by access types. The generic procedure is:

```
generic
   type Object is limited private;
   type Name   is access Object;
procedure Unchecked_Deallocation (X : in out Name);
```

It is instantiated as:

```
A_Record is
  record
    ...
    ...
  end record;
```

```
type A_Record_Pointer is access A_Record;

procedure Free is new Unchecked_Deallocation
                  (Object => A_Record;
                   Name   => A_Record_Pointer);
```

If we have:

```
Employee : A_Record_Pointer;
```

and the use of an allocator as:

```
Employee := new A_Record;
... -- use Employee
```

then the call,

```
Free (Employee);
```

has the effect that the object designated by Employee is no longer required; the run-time environment is to reclaim the storage the object occupies.

An implementation is not required to do anything but *recognize* Unchecked_Deallocation; it is not required to actually reclaim the memory.

15.4   Implementation-Dependent Features

Much of the material in this chapter (and in Chapter 17, Tasks as Interrupt Handlers) is implementation-defined, implementation-dependent, and implementation-specific. There is a bit of *caveat emptor* to this. Know your compiler builder and know the specific implementation! (Actually, this is somewhat true of *all* the tasking issues.) The implementation-dependent features are defined in appendix F of the Ada Language Reference Manual [ANS83] for a specific compiler.

Appendix F contains information such as:

- Implementation-dependent pragmas and attributes
- Implementation-dependent input-output
- Restrictions on representation clauses
- The specification of package System

At a minimum, package System must contain the following specification.

```
package System is
   type Address is ...
   type Name    is ...

   System_Name  : constant Name := ...

   Storage_Unit : constant := ...
   Memory_Size  : constant := ...
   Min_Int      : constant := ...
   Max_Int      : constant := ...
   Max_Digits   : constant := ...
   Max_Mantissa : constant := ...
   Fine_Delta   : constant := ...
   Tick         : constant := ...
   ...
   subtype Priority is Integer range ...
   ...
end System;
```

The names are generally self-explanatory. Additional details are spelled out clearly in the language reference manual [ANS83, 13.7], and need no further explanation.

Many of the pragmas are also implementation-dependent. Some of the pragmas of interest to us for machine level programming are:

- Pragma Pack: Specifies that storage minimization is to be the main criterion for representing an array or record type.

- Pragma Suppress: Allows the compiler to eliminate run time checks that are designed to detect conditions that would give rise to exceptions. There are a variety of options with this pragma.

- Pragma Controlled: Forbids automatic storage reclamation.

- Pragma Optimize: Specifies time or space as highest priority for optimization.

- Pragma Inline: Suggests that subprograms should be expanded inline

- Pragma Priority: Specifies priority of tasks.

- Pragma Shared: Specifies that every read or update of a variable is a synchronization point.

- Pragma Interface: Provides for interface between Ada and other languages.

In addition, any implementation may have its own pragmas. Pragmas are not allowed to influence the *correctness* of a program, only its relative *efficiency*.

Ada allows for machine code insertions in the context of the language itself (using record aggregates of record types that define the instructions), and also allows for interface to assembly language routines. An implementation may provide machine-dependent pragmas and attributes regarding registers and calling conventions.

15.5 Machine Level Input-Output

There are two methods for handling machine level input-output (IO): use of the the standard package Low_Level_IO or association of program variables with specific machine addresses to accomplish memory-mapped IO. The paragraphs below briefly discuss Low_Level_IO, then provide examples of memory-mapped IO.

15.5.1 Low__Level__IO

Input-output operations on a physical device may be handled by the procedures defined in the package Low_Level_IO as:

```
package Low_Level_IO is
   type Disk_Drive  is (DB0, DB1, ...); -- implementation-defined
   type Tape_Drive  is ...

   type Disk_Command is              -- implementation-defined
     record
       ... -- commands to the disk
     end record;

   type Disk_Status is               -- implementation-defined
     record
       ... -- status of the disk
     end record;
```

```
procedure Send_Control    (Device : in     Disk_Drive;
                           Data   : in out Disk_Command);
procedure Receive_Control (Device : in     Disk_Drive;
                           Data   : in out Disk_Status);

... -- and so on for other devices
end Low_Level_IO;
```

The (hypothetical) package above provides information needed to communicate with various devices. A skeleton is provided only for the disk. The Send_Control and Receive_Control procedures would be overloaded for each device.

The Disk_Command might contain information such as a read/write directive and a pointer to a data area. The Disk_Status might contain error information and completion or other status. How these procedures are used to interact with devices is implementation-dependent.

15.5.2 Memory-Mapped IO

Many processors do not have specific IO instructions. Devices are accessed via a set of registers that have addresses in the physical memory address space. Device handlers control the devices by writing to these registers. The devices return status by writing to the registers (mapped to the processor's memory); the status is then read by the device handler. The device also reads data to and from specified memory locations. The advantage to this approach is that access to IO device registers is controlled by the normal memory management mechanism; the device driver can use the regular instruction set to control the device.

A write to a memory location is then an output, while a read from a memory location is an input. Figure 15-1 illustrates this relationship with a keyboard and a display. A program reads a charcter from the keyboard by reading memory location 8#177562# and writes a character to the display by writing to memory location 8#177566#. We will assume a byte-addressable memory, with System.Storage_Unit being a byte. There must be some protocol between the program and the devices to synchronize the reading and writing. The partial example below will use polling to complete the illustration of memory-mapped IO (without interrupts). We assume the implementation uses one byte for Character representations, and 1 bit for Boolean representation.

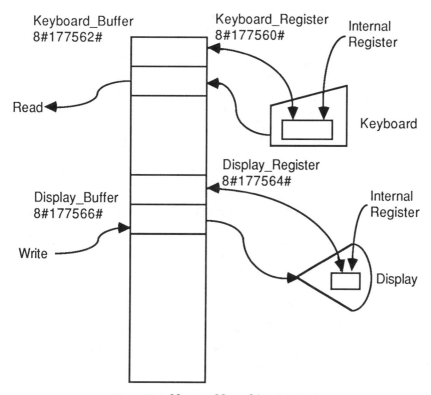

Figure 15-1. Memory_Mapped input/output

The first aspect of dealing with memory-mapped IO in an Ada device driver is to associate Ada object names with specific memory locations. This is done with an address clause. For example:

```
Keyboard_Buffer : Character;
for Keyboard_Buffer use at 8#177562#;
Display_Buffer : Character;
for Display_Buffer use at 8#177566#;
Internal_Char : Character;
```

An assignment such as

```
Internal_Char := Keyboard_Buffer;
```

reads a character from the keyboard into the internal variable.
An assignment such as

```
Display_Buffer := Internal_Char;
```

or

```
Display_Buffer := 'A';
```

is sufficient to display a character.

Notice that we never read from Display_Buffer or write to Keyboard_Buffer. The compiler will presumably recognize that the variable Keyboard_Buffer is associated with an external device rather than being a "normal" variable. This is needed so that we do not receive bogus compiler warnings or run-time errors for reading from a uninitialized variable.

In order to synchronize the reading and writing, suppose that each of the keyboard and display have a register, mapped to memory locations, that define the status of the external device. For each device, part of the status is whether or not the device has been activated. This is referred to as "active status." The device is activated by setting bit 15 to 1.

For the keyboard, the status also defines whether or not it has written to its output register (mapped to 8#177562# and hence to Keyboard_Buffer). This is referred to as "character status." When the keyboard has written a character, the character status is "set." We will refer to this as Char_Available. When the device handler reads from Keyboard_Buffer the status is automatically "reset" (to "0"). We will call the reset status Not_Available.

Similarly for the display in relation to Display_Buffer, we can have a character status of Char_Displayed or Not_Displayed.

Each of the registers, for the keyboard and display, is 16 bits long, bit 7 defining the character status of the buffer. Bit 15 defines the active status, and must be set to 1 in order to activate the device. This is shown in Figure 15-2. (The ordering of bytes in a word and the numbering of bits is implementation-dependent. The examples below are a hypothetical or possible implementation.)

Let's look at the use of length and address clauses to map Ada variables to memory locations. First the definition and length specification for an array to represent the register.

```
type Register_Type is array (0 .. 15) of Boolean;
for  Register_Type'Size use 16;
```

Now the keyboard and display register definitions:

The structure of the Keyboard and Display registers
is the same.

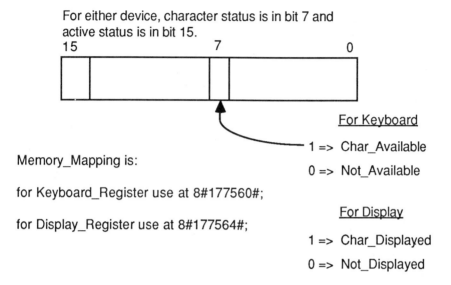

For either device, character status is in bit 7 and
active status is in bit 15.

For Keyboard

1 => Char_Available

0 => Not_Available

Memory_Mapping is:

for Keyboard_Register use at 8#177560#;

For Display

for Display_Register use at 8#177564#;

1 => Char_Displayed

0 => Not_Displayed

Figure 15-2. Keyboard/display internal register

```
Keyboard_Register : Register_Type;
for Keyboard_Register use at 8#177560#;
Display_Register : Register_Type;
for Display_Register use at 8#177564#;
```

And now the buffer definitions:

```
Keyboard_Buffer : Character;
for Keyboard_Buffer use at 8#177562#;
Display_Buffer : Character;
for Display_Buffer use at 8#177566#;
```

The declarations are shown with additional explanation (for the
keyboard only) in Figure 15-3.

Let's look at some basic use of the definitions above to activate
the devices and read and write the buffers.

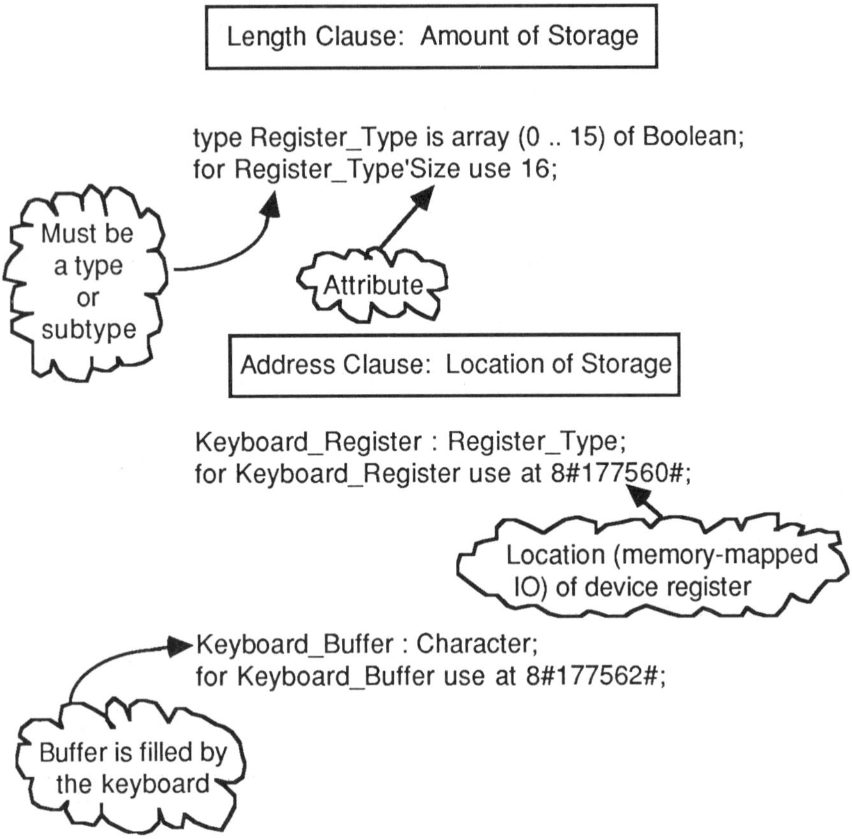

```
┌─────────────────────────────────────┐
│ Length Clause: Amount of Storage     │
└─────────────────────────────────────┘
```

type Register_Type is array (0 .. 15) of Boolean;
for Register_Type'Size use 16;

Must be a type or subtype

Attribute

```
┌─────────────────────────────────────┐
│ Address Clause: Location of Storage  │
└─────────────────────────────────────┘
```

Keyboard_Register : Register_Type;
for Keyboard_Register use at 8#177560#;

Location (memory-mapped IO) of device register

Keyboard_Buffer : Character;
for Keyboard_Buffer use at 8#177562#;

Buffer is filled by the keyboard

Figure 15-3. Length and address clauses

```
begin
   Keyboard_Register (15) := True;
   Display_Register  (15) := True;

   Internal_Char := Keyboard_Buffer; -- read from keyboard
   ... -- ignore the character status for now
   Display_Buffer := Internal_Char;  -- write to display
   ...
   ...
```

The code above can be made more readable by using "renames":

```
Keyboard_Active : Boolean renames Keyboard_Register (15);
Display_Active  : Boolean renames Display_Register  (15);
```

Then we would have:

```
Keyboard_Active := True;
Display_Active  := True;
```

The code fragment above depends upon Boolean being represented as a single bit. This may not be the case since the representation is implementation-dependent. (It also depends upon True being represented by a "1"; this is always correct, as the representation is defined by the language.)

The code fragments below show an alternate representation of the device registers, using records, a use of user-defined enumeration representations, and a derived type of the language-defined Boolean.

Here are the declarations, using length, enumeration and record representation clauses, to map the hardware to Ada high-level constructs.

```
type Activation_Level is new Boolean;
for Activation_Level'Size use 1;
-- definitions for the keyboard

type Char_Availability is (Not_Available, Char_Available);

for Keyboard_Status use
  record
    First_7 : array (0 .. 6) of Boolean; -- we don't care
    Char    : Char_Availability;
    Next_7  : array (0 .. 6) of Boolean; -- we don't care
    Active  : Activation_Level;
  end record;

for Char_Availability use (Not_Available => 0,
                           Char_Available => 1);

for Keyboard_Status use
  record at mod 2
    First_7 at 0 range 0 .. 6;
    Char    at 0 range 7 .. 7;
    Next_7  at 1 range 0 .. 6;
    Active  at 1 range 7 .. 7;
  end record;
```

```
...  -- similar definitions for the display
...
```

The definitions show a *possible* way to map the byte addressable memory to the device's 16-bit register. This issue is highly implementation-dependent. The enumeration and record definition and representation are illustrated in Figure 15-4.

```
type Activation_Level is new Boolean;
for Activation _Level'Size use 1;

type Char_Availability is (Not_Available, Char_Available);

type Keyboard_Status is
    record
        First_7  : array (0 .. 6) of Boolean; -- we don't care
        Char     : Char_Availability;
        Next_7   : array (0 .. 6) of Boolean; -- we don't care
        Active   : Activation_Level;
    end record;
```

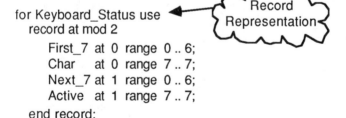

```
for Char_Availability use (Not_Available  => 0,
                           Char_Available => 1);
```

```
for Keyboard_Status use
    record at mod 2
        First_7 at 0 range 0 .. 6;
        Char    at 0 range 7 .. 7;
        Next_7 at 1 range 0 .. 6;
        Active  at 1 range 7 .. 7;
    end record;
```

Figure 15-4. Enumeration and record representation

Here are the definitions of the keyboard and display status registers:

```
Keyboard : Keyboard_Status;
Display  : Display_Status;
```

The following code fragments make use of the definitions to accomplish the input and output.

The activation code is:

```
Keyboard.Active := True;
Display.Active  := True;
```

The code to read a character from the keyboard is:

```
while Keyboard.Char = Not_Available loop
   null; -- busy wait
end loop;


Internal_Char := Keyboard_Buffer;
```

When the keyboard writes to Keyboard_Buffer, it changes (sets) Keyboard.Char to Char_Available. Reading the buffer (by the device handler) resets Keyboard.Char to Not_Available.

The similar code, and similar effect, for writing a character to the display is:

```
Display_Buffer := Internal_Char;

while Display.Char = Not_Displayed loop
   null; -- busy wait
end loop;
```

The keyboard and display may each have their own device handler, or (if the assumption is made that the display is much faster than the keyboard) both code fragments may be in a loop in a single Ada task.

The interface using polling is satisfactory if the processor has nothing else to do, or can do some useful work while polling (doing the work instead of the null statement). In addition, sometimes there may be no alternative to polling because of the characteristics of the device being used. More often, however, the processor will have other tasks to perform. If possible, a preferable interface is to use interrupts as shown in Chapter 17, Tasks as Interrupt Handlers.

Keys to Understanding

- Ada provides mechanisms for mapping Ada constructs to machine level representations of data.

- Ada allows an escape from its usual strong typing mechanism through the use of Unchecked_Conversion.

- There are are number of implementation-dependent issues related to low-level interfaces and representations. These issues include interface to other languages, tasking implementation, and Low_Level_IO.

- Don't write programs that are erroneous or contain incorrect order dependence. Avoid writing nonportable programs.

- Memory-mapped IO maps external device registers to memory locations. Ada allows the mapping of Ada variables to memory, hence allowing device handlers to be written at an abstract, high-level language level.

Case Four: Multiple Keyboard Handler (MKH)

> Objective: To illustrate machine-level interaction
> with an external hardware device

The MKH* case study illustrates a mode of interaction with external hardware that uses the Ada features introduced in Chapter 15.

16.1 Software Requirements Specification

The Multiple Keyboard Handler (MKH) is a component of a keyboard handler that accomplishes the machine-dependent interactions for a number of keyboards. The overall processing of the system is shown in Figure 16-1a. The handler accepts input on a character by character basis, buffers the input (character), and, when requested,

---

*This case study has been adapted from a problem posed and largely solved by Habermann [HAB83, page 353]. An important difference in this solution is that the intermediate buffers are encapsulated in the body of a package.

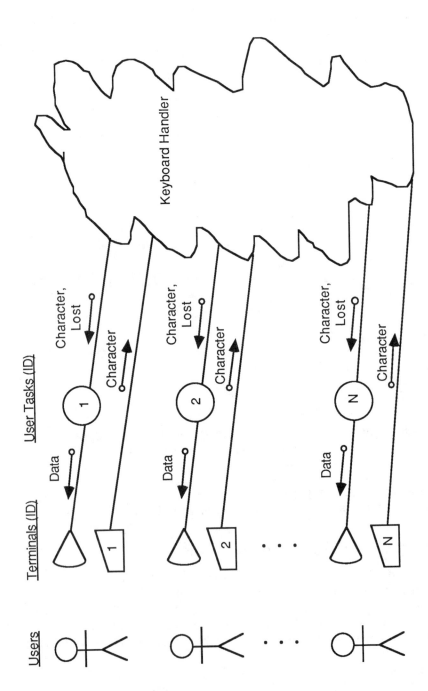

Users | **Terminals (ID)** | **User Tasks (ID)**

Data — 1 — Character, Lost — Character — Keyboard Handler

Data — 2 — Character, Lost — Character

Data — N — Character, Lost — Character

Figure 16-1a. MKH illustration

provides the input to user tasks. It also provides a count of characters lost in the handler since the last character delivered.

What the user tasks return to the users as data is of no direct concern to this problem. However, one likely chore of the user tasks is to echo, on a display, the characters as they are typed on the keyboard.

The MKH does not interact with the keyboards directly; it interacts with an Asynchronous Communications Interface (ACI) that handles the keyboards themselves. The ACI places information in a hardware buffer. For each character received from a keyboard, the ACI places the character and the keyboard number in the buffer. The buffer consists of a head pointer, a tail pointer, and 64 elements organized as a circular queue.

The ACI updates the hardware tail pointer when it puts a character into the buffer. (This is the sort of pointer we called "Insert" in Chapter 7.) The ACI can also read the head pointer (the one we called "Remove" in Chapter 7) and compare it with the tail pointer to determine if the buffer is full (using the alternate algorithm we developed in Chapter 7). The structure of the buffer and its hardware-dependent information is shown in Figure 16-1b. The Head is located at 8#500#, the Tail at 8#502#, the first element of the queue at 8#504#, and so on.

When the buffer is full, the ACI discards incoming characters from the keyboard. It does not notify either the keyboard or the MKH or this loss of data. To prevent this situation from occuring it is essential that the MKH operate fast enough to ensure that the buffer does not become full.

Since the MKH must remove characters from the hardware buffer as quickly as possible, without regard to requests from user tasks for their input, it must store the characters in an intermediate buffer internal to the MKH. Then, when requested, it provides the characters out of the intermediate buffer.

If the users do not ask for input at approximately the same rate (or faster) than the data arrive from the keyboards, the intermediate buffer will become full. When the buffer becomes full, the MKH is to discard characters (i.e., not overwrite the buffer) until the buffer is no longer full. The MKH is required to maintain a count of how many characters have been lost prior to once again being able to place information in the intermediate buffer. This count of lost characters is to be maintained for each keyboard. Hence, each character for each keyboard has associated with it a "lost count." The lost count contains the number of characters that were lost (for the originating keyboard) before this specific character was successfully

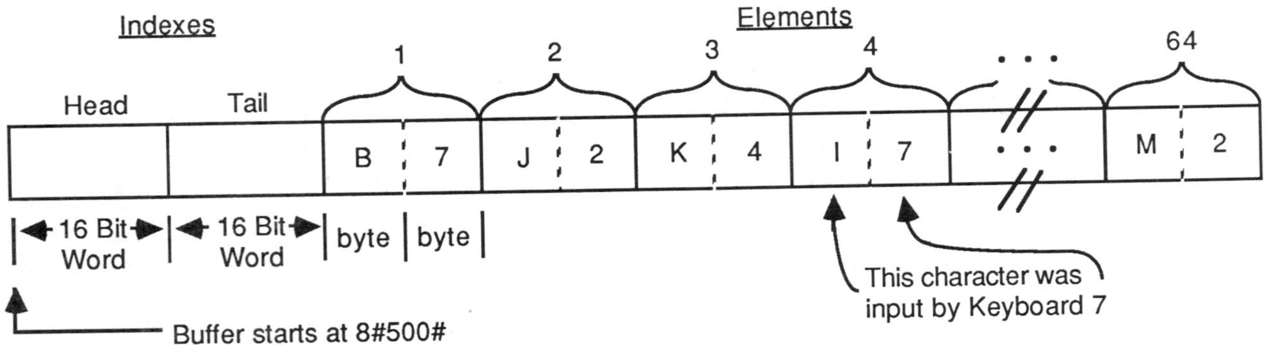

Figure 16-1b. Structure of the hardware buffer

- Head and Tail are each 16 bit integers

- Each element is 2 bytes consisting of:

  - A character (1 byte)

  - The number (1 byte, integer) of the keyboard that provided the character to the ACI

Indexes

Head   Tail

|← 16 Bit →|← 16 Bit →| byte | byte |
| Word | Word |

Buffer starts at 8#500#

Elements

1	2	3	4		64
B	J	K	I		M
7	2	4	7		2

This character was input by Keyboard 7

stored. In a well designed handler, the lost count will almost always be zero.

The interface between the user tasks and the MKH is that the user tasks request a character by providing the identification of the keyboard for which they are responsible. The MKH returns a character and the associated lost count discussed above. If no character for the requesting keyboard is available, the user task is forced to wait until a character does become available.

In summary, the MKH provides the following two functions:

- Empty the hardware buffer before it fills.

- Provide a character from a given keyboard to the requesting user programs.

Figure 16-1c illustrates the interfaces between the MKH, the ACI, and the users.

16.2 MKH Environment

Figure 16-2 is the context diagram for the MKH. The specific machine level values were shown in Figure 16-1b.

16.3 Top-Level Design

This section presents the graphical design and the Ada package specifications.

16.3.1 Graphical Design

The hardware ACI should be served by a single process since its primary function is to empty the hardware buffer before it is filled by the ACI: otherwise characters from the keyboards would be lost.

We must also have a process to serve the users, taking information from the intermediate buffer.

We will address the intermediate buffer as a separate entity, providing the interface between the ACI process and the process to serve the users.

Figure 16-3a shows the process graph for the MKH. The ACI mythical hardware task and the user tasks are included to show the context for the MKH; they are not part of the problem to be solved.

The buffers are shown as clouds to illustrate that their structure is as yet undefined. However, some important preliminary decisions have been made about the buffer-task interaction; namely that, each of the buffers will raise an exception, propagating it to the

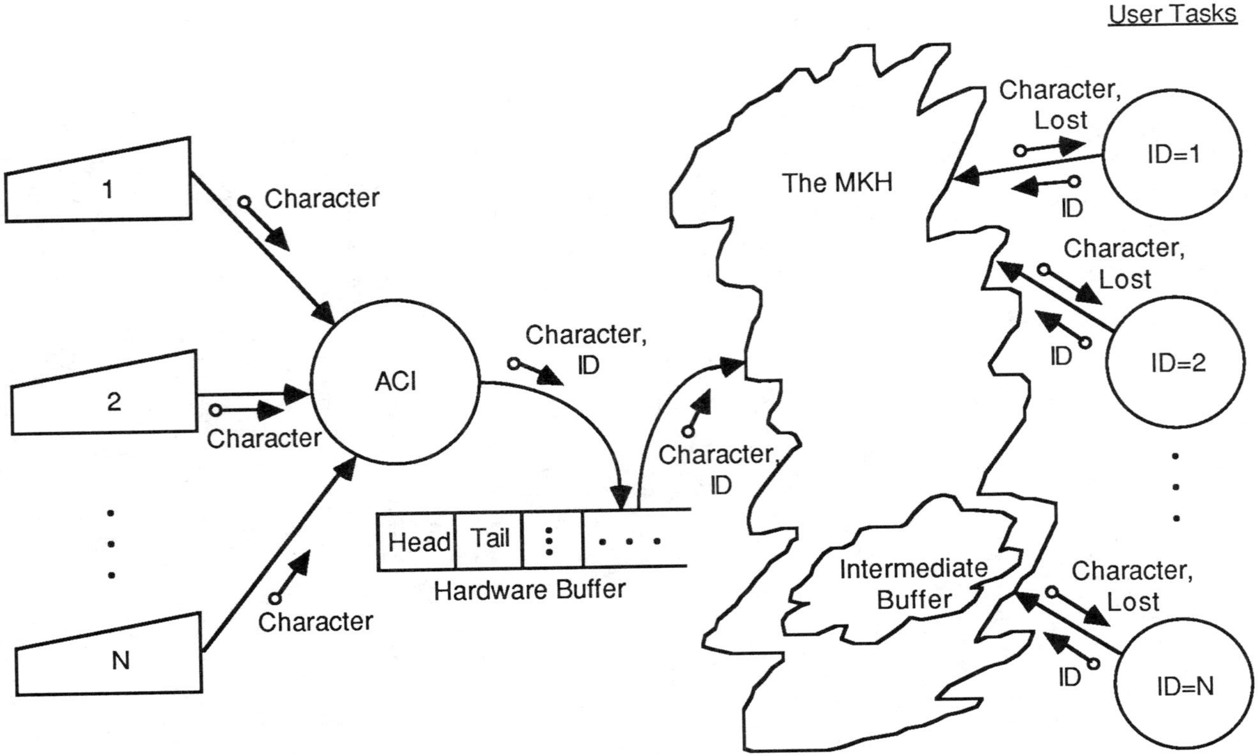

Figure 16-1c. MKH interfaces

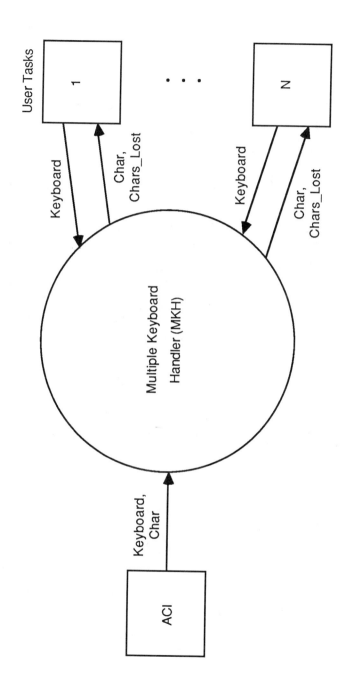

Figure 16-2. MKH context diagram

411

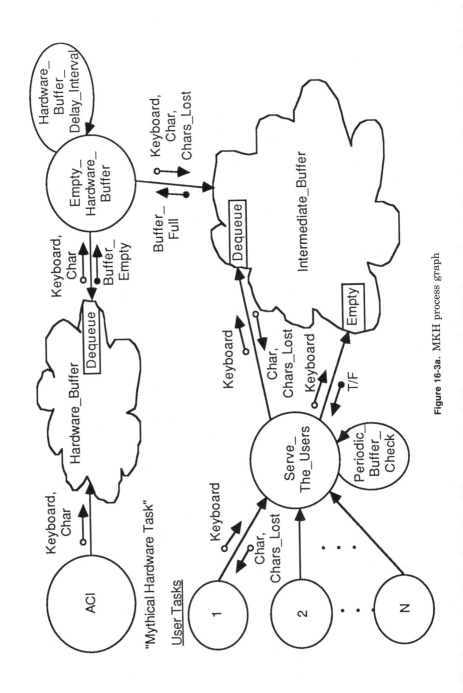

Figure 16-3a. MKH process graph

Empty_Hardware_Buffer process, on the conditions of empty (Hardware_Buffer) and full (Intermediate_Buffer).

The interaction between the Empty_Hardware_Buffer process and the Hardware_Buffer is based on the use of an unprotected buffer using the alternate algorithm that we discussed in Chapter 7, i.e., the buffer algorithm that does not explicity count the number of items in the buffer. In order to have this interaction, it must poll the buffer, delaying (for Hardware_Buffer_Delay_Interval as shown in Figure 16-3a) when it finds the buffer is empty.

In order to effectively use the buffer without contention for access to the data, Empty_Hardware_Buffer should be a single task. Further, it should be a high-priority task: higher than the users and higher than the interface to the users. This will ensure that it is not held up, and losing characters, while some other task is processing.

The next aspect to be considered is the design of the intermediate buffer (called Intermediate_Buffer on the process graph); the interface between Empty_Hardware_Buffer and the interface to the users. The most important issue in the design of the intermediate buffer is that Empty_Hardware_Buffer must not be held up (for example, queued for a rendezvous) waiting for a busy Serve_The_Users process.

A natural way to implement the intermediate buffer is to use the same sort of buffer that is used for the interaction with the hardware. The advantage of this sort of buffer is that the Empty_Hardware_Buffer is not held in a rendezvous while some encapsulating task is busy serving an other user. Although we no not want to do too much design of the buffer at this point, we will make the decision that it should be encapsulated in a package, rather than directly visible. As discussed in Chapter 7, this allows the design of a using task (in this case Empty_Hardware_Buffer) to be independent of the details of buffering. The mechanism for letting Empty_Hardware_Buffer know that the buffer is full is to return the exception Buffer_Full.

The structure of the intermediate buffer should be addressed in conjunction with the design of the interface to the users. We have two options for the process Serve_The_Users: either a set of tasks (one for each user) or a single task with an entry for each user.

Let's first consider the design of the internals of the Intermediate_Buffer. In order to prevent having to search a large buffer for the next data associated with a particular keyboard, it is natural to have a number of distinct buffers, one for each keyboard. Although this does not *force* us to use multiple tasks to access the Intermediate_Buffer, it does *allow* us to do so and has an attractive symmetry. Therefore, we will present the design with an array of tasks, reserving the alternative for the exercises.

(Remember that the method of using Insert/Remove to determine buffer-full/buffer-empty is safe only for two tasks, a producer and a consumer, accessing the buffer. If we had one large buffer, rather than a buffer for each keyboard, we would be forced to use a single Serve_The_User with a family of entries.)

The size of the buffer should be chosen based on likely input rates from the keyboard. It must be small enough to be space efficient, but large enough to only rarely become full. When it is full, it must return an indication to the task attempting to queue data.

Figure 16-3b shows some of the detail of the approach to the user interface. It illustrates that we have multiple intermediate buffers, each being served by a single task, User_Server (i), of an array of tasks. The solution to follow will encapsulate things so that the actual mechanism of accessing the buffers is hidden from the producer (Empty_Hardware_Buffer) and consumer [User_Server (i)].

Minispecifications for the MKH Processes

This section presents minispecifications for:

- Empty_Hardware_Buffer
- User_Server (i)

The process interactions are shown in Figures 16-3a and 16-3b.

Empty__Hardware__Buffer

Empty_Hardware_Buffer takes information from Hardware_Buffer and places it in the Intermediate_Buffer. If the hardware buffer is empty (indicated by the raising of the Buffer_Full exception), Empty_Hardware_Buffer delays for Hardware_Buffer_Delay_Interval—that is its response to this exception. We assume that the implementation of the Ada run-time environment will cause a scheduling event to occur upon the expiration of the delay of this task. Since it will be the highest priority task in the system, it will gain control to access the buffer. (If we have a separate processor for this task, such issues are not of concern.) The length of time for the Hardware_Buffer_Delay_Interval should be chosen carefully, based upon the speed of the ACI and maximum keyboard input rates. It is necessary to balance loss of characters with unnecessary polling of the buffer.

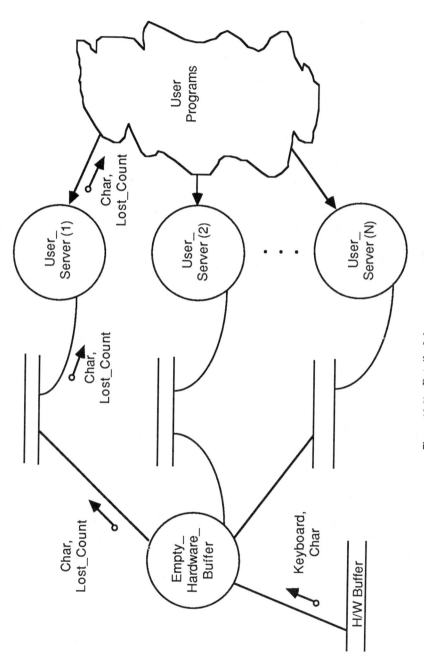

Figure 16-3b. Detail of the user interface approach

If the Intermediate_Buffer is full (raises the Buffer_Full exception), Empty_Hardware_Buffer increments the Chars_Lost value for the keyboard for which the buffer is full. (The buffer may be full for some keyboards, while having storage available for others). The incrementing of the Chars_Lost is the response to this exception.

User__Server (i)

The User_Server is an array of identical tasks; each of them is very simple. User_Server checks to see if the buffer (for the keyboard for which it is responsible) is empty.

If the buffer *is not* empty, the task is prepared to accept a call from the user task that it serves. When the call is made, User_Server obtains the data from the intermediate buffer and provides it to the caller.

If the buffer *is* empty, the task delays for Periodic_Buffer_Check before once again checking the buffer. The amount of delay will depend on the characteristics of a specific system, but should be chosen to be as large as possible (to conserve processor resources by avoiding frequent polling) consistent with no significant delay in service to the user tasks. (For example, if the user tasks are echoing the character to a screen, it should appear without noticeable delay.)

16.3.2   Package Specifications

This section presents the specifications for:

- Definitions
- Intermediate_Buffer
- Handle_Asynch_Keyboard_Interface
- User_Interface

Figure 16-4 shows the relationships between the major packages and the main procedure. The packages also depend upon Definitions.

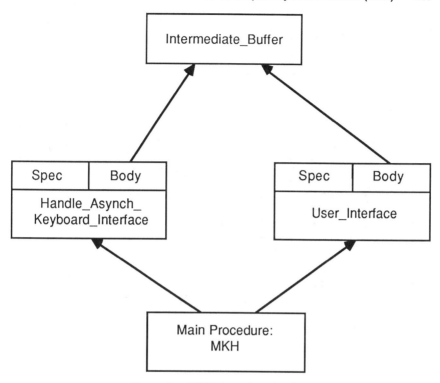

Figure 16-4. MKH dependency graph

16.3.2.1 Definitions.

```
with System;
package Definitions is
   Hardware_Buffer_Location : constant := 8#500#;
   Hardware_Buffer_Size     : constant := 64;
   Intermediate_Buffer_Size : constant := 30;
   Number_Of_Keyboards      : constant := 3;

   type Keyboard_Index is range 1 .. Number_Of_Keyboards;
   for Keyboard_Index'Size use 8;
   Serve_Hardware_Priority : constant System.Priority := 10;
   Serve_User_Priority     : constant System.Priority :=  8;
end Definitions;
```

16.3.2.2 Intermediate__Buffer.

Abstract Algorithm:

----- Enqueue -----

For the indicated Keyboard, if the buffer is full, raise the
Buffer_Full exception.
Otherwise, store the Char and Chars_Lost.

----- Dequeue -----

For the indicated Keyboard, provide the Char and Chars_Lost,
in a first-in first-out manner.

----- Empty -----

For the indicated Keyboard, indicate whether the buffer is empty.

Specification:

```
with Definitions;  use Definitions;
package Intermediate_Buffer is
   procedure Enqueue (Keyboard    : in Keyboard_Index;
                      Char        : in Character;
                      Chars_Lost  : in Natural);
   procedure Dequeue (Keyboard    : in Keyboard_Index;
                      Char        : out Character;
                      Chars_Lost  : out Natural);
   function Empty (Keyboard : Keyboard_Index) return Boolean;

   Buffer_Full : exception;
end Intermediate_Buffer;
```

16.3.2.3 Handle__Asynch__Keyboard__Interface.

Abstract Algorithm:

```
loop
  get the information from the hardware buffer;

  send the information (including the count of
  lost characters) to the intermediate buffer,
  keeping track of lost characters;
end loop;
```

Specification:

```
package Handle_Asynch_Keyboard_Interface is

  -- Calls Intermediate_Buffer.Enqueue

  -- Contains hardware dependent task to remove
  -- characters from a buffer
end Handle_Asynch_Keyboard_Interface;
```

16.3.2.4 User__Interface.

Abstract Algorithm:

```
loop
  select
    when the intermediate buffer for a keyboard
    is not empty =>
      accept a request for data and
      provide the Char and Chars_Lost;
  or
    when the intermediate buffer for a keyboard
    is empty =>
      delay appropriate interval;
  end select;
end loop;
```

Specification:

```
with Definitions;  use Definitions;
package User_Interface is
  procedure Read_Keyboard
     (Keyboard        : in Keyboard_Index;
      Char            : out Character;
      Chars_Lost      : out Natural);

  -- Calls Intermediate_Buffer.Empty
  -- Calls Intermediate_Buffer.Dequeue
end User_Interface;
```

16.4 Detailed Design

The structure graph of Figure 16-5 provides an overview of the components of the MKH. Figure 16-5a shows the overall structure, deferring the detail of the intermediate buffer. Figure 16-5b shows the intermediate buffer in detail.

This section presents the detailed design for:

- Intermediate_Buffer
- Handle_Asynch_Keyboard_Interface
- User_Interface

The designs below assume the existance of a generic buffer called Queue_Type_Manager that has generic parameters of the index to the buffer and the type of object being buffered. This is the buffer discussed in Section 7.1.3.2.

16.4.1 Intermediate__Buffer

```
with Queue_Type_Manager; -- assume appropriate generic buffer
package body Intermediate_Buffer is
  type Intermediate_Buffer_Index is
       range 1 .. Intermediate_Buffer_Size + 1;

  type Intermediate_Buffer_Element is
    record
      Char        : Character;
      Chars_Lost  : Natural;
    end record;
```

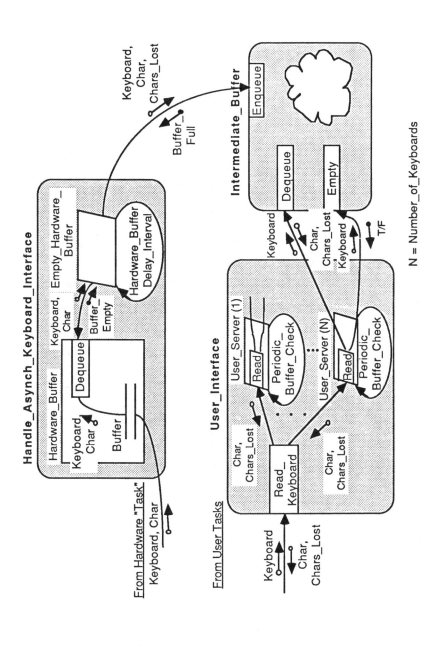

Figure 16-5a. MKH structure graph

N = Number_of_Keyboards

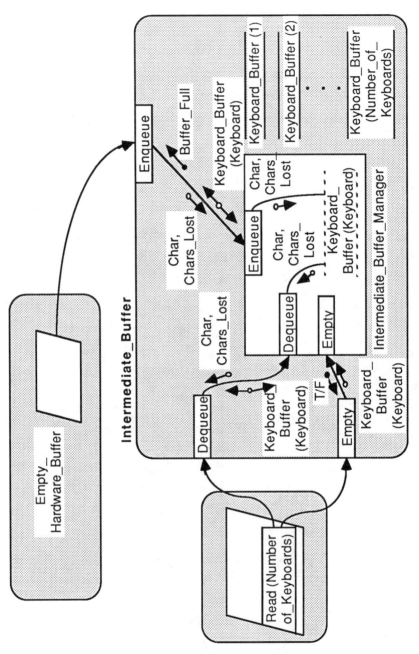

Figure 16-5b. MKH structure graph—detail of Intermediate_Buffer

```
package Intermediate_Buffer_Manager is new Queue_Type_Manager
         (Index          => Intermediate_Buffer_Index,
          Buffered_Type => Intermediate_Buffer_Element);

Keyboard_Buffer : array (Keyboard_Index) of
                     Intermediate_Buffer_Manager.Queue_Buffer;


procedure Enqueue (Keyboard   : in Keyboard_Index;
                   Char       : in Character;
                   Chars_Lost : in Natural) is separate;
procedure Dequeue (Keyboard   : in Keyboard_Index;
                   Char       : out Character;
                   Chars_Lost : out Natural) is separate;

function Empty (Keyboard : Keyboard_Index) return Boolean is
begin
   return Intermediate_Buffer_Manager.Empty (Keyboard_Buffer (Keyboard));
end Empty;
end Intermediate_Buffer;
```

The Intermediate_Buffer_Manager, as an instantiation of Queue_
Type_Manager with the appropriate types, provides the resources for
creation and manipulation of the multiple intermediate buffers. The
actual buffers, literally the actual storage areas, are created as
Keyboard_Buffer—an array of buffers of type exported by
Intermediate_Buffer_Manager.

The function Empty calls on the services of Intermediate_
Buffer_Manager, using a parameter of a specific buffer picked from
the array of buffers; the choice of a specific buffer is based on its
own input parameter, Keyboard.

```
separate (Intermediate_Buffer)
   procedure Enqueue (Keyboard   : in Keyboard_Index;
                      Char       : in Character;
                      Chars_Lost : in Natural) is
   begin
      select one of the keyboard buffers, using Keyboard as an index;

      enqueue Char and Chars_Lost into the buffer by using the
      services of Intermediate_Buffer_Manager.Enqueue;
```

```
exception
  when Intermediate_Buffer_Manager.Buffer_Full =>
    raise Buffer_Full;
end Enqueue;
```

When the exception Intermediate_Buffer_Manager.Buffer_Full is raised, Enqueue does not simply pass it along (since its name is not known to the task Empty_Hardware_Buffer), but rather transforms it into the exception exported by the package Intermediate_Buffer: Buffer_Full. This is better than forcing the Empty_Hardware_Buffer package to include an exception handler that used "when others = > delay ...".

```
separate (Intermediate_Buffer)
  procedure Dequeue (Keyboard   : in Keyboard_Index;
                     Char       : out Character;
                     Chars_Lost : out Natural) is
  begin
    select one of the keyboard buffers, using Keyboard as an index;

    dequeue Char and Chars_Lost from buffer by using the
    services of Intermediate_Buffer_Manager.Dequeue;
  end Dequeue;
```

This procedure depends upon the proper use the exported function Empty. If this procedure is improperly used, it will attempt to access an empty buffer, obtaining the exception Intermediate_Buffer_Manager.Buffer_Empty. This exception will be propagated to the caller.

16.4.2 Handle_Asynch_Keyboard_Interface

```
with Definitions; use Definitions;
with Queue_Type_Manager;
package body Handle_Asynch_Keyboard_Interface is
  type Hardware_Buffer_Index is range 1 .. Hardware_Buffer_Size;

  type Hardware_Buffer_Element is
    record
      Char     : Character;
      Keyboard : Keyboard_Index;
    end record;
```

```
for Hardware_Buffer_Index'Size use 16;
for Hardware_Buffer_Element use
   record at mod 2; -- byte is storage unit
      Char     at 0 range 0 .. 7;
      Keyboard at 1 range 0 .. 7;
   end record;

package Hardware_Buffer_Manager is new
      Queue_Type_Manager (Index          => Hardware_Buffer_Index,
                          Buffered_Type => Hardware_Buffer_Element);

Hardware_Buffer : Hardware_Buffer_Manager.Queue_Buffer;
for Hardware_Buffer use at Hardware_Buffer_Location;

task Empty_Hardware_Buffer is

   pragma Priority (Serve_Hardware_Priority);
   -- Gets characters from the Hardware_Buffer
   -- Calls Intermediate_Buffer.Enqueue
end Empty_Hardware_Buffer;

task body Empty_Hardware_Buffer is separate;
end Handle_Asynch_Keyboard_Interface;
```

The use of the priority pragma establishes a (high) priority for the task that interacts with the hardware. Except when it is delaying, it will have control to execute, not being suspended while other tasks execute. (This implies that the run-time environment makes a scheduling decision at the expiration of the delay statement, in order to determine that a high-priority task is ready to execute. Some implementations do not make this scheduling decision. This is an area in which you should be certain to understand the characteristics of the implementation of your compiler and run-time environment.)

The index to the hardware buffer is Hardware_Buffer_Index. Its size is specified as being 16 bits. The structure of the items in the buffer as is defined as Hardware_Buffer_Element. Its bit-level layout is specified by the record representation clause. The Keyboard has been previously defined (in package Definitions) as requiring 8 bits. We assume the predefined type Character is one byte. Remember that the buffer itself consists of a Head (or Remove) index, a Tail (or Insert) index, and 64 elements.

The next step is to instantiate the same generic buffer we used in the Intermediate_Buffer. This establishes a Hardware_Buffer_

Manager. The type Queue_Buffer, imported from the Hardware_ Buffer_Manager, has the desired structure of Remove, Insert, and 64 elements. Finally, we define the actual buffer, Hardware_Buffer, and ensure that it will be located at the appropriate location in memory.

These steps make use of the methods described in Chapter 15, and allow us to meet the low-level hardware interface requirements of the problem specification.

```
with Intermediate_Buffer;
separate (Handle_Asynch_Keyboard_Interface)

    initialize Chars_Lost (for each keyboard) to zero;

  task body Empty_Hardware_Buffer is
  -- Takes characters from the Hardware_Buffer and places them
  -- in the intermediate buffer, along with the count of
  -- characters lost. Keeps track of characters lost as a
  -- result of the intermediate buffer being full

    Hardware_Buffer_Delay_Interval : constant := 0.1;
  begin
    loop
      Handle_Buffer_Exceptions:
      begin
        get a character and keyboard number from hardware buffer;

        send the character and the number of characters lost to
        the intermediate buffer (for specified keyboard);

        set Chars_Lost for this keyboard to 0;
      exception
        when Hardware_Buffer_Manager.Buffer_Empty =>
          delay Hardware_Buffer_Delay_Interval;
        when Intermediate_Buffer.Buffer_Full      =>
          increment Chars_Lost for this keyboard;
      end Handle_Buffer_Exceptions;
    end loop;
  end Empty_Hardware_Buffer;
```

The type definitions and instantiation of the buffer package could have been deferred until the task body. However, there being no other tasks in this package (indeed, since the package exists only to encapsulate the task), it is safe to have the buffer itself outside the task body.

Further, it is clearer to finish the declarations needed for the proper functioning of the task *before* the task itself is declared. The task itself can concentrate on the active operations of the device handler. (This is a close issue; one can also make a good arguement for placing the declarations in the task body. What is important is to recognize that you can do it either way.)

16.4.3 User—interface

```
package body User_interface is
  task type Serve_The_Users is
    pragma Priority (Serve_User_Priority);

    entry Keyboard_Is  (The_Keyboard : in Keyboard_Index);
    entry Read  (Char : out Character; Chars_Lost : out Natural);
    -- Calls Intermediate_Buffer.Dequeue
  end Serve_The_Users;

  User_Server : array (Keyboard_Index) of Serve_The_Users;

  task body Serve_The_Users is separate;

  procedure Read_Keyboard
      (Keyboard   : in Keyboard_Index;
       Char       : out Character;
       Chars_Lost : out Natural) is
  begin
    User_Server (Keyboard).Read (Char, Chars_Lost);
  end Read_Keyboard;
begin -- initialize User_Interface
  for This_Keyboard in Keyboard_Index loop
    User_Server (This_Keyboard).Keyboard_Is (This_Keyboard);
  end loop;
end User_Interface;
```

The use of the pragma Priority establishes that all the tasks that serve the users will have lower priority than the task that serves the hardware.

The "Keyboard_Index" is specified in the package Definitions, with range dependent upon the value of Number_Of_Keyboards. We will use a task type to establish a template for the User_Server tasks. The User_Server array is the set of tasks that actually provide the service.

The entrance procedure uses the input parameter of the keyboard requesting service to select the approriate task.

It will be necessary for the User_Server tasks to know for which keyboard they provide service; they are initialized by the initialization part of the package body. (This detail of initialization is not shown in the structure graph of Figure 16-5 since it does not have to do with the overall structure of the problem.)

A nice feature of this solution, using an array of tasks, is that it is very short, and is easy to change: taking only a new value of "Number_Of_Keyboards."

```
with Intermediate_Buffer;
separate (User_Interface)
  task body Serve_The_Users is
    My_Keyboard : Keyboard_Index;
    Periodic_Buffer_Check : constant := 0.2;
  begin
    accept Keyboard_Is (The_Keyboard : in Keyboard_Index) do
      My_Keyboard := The_Keyboard;
    end Keyboard_Is;

    loop
      select
        when the Intermediate_Buffer for My_Keyboard is not empty =>
          accept Read (Char : out Character; Chars_Lost : out Natural)
            from the Intermediate_Buffer, Dequeue a Char and Chars_Lost
            for the indicated keyboard;
          end Read;
      or
        when the Intermediate_Buffer for My_Keyboard is empty =>
          delay Periodic_Buffer_Check;
      end select;
    end loop;
  end Serve_The_Users;
```

16.5 Code

This section presents the code for:

- Enqueue and Dequeue
- Empty_Hardware_Buffer

- Serve_The_Users

16.5.1 Enqueue and Dequeue

```
separate (Intermediate_Buffer)
  procedure Enqueue (Keyboard    : in Keyboard_Index;
                     Char        : in Character;
                     Chars_Lost  : in Natural) is
  begin
    Intermediate_Buffer_Manager.Enqueue
                    (Keyboard_Buffer (Keyboard), (Char, Chars_Lost));
  exception
    when Intermediate_Buffer_Manager.Buffer_Full =>
      raise Buffer_Full;
  end Enqueue;

separate (Intermediate_Buffer)
  procedure Dequeue (Keyboard    : in Keyboard_Index;
                     Char        : out Character;
                     Chars_Lost  : out Natural) is

    User_Data : Intermediate_Buffer_Element;
  begin
    Intermediate_Buffer_Manager.Dequeue
                    (Keyboard_Buffer (Keyboard), User_Data);

    Char       := User_Data.Char;
    Chars_Lost := User_Data.Chars_Lost;
  end Dequeue;
```

These entrance procedures use the input value of the keyboard identification to select one of the intermediate buffers. Then the buffer manager is used to either enqueue or dequeue the data for the buffer.

16.5.2 Empty__Hardware__Buffer

```
with Intermediate_Buffer;
separate (Handle_Asynch_Keyboard_Interface)
  task body Empty_Hardware_Buffer is
  -- Takes characters from the hardware buffer and places them
  -- in the intermediate buffer, along with the count of
  -- characters lost. Keeps track of characters lost as a
  -- result of the intermediate buffer being full

    Chars_Lost : array  (Keyboard_Index) of Natural :=  (others => 0);
    Hardware_Buffer_Delay_Interval : constant := 0.1;
    Input : Hardware_Buffer_Element;
  begin
    loop
      Handle_Buffer_Exceptions:
      begin
        -- From hardware buffer
        Hardware_Buffer_Manager.Dequeue (Hardware_Buffer, Input);

        -- To intermediate buffer  (for specified Keyboard)
        Intermediate_Buffer.Enqueue
          (Input.Keyboard, Input.Char, Chars_Lost (Input.Keyboard));

        Chars_Lost (Input.Keyboard) := 0;
      exception
        when Hardware_Buffer_Manager.Buffer_Empty =>
          delay Hardware_Buffer_Delay_Interval;

        when Intermediate_Buffer.Buffer_Full      =>
          Chars_Lost (Input.Keyboard) :=
                        Chars_Lost (Input.Keyboard) + 1;
      end Handle_Buffer_Exceptions;
    end loop;
  end Empty_Hardware_Buffer;
```

Chars_Lost is the array where we keep the record of lost characters for each keyboard.

The task gets some input from the hardware buffer, using the services of the buffer manager in the type manager style. In the usual case, processing continues. In the exceptional case, the exception Buffer_Empty (from the hardware buffer) is handled by a delay. At the expiration of the delay, this task will be resumed since it is the highest priority task in our system. (As indicated earlier, we assume a scheduling event at the expriation of the delay.)

The call to the intermediate buffer has three parameters:

- The keyboard identification, which is part of the input
- The character input
- The number of characters lost, for the input keyboard

In the usual case, the information will be stored in the appropriate intermediate buffer for the keyboard; therefore the count of lost characters is set to zero. In the exceptional case, the Buffer_Full exception (from the intermediate buffer) will be handled by incrementing the lost count for the keyboard being handled.

16.5.3 Serve_The_Users

```
with Intermediate_Buffer;
separate (User_Interface)
  task body Serve_The_Users is
    My_Keyboard : Keyboard_Index;
    Periodic_Buffer_Check : constant := 0.2;
    My_Buffer_Empty       : Boolean;
  begin
    accept Keyboard_Is (The_Keyboard : in Keyboard_Index) do
      My_Keyboard := The_Keyboard;
    end Keyboard_Is;

    loop
      My_Buffer_Empty := Intermediate_Buffer.Empty (My_Keyboard);
      select
        when not My_Buffer_Empty =>
          accept Read  (Char : out Character; Chars_Lost : out Natural) do
            Intermediate_Buffer.Dequeue (My_Keyboard, Char, Chars_Lost);
          end Read;
      or
        when My_Buffer_Empty =>
          delay Periodic_Buffer_Check;
      end select;
    end loop;
  end Serve_The_Users;
```

The first rendezvous is the initializing call, whereby each task of the type finds out its own identification. It then loops to accomplish its main job. It sends its own identification to the buffer manager to get information for its user task.

16.6 Discussion

Let's look at the overall decomposition and encapsulation of function in this problem. There are three major conponents:

- Intermediate_Buffer
- Handle_Asynch_Keyboard_Interface
- User_Interface

The Intermediate_Buffer encapsulates the buffers themselves, and the buffering methods. Its use of a type manager approach to creating multiple buffers is a good illustration of a type manager. The creation of multiple object managers, even using a generic, would be awkward. The fact that there are multiple buffers, or that a type manager approach is used, or that a generic buffer manager is used, is hidden from the tasks that access the buffer.

Handle_Asynch_Keyboard_Interface encapsulates the hardware buffer. How it goes about its job is hidden. It uses the same generic buffer package, and the same type manager approach, as used in the Intermediate_Buffer. It could effectively have used an object manager. In fact, we generally prefer object managers for single buffers; in this problem we used the type manager to demonstrate how the same buffering paradigm could be used for different purposes. It also illustrated the interaction of representation clauses, a type manager buffer, and a generic buffer.

The User_Interface package hides details from the user tasks. They do not, and should not, know how the buffering is handled (whether it is in the package or a in separate package) or how many tasks are used to interact with the user tasks. The exercises will show that the implementation of this package can change quite dramatically, with no effect on the using task.

16.7 Exercises

Exercise 16.1. Use a single task with a family of entries rather than an array of tasks to serve users. This involves a modification of the body of User_Interface. Does anything outside the package body have to change?

Exercise 16.2. Eliminate the server (or user interface) tasks altogether. The entrance procedure can access the intermediate buffer directly (polling the buffer as needed). Since the code of the entrance procedure is reentrant, each of the user tasks essentially has its own procedure doing the polling of the intermediate buffer. Does anything outside the package body have to change?

Exercise 16.3. Simulate the actions of the ACI and the users. We might well wish to do this in order to test the operation of the system.

Exercise 16.4. Use an object manager for the hardware buffer. Does this make access to the buffer easier? Does anything outside the package body of the handler have to change?

Exercise 16.5. Use multiple instantiations of an object manager for the intermediate buffer. Does this make access to the buffers easier? How easy and clear is it to create the buffers? Does anything outside the package body of the buffer have to change?

Exercise 16.6. Using the simulated hardware and users of Exercise 16.3, evaluate the efficiency of the original solution and the alternatives presented in the first two exercises. Evaluate the efficiency of the buffering alternatives in the next exercises.

16.8 Partial Solutions to Exercises

Solution 16.1 Single Task to Serve All Users. The use of a single task to serve all users is an interesting alternative both in its own right and in that it illustrates the conceptual similarity between an array of tasks and a single task with a family of entries. Further, if we have a single processor, efficiency considerations regarding the speed of the processor and characteristics of a specific implementation (context switch time, implementation of a rendezvous, and so on) become important and may influence our design.

If we have a single task for all users, the appropriate method is to have a family of entries, since each of the entries will perform essentially the same function. We will show all the design steps for this solution. Serve_The_Users will no longer be a task type used for the declaration of an array of tasks; it will be a single task with a family of entries. The modifications to the earlier solution are restricted to the body of the user interface package.

Here is a minispecification for the new process.

Serve__The__Users

Serve_The_Users checks to see which of the keyboards has information available. It prepares to rendezvous with any keyboard that has information in the buffer at the time of the check. If it is called by any of the keyboards, it services the call, rechecks the buffer (for all keyboard information), and once again prepares to rendezvous with any keyboard for which the buffer has information. If more than one keyboard desires service (and has information available) Serve_The_Users makes a nondeterministic choice of which one to serve.

If no keyboard is served for an interval of Periodic_Buffer_Check, Serve_The_Users "times out" and rechecks the buffer to determine keyboard information availability.

Here is an abstract algorithm for the encapsulating package:

Abstract Algorithm:

```
loop
   select
     when the intermediate buffer for a keyboard
     is not empty =>
       accept ...
         provide the Char and Chars_Lost;
     or
       (same for this keyboard)
     or
       and so on ...
     or
       delay ...;
   end select;
end loop;
```

Here is the detailed design. The structure graph is shown in Figure 16-6.

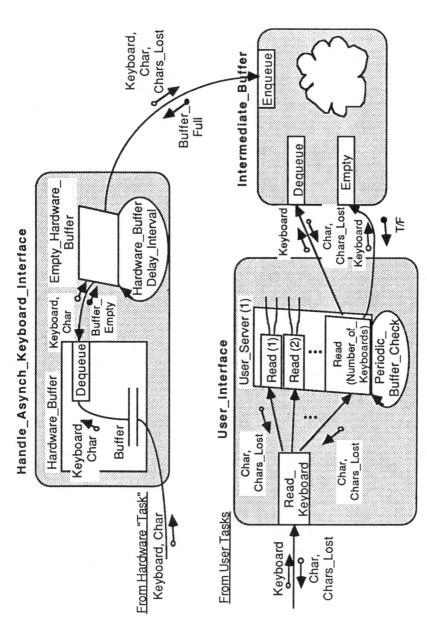

Figure 16-6. MKH structure graph—alternate design of User_Interface package body

435

```
package body User_interface is
  task Serve_The_Users is
    pragma Priority (Serve_User_Priority);

    entry Read (Keyboard_Index) -- note the entry to the family
                     (Char : out Character; Chars_Lost : out Natural);

    -- Calls Intermediate_Buffer.Dequeue
  end Serve_The_Users;

  task body Serve_The_Users is separate;

  procedure Read_Keyboard
      (Keyboard   : in Keyboard_Index;
       Char       : out Character;
       Chars_Lost : out Natural) is
  begin
    Serve_The_Users.Read (Keyboard) (Char, Chars_Lost);
  end Read_Keyboard;
end User_Interface;

with Intermediate_Buffer;
separate (User_Interface)
  task body Serve_The_Users is
    Periodic_Buffer_Check : constant := 0.2;
  begin
    loop
      select
        when the Intermediate_Buffer for this keyboard is not empty =>
          accept Read (for this keyboard) (Char       : out Character;
                                           Chars_Lost : out Natural) do

            get the Char and Chars_Lost (for this keyboard) from
            Intermediate_Buffer.Dequeue;
          end Read;
      or
        same for next keyboard ...
      or
        and the next keyboard, etc.
```

```
    or
      delay Periodic_Buffer_Check;
    end select;
  end loop;
end Serve_The_Users;
```

Here is the coded solution for the task body:

```
with Definitions;  use Definitions;
with Intermediate_Buffer;
separate (User_Interface)
  task body Serve_The_Users is
    Periodic_Buffer_Check : constant := 0.2;
  begin
    loop
      select
        when not Intermediate_Buffer.Empty (1) =>
          accept Read (1) (Char       : out Character;
                           Chars_Lost : out Natural) do
            Intermediate_Buffer.Dequeue  (1, Char, Chars_Lost);
          end Read;
      or
        when not Intermediate_Buffer.Empty (2) =>
          accept Read (2) (Char       : out Character;
                           Chars_Lost : out Natural) do
            Intermediate_Buffer.Dequeue  (2, Char, Chars_Lost);
          end Read;
      or
        when not Intermediate_Buffer.Empty (3) =>
          accept Read (3) (Char       : out Character;
                           Chars_Lost : out Natural) do
            Intermediate_Buffer.Dequeue  (3, Char, Chars_Lost);
          end Read;
      or
        delay Periodic_Buffer_Check;
      end select;
    end loop;
  end Serve_The_Users;
```

An alternate approach to the above use of a select statement with an alternative for each entry in a family is to introduce a polling solution to check the calls on the family of entries. It would look like this.

```
loop
  for I in 1 .. Number_Of_Keyboards loop
    select
      when not Intermediate_Buffer.Empty (I) =>
        accept Read (I) (Char      : out Character;
                         Chars_Lost : out Natural) do
          Intermediate_Buffer.Dequeue  (I, Char, Chars_Lost);
        end Read;
    else
      null;
    end select;
  end loop;

  delay Periodic_Buffer_Check;
end loop;
```

This has the advantages of being more concise and of allowing the single parameter "Number_Of_Keyboards" (from the package Definitions) to specify the family of entries. However, it has the unpleasant characteristic of continually polling the users. Whether or not this is suitable depends upon the exact characteristics of the problem. For example, this might be appropriate in a busy system with balanced demands among users; it would be inappropriate in a system in which typically only a few users were active while the others had long periods of dormancy.

Exercise 16.2 is not solved here.

Solution 16.3 ACI and User Simulation. We first need modifications to the specification of the package Handle_Asynch_Keyboard_Interface. This will allow the simulation to access the "hardware buffer." We could alternatively have included the simulation within the body of the package, but we prefer to group the simulations together in their own package, external to the remainder of the MKH.

```
with Definitions; use Definitions;

package Handle_Asynch_Keyboard_Interface is
  -- Enqueue allows the simulation of the ACI to place information
  -- in the ''hardware'' buffer
```

```
procedure Enqueue (Keyboard : in Keyboard_Index;
                   Char     : in Character);

-- Calls Intermediate_Buffer.Enqueue
end Handle_Asynch_Keyboard_Interface;
```

Then the body needs some modification with an entrance procedure to access the buffer:

```
with Queue_Type_Manager;
package body Handle_Asynch_Keyboard_Interface is
  -- most of the package body is the same
  procedure Enqueue (Keyboard : in Keyboard_Index;
                     Char     : in Character) is
  -- This procedure is part of the simulation of the keyboards
  begin
    Hardware_Buffer_Manager.Enqueue (Hardware_Buffer, (Keyboard, Char));
  exception
    when Hardware_Buffer_Manager.Buffer_Full =>
      null; -- the characters are lost
  end Enqueue;
end Handle_Asynch_Keyboard_Interface;
```

Now we can write the simulation package. It uses the previously established interface to the user interface. It does not matter to the simulation (or the users) whether the user interface is accomplished by an array of tasks or a single task with a family of entries.

```
-- Here is the main part of the simulation

package Simulator is
  -- Calls Handle_Asynch_Keyboard_Interface.Enqueue
  -- Calls User_Interface.Read_Keyboard
end Simulator;

with Definitions;   use Definitions;
with Handle_Asynch_Keyboard_Interface;
with User_Interface;
package body Simulator is

  task type Simulate_Keyboard is
    entry Keyboard_Is (The_Keyboard : in Keyboard_Index);
    -- Calls Handle_Asynch_Keyboard_Interface.Enqueue
  end Simulate_Keyboard;
```

```
    task type Simulate_User is
      entry Keyboard_Is (The_Keyboard : in Keyboard_Index);
      -- Calls User_Interface.Read_Keyboard
    end Simulate_User;

    task body Simulate_Keyboard is separate;
    task body Simulate_User is separate;

    Keyboard : array (Keyboard_Index) of Simulate_Keyboard;
    User     : array (Keyboard_Index) of Simulate_User;
begin -- Simulator
    -- initialize simulations with keyboard numbers

    for This_Keyboard in Keyboard_Index loop
      Keyboard (This_Keyboard).Keyboard_Is (This_Keyboard);
      User     (This_Keyboard).Keyboard_Is (This_Keyboard);
    end loop;
end Simulator;

separate (Simulator)
    task body Simulate_Keyboard is
      My_Keyboard : Keyboard_Index;
    begin
      accept Keyboard_Is (The_Keyboard : in Keyboard_Index) do
        My_Keyboard := The_Keyboard;
      end Keyboard_Is;

      loop
        -- type the character
        for Char in 'a' .. 'z' loop
          Handle_Asynch_Keyboard_Interface.Enqueue (Char, Keyboard);
        end loop;
      end loop;
    end Simulate_Keyboard;

separate (Simulator)
    task body Simulate_User is
      Char        : Character;
      Chars_Lost  : Natural;
      My_Keyboard : Keyboard_Index;
```

```
begin
  accept Keyboard_Is (The_Keyboard : in Keyboard_Index) do
    My_Keyboard := The_Keyboard;
  end Keyboard_Is;

  loop
    User_Interface.Read_Keyboard  (My_Keyboard, Char, Chars_Lost);
    -- do whatever the user does with the information
  end loop;
end Simulate_User;
```

Keys to Understanding

- Representation clauses can allow Ada programs to interact with hardware devices in very detailed ways. Once the specifications are defined, the interface remains at a high level of abstraction—using Ada constructs.

- An effective interface to a hardware device can be established by using polling of a hardware buffer.

- The hardware buffer must be polled often enough that it does not become full.

- The task polling the hardware buffer must not be held up waiting for a rendezvous with some other task. The implication of this is that the interface between the task polling the hardware buffer and the user interface processing must not involve a buffer encapsulated in a task.

- A generic type manager approach to buffering can be effectively used to create multiple buffers.

- Proper encapsulation of design decisions allows considerable change to take place without affecting any processes outside the body of the package being modified.

CHAPTER 7

Tasks as Interrupt Handlers

Objective: To demonstrate how tasks can be used to handle interrupts from external devices

Ada has a consistent concept and notation for handling all aspects of concurrency, including interacting with the true concurrency of external devices. Just as tasks communicate via calls to entries of other tasks, external devices communicate with an Ada program through "calls" to entries of tasks. We call such tasks *interrupt tasks*. The sections below first describe the interrupt process in general, and then provide a discussion of interrupts in Ada. The final section reworks an example from Chapter 15 to illustrate how interrupts can be used in device drivers.

17.1 The Interrupt Process

An interrupt is an asynchronous signal from an external device that causes the execution of a sequence of instructions not in the normal sequence.

The sections below first provide some motivation for the interrupt mechanism, then describe the interrupt process in some detail. The discussion generally follows that of Mick and Brick [MIC80, page 207].

17.1.1   Motivation for Interrupts

A real-time system must have some mechanism for communicating with external devices. In Chapter 15 we saw an example of the use of polling to accomplish the interaction by repeated interrogation of a flag associated with an event. When the device is ready for service (or has accomplished its task) it sets the flag. This is easy to understand and only requires simple hardware for implementation.

However, the method trades hardware for software. The program must explicitly account for the checking of the flags. This takes some extra instructions (and memory) and (more importantly) uses processor resources for checking the flags when no service is required. In summary, "The polling method has low system through-put, high real time overhead and slow response time." [MIC80].

The alternative to polling is to have the external device generate an interrupt request signal that is passed to the processor. This *suspends the execution of the current process* and initiates the execution of an alternate sequence of instructions, the interrupt service routine. The suspended process later resumes execution.

Although the interrupt mechanism requires more hardware, it has many advantages. First, there is no overhead associated with checking flags. This should increase system throughput. Second, response time is typically faster since the interrupt will be serviced at any time, not just when a flag is checked. Third, there are some memory savings.

Most important, however, is the fact that the interrupt mechanism is hidden from individual processes. In the polling approach, processing that has nothing to do with the external device is performed in the intervals between checking of the flags. In the interrupt approach, such processing is in separate tasks (or processes) that simply perform their function without regard to the external device. When an interrupt occurs, such processes are interrupted and later resumed in a transparent manner.

In summary, the interrupt approach provides fast real-time response, high throughput, and is efficient in use of processor resources.

17.1.2 Interrupt Sequence of Events

There are many possible ways to accomplish the details of handling interrupts. The mechanism below is one approach.

Before we discuss the sequence of events, let's introduce the idea of *processor state* and *context switching*. The processor state is the information needed by a process to execute. This information includes the state of all processor registers (accumulators, index registers, program counter, and so on) and the status (flags, condition codes, overflow indicators, and so on). The status is often contained in a *program status word*. The processor state for any individual process is called its context. When an interrupt occurs, the execution environment is changed; this is the context switch.

There are six events that occur in response to an interrupt. They are:

- Interrupt recognition

- Save status

- Interrupt masking

- Interrupt acknowledge

- Interrupt service routine

- Restore and return

Most of these events are performed by the implementation-supplied run time environment. An implementation may require a user to provide some small amount of assembly language code to fine-tune the environment to a specific application. The run time environment works in cooperation with the Ada interrupt handlers to perform the processing for each interrupt.

Interrupt Recognition: At the conclusion of each instruction, the hardware of the processor checks (during the machine instruction fetch cycle) to see if the interrupt request line indicates that an external device requires service. If so, the processor determines *which* device requires service (and may also obtain the address of a specific interrupt handler), possibly in accordance with a priority mechanism.

Status: The next step is to save the context of the currently executing process. If the interrupted process will definately be resumed after the execution of the interrupt handler, this need not be a full context switch. The processor typically saves only a minimum set of flags and registers that are likely to be needed by the interrupt service routine. If a full context switch is required, the remaining information is saved by the software.

This notion of saving status is important for optimization of interrupts in Ada. An implementation may recognize, or allow the programmer to specify with a pragma, situations in which a full context switch is not required.

Interrupt Masking: The processor is set to a state such that additional interrupts are ignored. (They were also ignored during the two steps above.) This step may overlap earlier steps. If the hardware supports priorities, higher priority interrupts may be allowed to occur.

Interrupt Acknowledge: The processor lets the interrupting device know that the interrupt is being serviced.

Interrupt Service Routine: The processor calls the interrupt service routine. The interrupt service routine performs the actions necessary to service the interrupt. We will see below that a call to the interrupt service routine is a call to a task entry. Therefore, the interrupt service routine is actually written in Ada. The way in which the appropriate task/entry is identified is highly machine- and implementation-dependent.

Restore and Return: At the conclusion of execution of the interrupt service routine, the state of the processor is returned to that before the interrupt occured. That is, all the flags and registers are restored to establish the context of the process that had been executing when the interrupt occured. The process is then resumed. The execution of the interrupt process has been completely invisible (except for timing) to the process.

The interrupt task itself will typically loop back to again wait at the accept statement, ready to handle the next interrupt.

Actually, this process may be somewhat more complex than indicated, since the interrupted process may not be the process that is resumed. This may occur if the execution of the interrrupt service routine freed resources that allow a higher priority process to execute. The higher priority process will execute, requiring a full context switch. This situation is implementation-dependent.

17.2   Interrupts in Ada

Interrupts are accomplished through use of the rendezvous mechanism. An entry is associated with an interrupt. The occurrance of the interrupt acts as an entry call by a *mythical hardware task* that has a higher priority than any software task. The entry is associated with an interrupt by the use of an address clause. (This is another use of the address representation clause discussed in Chapter 15.) Here is a simple example:

```
task Interrupt_Handler is
  entry Display_Interrupt;
  for Display_Interrupt use at 8#40#;
end Interrupt_Handler;

task body Interrupt_Handler is
begin
  loop
    ...
    ...
    accept Display_Interrupt;
    ... -- actions in response to interrupt
    ...
  end loop;
end Interrupt_Handler;
```

The accept statement may contain a sequence of statements.

```
...
  accept Display_Interrupt do
    ...
  end Display_Interrupt;
...
```

The use clause assumes that Integer is acceptable for an address. It may be necessary to explicitly convert to the implementation-defined type of Address by withing the package System and having a use clause as:

```
for Display_Interrupt use at System.Address (8#40#);
```

The entry may also have parameters. They may be only of mode *in*. Their meaning is implementation-dependent. The accept statement may be in a select statement, including one with a terminate alternative. The idea of a "sibling" task, as defined in Chapter 12, and of termination rules in general are implementation-dependent. There may be several priorities of interrupts. Of course, the exact effect is implementation-dependent. Ordinary calls (from other Ada tasks) to the entry are allowed. These basic ideas are summarized in Figure 17-1.

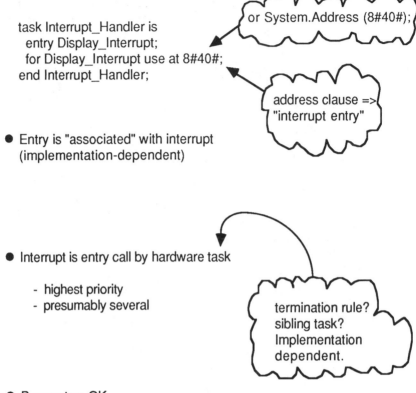

Figure 17-1. Handling interrupts

What happens if an interrupt occurs while it (the same interrupting device) is being serviced? Ada caters to the possibility that interrupts are queued; the calls are then queued just like ordinary entry calls. Usually, however, the interrupt signals will correspond to ordinary entry calls, and hence be lost. Therefore, the handler is only available for execution *while it is waiting at the accept statement*. (What *does not* happen is a recursive execution of the primary handler, as may be allowed with assembly language interrupt handlers.) An implementation may allow the user to provide an alternate entry to be called if there is no possible immediate rendezvous with the primary handler. Then the *alternate* handler may be executed, interrupting the *primary* handler. This sort of mechanism is implementation-dependent.

The rules above imply that a task with an interrupt entry should spend almost all of its existance waiting at the accept for the entry. The accept statement itself should be short, and there should be little code outside the body of the accept. All the code should be concerned with the actions of interrupt handling; the application code, the functions to be performed while awaiting the interrupt, should be in a different task.

17.3 Keyboard/Display with Interrupts

In Chapter 15 we illustrated some issues about machine level constructs by showing a device driver for passing characters from a keyboard to a display. That method used polling. Let's see how we would do the same thing using interrupts. Figure 17-2 illustrates the situation. The display generates an interrupt, which causes transfer (in some machine- and implementation-dependent way) to the interrupt handler. In our situation, this will be an accept statement corresponding to an interrupt entry. Although not shown, a similar situation exists for the keyboard.

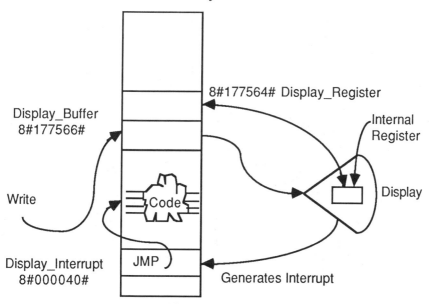

Figure 17-2. Memory_Mapped input/output

The process for reading from the keyboard and writing to the display is:

1. The keyboard places a character in the buffer and then interrupts the processor.

2. The device driver takes the character out of the keyboard buffer and places it into the display buffer. This simultaneously alerts the display that a character is to be displayed.

3. The display displays the character, interrupting the processor when complete.

4. The device driver is ready for another character from the keyboard.

5. The interaction may be more complicated than this for any specific set of devices, but we will use this simple interaction to illustrate the general nature of interrupt handling.

Here is the revised version of the device driver from Chapter 15. We will first illustrate the use of a single task, then of two separate tasks.

Single Task: Version One: Here is our first version of the single task device driver.

```
task Device_Driver is
   entry Keyboard_Interrupt;
   entry Display_Interrupt;

   for Keyboard_Interrupt use at 8#000036#;
   for Display_Interrupt  use at 8#000040#;
end Device_Driver;

task body Device_Driver is
   Keyboard_Buffer : Character;
   for Keyboard_Buffer use at 8#177562#;
   Display_Buffer : Character;
   for Display_Buffer use at 8#177566#;
begin
   loop
     accept Keyboard_Interrupt;
       Display_Buffer := Keyboard_Buffer;

     accept Display_Interrupt;
   end loop;
end Device_Driver;
```

This would be fine in the common case in which the display is much faster than a person typing at a keyboard. However, in order to cater to a variety of speeds (maybe the keyboard will be replaced by a high-speed communication line) or to allow for buffering of characters when the display is blocked, we might want to use a selective wait to be able to accept *either* interrupt.

Single Task: Version Two: The specification is unchanged, while the body of the task changes to:

```
with Buffer; -- a Buffer of the sort discussed in Chapter 7
task body Device_Driver is
   ... -- the same as before
begin
   loop
      select
         accept Keyboard_Interrupt do
            Buffer.Enqueue (Keyboard_Buffer);
         end Keyboard_Interrupt;
      or
         accept Display_Interrupt do
            Buffer.Dequeue (Display_Buffer);
         end Display_Interrupt;
      end select;
   end loop;
end Device_Driver;
```

This solution allows for other than fixed alternating interaction.

There are many options for the buffer; perhaps the most desirable for many situations is the sort of buffer using the algorithm with no explicit count of items in the buffer; this was discussed in Chapter 7 and used in Chapter 15. Placing the buffering/unbuffering in the accept statement ensures that it is not preempted by some higher priority task—unless preempted by some higher priority interrupt in some implementation-dependent manner.

An alternate approach that has a similar effect is to use two tasks.

Two Tasks:

```
task Keyboard_Driver is
  entry Keyboard_Interrupt;

  for Keyboard_Interrupt use at 8#000036#;
end Keyboard_Driver;

task Display_Driver is
  entry Display_Interrupt;
  for Display_Interrupt  use at 8#000040#;
end Display_Driver;

with Buffer;
task body Keyboard_Driver is
  ... -- declarations only for Keyboard
begin
  loop
    accept Keyboard_Interrupt do
      Buffer.Enqueue (Keyboard_Buffer);
    end Keyboard_Interrupt;
  end loop;
end Keyboard_Driver;

with Buffer;
task body Display_Driver is
  ... -- declarations only for Display
begin
  loop
    accept Display_Interrupt do
      Buffer.Dequeue (Display_Buffer);
    end Keyboard_Interrupt;
  end loop;
end Display_Driver;
```

Now we have two tasks, one for each device. One task puts characters in the buffer, the other removes them. The two tasks might well be encapsulated in a device driver package; the package might contain an instantiation of an appropriate buffer, removing the need to "with" the buffer.

This solution nicely accommodates variability in speed of the devices, allows for buffering, allows for literal concurrency when possible, and in general seems to be nicely balanced. Whether or not it is preferable to the earlier solution with two accept statements in a selective wait is dependent upon a specific application and upon a specific implementation.

17.4 Exercises

Exercise 17.1 HLCS with Interrupts.

Purpose: To illustrate the use of interrupts in the context of a case study

Problem: Revise the Hot Line Communication System solution of Chapter 3 to handle interrupts from the external keyboard and display, rather than using the services of the pre-defined packages.

Solution: The general approach is to use the methods of this chapter within the task bodies, rather than make use of the Executive services provided in the HLCS Environment of Chapter 3. This also requires changes to many of the declarations. Some of the declaration changes are simply comments, and do not actually require any recompilation of code using the unit being changed. Assume here that System.Address is Integer. Package Definitions is unchanged from Chapter 3 and is not repeated. Figure 17-3 is a structure graph of this situation. It is a modification of the structure graph of Figure 3-5.

```
package Hardware_Dependent_Package is

    Red_Keyboard_Buffer_Address      : constant := 16#00A0#;
    Red_Keyboard_Interrupt_Address   : constant := 16#00A4#;

    Blue_Keyboard_Buffer_Address     : constant := 16#00B0#;
    Blue_Keyboard_Interrupt_Address  : constant := 16#00B4#;

    Red_Display_Buffer_Address       : constant := 16#00C0#;
    Red_Display_Interrupt_Address    : constant := 16#00C4#;

    Blue_Display_Buffer_Address      : constant := 16#00D0#;
    Blue_Display_Interrupt_Address   : constant := 16#00D4#;
end Hardware_Dependent_Package;
```

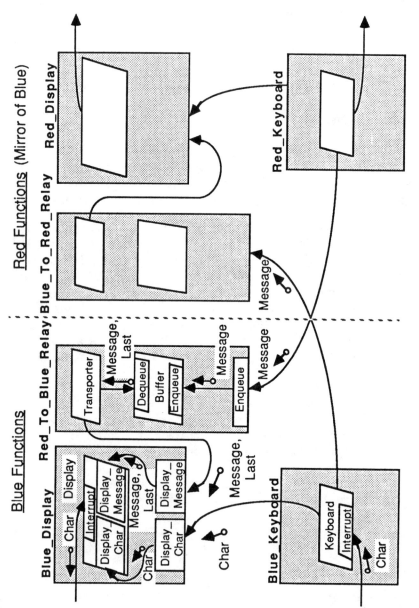

Figure 17-3. HLCS structure graph

454

```
---------- Blue_Display ----------

with Definitions; use Definitions;
package Blue_Display is
   procedure Display_Line (Line : in Line_Type;
                           Last : in Boolean);
   procedure Display_Char (Char : in Character);
   -- Contains hardware-dependent task to interact
   -- with display
end Blue_Display;


---------- Blue Keyboard ----------

package Blue_Keyboard is
   -- Calls
     -- Blue_Display.Display_Char
     -- Blue_To_Red_Relay.Enqueue

   -- Contains machine-dependent task to
   -- interact with the keyboard
end Blue_Keyboard;


---------- Blue_Display package body ----------

with Hardware_Dependent_Package; use Hardware_Dependent_Package;
package body Blue_Display is
   task Display is
      entry Display_Line (Line : in Line_Type; Last : in Boolean);
      entry Display_Char (Char : in Character);

      entry Display_Interrupt;
      for Display_Interrupt use at Blue_Display_Interrupt_Address;
   end Display;

   task body Display is
      Line : Line_Type;
      Last : Boolean;

      Display_Buffer : Character;
      for Display_Buffer use at Blue_Display_Buffer_Address;
```

```
begin
  loop
    select
      accept Display_Line (Line : in Line_Type;
                           Last : in Boolean) do
        Display.Line := Line;
        Display.Last := Last;
      end Display_Line;

      Display_All_Lines_Loop: loop
        Display_The_Line_Loop:
        for I in Message'Range loop
          Display_Buffer := Line (I);

          accept Display_Interrupt;

          exit Display_The_Line_Loop when Line (I) = ASCII.CR;
        end loop Display_The_Line_Loop;

        Display_Buffer := ASCII.LF;

        accept Display_Interrupt;

        exit Display_All_Lines_Loop when Last;

        accept Display_Line (Line : in Line_Type;
                             Last : in Boolean) do
          Display.Line := Line;
          Display.Last := Last;
        end Display_Line;
      end loop Display_All_Lines_Loop;
    or
      when Display_Line'Count = 0 =>
        accept Display_Char (Char : in Character) do
          Display_Buffer := Char;
        end Display_Char;

        accept Display_Interrupt;
```

```
            Display_The_Line_Loop:
            while Display_Buffer /= ASCII.CR loop
              accept Display_Char (Char : in Character) do
                Display_Buffer := Char;
              end Display_Char;

              accept Display_Interrupt;
            end loop Display_The_Line_Loop;

            Display_Buffer := ASCII.LF;
            accept Display_Interrupt;
        or
          terminate;
        end select;
      end loop;
  end Display;

  procedure Display_Line ...

  procedure Display_Char ...
end Blue_Display;

---------- Blue_Keyboard package body ----------

with Definitions; use Definitions;
with Blue_To_Red_Relay;
with Hardware_Dependent_Package; use Hardware_Dependent_Package;
package body Blue_Keyboard is
  task Keyboard is
    entry Keyboard_Interrupt;
    for Keyboard_Interrupt use at Blue_Keyboard_Interrupt_Address;
    -- Calls
      -- Blue_Display.Display_Char
      -- Blue_To_Red_Relay.Enqueue
  end Keyboard;

  task body Keyboard is
    Line : Line_Type;

    Keyboard_Buffer : Character;
    for Keyboard_Buffer use at Blue_Keyboard_Buffer_Address;
```

```
begin
  loop
    Build_Message:
    for I in Message'Range loop
      accept Keyboard_Interrupt;
      Line (I) := Keyboard_Buffer;

      Blue_Display.Display_Char (Line (I));

      exit Build_Message when Line (I) = ASCII.CR;
    end loop Build_Message;

    Blue_To_Red_Relay.Enqueue (Line);
  end loop;
  end Keyboard;
end Blue_Keyboard;
```

Exercise 17.2 Generic HLCS with Interrupts.

Purpose: To illustrate the use of interrupts in a generic solution

Problem: Same as Exercise 17.1 above, but start from the base of the generic HLCS given as the solution to Exercise 3.1.

Solution: Since the tasks are in generic packages, the location of the interrupt entries will have to be generic parameters. The Hardware_Dependent_Package is unchanged from the example above and is not repeated.

```
---------- generic Display_Handler ----------

with System; use System;
with Definitions; use Definitions;
generic
  Display_Interrupt_Address : Address;
  Display_Buffer_Address    : Address;
```

```
package Display_Handler is
  procedure Display_Message (Message : in Message_Type;
                             Last    : in Boolean);
  procedure Display_Char    (Char    : in Character);

  -- Contains hardware-dependent task to interact
  -- with display
end Display_Handler;


---------- generic Keyboard_Handler ----------

with System;      use System;
with Definitions; use Definitions;
generic
  Keyboard_Interrupt_Address : Address;
  Keyboard_Buffer_Address    : Address;
  with procedure Display_Char (Char : in Character);
  with procedure Buffer_Enqueue_Message (Message : in Message_Type);
package Keyboard_Handler is
  -- Calls
    -- Display_Char
    -- Buffer_Enqueue_Message

  -- Contains machine-dependent task to
  -- interact with the keyboard
end Keyboard_Handler;

---------- Display_Handler package body ----------

with Definitions; use Definitions;
package body Display_Handler is
  task Display is
    entry Display_Message (Message : in Message_Type;
                           Last    : in Boolean);
    entry Display_Char (Char : in Character);

    entry Display_Interrupt;
    for Display_Interrupt use at Display_Interrupt_Address;
  end Display;
```

```
task body Display is
  Message : Message_Type;
  Last    : Boolean;

  Display_Buffer : Character;
  for Display_Buffer use at Display_Buffer_Address;
begin
  loop
    select
      accept Display_Message (Message : in Message_Type;
                              Last    : in Boolean) do
        Display.Message := Message;
        Display.Last := Last;
      end Display_Message;

      Display_All_Messages_Loop:
      loop
        Display_The_Message_Loop:
        for I in Message'Range loop
          Display_Buffer := Message (I);

          accept Display_Interrupt;
          exit Display_The_Message_Loop when Message (I) = ASCII.CR;
        end loop Display_The_Message_Loop;

        Display_Buffer := ASCII.LF;

        accept Display_Interrupt;
        exit Display_All_Messages_Loop when Last;

        accept Display_Message (Message : in Message_Type;
                                Last    : in Boolean) do
          Display.Message := Message;
          Display.Last := Last;
        end Display_Message;
      end loop Display_All_Messages_Loop;
    or
      when Display_Message'Count = 0 =>
        accept Display_Char (Char : in Character) do
          Display_Buffer := Char;
        end Display_Char;

        accept Display_Interrupt;
```

```
        Display_The_Message_Loop_2:
        while Display_Buffer /= ASCII.CR loop
          accept Display_Char (Char : in Character) do
            Display_Buffer := Char;
          end Display_Char;

          accept Display_Interrupt;
        end loop Display_The_Message_Loop_2;

        Display_Buffer := ASCII.LF;
        accept Display_Interrupt;
    or
      terminate;
    end select;
  end loop;
end Display;

  procedure Display_Message ...

  procedure Display_Char ...
end Display_Handler;

---------- Display_Handler instantiations ----------

with Display_Handler;
with Hardware_Dependent_Package;        use Hardware_Dependent_Package;
package Blue_Display is new Display_Handler
        (Display_Interrupt_Address => Blue_Display_Interrupt_Address,
         Display_Buffer_Address    => Blue_Display_Buffer_Address);

with Display_Handler;
with Hardware_Dependent_Package;        use Hardware_Dependent_Package;
package Red_Display is new Display_Handler
        (Display_Interrupt_Address => Red_Display_Interrupt_Address,
         Display_Buffer_Address    => Red_Display_Buffer_Address);

---------- Keyboard package body ----------

with Definitions; use Definitions;
```

```
package body Keyboard_Handler is
  task Keyboard is
    entry Keyboard_Interrupt;
    for Keyboard_Interrupt use at Keyboard_Interrupt_Address;
    -- Calls
      -- Display_Char
      -- Buffer_Enqueue_Message
  end Keyboard;

  task body Keyboard is
    Message : Message_Type;

    Keyboard_Buffer : Character;
    for Keyboard_Buffer use at Keyboard_Buffer_Address;
  begin
    loop
      Build_Message:
      for I in Message'Range loop
        accept Keyboard_Interrupt;
        Message (I) := Keyboard_Buffer;
        Display_Char (Message (I));
        exit Build_Message when Message (I) = ASCII.CR;
      end loop Build_Message;

      Buffer_Enqueue_Message (Message);
    end loop;
  end Keyboard;
end Keyboard_Handler;

----------Keyboard instantiations ----------

with Keyboard_Handler;
with Hardware_Dependent_Package;          use Hardware_Dependent_Package;
with Blue_Display;
with Blue_To_Red_Relay;
package Blue_Keyboard is new Keyboard_Handler
    (Keyboard_Interrupt_Address => Blue_Keyboard_Interrupt_Address,
     Keyboard_Buffer_Address    => Blue_Keyboard_Buffer_Address,
     Display_Char               => Blue_Display.Display_Char,
     Buffer_Enqueue_Message     => Blue_To_Red_Relay.Enqueue);
```

```
with Keyboard_Handler;
with Hardware_Dependent_Package;          use Hardware_Dependent_Package;
with Red_Display;
with Red_To_Blue_Relay;
package Red_Keyboard is new Keyboard_Handler
   (Keyboard_Interrupt_Address => Red_Keyboard_Interrupt_Address,
    Keyboard_Buffer_Address    => Red_Keyboard_Buffer_Address,
    Display_Char               => Red_Display.Display_Char,
    Buffer_Enqueue_Message     => Red_To_Blue_Relay.Enqueue);
```

Keys to Understanding

- An address clause associates a task entry with a hardware interrupt. The association is implementation-dependent and may include parameters.

- An interrupt may be considered to be a "mythical hardware task" that has a higher priority than any software task. The hardware interrupts themselves may have relative priority.

- A task is able to immediately service the interrupt only if it is waiting at the *accept* (corresponding to the interrupt entry) at the time of call.

- Interrupts will typically be treated as conditional calls, being handled only if an interrupt task is at its entry point, but may also have the effect of timed or unconditional calls. An implementation may provide for alternate handlers.

- A typical implementation will provide a run-time environment, potentially incorporating some "user-written" code, to capture the interrupt before issuing the appropriate entry call.

- The methods of handling interrupts will be highly implementation-dependent.

Case Five: Remote Temperature Sensor (RTS)

Objective:	To illustrate many features of Ada in the design of a complex system that interacts with three external devices using interrupts

This is the final case study of the book. It is somewhat more complex than previous examples, particularly in that it involves more tasks and interaction with a larger number of different external devices than before.

The sections below follow the usual format.

18.1   Software Requirements Specification

The Remote Temperature Sensor is part of a monitoring system for evaluating and controlling the temperature of a set of furnaces. Figure 18-1 illustrates the RTS situation.

The RTS is implemented in a microprocessor at a location close to the furnaces. The role of the RTS is to obtain and report the furnace temperatures, as directed to do so. It is controlled by, and sends messages to, a remote host computer.

The remote host computer specifies the frequency of temperature readings (in number of readings per hour) for each furnace. The RTS obtains the temperature by interacting with a digital thermometer. The digital thermometer provides the temperature of a specified furnace. The temperature values are transmittted to the remote host computer. This is shown in Figure 18-1.

The specific operations performed by the RTS are:

- Receives and stores orders (control packets) from the host computer. The control packets contain:

  Furnace number

  Frequency of reading the temperature of the furnace

- Keeps track of time
- Queries the digital thermometer and stores temperatures
- Transmits furnace number and temperature (data packets) to the host computer
- Handles the message protocol with the host computer

The characteristics of the host computer are:

- It is remote from the RTS and digital thermometer.
- It transmits control packets to control the frequency of reading the temperature of each furnace.
- It receives messages in a simple format. The messages contain:

  Furnace number

  Temperature of the given furnace

- It implements the message protocol with the RTS.

The digital thermometer accepts an input as a furnace number in the range 0–15, and provides an output of the temperature of the furnace in the range 0–1000 degrees Centigrade. It generates an interrupt to the RTS after it has placed the temperature in a designated hardware buffer.

The RTS and host computer exchange messages. The host computer sends control packets (CPs) to the RTS, and the RTS sends data packets (DPs) to the host computer. The message formats and the message exchange protocol are highly simplified for the purposes of this case study. The formats are:

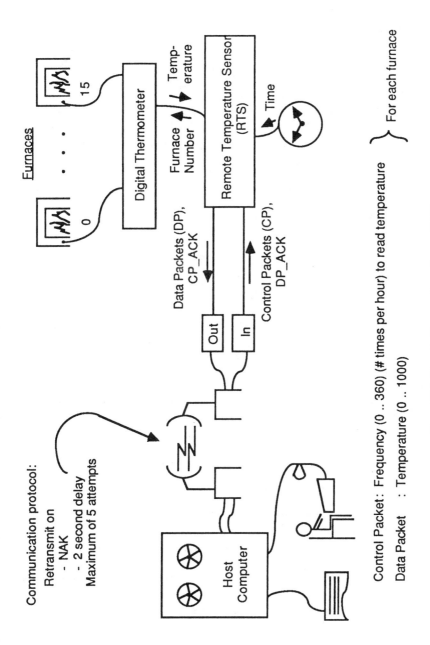

Communication protocol:
Retransmit on
- NAK
- 2 second delay
Maximum of 5 attempts

Furnaces

Digital Thermometer

15

0

Temp-
erature

Furnace
Number

Remote Temperature Sensor
(RTS)

Time

For each furnace

Data Packets (DP),
CP_ACK

Control Packets (CP),
DP_ACK

Out

In

Host
Computer

Control Packet: Frequency (0 .. 360) (# times per hour) to read temperature

Data Packet   : Temperature (0 .. 1000)

Figure 18-1. Remote Temperature Sensor (RTS)

467

- CP Format—(STX) (FF) (RPH) (ETX)
- DP Format—(STX) (FF) (TTTT) (ETX)

where

$\quad$ FF = furnace number in range 0–15

$\quad$ RPH = readings per hour (frequency of reading temperature) in range 0–360.

$\quad$ TTTT = temperature in range 0–1000 degrees Centigrade

$\quad$ STX = start of text

$\quad$ ETX = end of text

The message protocol for the RTS is:

Receive: Receive a message and check for validity:

- If valid, send acknowledgement (ACK)
- If invalid, send negative acknowledgement (NAK)

The criteria for validity are that the message must have an STX, and the two fields of the message must contain numbers in the correct range. The messages are transmitted as a continous sequence of ASCII characters.

CP_ACK represents either an acknowledgement or negative acknowledgement (i.e., an ACK or NAK) of a control packet sent from the host to RTS. Similarly, DP_ACK represents an ACK or NAK of a data packet sent from RTS to the host.

Transmit: Transmit the message, and wait for one of three events:

- Receive acknowledgement (ACK) => Send next message
- Receive negative acknowledgement (NAK) => Retransmit message
- Time-out (2-second delay) => Retransmit message

If the message is transmitted 5 times without an acknowledgement, it is discarded and the next available message is transmitted.
The processing of the RTS is as follows:

- *Receive.* At any time, receive control packets from the host. Buffer up to six control packets at a time. When the buffer is full, discard additional incoming messages. Generate ACK or NAK for incoming control packets from the host computer. At any time, receive ACKs and NAKs of data packets.

- *Read temperature.* Read the temperature of each of the furnaces in accordance with its specified frequency. (This implies a requirement to build and maintain a control table containing the frequency with which each furnace is to be read.) Query the digital thermometer to determine the temperature of the furnace. Store the necessary information for a data packet in a buffer.

- *Buffer messages.* Provide a buffer for the data packet information. Buffer up to 100 furnace/temperature readings, overwriting the oldest information when necessary. The queue discipline is first-in-first-out (FIFO). (In order to store the information as compactly as possible, the buffer is to contain information in numeric, rather than ASCII, format.)

- *Transmit.* Whenever there is information in the buffer, build data packets and transmit them to the host computer in accordance with the communication protocol. Transmit ACK or NAK for the control packets from the host computer.

The processing described above is dependent upon four adaptation parameters (system parameters) that must be easy to modify. The parameters should be isolated and easy to identify in the code. The only changes necessary to modify the parameters is to be a change in one location and a recompilation of the code. These parameters and default values are:

- Size of the input buffer for control packets: 6 messages
- Size of the storage buffer for data packets: 100 furnace readings
- Time-out before retransmit of a data packet: 2 seconds
- Number of transmission retrys before discarding a message: 5 attempts

18.2   RTS Environment

The context diagram shown in Figure 18-2 summarizes the interfaces between the RTS and the external devices. Control packets (CP) and acknowledgements of data packets (DP_ACK) are received from the host computer. Positive or negative acknowledgements of the control packets (CP_ACK) are returned to the host. A furnace number, representing the furnace for which the temperature is to be read, is sent from RTS to the digital thermometer. A temperature reading for the given furnace is received from the digital thermometer. A data packet (DP) is constructed and sent to the host computer.

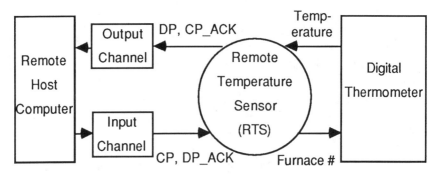

CP -- Control Packet (Host ➔ RTS)

DP -- Data Packet (RTS ➔ Host)

_ACK -- ACK or NAK

Figure 18-2. RTS context diagram

The RTS interacts with the input channel, output channel, and digital thermometer through the interrupt mechanism discussed in Chapter 17. The interrupt locations and buffer addresses for the various devices are shown below. The addresses are given in hexadecimal.

Output Channel:

- Interrupt address: 00A0
- Buffer address: 00A2

Digital Thermometer:

- Interrupt address: 00B0
- Buffer address (Temperature): 00B2
- Buffer address (Furnace): 00B4

Input Channel:

- Interrupt address: 00A4
- Buffer address: 00A6

18.3 Top-Level Design

As usual, we first present the graphical design, followed by the package specifications.

18.3.1 Graphical Design

The preliminary decomposition of the RTS into processes is shown in Figure 18-3a. As we have discussed previously, there is an almost automatic assignment of a process to each external device. We include the functionality of the system with those processes, later separating concerns and identifying additional concurrency through decomposition of the original processes.

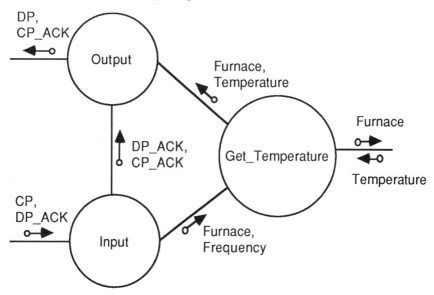

Figure 18-3a. Preliminary RTS process graph

The functions of the three processes are clear from their names and the data being passed. Of greater interest is the next level of decomposition shown in Figure 18-3b. The Input becomes:

- Input_Channel_Handler
- Input_Message_Buffer
- Input_Analyzer

Get_Temperature becomes:

- Temperature_Reading_Sequencer
- DT_Handler
- Furnace_Sequencer

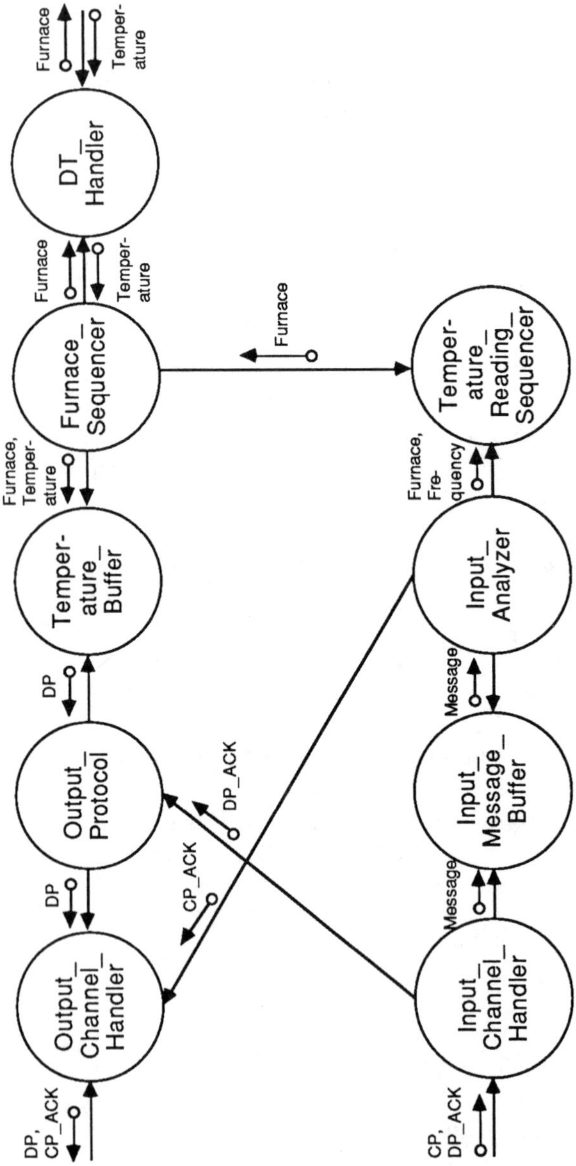

Figure 18-3b. Final RTS process graph

Output becomes:

- Temperature_Buffer
- Output_Protocol
- Output_Channel_Handler

This decomposition is a good example of process abstraction. It is also a somewhat different form of process abstraction than the "edges-in" approach of the ATDS case study in Chapter 9. We first decomposed the context diagram into Input, Output, and Get_Temperature processes. These processes turned out to be concurrent programs, decomposable into the processes shown above. Cherry [CHE86] similarly distinguishes between processes that are sequential programs and processes that are concurrent programs, making the decompostion process explicit with a "hierarchical" process graph. He relies heavily on process abstraction as a foundation for Ada design.

Minispecifications for the Remote Temperature Sensor

Input_Channel_Handler

The Input_Channel_Handler takes CPs and DP_ACKs from the input channel. When it receives a DP_ACK, it sends it to Output_Protocol. When it receives an ASCII.STX, it creates a message and sends it to the Input_Message_Buffer. It discards all other characters in the input stream.

Input_Message_Buffer

The Input_Message_Buffer buffers messages in such a manner as to never block the Input_Channel_Handler when the buffer is full. The message is simply ignored.

Input_Analyzer

The Input_Analyzer takes messages from the buffer and determines whether or not they are valid.

Depending on the outcome it sends either an acknowledgement or negative acknowledgement to the Output_Channel_Handler.

For valid messages, it sends the validated furnace number and frequency of temperature reading to the Temperature_Reading_Sequencer.

Temperature_Reading_Sequencer

The Temperature_Reading_Sequencer maintains the control information, i.e., the information necessary to determine when it is time to read the temperature of a furnace. It blocks the Furnace_Sequencer until time to read, then provides the appropriate furnace number.

DT_Handler

The DT_Handler receives a furnace number and uses it in its interactions with the digital thermometer to obtain the temperature of the furnace. It passes this temperature back to the caller at the conclusion of the rendezvous.

Furnace_Sequencer

The Furnace_Sequencer gets a furnace number from Temperature_Reading_Sequencer, uses DT_Handler to find the associated temperature, and passes both items to the Temperature_Buffer.

Temperature_Buffer

The Temperature_Buffer is more than a simple buffer; it enqueues temperature information, but on a dequeue it provides a Data Packet. If the buffer is full when new temperature information is presented, it overwrites the oldest information in the buffer.

Output_Protocol

The Output_Protocol process controls the transmission and retransmission of Data Packets, depending upon timing and the acknowledgement received from the host computer. It implements the protocol specified in the problem statement.

Output_Channel_Handler

The Output_Channel_Handler transmits DPs and CP_ACKs. It gives preference to CP_ACKs (since they are shorter).

18.3.2   Package Specifications

This section presents the specifications for:

- Definitions
- Hardware_Dependent_Package
- Message_Analyzer

- Receiver
- Temperature_Reading_Sequencer
- Temperature_Buffer
- Temperature_Reader
- Transmitter

Figure 18-4 shows the relationship between the major packages. Most of the packages depend upon Definitions. The order of presentation below is that of a typical compilation order.

In Chapter 9, we defined three catagories of packages:

- Application
- Communication
- Helper

We can use the same catagories to define the packages in this case study.

- Application: The Receiver, Temperature_Reader, and Transmitter do the work of the system.
- Communication: The Temperature_Reading_Sequencer and Temperature_Buffer provide for communication between the application packages. However, they are also helpers.
- Helper: The first class of helper packages are Definitions and Hardware_Dependent_Package. They are needed by many of the other packages and provide the context in which the other packages operate. They can be thought of as "environment" packages. The helpers in the sense of information hiding and abstraction that was discussed in Chapter 9 are Message_Analyzer, Temperature_Reading_Sequencer, and Temperature_Buffer.

The helping packages *hide* or *encapsulate* information and perform the nitty-gritty functions whose detail we wish to defer—i.e., how to validate a message, how to determine the next furnace to read, and how to buffer messages. An effective way to handle such details is to encapsulate them in a package and provide a specification (with a general idea of what the package is to accomplish), but defer the design and implementation until some later time. The application packages can be fully designed (even coded, if we desire) without concern about the detailed workings of the helper packages. When we look at the detailed design, we will see that the helper packages are presented last.

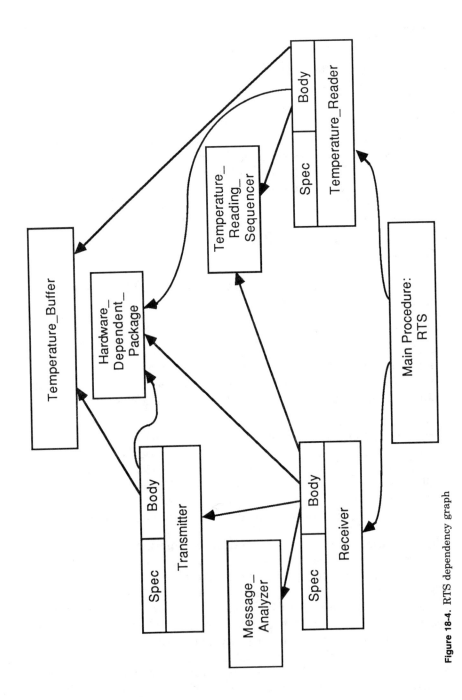

Figure 18-4. RTS dependency graph

18.3.2.1 Definitions.

```
--  Global definitions  ----

package Definitions is
  Max_CP_Chars       : constant := 7;
  Max_DP_Chars       : constant := 8;
  Max_Furnace        : constant := 15;
  Max_Temp           : constant := 1000;
  Max_CP_Msgs        : constant := 6;
  Max_IDP            : constant := 100;
  Highest_Frequency  : constant := 360;
  Max_Retry          : constant := 5;

  Re_Tx_Delay        : constant Duration := 2.0;
  Read_Temp_Period   : constant Duration := 5.0;

  subtype DP_Format    is String (1 .. Max_DP_Chars);
  subtype Message_Type is String (1 .. Max_CP_Chars - 2);

  subtype Furnace_Type   is Natural range 0 .. Max_Furnace;
  subtype Temp_Type      is Natural range 0 .. Max_Temp;
  subtype Frequency_Type is Natural range 0 .. Highest_Frequency;
end Definitions;
```

18.3.2.2 Hardware__Dependent__Package.

```
package Hardware_Dependent_Package is
  Output_Interrupt              : constant := 16#00A0#;
  Output_Location               : constant := 16#00A2#;

  Digital_Thermometer_Interrupt : constant := 16#00B0#;
  Furnace_Location              : constant := 16#00B2#;
  Temperature_Location          : constant := 16#00B4#;

  Input_Interrupt               : constant := 16#00A4#;
  Input_Location                : constant := 16#00A6#;
end Hardware_Dependent_Package;
```

18.3.2.3 Message__Analyzer.

Abstract Algorithm:

```
determine validity of message;
if the message is valid then
  return the furnace number and frequency;
else
  raise Invalid_Message exception;
end if;
```

Specification:

```
with Definitions; use Definitions;
package Message_Analyzer is
  procedure Analyze_Message (Message   : in  Message_Type;
                             Furnace   : out Furnace_Type;
                             Frequency : out Frequency_Type);

  Invalid_Message : exception;
end Message_Analyzer;
```

18.3.2.4 Receiver.

Abstract Algorithm:

```
----- Input_Channel_Handler -----

loop
  accept a character from the input stream;

  if the character is a DP_ACK then
    send it to the Transmitter;
  elsif the character is an ASCII.STX then

    for the length of a message loop
      accept a character from the input stream;
      put the character in a message;
    end loop;

    put the message in a buffer;
  end if;
end loop;
```

```
    put the message in a buffer;
  end if;
end loop;
```

----- Input_Analyzer -----

```
loop
  take messages out of the buffer;
  determine validity of message (using Message_Analyzer)

  if the message is valid then
    send acknowledgement to Transmitter;
    send furnace number and frequency to
      Temperature_Reading_Sequencer;
  else -- message is invalid
    send negative acknowledgement to Transmitter;
  end if;
end loop;
```

Specification:

```
package Receiver is
  -- Calls
    -- Transmitter.DP_Acknowledgement
    -- Message_Analyzer.Analyze_Message
    -- Transmitter.CP_Acknowledgement
    -- Temperature_Reading_Sequencer.Control_Information
end Receiver;
```

18.3.2.5   Temperature__Reading__Sequencer.

Abstract Algorithm:

```
loop
  select
    accept and store control information;
    keep track of number of active furnaces;
  or
    when no control information is available and
        there is at least one active furnace =>
```

```
      accept a request for next furnace to be read do
         find the next furnace to be read;
         update next time-to-read for this furnace;
         delay until it is time to read;
         return the furnace number;
      end a request for next furnace to be read;
   end select;
end loop;
```

Note: There are many possible algorithms for this part of the solution. This one has the potentially undesirable aspect that it may occasionally delay for as long as 1 hour before receiving new control information. We assume this is acceptable. In this algorithm's favor is its nice behavior when no furnaces are actively to be read (frequency of zero readings per hour). In this case, it simply waits for control information; other algorithms might require polling. Of even greater favor for this algorithm is its simplicity.

Specification:

```
with Definitions; use Definitions;
package Temperature_Reading_Sequencer is
   procedure Control_Information (Furnace   : in Furnace_Type;
                                  Frequency : in Frequency_Type);
   procedure Which_To_Read (Furnace : out Furnace_Type);
end Temperature_Reading_Sequencer;
```

18.3.2.6 Temperature_Buffer.

Abstract Algorithm:

```
loop
  select
    accept enqueue temperature information;
    enqueue the temperature information;
  or
    accept dequeue a Data Packet do
      dequeue temperature information;
      build a Data Packet;
      return the Data Packet;
    end dequeue a Data Packet;
  end select;
end loop;
```

Specification:

```
with Definitions; use Definitions;
package Temperature_Buffer is
   procedure Enqueue (Furnace     : in Furnace_Type;
                      Temperature : in Temp_Type);
   procedure Dequeue (Data_Packet : out DP_Format);
end Temperature_Buffer;
```

18.3.2.7   Temperature__Reader.

Abstract Algorithm:

```
----- Furnace_Sequencer -----

loop
   determine what furnace is to be read (blocking on
     an entry in Temperature_Reading_Sequencer until
     it is time to read the furnace);

   get the temperature from DT_Hander;

   enqueue the furnace number and temperature;
end loop;

----- DT_Handler -----

loop
   accept Read_Temperature do
     take furnace number from caller;
     get the temperature from the digital thermometer;
     return the temperature to the caller;
   end Read_Temperature;
end loop;
```

Specification:

```
package Temperature_Reader is
   -- Calls
     -- Temperature_Reading_Sequencer.Which_To_Read
     -- Temperature_Buffer.Enqueue
end Temperature_Reader;
```

18.3.2.8 Transmitter.

Abstract Algorithm:

----- Output_Protocol -----

```
loop
  get a DP from the buffer;

  Transmit_The_DP:
    for specified number of times loop
      send the DP to Output_Channel_Handler;

      select
        accept a DP acknowledgement;
      or
        delay specified delay interval;
      end select;

      if positive acknowledgement then
        exit Transmit_The_DP;
      end if;
    end loop Transmit_The_DP;
end loop;
```

----- Output_Channel_Handler -----

```
loop
  select
    accept a CP acknowledgement;
    transmit the acknowledgement;
  or
    when there are no CP acknowledgements pending =>
      acceot Transmit_DP do
        take a Data Packet from caller;
        transmit the Data Packet;
      end Transmit_DP;
  end select;
end loop;
```

Specification:

```
package Transmitter is
  procedure DP_Acknowledgement (DP_ACK : in Character);
  procedure CP_Acknowledgement (CP_ACK : in Character);
  -- Calls Temperature_Buffer.Dequeue
end Transmitter;
```

18.4   Detailed Design

This section presents the detailed design for:

- Receiver
- Temperature_Reader
- Transmitter
- Message_Analyzer
- Temperature_Reading_Sequencer
- Temperature_Buffer

The packages will be presented in the order indicated. The first three packages are the main work of the RTS. The final three are more of the sort of "helper" packages; they contain the small details of how things are accomplished. We will defer such detail until the end.

Figure 18-5 provides an overview of the detailed design. Figures 18-5a through 18-5e provide the needed detail within the packages.

18.4.1   Receiver

```
with Definitions;              use Definitions;
with Hardware_Dependent_Package;  use Hardware_Dependent_Package;
with Non_Blocking_Bounded_Buffer;
package body Receiver is
  package Input_Message_Buffer is new Non_Blocking_Bounded_Buffer
                            (Buffer_Size   => Max_CP_Msgs,
                             Buffered_Type => Message_Type);
  -- Input_Message_Buffer does not block on an enqueue
```

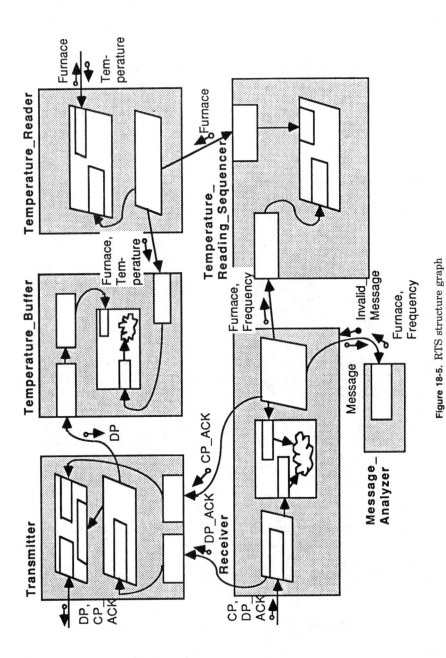

Figure 18-5. RTS structure graph

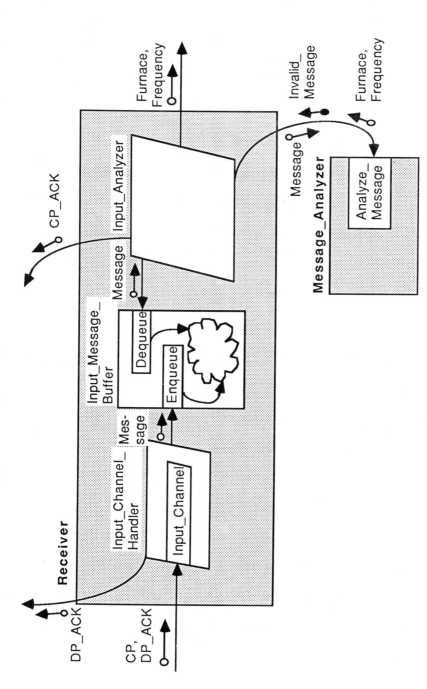

Figure 18-5a. RTS structure graph

485

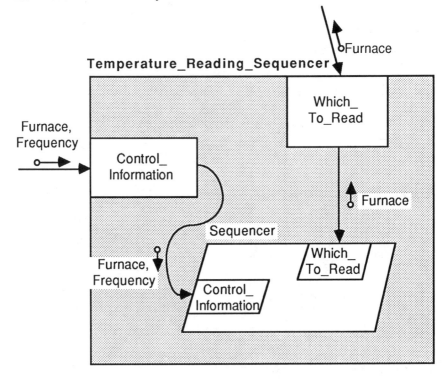

Figure 18-5b. RTS structure graph

```
task Input_Channel_Handler is
   -- Calls
      -- Transmitter.DP_Acknowledgement
      -- Input_Message_Buffer.Enqueue

   entry Input_Channel;
   for Input_Channel use at Input_Interrupt;
end Input_Channel_Handler;

task Input_Analyzer is
   -- Calls
      -- Input_Message_Buffer.Dequeue
      -- Message_Analyzer.Analyze_Message
      -- Transmitter.CP_Acknowledgement
      -- Temperature_Reading_Sequencer.Control_Information
end Input_Analyzer;
```

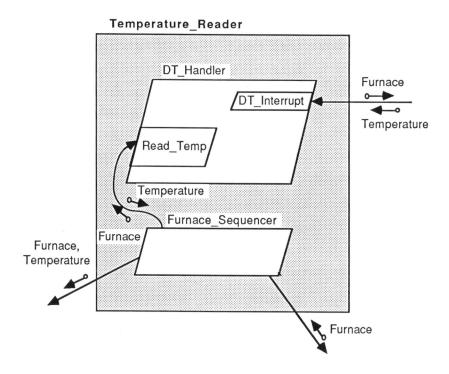

Figure 18-5c. RTS structure graph

```
    task body Input_Channel_Handler is separate;
    task body Input_Analyzer        is separate;
end Receiver;
```

We assume the existance of a generic buffer of the general sort described in Chapter 7. It has the characteristic that it does not block the caller to an enqueue when the buffer is full. It accomplishes this by issuing a *conditional* entry call (in the usual entrance procedure of Enqueue) to the internal task controlling access to the buffer. If the buffer is full, the task will not be prepared to accept a call to Enqueue, the conditional call will fail, and the entrance procedure will simply return control. The end result is that when the buffer is full, the message is discarded.

Temperature_Buffer

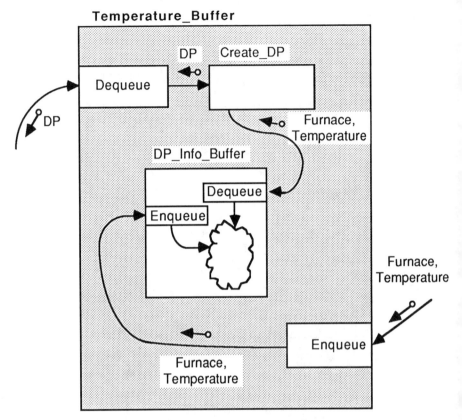

Figure 18-5d. RTS structure graph

```
with Transmitter;
separate (Receiver)
task body Input_Channel_Handler is
  Input_Character : Character;
  Input_Message    : Message_Type;
begin
  loop
    accept Input_Channel;
    get the Input_Character;

    if the Input_Character is an  ASCII.ACK or ASCII.NAK then
      send it to Transmitter.DP_Acknowledgement;
    elsif the Input_Character is an  ASCII.STX then
```

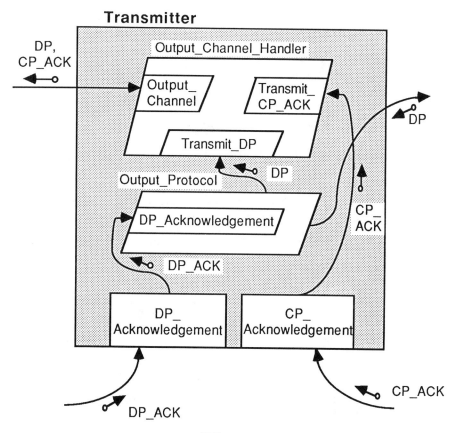

Figure 18-5e. RTS structure graph

```
Build_Input_Message:
for I in Message_Type'Range loop
   accept Input_Channel;
   build the Input_Message ;
  end loop Build_Input_Message;

   send the Input_Message  to Input_Message_Buffer.Enqueue;
  end if;
 end loop;
end Input_Channel_Handler;

with Message_Analyzer;
with Transmitter;
with Temperature_Reading_Sequencer;
separate (Receiver)
```

```
task body Input_Analyzer is
  Input_Message  : Message_Type;
  Furnace    : Furnace_Type;
  Frequency : Frequency_Type;
begin
  loop
    Input_Message_Buffer.Dequeue (Input_Message);

    Limit_Invalid_Message_Exception:
    begin
      using Message_Analyzer.Analyze_Message, find the
        values of Furnace and Frequency while determining
        if a message is valid (an exception will be raised
        when a message is invalid);

        send the Furnace and Frequency to
          Temperature_Reading_Sequencer;

        send Transmitter a positive acknowledgement;
      exception
        when Message_Analyzer.Invalid_Message =>
          send Transmitter a negative acknowledgement;
      end Limit_Invalid_Message_Exception;
    end loop;
end Input_Analyzer;
```

18.4.2 Temperature_Reader

```
with Definitions;                use Definitions;
with Hardware_Dependent_Package; use Hardware_Dependent_Package;
package body Temperature_Reader is
  task DT_Handler is
    entry DT_Interrupt;
    for DT_Interrupt use at Digital_Thermometer_Interrupt;
    entry Read_Temp (Furnace     : in  Furnace_Type;
                     Temperature : out Temp_Type);
  end DT_Handler;
```

```
   task Furnace_Sequencer is
     -- Calls
       -- Temperature_Reading_Sequencer.Which_To_Read
       -- DT_Handler.Read_Temp
       -- Temperature_Buffer.Enqueue
   end Furnace_Sequencer;

   task body DT_Handler        is separate;
   task body Furnace_Sequencer is separate;
end Temperature_Reader;

separate (Temperature_Reader)
  task body DT_Handler is
  begin
    loop
      accept Read_Temp (Furnace     : in  Furnace_Type;
                        Temperature : out Temp_Type) do
        use the Furnace to get the Temperature from
          digital thermometer;
      end Read_Temp;
    end loop;
  end DT_Handler;

with Temperature_Reading_Sequencer;
with Temperature_Buffer;
separate (Temperature_Reader)
  task body Furnace_Sequencer is
    Furnace     : Furnace_Type;
    Temperature : Temp_Type;
  begin
    loop
      block on a call to Temperature_Reading_Sequencer.Which_To_Read
      to obtain the furnace number;

      use the furnace number to get the temperature from
        DT_Handler.Read_Temp;

      send the furnace number and temperature to
        Temperature_Buffer.Enqueue;
      end loop;
    end Furnace_Sequencer;
```

18.4.3 Transmitter

```
with Definitions;                    use Definitions;
with Hardware_Dependent_Package; use Hardware_Dependent_Package;
package body Transmitter is
  task Output_Channel_Handler is
    entry Transmit_DP      (DP     : in DP_Format);
    entry Transmit_CP_ACK (CP_ACK : in Character);
    entry Output_Channel;
    for Output_Channel use at Output_Interrupt;
  end Output_Channel_Handler;

  task Output_Protocol is
    -- Calls
      -- Output_Channel_Handler.Transmit_DP

    entry DP_Acknowledgement (DP_ACK : in Character);
  end Output_Protocol;

  task body Output_Channel_Handler is separate;
  task body Output_Protocol        is separate;

  procedure DP_Acknowledgement (DP_ACK : in Character) is
  begin
    Output_Protocol.DP_Acknowledgement (DP_ACK);
  end DP_Acknowledgement;

  procedure CP_Acknowledgement (CP_ACK : in Character) is
  begin
    Output_Channel_Handler.Transmit_CP_ACK (CP_ACK);
  end CP_Acknowledgement;
end Transmitter;
```

```
separate (Transmitter)
  task body Output_Channel_Handler is
  begin
    loop
      select
        when Transmit_CP_ACK'Count = 0 =>
          accept Transmit_DP (DP : in DP_Format) do
            for I in DP'Range loop
              transmit a character in the Data Packet;
            end loop;
          end Transmit_DP;
      or
        accept Transmit_CP_ACK (CP_ACK : in Character) do
          transmit the CP_ACK;
        end Transmit_CP_ACK;
      end select;
    end loop;
  end Output_Channel_Handler;

with Temperature_Buffer;
separate (Transmitter)
  task body Output_Protocol is
    DP      : DP_Format;
    DP_ACK : Character;
  begin
    loop
      dequeue a Data Packet (DP) from Temperature_Buffer.Dequeue;

      DP_ACK := ASCII.NAK; -- NAK until positive acknowledgement

      Transmit_The_DP:
      for I in 1 .. Max_Retry loop
        send the DP to Output_Channel_Handler.Transmit_DP;

        select
          accept DP_Acknowledgement (DP_ACK : in Character) do
            Output_Protocol.DP_ACK := DP_Acknowledgement.DP_ACK;
          end DP_Acknowledgement;
        or
          delay Re_Tx_Delay; -- Wait for timeout
        end select;
```

```
        exit Transmit_The_DP when DP_ACK = ASCII.ACK;
      end loop Transmit_The_DP;
    end loop;
  end Output_Protocol;
```

18.4.4 Message__Analyzer

```
package body Message_Analyzer is
  procedure Analyze_Message (Message   : in  Message_Type;
                             Furnace   : out Furnace_Type;
                             Frequency : out Frequency_Type)
                                                    is separate;
end Message_Analyzer;

separate (Message_Analyzer)
  procedure Analyze_Message (Message   : in  Message_Type;
                             Furnace   : out Furnace_Type;
                             Frequency : out Frequency_Type) is
  begin
    calculate Furnace   using the attribute Integer'Value;
    calculate Frequency using the attribute Integer'Value;

    (If the Furnace or Frequency are not in the correct range, use
      of the attribute will raise Constraint_Error -- this indicates
      an invalid message.)

  exception
    when Constraint_Error => -- raised on invalid values in the message
      raise Invalid_Message;
  end Analyze_Message;
```

18.4.5 Temperature__Reading__Sequencer

```
with Calendar;  use Calendar;
package body Temperature_Reading_Sequencer is
  task Sequencer is
    entry Control_Information (Furnace   : in Furnace_Type;
                               Frequency : in Frequency_Type);
    entry Which_To_Read (Furnace : out Furnace_Type);
  end Sequencer;

  task body Sequencer is separate;
```

```
procedure Control_Information (Furnace    : in Furnace_Type;
                               Frequency : in Frequency_Type) is
begin
   Sequencer.Control_Information (Furnace, Frequency);
end Control_Information;

procedure Which_To_Read (Furnace : out Furnace_Type) is
begin
   Sequencer.Which_To_Read (Furnace);
end Which_To_Read;
end Temperature_Reading_Sequencer;

separate (Temperature_Reading_Sequencer)
   task body Sequencer is
      type Control_Element is
        record
          Time_To_Read : Time;
          Frequency    : Frequency_Type;
        end record;

      Control_Table : array (Furnace_Type) of Control_Element;
      Number_Active : Natural := 0;
      procedure Establish_Next_Furnace (Furnace : out Furnace_Type)
                                                   is separate;
   begin
     loop
       select
         accept Control_Information (Furnace    : in Furnace_Type;
                                     Frequency : in Frequency_Type) do
             if Frequency is 0 then
               if this causes a furnace to be deactivated then
                 deactivate the furnace;
                 decrement Number_Active;
               end if;
             else -- Frequency is not zero
               if this causes a furnace to be activated then
                 increment Number_Active;
               end if;

               set this furnace's Time_To_Read to the current time;
               set this furnace's Frequency to the new Frequency;
             end if;
         end Control_Information;
       or
```

```
          when at least one furnace is active and
               there are no calls to Control_Information  =>
            accept Which_To_Read (Furnace : out Furnace_Type) do
               Establish_Next_Furnace (Furnace);
             end Which_To_Read;
        end select;
      end loop;
  end Sequencer;


separate (Temperature_Reading_Sequencer.Sequencer)
   procedure Establish_Next_Furnace (Furnace : out Furnace_Type) is
      -- use and set information in Sequencer.Control_Table

   Time_Interval : constant := 3600.0;

   Next_Furnace is the next furnace to be read (this procedure
   finds the number of the next furnace)

   Earliest is the Time_To_Read for the next furnace to be read

   Initialize Earliest to a time larger than the next time to
   read of any furnace

   begin
     Find_Next_Furnace:
     for all the furnaces loop
       if Frequency of this furnace is not zero and
          Time_To_Read of this furnace is less than Earliest then
          set Earliest to this furnace's Time_To_Read;
          set Next_Furnace to this furnace number;
        end if;
     end loop Find_Next_Furnace;

     delay until it is time to read the Next_Furnace;
     update the Time_To_Read of the furnace;
     return the number of the furnace to be read;
   end Establish_Next_Furnace;
```

18.4.6 Temperature_Buffer

```
with Generic_Overwriting_Bounded_Buffer;
package body Temperature_Buffer is
  type IDP is
    record
      Furnace     : Furnace_Type;
      Temperature : Temp_Type;
    end record;

  package DP_Info_Buffer is new Generic_Overwriting_Bounded_Buffer
      (Buffer_Size  => Max_IDP,
       Buffered_Type => IDP);
  -- DP_Info_Buffer overwrites oldest message

  procedure Create_DP (DP : out DP_Format) is separate;
  procedure Enqueue (Furnace     : in Furnace_Type;
                     Temperature : in Temp_Type) is
  begin
    DP_Info_Buffer.Enqueue ( (Furnace, Temperature) );
  end Enqueue;

  procedure Dequeue (Data_Packet : out DP_Format) is
  begin
    Create_DP (Data_Packet);
  end Dequeue;
end Temperature_Buffer;

separate (Temperature_Buffer)
  procedure Create_DP (DP : out DP_Format) is
    Furnace     : Furnace_Type;
    Temperature : Temp_Type;
  begin
    dequeue Temperature_Data (i.e., Furnace and Temperature);

    build the ASCII information in a DP using the attribute
      Integer'Image for both Temperature and Furnace;

    DP (1) := ASCII.STX;
    DP (8) := ASCII.ETX;
  end Create_DP;
```

18.5 Code

This section presents the code for the separate tasks and procedures of:

- Receiver
- Temperature_Reader
- Transmitter
- Message_Analyzer
- Temperature_Reading_Sequencer
- Temperature_Buffer

18.5.1 Receiver

```
with Transmitter;
separate (Receiver)
task body Input_Channel_Handler is
  Input_Character : Character;
  Input_Message   : Message_Type;

  Input_Buffer : Character := ' ';  -- Dummy Character
  for Input_Buffer use at Input_Location;
begin
  loop
    accept Input_Channel;
    Input_Character := Input_Buffer;

    if ((Input_Character = ASCII.ACK) or
        (Input_Character = ASCII.NAK)) then
      Transmitter.DP_Acknowledgement (Input_Character);
    elsif (Input_Character = ASCII.STX) then

      Build_Input_Message:
      for I in Message_Type'Range loop
        accept Input_Channel;
        Input_Message  (I) := Input_Buffer;
      end loop Build_Input_Message;

      Input_Message_Buffer.Enqueue (Input_Message);
    end if;
  end loop;
end Input_Channel_Handler;
```

```
with Message_Analyzer;
with Transmitter;
with Temperature_Reading_Sequencer;
separate (Receiver)
task body Input_Analyzer is
  Input_Message  : Message_Type;
  Furnace    : Furnace_Type;
  Frequency : Frequency_Type;
begin
  loop
    Input_Message_Buffer.Dequeue (Input_Message);

    Limit_Invalid_Message_Exception:
    begin
      Message_Analyzer.Analyze_Message (Input_Message,
                                        Furnace,
                                        Frequency);
      Temperature_Reading_Sequencer.Control_Information
                                        (Furnace, Frequency);
      Transmitter.CP_Acknowledgement (ASCII.ACK);
    exception
      when Message_Analyzer.Invalid_Message =>
        Transmitter.CP_Acknowledgement (ASCII.NAK);
    end Limit_Invalid_Message_Exception;
  end loop;
end Input_Analyzer;
```

18.5.2   Temperature_Reader

```
separate (Temperature_Reader)
  task body DT_Handler is
    Furnace : Furnace_Type;
    for Furnace use at Furnace_Location;
    Temperature : Temp_Type;
    for Temperature use at Temperature_Location;
```

```
begin
  loop
    accept Read_Temp (Furnace     : in  Furnace_Type;
                      Temperature : out Temp_Type) do
      DT_Handler.Furnace := Furnace;
      accept DT_Interrupt;
      Temperature := DT_Handler.Temperature;
    end Read_Temp;
  end loop;
end DT_Handler;

with Temperature_Reading_Sequencer;
with Temperature_Buffer;
separate (Temperature_Reader)
  task body Furnace_Sequencer is
    Furnace     : Furnace_Type;
    Temperature : Temp_Type;
  begin
    loop
      Temperature_Reading_Sequencer.Which_To_Read (Furnace);
      DT_Handler.Read_Temp (Furnace, Temperature);
      Temperature_Buffer.Enqueue (Furnace, Temperature);
    end loop;
  end Furnace_Sequencer;
```

18.5.3 Transmitter

```
separate (Transmitter)
  task body Output_Channel_Handler is
    Output_Buffer : Character;
    for Output_Buffer use at Output_Location;
  begin
    loop
      select
        when Transmit_CP_ACK'Count = 0 =>
          accept Transmit_DP (DP : in DP_Format) do
            for I in DP'Range loop
              Output_Buffer := DP (I);
              accept Output_Channel;
            end loop;
          end Transmit_DP;
      or
```

```
          accept Transmit_CP_ACK (CP_ACK : in Character) do
            Output_Buffer := CP_ACK;
            accept Output_Channel;
          end Transmit_CP_ACK;
        end select;
      end loop;
  end Output_Channel_Handler;

with Temperature_Buffer;
separate (Transmitter)
  task body Output_Protocol is
    DP      : DP_Format;
    DP_ACK : Character;
  begin
    loop
      Temperature_Buffer.Dequeue (DP);

      DP_ACK := ASCII.NAK; -- NAK until positive acknowledgement
      Transmit_The_DP:
      for I in 1 .. Max_Retry loop
        Output_Channel_Handler.Transmit_DP (DP);

        select
          accept DP_Acknowledgement (DP_ACK : in Character) do
            Output_Protocol.DP_ACK := DP_Acknowledgement.DP_ACK;
          end DP_Acknowledgement;
        or
          delay Re_Tx_Delay; -- Wait for timeout
        end select;

        exit Transmit_The_DP when DP_ACK = ASCII.ACK;
      end loop Transmit_The_DP;
    end loop;
  end Output_Protocol;
```

18.5.4 Message—Analyzer

```
separate (Message_Analyzer)
  procedure Analyze_Message (Message   : in  Message_Type;
                             Furnace   : out Furnace_Type;
                             Frequency : out Frequency_Type) is
```

```
begin
  Furnace    := Integer'Value (Message (1 .. 2) );
  Frequency := Integer'Value (Message (3 .. 5) );
exception
  when Constraint_Error => -- raised on invalid values in the message
    raise Invalid_Message;
end Analyze_Message;
```

18.5.5   Temperature_Reading_Sequencer

```
separate (Temperature_Reading_Sequencer)
  task body Sequencer is
    type Control_Element is
      record
        Time_To_Read : Time;
        Frequency    : Frequency_Type;
      end record;

    Control_Table : array (Furnace_Type) of Control_Element;
    Number_Active : Natural := 0;
    procedure Establish_Next_Furnace (Furnace : out Furnace_Type)
                                                      is separate;
  begin
    loop
      select
        accept Control_Information (Furnace   : in Furnace_Type;
                                    Frequency : in Frequency_Type) do
          if Frequency = 0 then
            if Control_Table (Furnace).Frequency /= 0 then
              Control_Table (Furnace).Frequency := 0;
              Number_Active := Number_Active - 1;
            end if;
          else -- Frequency is not zero
            if Control_Table (Furnace).Frequency = 0 then
              Number_Active := Number_Active + 1;
            end if;

            Control_Table (Furnace).Time_To_Read := Clock;
            Control_Table (Furnace).Frequency := Frequency;
          end if;
        end Control_Information;
      or
```

```
          when Number_Active > 0 and
               Control_Information'Count = 0 =>
            accept Which_To_Read (Furnace : out Furnace_Type) do
              Establish_Next_Furnace (Furnace);
            end Which_To_Read;
        end select;
      end loop;
  end Sequencer;


separate (Temperature_Reading_Sequencer.Sequencer)
  procedure Establish_Next_Furnace (Furnace : out Furnace_Type) is

    -- use and set information in Sequencer.Control_Table

    Time_Interval           : constant := 3600.0;
    Very_Long_Time_Interval : constant := Time_Interval + 1.0;

    Next_Furnace : Furnace_Type;
    Earliest     : Time := Clock + Duration (Very_Long_Time_Interval);
  begin
    Find_Next_Furnace:
    for This_Furnace in Furnace_Type loop
      if Control_Table (This_Furnace).Frequency /= 0 and
         Control_Table (This_Furnace).Time_To_Read < Earliest then

        Earliest := Control_Table (This_Furnace).Time_To_Read;
        Next_Furnace := This_Furnace;
      end if;
    end loop Find_Next_Furnace;

    delay Control_Table (Next_Furnace).Time_To_Read - Clock;

    Control_Table (Next_Furnace).Time_To_Read :=
        Control_Table (Next_Furnace).Time_To_Read +
        Duration (Time_Interval / Control_Table (Next_Furnace).Frequency);

    Furnace := Next_Furnace;
  end Establish_Next_Furnace;
```

18.5.6 Temperature__Buffer

```
separate (Temperature_Buffer)
  procedure Create_DP (DP : out DP_Format) is
    Temperature_Data : IDP;
    Furnace      : Furnace_Type;
    Temperature : Temp_Type;
  begin
    DP_Info_Buffer.Dequeue (Temperature_Data);

    Furnace      := Temperature_Data.Furnace;
    Temperature := Temperature_Data.Temperature;

    if Temperature < 10 then
      DP (6 .. 7) := Integer'Image (Temperature);
      DP (4 .. 6) := "000";
    elsif Temperature < 100 then
      DP (5 .. 7) := Integer'Image (Temperature);
      DP (4 .. 5) := "00";
    elsif Temperature < 1000 then
      DP (4 .. 7) := Integer'Image (Temperature);
      DP (4 .. 4) := "0";
    else -- Temperature = 1000 then
      DP (3 .. 7) := Integer'Image (Temperature);
    end if;

    if Furnace < 10 then
      DP (2 .. 3) := Integer'Image (Furnace);
      DP (2 .. 2) := "0";
    else
      DP (1 .. 3) := Integer'Image (Furnace);
    end if;

    DP (1) := ASCII.STX;
    DP (8) := ASCII.ETX;
  end Create_DP;
```

18.6 Discussion

The RTS is a large design problem in concurrency. The RTS is called upon to interact with three external devices, with the transmit and receive sides of the system interacting via a specified communication protocol. Many design decisions were made during the development of a solution. These decisions were expressed in the minispecifications, abstract algorithms, and pseudocode intermixed with the Ada control constructs convey the nature of what is being accomplished. Nonetheless, a few points are worthy of discussion.

The "Temperature_Buffer" is not simply a buffer; it does some significant amount of processing in terms of storing the furnace and temperature data in an internal format, then building a message in an external, ASCII, format when a user wishes to remove data. Since it does this additional work, we characterize it as a helper package rather than a communication package. (The process graph hints at this complexity early in the design; the input and output of the buffer are not the same. See Figure 18-3b.) The hiding of the details of the buffer structure and associated transformations is an important design decision.

In this book, we have placed an emphasis on concurrency issues rather than design issues, but the nature of the case studies tends to illustrate certain design principles in any event. The principle applied here is that of information hiding [PAR72]: a module should let its user know everything needed for proper use of the module, *and nothing more.* Certain design methods might consider the Temperature_Buffer to be a form of "abstract data type," or a "resource," or an "object" that has certain operations that may be performed upon it.

The RTS design used both process and data abstraction to accomplish decomposition into Ada components. Wegner [WEG84] has characterized both forms of abstraction as "object oriented." Indeed, we could have considered the three major processes of Figure 18-3a to be Input Channel, Thermometer, and Output Channel "objects" in the sense of object-oriented design [BOO87]. However, our later decomposition follows more nearly the guidelines of Buhr [BUH84], Cherry [CHE86], and Nielsen [NIE88].

The interaction between the Output_Protocol and the Output_Channel_Handler is interesting in that the handler does not simply take the data and transmit it; instead, it holds the caller (Output_Protocol) *in the rendezvous* while the transmission takes place. This is done in order to ensure accurate timing for the retransmit delay in Output_Protocol.

Output_Protocol has another interesting characteristic: it makes calls and is also a called task. This is certainly legal, and sometimes appropriate, but is actually relatively rare. Most of the tasks we have seen are either strictly caller or strictly called. (Our only previous exception in a case study was the Serve_The_Users task in the MKH problem in Chapter 16. It was called by users and called a package in order to obtain data from a buffer. In fact, this is only a partial exception since it turned out that the package encapsulating the data structure did not use an internal task; it accessed the data buffer directly.)

Output_Protocol is conveniently a caller to obtain information from a buffer task and to call (so that it may be held in a rendezvous) the Output_Channel_Handler. It is conveniently called in order to either time-out or receive an acknowledgement from a task that is a natural caller—the Input_Channel_Handler. If we wish to modify the caller/called relationship so that they are both callers, we could place a buffer (strictly called) between them. This is a design decision.

The entire interaction between these two tasks is complex; we want to neither hold up the input side of the communication while waiting for a message transmission (which the current design takes the risk of), nor to risk the loss of an acknowledgement. There are a number of alternate designs for this interaction, some of which are suggested as exercises.

There are many other complex interactions. In fact, that is the point of this case study. The timing and synchronization, the caller/called decisions, the use of step-wise refinement, and so on, make this a case worth your continued study.

18.7 Exercises

Exercise 18.1. Analyze alternative interactions between the Input_Channel_Handler and the Output_Protocol. For example, have the Input_Channel_Handler issue a conditional or timed entry call. Have the entrance procedure of the Transmitter package issue the conditional or timed entry call. Change the direction of call, i.e., have the Output_Protocol task call the Input_Channel_Handler. What is the effect of each change?

Exercise 18.2. Place an intermediary between the Input_Channel_Handler and Output_Protocol. What sort of an intermediary should it be? Note that if the intermediary is a buffer, Output_Protocol becomes a pure caller. What are the alternatives regarding timed and conditional entry calls in this situation? Can there ever be more than one DP acknowledgement outstanding? What about errors on the communication line causing false acknowledgements?

Exercise 18.3. Is the ACK/NAK scheme for transmissions secure in the face of various sorts of line errors and failures? What problems arise because of the simplistic ACK/NAK scheme with only a single message outstanding? Fix the problems by implementing a message numbering scheme, and ACK/NAK by message number. Allow several messages to be outstanding, waiting for ACK or NAK.

Exercise 18.4. Instead of sending a single message for each temperature reading, "batch" the readings into a periodic transmission of a single message.

Exercise 18.5. Implement an error detection scheme as part of the message construction and processing. NAK messages with errors.

Exercise 18.6. There are many additional alternate algorithms and other design decisions to be made in this problem. You can benefit from thinking about and implementing various alternatives. No solutions are presented here.

Keys to Understanding

- The Remote Temperature Sensor bears considerable similarity to actual real-time systems; it is a good approximation to the level of complexity of task interactions.

- Both process abstraction and data abstraction are important to software design.

- The task interaction mechanisms we have discussed throughout the book—caller/called, uncoupling with intermediaries, buffers, and so on—continue to be important.

- The development approach—of top-level design (graphical and specification), detailed design, and code—is particularly applicable and important to a large problem like the RTS.

- The development approach is an application of step-wise refinement: the deferral of unnecessary detail at each stage of the development, while addressing additional problems and completing detail at a later stage.

- The notion of the "helper" package with details encapsulated in the package body assists the deferral of detail.

- The Ada model of concurrency, taken together with other advanced Ada features, provides an effective tool for the implementation of real-time systems.

- If you have read this far, and worked the exercises and case studies, you "Understand Concurrency in Ada!"

The Cobbler Problems

The purpose of the cobbler problems is to use a single problem to introduce many Ada concepts. We will start with a very simple statement of the problem and then build a series of exercises to elaborate on the problem. The situation will build in complexity to a certain point where we will no longer make the problem larger, but rather will consider alternative solutions. The solutions are presented in Appendix B.

One of the principal topics to be illustrated in the series of problems is the major models of client-server interaction.

In the client-server model of task interaction, we have a very general situation in which the client gives the server a "request" (a message to be encrypted or transmitted, an equation to be solved, a request for resources, a worn pair of boots, and so on) and then receives a "product" (the encrypted or transmitted form of the message, the result of solving the equation, the resources, or the repaired boots).

The model is even more general than the sort of interactions specified. For example, similar methods may be used to ensure that a task attempting to release resources has the authority to do so, i.e., either had requested the resources in the first place or has been granted permission to release the resources by the original requester.

An essential aspect of the interaction is that the product returned to a task generally must be associated with the original request. For example, if a series of tasks submitted messages to be encrypted, we generally want each task to receive the encrypted version of its own plain text message. Similarly, we want the solution to an equation returned only to the original requester.

There are three paradigms for the client-server interaction:

- Waiting model: The client waits for service, i.e., the service is performed during the rendezvous.

- Mailbox model: The client provides the address of a task that serves as a mailbox. The server returns the product or result to the mailbox. The client retrieves the product from the mailbox.

- Receipt model: The server accepts a request for service and issues a receipt. The client later uses the receipt to retrieve a product.

In each case, the client is assured that it receives its own result. In the problems below, the client-server relationship will be demonstrated by a customer (client) and a cobbler shop (server).

Problem Statement

A customer (potentially many customers, but just one for now) has a pair of boots to be repaired. He goes to a cobbler shop to have them repaired. He waits for the boots to be repaired, then goes about his business.

His boots may be of any of the types: cowboy, ski, or waders. The boot status is any of: brand new, worn, or repaired. The way the cobbler repairs the boots is to change the condition of the boots from worn to repaired. The cobbler will not repair boots unless they are worn.

Here are the problems:

Cobbler__1.

Purpose: To establish the basic cobbler problem

Problem: Implement the basic cobbler task interactions. Implement both tasks in the declarative part of a procedure. Do you have an option as to which task is the calling task? This is the first of the three client-server paradigms to be illustrated: the waiting model.

Cobbler__2.

Purpose: To illustrate methods of using a task specification in a package specification

Problem: Let there be three customers.

Put the customers in one package and the cobbler in a separate package. Make both packages library units. Put the cobbler task specification in the package specification. Have the customers make unconditional, timed, and conditional entry calls on the entry. (Each customer makes a different type of entry call.)

Also rename the entry as a procedure so that customers who do not wish to make timed or conditional calls have the same interface as the previous example.

Cobbler__3.

Purpose: To illustrate the use of entrance procedures, including with conditional and timed entry calls

Problem: Put the cobbler task specification in the package body. Provide entrance procedures for three types of calls: conditional, timed, and unconditional. Return a parameter that tells the caller whether the call resulted in a rendezvous. Which is preferable—the placement of a task specification in the package specification, or its placement in the body with the use of entrance procedures?

Cobbler__4.

Purpose: To use an exception as a replacement for a status parameter

Problem: Instead of a parameter, the cobbler package is to raise an exception that tells the caller whether the call resulted in a rendezvous. Which is preferable—the exception or the parameter?

Cobbler__5.

Purpose: To use several tasks to provide service in a manner that is hidden from customers of the serving package

Problem: The cobbler shop has become successful. There are now two cobblers, Dick and Jane. They are identical in their functioning; therefore, use a task type and task object declarations.

Have the entrance procedure deliver boots to either Dick or Jane, whichever one is available. Keep in mind that the entrance procedure is reentrant and can be simultaneously used by multiple tasks. Make the user interface identical to that of COBBLER_1.

Cobbler__6.

Purpose: To illustrate uncoupling of the interaction between the Customers and the Cobbler_Shop

Problem: Allow the customer to perform alternate actions while the boots are being repaired. Provide for buffering of boots in the cobbler shop, and allow customers to deliver boots for repair, picking them up at some later time.

Assume (for the moment) that the customers are not fussy; they don't care if they get back the same pair of boots. (This violates our usual assumption, but will simplify the problem for a moment.)

Cobbler__7.

Purpose: To demonstrate the difference between a "type manager" and an "object manager" in the context of simple buffers

Problem: Make one of the buffers to be of the style "type manager" (this is not easy to do) and the other to be of the style "object manager." Remember that the buffers must cater to multiple simultaneous users.

Cobbler__8.

Purpose: To show a generic style for a type manager buffer

Problem: Create a generic buffer of style type manager.

Cobbler__9.

Purpose: To implement a coordinating task, with a time-out condition

Problem: Using COBBLER_6 as a base, have the cobbler shop output a message if no one has dropped off boots in 60 minutes. (You will need a coordinating task to take the boots from the customer and put them in the buffer.)

Cobbler_10.

Purpose: To illustrate provision of priority service using a family of entries

Problem: Modify the coordinator to have separate entries, depending on the type of boots to be repaired. Prioritize the entries so that cowboys get best service and fisherman (wading boots) get poorest service.

Cobbler_11.

Purpose: To use an array of tasks with an initializing entry

Problem: The cobbler shop is even more successful; there are now 200 cobblers! The cobblers will now be known by their employee numbers. Let them know what their numbers are by an initializing entry. (You should use a task type and array of tasks.) Use COBBLER_6 as a starting point.

Cobbler_12.

Purpose: To illustrate the use of an agent task (created through the use of an allocator) to serve as a "mailbox"

Problem: The agent or mailbox is a buffer, being called by both the server and (later) by the client. This is the second of the three client-server paradigms to be illustrated.

The customers are complaining; they want their own boots back after all. Use COBBLER_6 as a starting point. Have the customers create agent tasks as mailboxes and give both the boots and the address of the mailbox to the cobbler shop. The mailbox is to be of the form of a buffer, storing a single item. The cobblers return the repaired boots to the mailbox, rather than a storage area in the cobbler shop. The customer later calls his agent to retrieve the boots. The agent is to get the item from a cobbler, return it to its customer, and then terminate.

This problem brings us back to the usual assumption of the client-server model that the product is associated with the request. You may wish to revise problems 6–11 to use this method.

Must the customers be all of the same type? Can the customer do other things while the boots are being repaired? Would it make sense for the customer to poll his mailbox? What happens to the mailbox when its function is complete?

Cobbler__13.

Purpose: To illustrate the use of a generic approach to allow a helper package to gain visibility to a type definition in the unit requiring the help

Problem: Use a generic package to define the agent used in COB-BLER_12. Instantiate the package in the Cobbler_Shop.

Cobbler__14.

Purpose: To combine several aspects of previous problems

Problem: Combine problems 8, 9, and 13, i.e., have each customer create its own mailbox, with the cobbler shop using a generic type manager. Establish a coordinating task in the cobbler shop to take the boots from the customers and place them in the buffer for the cobblers. The coordinating task need not time out when no boots have arrived.

Since we have changed the problem so much, it is worth restating the cobbler problem in its entirety.

A cobbler shop has a clerk to take orders from customers, and two cobblers who actually do the repairs. The clerk takes the address of the customer, attaches it to the boots, and puts the job (boots and address ticket) on a shelf of boots to be repaired. The shop has storage for 100 pair of boots awaiting repair. Each cobbler takes jobs from the shelf, repairs the boots, and mails the repaired boots to the address on the ticket.

(This problem is essentially the same as a problem in Barnes, [Bar84, page 251]. The problem generated so much spirited discussion in an advanced tasking class, that I began to use modifications of it to illustrate various issues and paradigms. Hence, this problem is the foundation for the cobbler series. Since we are using the problem to illustrate more points than did Barnes, our solution is somewhat more elaborate.)

Cobbler__15.

Purpose: To allow the customer to be a called task, while still using a mailbox agent to receive the boots from the cobbler shop

Problem: Suppose each customer has two pair of boots, and was able to proceed on his task if either pair was mended. Modify the code of the customer to wait for either of two mailboxes. Is this as general and flexible as the previous scheme—for the customer? for the cobbler? for the interaction in general? What sort of changes did you have to make to the customers?

Cobbler__16.

Purpose: To illustrate the "receipt" model of task interaction

Problem: Get rid of the mailbox task. Instead, give each customer a receipt for each pair of boots. Make the receipt secure so that you are certain the proper customer is getting the boots (i.e., the receipt cannot be copied). This is the third of the three client-server paradigms to be illustrated.

This involves major changes to the structure of the solution. For example, there must be consideration of generation or storage of receipts, the method of controlling and validating receipts, the sort of exceptions that are to be raised in certain circumstances, and so on.

B

Cobbler Solutions

This appendix provides solutions to the cobbler problems. The purpose and problem are restated, followed by

- Approach:
- Solution:
- Discussion:

The Approach outlines a general strategy or method of handling some interesting aspect of the problem; it is not an algorithm or complete outline of a solution.

The Solution is the code to solve the problem. A few of the solutions are presented with the complete code. However, there is considerable duplication between the problems, so most solutions are presented in abbreviated form, focusing on the new material. Code and explanatory textual material are interspersed.

The Discussion highlights interesting overall aspects of the case study.

The last few problems consist only of discussion and ideas about additional exercises.

Here is a restatement of the original problem:

Problem Statement

A customer (potentially many customers, but just one for now) has a pair of boots to be repaired. He goes to a cobbler shop to have them repaired. He waits for the boots to be repaired, then goes about his business.

His boots may be of any of the types: cowboy, ski, or waders. The boot status is any of: brand new, worn, or repaired. The way the cobbler repairs the boots is to change the condition of the boots from worn to repaired. The cobbler will not repair boots unless they are worn.

Cobbler__1.

Purpose: To establish the basic cobbler problem

Problem: Implement the basic cobbler task interactions. Implement both tasks in the declarative part of a procedure. Do you have an option as to which task is the calling task? This is the first of the three client-server paradigms to be illustrated: the waiting model.

Approach: At a minimum, we need a type definition for the boots, a boots object (i.e., the boots themselves), and an indicator of the degree of needed repair. Since, after their interaction in the cobbler shop, the customer and the cobbler will go their separate ways, they should be implemented as tasks.

Use two tasks in a procedure.

Solution:

```
procedure The_Cobbler_Shop is
   type Boot_Status is (Brand_New, Worn, Repaired);
   type Boots_Style is (Cowboy, Ski, Waders);
   type Pair_Of_Boots is
     record
       Style  : Boots_Style;
       Status : Boot_Status;
     end record;

   task Cobbler_Shop is
     entry Repair_Boots (Boots : in out Pair_Of_Boots);
   end Cobbler_Shop;
   task body Cobbler_Shop is separate;
```

```
   task Customer is
     -- Calls
       -- Cobbler_Shop.Repair_Boots
   end Customer;
   task body Customer is separate;
begin
  null;
end The_Cobbler_Shop;


separate (The_Cobbler_Shop)
  task body Cobbler_Shop is
  begin
    loop
      accept Repair_Boots (Boots : in out Pair_Of_Boots) do

        if Boots.Status = Worn then
          Boots.Status := Repaired;
        end if;
      end Repair_Boots;
    end loop;
  end Cobbler_Shop;


separate (The_Cobbler_Shop)
  task body Customer is
    Boots : Pair_Of_Boots;
    procedure Purchase_Boots (Boots : out Pair_Of_Boots)
                                              is separate;
    procedure Abuse_Boots (Boots : in out Pair_Of_Boots)
  begin
    Purchase_Boots (Boots);
    loop
      Abuse_Boots (Boots);
      Cobbler_Shop.Repair_Boots (Boots);
    end loop;
  end Customer;
```

Discussion: There is not much structure to this simple problem. It is just two tasks in a procedure that also contains all the needed type information. Figure Cobbler_1 provides the process graph for this problem. Most of the solutions will include process graphs in order to present a graphical illustration of the situation. They will be mentioned in the discussion only if necessary. Many of the solutions will have the same process graph as previous solutions; these will not be discussed.

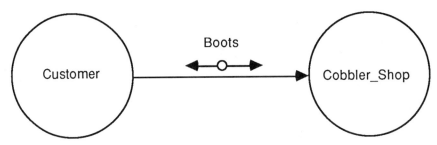

Figure Cobbler__1.

The customer must be the caller; the cobbler takes actions during the rendezvous to repair the boots. If the cobbler were to be the caller, there is no way to take the boots, repair them, and return them to the customer. In addition, there are potentially many (in fact, arbitrarily many) customers. Even further, only the customers know when they have boots to be repaired; we don't want the cobbler to have to know and visit all his potential customers, checking to see if they had boots to be repaired.

Note that the customer waits for the cobbler to repair the boots.

This is one of three major models of this sort of task interaction. We call this the "waiting" model. We will later see examples of the "delivery" model and the "receipt" model. In the latter two models, the customer does not have to wait for the boots, but takes other action while the boots are being repaired.

Cobbler__2.

Purpose: To illustrate methods of using a task specification in a package specification

Problem: Let there be three customers.

Put the customers in one package and the cobbler in a separate package. Make both packages library units. Put the cobbler task specification in the package specification. Have the customers make unconditional, timed, and conditional entry calls on the entry. (Each customer makes a different type of entry call.)

Also rename the entry as a procedure so that customers who do not wish to make timed or conditional calls have the same interface as the previous example.

Approach: The solution must be considerably restructured as indicated in the problem statement. Remember to have the customers do something different depending upon whether or not the boots were mended, i.e., whether or not the call was successful.

We will now call the task that does the repair work "Cobbler", and call the enclosing package "Cobbler_Shop". The entry to Cobbler is called "Repair", but the procedure renaming the entry is Repair_Boots, to retain the same user interface as in COBBLER_1.

Solution: The package specification contains the task specification and a procedure renaming the Repair entry to the Cobbler task.

```
package Cobbler_Shop is
type Boot_Status is (Brand_New, Worn, Repaired);
type Boots_Style is (Cowboy, Ski, Waders);
type Pair_Of_Boots is
  record
    Style  : Boots_Style;
    Status : Boot_Status;
  end record;

  task Cobbler is
    entry Repair (Boots : in out Pair_Of_Boots);
  end Cobbler;

  procedure Repair_Boots (Boots : in out Pair_Of_Boots)
                              renames Cobbler.Repair;
end Cobbler_Shop;
```

The three customer tasks will be in a package Customers, making calls on the entry in the visible task Cobbler.

```
package Customers is
    -- Calls
    -- Cobbler_Shop.Cobbler.Repair
    -- Cobbler_Shop.Repair_Boots (same call)
end Customers;
```

The separate task is unchanged except for its name and the separate clause.

```
separate (Cobbler_Shop)
  task body Cobbler is
  begin
    loop
      accept Repair_Boots (Boots : in out Pair_Of_Boots) do

        if Boots.Status = Worn then
          Boots.Status := Repaired;
        end if;
      end Repair_Boots;
    end loop;
  end Cobbler;
```

The three customer task specifications appear in the Customer package body. The package body "withs" the Cobbler_Shop.

```
with Cobbler_Shop;
package body Customers is
  task Customer is
    -- Calls
      -- Cobbler_Shop.Cobbler.Repair
      -- Cobbler_Shop.Repair_Boots (same call)
  end Customer;

  task Impatient_Customer is
    -- Calls
      -- Cobbler_Shop.Cobbler.Repair
  end Impatient_Customer;

  task Very_Impatient_Customer is
    -- Calls
      -- Cobbler_Shop.Cobbler.Repair
  end Very_Impatient_Customer;
```

The procedures to purchase and abuse boots can be common to all three tasks since they are reentrant. (Remember that all procedures in Ada are reentrant.) They are therefore placed in the body of the Customer package, preceding the bodies of the customer tasks.

(An alternative approach is to place them in a separate package, "withed" by the Customer package body. Since there are only two procedures, and they are closely tied to the functional processing of Customer, we chose to place them here.)

```
procedure Purchase_Boots
            (Boots :    out Cobbler_Shop.Pair_Of_Boots) is separate;
procedure Abuse_Boots
            (Boots : in out Cobbler_Shop.Pair_Of_Boots) is separate;
```

The task bodies are separate.

```
task body Customer                is separate;
task body Impatient_Customer      is separate;
task body Very_Impatient_Customer is separate;
end Customers;
```

The first customer does an unconditional call on the cobbler, using both a direct call to the entry in the task in the package, and a call to the procedure renaming the entry.

```
separate (Customers)
  task body Customer is
    Boots : Cobbler_Shop.Pair_Of_Boots;
  begin
    Purchase_Boots (Boots);
    loop
      Abuse_Boots (Boots);
      Cobbler_Shop.Cobbler.Repair (Boots);
      Abuse_Boots (Boots);
      Cobbler_Shop.Repair_Boots (Boots); -- use the renamed entry
    end loop;
  end Customer;
```

The next two tasks make timed and conditional calls.

```
separate (Customers)
  task body Impatient_Customer is
    Minute : constant := 60.0;
    Boots : Cobbler_Shop.Pair_Of_Boots;
  begin
    Purchase_Boots (Boots);
    loop
      Abuse_Boots (Boots);
      select
        Cobbler_Shop.Cobbler.Repair (Boots);
      or
```

```
        delay 1 * Minute;
        -- fix the boots without a cobbler
        -- (since the cobbler is not available)
        ...
      end select;
    end loop;
  end Impatient_Customer;

separate (Customers)
  task body Very_Impatient_Customer is
    Boots : Cobbler_Shop.Pair_Of_Boots;
  begin
    Purchase_Boots (Boots);
    loop
      Abuse_Boots (Boots);
      select
        Cobbler_Shop.Cobbler.Repair (Boots);
      else
        -- fix the boots without a cobbler
        ...
      end select;
    end loop;
  end Very_Impatient_Customer;
```

Discussion: Figure Cobbler_2 shows that each of the customers is
calling the same entry; they just use different styles of call (unconditional, timed, and conditional).

This solution has a structure more typical of a large real-time Ada
program: packages containing tasks to perform application functions
(The "Abuse_Boots" in the Customer presumably performs some useful function.), and tasks to perform services (The Cobblers).

To start the tasks executing, we must elaborate the packages. A
simple way to do so is to add a small procedure that elaborates Customers, which in turn elaborates the Cobbler_Shop. It is:

```
with Customers;
procedure The_Cobbler_Shop is
begin
  null;
end The_Cobbler_Shop;
```

The process graph in Figure Cobbler_2 does not show the package
structure or the use of the procedure renaming the entry, but does
show the additional tasks.

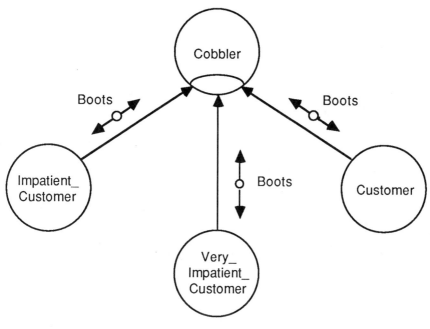

Figure Cobbler__2.

Cobbler__3.

Purpose: To illustrate the use of entrance procedures, including with conditional and timed entry calls

Problem: Put the cobbler task specification in the package body. Provide entrance procedures for three types of calls: conditional, timed, and unconditional. Return a parameter that tells the caller whether the call resulted in a rendezvous. Which is preferable—the placement of a task specification in the package specification, or its placement in the body with the use of entrance procedures?

Approach: We will return a Boolean parameter to indicate whether or not the calls to Cobbler.Repair were successful, i.e., whether or not the boots were mended. The entrance procedures accomplish the timed an conditional calls, appropriately setting the parameter to true or false. The Customers should check the parameter to know whether or not the boots were mended.

Note: Portions of the problem that are repeated from the previous solution are indicated by a partial code fragment and ...

Solution: The specification of Cobbler_Shop now contains only the type definitions and the three entrance procedures.

```
package Cobbler_Shop is
  type Boot_Status is ...
  type Boots_Style is ...
  type Pair_Of_Boots is ...
  procedure Repair_Boots                 (Boots  : in out Pair_Of_Boot
  procedure Impatient_Repair_Boots       (Boots  : in out Pair_Of_Boot
                                          Mended : out Boolean);
  procedure Very_Impatient_Repair_Boots (Boots  : in out Pair_Of_Boot
                                          Mended : out Boolean);
end Cobbler_Shop;
```

The package Customers indicates its new set of called procedures.

```
package Customers is
  -- Calls
    -- Cobbler_Shop.Repair_Boots
    -- Cobbler_Shop.Impatient_Repair_Boots
    -- Cobbler_Shop.Very_Impatient_Repair_Boots
end Customers;
```

The Cobbler task specification and body are unchanged; we will not show them in this example.

```
package body Cobbler_Shop is
  ...
  ...
```

The entrance procedures enforce the timed and conditional calls.

```
  procedure Repair_Boots (Boots  : in out Pair_Of_Boots) is
  begin
    Cobbler.Repair (Boots);
  end Repair_Boots;

  procedure Impatient_Repair_Boots (Boots  : in out Pair_Of_Boots;
                                    Mended : out Boolean) is
    Minute : constant := 60.0;
```

```
begin
  select
    Cobbler.Repair (Boots);
    Mended := True;
  or
    delay 1 * Minute;
    Mended := False;
  end select;
end Impatient_Repair_Boots;

procedure Very_Impatient_Repair_Boots (Boots   : in out Pair_Of_Boots;
                                       Mended : out Boolean) is
begin
  select
    Cobbler.Repair (Boots);
    Mended := True;
  else
    Mended := False;
  end select;
end Very_Impatient_Repair_Boots;
end Cobbler_Shop;
```

The only changes to package body Customers are the comments reflecting the new calls (since the code for the task bodies is separate.) We will not show this package body here.

The task body Customer now only calls the entrance procedure. Notice that the call is syntactically the same whether there is a call to an entry in a task (as in COBBLER_1), a call to an entry renamed as a procedure (as in COBBLER_2), or to a procedure in a package, as shown below.

```
separate (Customers)
  task body Customer is
    ...
    Cobbler_Shop.Repair_Boots (Boots);
    ...
  end Customer;
```

The impatient customers must check the parameter to achieve the same effect as in COBBLER_2.

```
separate (Customers)
  task body Impatient_Customer is
    ...
    Cobbler_Shop.Impatient_Repair_Boots (Boots, Mended);

    if not Mended then
      -- fix the boots without a cobbler
          ...
    end if;
    ...
  end Impatient_Customer;

separate (Customers)
  task body Very_Impatient_Customer is
    ...
    Cobbler_Shop.Very_Impatient_Repair_Boots (Boots, Mended);

    if not Mended then
      -- fix the boots without a cobbler
          ...
    end if;
    ...
  end Very_Impatient_Customer;
```

Discussion: The advantage of hiding the task specification in the package body is that it conceals information that is typically not needed by users of the package. It prevents inappropriate timed or conditional calls, prevents any attempt by external users to abort the serving task, and provides a uniform procedural interface between packages.

The disadvantage of hiding the task specification is that it makes necessary timed and conditional calls somewhat awkward as a result of the extra parameter and the need to explicitly check its value. This is made somewhat less awkward in the example to follow.

We will typically use entrance procedures. If there were a specific reason why showing the task specification in the package specification would be useful, we would do so.

Cobbler__4.

Purpose: To use an exception as a replacement for a status parameter

Problem: Instead of a parameter, the cobbler package is to raise an exception that tells the caller whether the call resulted in a rendez-vous. Which is preferable—the exception or the parameter?

Approach: We will delete the status parameter from the procedures exported by Cobbler_Shop. Instead, it will export the name of an exception that will be raised when the boots are not mended. The Customers need not have an extra local "Mended" variable or related check on its status, but must instead handle the exceptional situation.

Solution: The impatient procedures no longer have the parameter "Mended".

```
package Cobbler_Shop is
   type Boot_Status is ...
   type Boots_Style is ...
   type Pair_Of_Boots is ...
   procedure Repair_Boots ...
   procedure Impatient_Repair_Boots      (Boots  : in out Pair_Of_Boots);
   procedure Very_Impatient_Repair_Boots (Boots  : in out Pair_Of_Boots);
```

The package specification must now export an exception.

```
Not_Mended : exception; -- raised by Impatient_Repair_Boots and
                        -- Very_Impatient_Repair_Boots when boots
                        -- are not mended
end Cobbler_Shop;
```

There are changes to the entrance procedures. Instead of setting the parameter to either true or false, they raise the exception Not_Mended when the call to Cobbler is not completed.

```
package body Cobbler_Shop is
   ...
   -- the entrance procedures are:

   procedure Impatient_Repair_Boots (Boots  : in out
                                     Pair_Of_Boots) is
      Minute : constant := 60.0;
```

```
begin
  select
    Cobbler.Repair (Boots);
  or
    delay 1 * Minute;
    raise Not_Mended;
  end select;
end Impatient_Repair_Boots;

procedure Very_Impatient_Repair_Boots (Boots  : in out
                                       Pair_Of_Boots) is
begin
  select
    Cobbler.Repair (Boots);
  else
    raise Not_Mended;
  end select;
end Very_Impatient_Repair_Boots;
end Cobbler_Shop;
```

The other changes are in the body of the Customer tasks. The
first example shows the handling of the exception at the end of the
task.

```
task body Impatient_Customer is
  ...
  -- there is no declaration of a local variable Mended
begin
  ...
  -- the call has one less parameter
  Cobbler_Shop.Impatient_Repair_Boots (Boots);
  -- there is no check on Mended
  ...
exception
  when Cobbler_Shop.Not_Mended =>
    -- fix the boots without a cobbler
      ...
    -- this handler could be a local block as shown below
end Impatient_Customer;
```

This example shows how the exception is handled in a local block.
This block will be within the main loop in the body of the task.
This example is exactly analogous to the way the situation of "boots
not mended" is handled in COBBLER_3.

```
task body Very_Impatient_Customer is
  ...
begin
  ...
  Fix_The_Boots_Somehow:
  begin
    Cobbler_Shop.Very_Impatient_Repair_Boots (Boots);
  exception
    when Cobbler_Shop.Not_Mended =>
      -- fix the boots without a cobbler
      ...
  end Fix_The_Boots_Somehow;
  ...
end Very_Impatient_Customer;
```

Discussion: The solution with exceptions is preferred to the solution with the extra parameter in the procedure.

The use of exceptions clearly distinguishes the usual logic (i.e., the call to the cobbler shop without an extra parameter) from the exceptional or unusual situation. There is no explicit "if ... then ... else ... end if;" logic to check an extra parameter.

Another difference is that the user of the Cobbler_Shop package cannot make a logical error by erroneously failing to check for the mended/not mended condition: the using task will simply fail on the unhandled exception.

Cobbler_5.

Purpose: To use several tasks to provide service in a manner that is hidden from customers of the serving package

Problem: The cobbler shop has become successful. There are now two cobblers, Dick and Jane. They are identical in their functioning; therefore, use a task type and task object declarations.

Have the entrance procedure deliver boots to either Dick or Jane, whichever one is available. Keep in mind that the entrance procedure is reentrant and can be simultaneously used by multiple tasks. Make the user interface identical to that of COBBLER_1.

Approach: There are several ways to solve this problem, all somewhat awkward. We will take the approach that the entrance procedure will poll the two cobbler tasks, Dick and Jane. Conditional calls will be issued repeatedly, until the boots are mended.

Solution: We now have only a single entrance procedure, Repair_ Boots, in the package specification.

```
package Cobbler_Shop is
   type Boot_Status is ...
   type Boots_Style is ...
   type Pair_Of_Boots is ...
   procedure Repair_Boots (Boots : in out Pair_Of_Boots);
end Cobbler_Shop;

package Customers is
   -- Calls
      -- Cobbler_Shop.Repair_Boots
end Customers;
```

We will use a task type to define a template for the two working cobblers, Dick and Jane.

```
package body Cobbler_Shop is
    task type Cobbler is
      entry Repair (Boots : in out Pair_Of_Boots);
    end Cobbler;

    Dick, Jane : Cobbler;

    task body Cobbler is separate;
```

Here is the major new item in this cobbler problem.

```
    procedure Repair_Boots (Boots : in out Pair_Of_Boots) is
    begin
      Repair_The_Boots:
      loop
        select
          Dick.Repair (Boots);
          exit Repair_The_Boots;
```

```
      else
        select
          Jane.Repair (Boots);
          exit Repair_The_Boots;
        else
          null;
        end select;
      end select;
    end loop Repair_The_Boots;
  end Repair_Boots;
end Cobbler_Shop;
```

The task body Cobbler is identical to the previous cobbler.

```
separate (Cobbler_Shop)
  task body Cobbler is ...
```

We will also use a task type for the customers.

```
with Cobbler_Shop;
package body Customers is
  task type Customer is
    -- Calls
      -- Cobbler_Shop.Repair_Boots
  end Customer;

  Customer_1, Customer_2, Customer_3 : Customer;

  procedure Purchase_Boots ...
  procedure Abuse_Boots    ...

  task body Customer is separate;
end Customers;
```

Except that it does not contain the specification of the procedures Purchase_Boots and Abuse_Boots, the body of customer is the same as in the first problem, COBBLER_1.

```
separate (Customers)
  task body Customer is ...
```

Discussion: Figure Cobbler_5 illustrates that each of the customers may interact directly with each of the cobblers. The first customer goes to Dick, the second to Jane, and later customers (if Dick and Jane are still busy) must poll while waiting. This is clumsy. It is also an asymmetric solution in regard to Dick and Jane; Dick always gets the first customer when neither are busy.

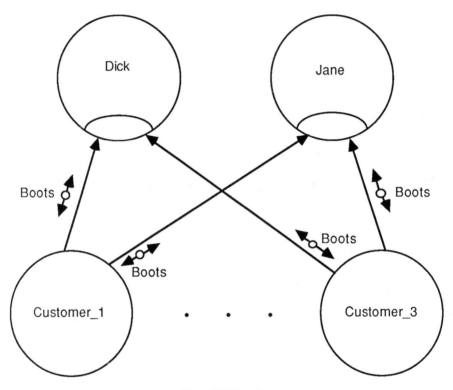

Figure Cobbler__5.

A better solution would be to assign a cobbler directly to a customer. As an additional exercise, you might want to think about how to do this.

Buhr addresses alternate methods. One approach uses two calls, one to request a server and the next to request service [BUH84, p. 78]. The other approach involves servers that are created through the evaluation of allocators; the address of a server is provided to the client [BUH84, p. 162].

In COBBLER_6 we address a slightly different aspect of the problem, combining the use of multiple servers with the ability of the client to take other actions while his boots are being repaired.

Cobbler__6.

Purpose: To illustrate uncoupling of the interaction between the Customers and the Cobbler_Shop

Problem: Allow the customer to perform alternate actions while the boots are being repaired. Provide for buffering of boots in the cobbler shop, and allow customers to deliver boots for repair, picking them up at some later time.

Assume (for the moment) that the customers are not fussy; they don't care if they get back the same pair of boots. (This violates our usual assumption, but will simplify the problem for a moment.)

Approach: The entrance procedures will put the worn boots into a buffer. Dick and Jane will take worn boots from the buffer and return repaired boots to a different buffer. The entrance procedure will take boots from the latter buffer when the customer calls to pick up boots.

Solution: We add appropriate entrance procedures to the package specification:

```
package Cobbler_Shop is
  type Boot_Status is ...
  type Boots_Style is ...
  type Pair_Of_Boots is ...
  procedure Deliver_Boots (Boots : in     Pair_Of_Boots);
  procedure Pick_Up_Boots (Boots :     out Pair_Of_Boots);
end Cobbler_Shop;

package Customers is
  -- Calls
    -- Cobbler_Shop.Deliver_Boots
    -- Cobbler_Shop.Pick_Up_Boots
end Customers;
```

We add packages to buffer the boots. We will not show the bodies, as they are exactly the same as the buffer packages that we discussed extensively in Chapter 7.

```
package body Cobbler_Shop is
  package Worn_Boots is
    procedure Enqueue (Boots : in    Pair_Of_Boots);
    procedure Dequeue (Boots :    out Pair_Of_Boots);
  end Worn_Boots;

  package Repaired_Boots is
    procedure Enqueue (Boots : in    Pair_Of_Boots);
    procedure Dequeue (Boots :    out Pair_Of_Boots);
  end Repaired_Boots;

  task type Cobbler is
    -- Calls
      -- Worn_Boots.Dequeue
      -- Repaired_Boots.Enqueue
  end Cobbler;

  Dick, Jane : Cobbler;

  task body Cobbler is separate;

  package body Worn_Boots     is separate;
  package body Repaired_Boots is separate;
```

The entrance procedures no longer interact directly with the cobblers, but rather enqueue and dequeue the boots from the buffers.

```
  procedure Deliver_Boots (Boots : in    Pair_Of_Boots) is
  begin
    Worn_Boots.Enqueue (Boots);
  end Deliver_Boots;

  procedure Pick_Up_Boots (Boots :    out Pair_Of_Boots) is
  begin
    Repaired_Boots.Dequeue (Boots);
  end Pick_Up_Boots;
end Cobbler_Shop;
```

The cobblers now also interact only with the buffers, rather than
directly with the entrance procedures. This makes them strictly
calling tasks.

```
separate (Cobbler_Shop)
  task body Cobbler is
    Boots : Pair_Of_Boots;
  begin
    loop
      Worn_Boots.Dequeue (Boots);

      if Boots.Status = Worn then
        Boots.Status := Repaired;
      end if;

      Repaired_Boots.Enqueue (Boots);
    end loop;
  end Cobbler;

with Cobbler_Shop;
package body Customers is
  task type Customer is
    -- Calls
      -- Cobbler_Shop.Deliver_Boots
      -- Cobbler_Shop.Pick_Up_Boots
  end Customer;

  Customer_1, Customer_2, Customer_3 : Customer;

  procedure Purchase_Boots ...
  procedure Abuse_Boots    ...

  task body Customer is separate;
end Customers;
```

The customers now can do work between the time they deliver the boots, and when they pick them up. This is an important difference from the earlier solutions.

```
separate (Customers)
  task body Customer is
    Boots : Cobbler_Shop.Pair_Of_Boots;
  begin
    Purchase_Boots (Boots);
    loop
      Abuse_Boots (Boots);
      Cobbler_Shop.Deliver_Boots (Boots);
```

```
        -- can do some work here, as long as the
        -- boots are not needed!
        ...
        Cobbler_Shop.Pick_Up_Boots (Boots);
      end loop;
   end Customer;
```

Discussion: Figure Cobbler_6 illustrates how the buffers provide an intermediate repository between the customers and cobblers. If the customers are really satisfied with any boots, this is a nice solution.

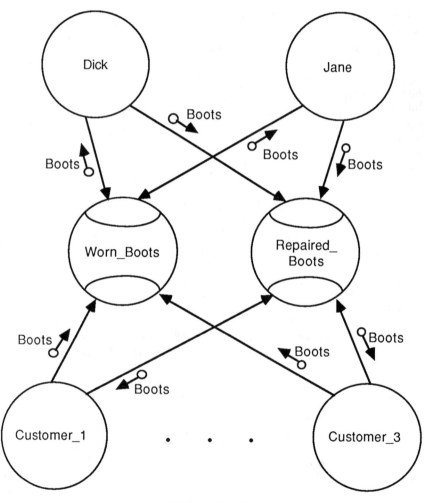

Figure Cobbler__6.

The customers block when the Cobbler_Shop is full or when no boots are currently ready for pickup. This solution could be combined with COBBLER_3 to allow for conditional delivery or pickup (additional exercise). The customer would not block, but would instead poll.

Cobbler__7.

Purpose: To demonstrate the difference between a "type manager" and an "object manager" in the context of simple buffers

Problem: Make one of the buffers to be of the style "type manager" (this is not easy to do) and the other to be of the style "object manager." Remember that the buffers must cater to multiple simultaneous users.

Approach: The difficulty in this problem is that the type manager buffer must protect against multiple users of the same buffer. There are various solutions to this, but the most elegant is that proposed by Barnes [BAR84, p. 249]. This also illustrates the use of a task type as a private type and the passing of a task as a parameter to a procedure.

As usual, the type of a buffer is to be exported by the buffering type manager. However, this type will be private, implemented as a task type. The task will ensure that the package acts as a monitor, providing mutually exclusive access for multiple users of the same buffered object.

Solution: The package specification for Cobbler_Shop is unchanged.

```
package Cobbler_Shop is ... end Cobbler_Shop;
```

We will make the worn boots buffer into the type manager. A number of changes will be caused by the different approach.

```
package body Cobbler_Shop is
  package Worn_Boots is
    type Bounded_Buffer is limited private;

    procedure Enqueue (Buffer   : in out Bounded_Buffer;
                       In_Item  : in      Pair_Of_Boots);
    procedure Dequeue (Buffer   : in out Bounded_Buffer;
                       Out_Item : out     Pair_Of_Boots);
```

```
      private
         task type Bounded_Buffer is
            entry Enqueue (In_Item  : in  Pair_Of_Boots);
            entry Dequeue (Out_Item : out Pair_Of_Boots);
         end Bounded_Buffer;
      end Worn_Boots;
```

Here is the actual buffer, of the type exported by the package Worn_Boots (the type manager).

```
      Worn_Boots_Shelf : Worn_Boots.Bounded_Buffer;
```

Except for enqueueing the boots, the rest of the package is unchanged.

```
      ...
      procedure Deliver_Boots (Boots : in   Pair_Of_Boots) is
      begin
        Worn_Boots.Enqueue (Worn_Boots_Shelf, Boots);
      end Deliver_Boots;
      ...
    end Cobbler_Shop;
```

The body of Worn_Boots has appropriate entrance procedures, calling the task Bounded_Buffer. This task is exactly the same as the bounded buffers we saw previously in Chapter 7.

```
    separate (Cobbler_Shop)
    package body Worn_Boots is
      task body Bounded_Buffer is separate;

      procedure Enqueue (Buffer   : in out Bounded_Buffer;
                         In_Item  : in     Pair_Of_Boots) is
      begin
        Buffer.Enqueue (In_Item);
      end Enqueue;

      procedure Dequeue (Buffer   : in out Bounded_Buffer;
                         Out_Item : out    Pair_Of_Boots) is
      begin
        Buffer.Dequeue (Out_Item);
      end Dequeue;
    end Worn_Boots;
```

The only change in the body of Cobbler is the call to the dequeue of Worn_Boots.

```
separate (Cobbler_Shop)
  task body Cobbler is
    Boots : Pair_Of_Boots;
  begin
    ...
      Worn_Boots.Dequeue (Worn_Boots_Shelf, Boots);
    ...
  end Cobbler;
```

For completeness, we show the body of Bounded_Buffer.

```
separate (Cobbler_Shop.Worn_Boots)
  task body Bounded_Buffer is

    Buffer_Size : constant := 100;

    Buffer : array (1 .. Buffer_Size) of Pair_Of_Boots;
    Insert, Remove : Positive range 1 .. Buffer_Size := 1;
    Count          : Natural  range 0 .. Buffer_Size := 0;
  begin
    loop
      select
        when Count < Buffer_Size =>
          accept Enqueue (In_Item : in Pair_Of_Boots) do
            Buffer (Insert) := In_Item;
          end Enqueue;
          Insert := (Insert mod Buffer_Size) + 1;
          Count  := Count + 1;
      or
        when Count > 0 =>
          accept Dequeue (Out_Item : out Pair_Of_Boots) do
            Out_Item := Buffer (Remove);
          end Dequeue;
          Remove := (Remove mod Buffer_Size) + 1;
          Count  := Count - 1;
      or
          terminate;
      end select;
    end loop;
  end Bounded_Buffer;
```

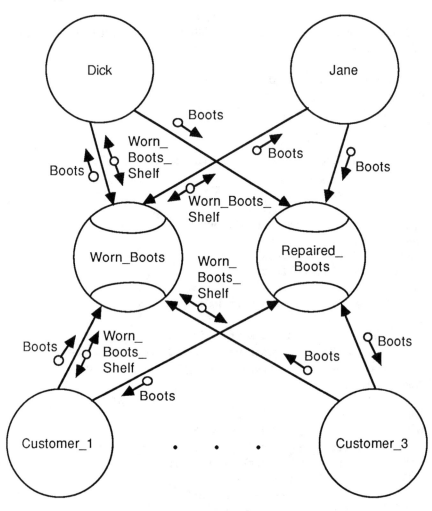

Figure Cobbler__7.

Discussion: Figure Cobbler_7 clearly illustrates the use of a type manager. The actual storage is called Worn_Boots_Shelf, and must be passed as a parameter to the buffer implemented as a type manager—Worn_Boots. You should compare this to Figure Cobbler_6, which does not require the extra parameter since the actual storage is located inside the object manager style buffer.

The difficulty in making the buffer a type manager is that of ensuring mutually exclusive access between different tasks using the same buffer object. It is not easy to keep track of the state of the buffer, since the code of the buffer manager can be reentrantly used by many tasks accessing several different buffer objects.

The use of a task as the buffer type itself is a very elegant solution to the problems noted; it associates a task with each buffer in order to maintain its state.

To fully appreciate this approach, you must attempt to find an alternative. The difficulty lies in attempting to keep track of the Insert and Remove indexes (and the Count), for each of the multiple buffers.

Why do we use a type manager in this problem? Well, the truth is that we are doing it for illustration of how to create a type manager. In problems of this sort, in which only one buffer of the type is created, it is better to use an object manager; the users need not be concerned with creating an object of the type Bounded_Buffer, the interfaces are simpler (no buffer needs to be passed as a parameter), and the situation is conceptually somewhat easier to deal with since the buffer itself is completely encapsulated in the serving package. Chapter 16, the MKH case study, illustrates effective use of a type manager.

Cobbler__8.

Purpose: To show a generic style for a type manager buffer

Problem: Create a generic buffer of style type manager.

Approach: The size of the buffer and the type of the object buffered will be made generic. Much of the rest of the solution is unchanged.

Solution: Here is the generic package specification. We will now call it by a more general purpose name.

```
generic
   Buffer_Size : Natural := 100;
   type Buffered_Type is private;
package Monitor_Type_Manager is
   type Bounded_Buffer is limited private;

   procedure Enqueue (Buffer   : in out Bounded_Buffer;
                      In_Item  : in      Buffered_Type);
   procedure Dequeue (Buffer   : in out Bounded_Buffer;
                      Out_Item : out     Buffered_Type);
```

```
   private
     task type Bounded_Buffer is
       entry Enqueue (In_Item  : in  Buffered_Type);
       entry Dequeue (Out_Item : out Buffered_Type);
     end Bounded_Buffer;
 end Monitor_Type_Manager;
```

The body of the package, and the separate task body, now depend
upon the generic parameters. They are otherwise unchanged.

```
 package body Monitor_Type_Manager is
   task body Bounded_Buffer is separate;

   procedure Enqueue (Buffer   : in out Bounded_Buffer;
                       In_Item  : in     Buffered_Type) is
   begin
     Buffer.Enqueue (In_Item);
   end Enqueue;

   procedure Dequeue (Buffer   : in out Bounded_Buffer;
                       Out_Item : out    Buffered_Type) is
   begin
     Buffer.Dequeue (Out_Item);
   end Dequeue;
 end Monitor_Type_Manager;

 separate (Monitor_Type_Manager)
   task body Bounded_Buffer is

     Buffer : array (1 .. Buffer_Size) of Buffered_Type;
     Insert, Remove : Natural range 1 .. Buffer_Size := 1;
     Count          : Natural range 0 .. Buffer_Size := 0;
   begin
     loop
       select
         when Count < Buffer_Size =>
           accept Enqueue (In_Item : in Buffered_Type) do
             Buffer (Insert) := In_Item;
           end Enqueue;
           Insert := (Insert mod Buffer_Size) + 1;
           Count  := Count + 1;
         or
```

```
      when Count > 0 =>
        accept Dequeue (Out_Item : out Buffered_Type) do
          Out_Item := Buffer (Remove);
        end Dequeue;
        Remove := (Remove mod Buffer_Size) + 1;
        Count  := Count - 1;
    or
      terminate;
    end select;
  end loop;
end Bounded_Buffer;
```

The package specification for Cobbler_Shop is unchanged.

```
package Cobbler_Shop is ... end Cobbler_Shop;
```

The package body now withs, and instantiates, the generic type manager.

```
with Monitor_Type_Manager;
package body Cobbler_Shop is
  package Worn_Boots is new Monitor_Type_Manager
                          (Buffer_Size   => 100,
                           Buffered_Type => Pair_Of_Boots);
```

As before, here is the actual buffer.

```
  Worn_Boots_Shelf : Worn_Boots.Bounded_Buffer;
```

The remainder of the package, and the package body, is the same as in COBBLER_7.

Discussion: We made the package generic in the usual way. A nice aspect of the use of such a generic package is that it need not be nested in the body of the package making use of its services. In COBBLER_7, the package was nested inside the Cobbler_Shop since the buffer needed visibility to the type of the object to be buffered.

Even when the buffer is nested, the use of the separate clause cleanly separates specification from implementation, but recompilation of Cobbler_Shop implies recompilation of the body of the buffer. This is avoided in the generic approach. The latter approach also leads to better software reusability.

Cobbler__9.

Purpose: To implement a coordinating task, with a time-out condition

Problem: Using COBBLER_6 as a base, have the cobbler shop output a message if no one has dropped off boots in 60 minutes. (You will need a coordinating task to take the boots from the customer and put them in the buffer.)

Approach: The coordinating task will be called by the entrance procedure. The coordinating task, called Clerk, will put the boots into the Worn_Boots buffer.

Solution: The change is restricted to the body of package Cobbler_Shop. Nothing else need be shown.

```
package body Cobbler_Shop is
  package Worn_Boots is ...
  package Repaired_Boots is ...

  task Clerk is
    entry Store_Boots (Boots : in Pair_Of_Boots);
  end Clerk;

  task type Cobbler is ... end Cobbler;
  Dick, Jane : Cobbler;

  task body Clerk   is separate;
  task body Cobbler is separate;
  package body Worn_Boots     is separate;
  package body Repaired_Boots is separate;

  procedure Deliver_Boots (Boots : in    Pair_Of_Boots) is
  begin
    Clerk.Store_Boots (Boots);
  end Deliver_Boots;

  procedure Pick_Up_Boots ...
end Cobbler_Shop;
```

```
separate (Cobbler_Shop)
  task body Clerk is
    Minutes : constant := 60.0;
    Boots : Pair_Of_Boots;
  begin
    loop
      select
        accept Store_Boots (Boots : in Pair_Of_Boots) do
          Clerk.Boots := Boots;
        end Store_Boots;

        Worn_Boots.Enqueue (Boots);
      or
        delay 60 * Minutes;
        -- send a message to the appropriate place
      end select;
    end loop;
  end Clerk;
```

Discussion: The Clerk uses a select statement with a delay in order to meet the time-out requirement. Figure Cobbler_9 shows the role of the Clerk in interacting with the customers and the buffer.

Cobbler__10.

Purpose: To illustrate provision of priority service using a family of entries

Problem: Modify the coordinator to have separate entries, depending on the type of boots to be repaired. Prioritize the entries so that cowboys get best service and fisherman (wading boots) get poorest service.

Approach: The Clerk will provide three different entries, with priority service as required. We will use a family of entries. The entrance procedure will call the entry corresponding to the boot style.

Solution: The change is restricted to the body of package Cobbler_ Shop and its separate Clerk. Nothing else will be shown.

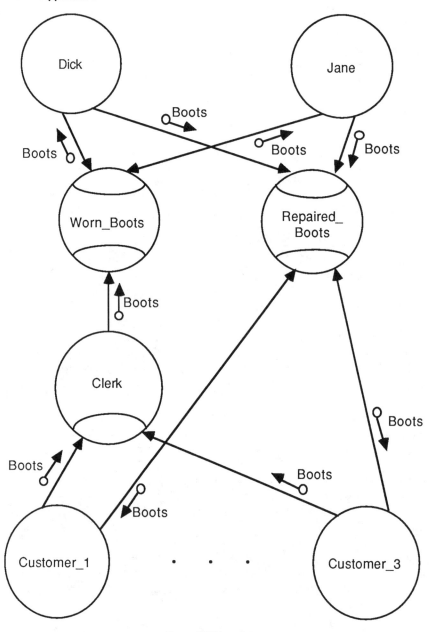

Figure Cobbler__9.

```
package body Cobbler_Shop is
   package Worn_Boots is ...
   package Repaired_Boots is ...
```

```
     task Clerk is
        entry Store_Boots (Boots_Style) (Boots :/in Pair_Of_Boots);
     end Clerk;

     task type Cobbler is ... end Cobbler;
     Dick, Jane : Cobbler;

     task body Clerk   is separate;
     task body Cobbler is separate;
     package body Worn_Boots     is separate;
     package body Repaired_Boots is separate;

     procedure Deliver_Boots (Boots : in    Pair_Of_Boots) is
     begin
        Clerk.Store_Boots (Boots.Style) (Boots);
     end Deliver_Boots;

     procedure Pick_Up_Boots ...
  end Cobbler_Shop;

separate (Cobbler_Shop)
   task body Clerk is
      Minutes : constant := 60.0;
      Boots   : Pair_Of_Boots;
   begin
      loop
        select
          accept Store_Boots (Cowboy) (Boots : in Pair_Of_Boots) do
            Clerk.Boots := Boots;
          end Store_Boots;

          Worn_Boots.Enqueue (Boots);
        or
          when Store_Boots (Cowboy)'Count = 0 =>
            accept Store_Boots (Ski) (Boots : in Pair_Of_Boots) do
              Clerk.Boots := Boots;
            end Store_Boots;

            Worn_Boots.Enqueue (Boots);
        or
```

```
            when Store_Boots (Cowboy)'Count = 0 and
                Store_Boots (Ski)'Count   = 0     =>
             accept Store_Boots (Waders) (Boots : in Pair_Of_Boots) do
                Clerk.Boots := Boots;
             end Store_Boots;

             Worn_Boots.Enqueue (Boots);
        or
          delay 60 * Minutes;
          -- send a message to the appropriate place
        end select;
      end loop;
   end Clerk;
```

Discussion: The Count attribute is used to prioritize the service. Since the calls are made in the entrance procedure, we will not have any problem with tasks leaving the queues as a result of the time-out of a timed entry call.

Note, however, that we could still have a problem as a result of a task on an entry queue being aborted. If we are concerned about this, we could have the entrance procedure create an agent task, using an allocator, to make the call. Then, even if the original customer were aborted, the rendezvous would still be completed.

Cobbler_11.

Purpose: To use an array of tasks with an initializing entry

Problem: The cobbler shop is even more successful; there are now 200 cobblers! The cobblers will now be known by their employee numbers. Let them know what their numbers are by an initializing entry. (You should use a task type and array of tasks.) Use COB-BLER_6 as a starting point.

Approach: The Cobbler task type needs an initializing entry that will be called to allow it to know its number. We then declare an array of such tasks and call each of them as part of the package initialization part. The task body accepts the call before it goes on about the rest of its business.

Solution: The changes are confined to the package body Cobbler_ Shop. None of the other units will be shown.

```
package body Cobbler_Shop is
```

We define an appropriate type as:

```
Number_Of_Cobblers : constant := 200;
type Cobbler_Range is range 1 .. Number_Of_Cobblers;

package Worn_Boots is ... end Worn_Boots;
package Repaired_Boots is ... end Repaired_Boots;
```

Here is the new task type specification and the array of tasks.

```
task type Cobbler is
   entry Number_Is (Number : in Cobbler_Range);

   -- Calls
     -- Worn_Boots.Dequeue
     -- Repaired_Boots.Enqueue
end Cobbler;

Cobblers : array (Cobbler_Range) of Cobbler;
```

The rest of the body is unchanged.

```
task body Cobbler is separate;

package body Worn_Boots     is separate;
package body Repaired_Boots is separate;

procedure Deliver_Boots ...
procedure Pick_Up_Boots ...
```

Except for the initialization!

```
begin -- initialize Cobbler_Shop
   for Cobbler_Number in Cobbler_Range loop
     Cobblers (Cobbler_Number).Number_Is (Cobbler_Number);
   end loop;
end Cobbler_Shop;

separate (Cobbler_Shop)
   task body Cobbler is
     Boots : Pair_Of_Boots;
```

We need local storage for the task to "remember" its number.

```
Number : Cobbler_Range;
begin
```

This is the only other change to the body of Cobbler.

```
accept Number_Is (Number : in Cobbler_Range) do
  Cobbler.Number := Number;
end Number_Is;

loop
  ... -- this is just like Cobbler_6
end loop;
end Cobbler;
```

Discussion: Figure Cobbler_11 shows that we now have many cobblers. We chose to not show the extra entry/initialization call, since it is not directly part of the solution to an application-oriented problem; it is an implementation detail. (If you want to draw process graphs that show this detail, that's fine too.)

The use of an array of tasks is a good way to have many simultaneous functions being executed. Although we do not use the capability in this problem, such tasks frequently need to identify themselves. For example, the package that stores repaired boots might take the employee number as part of the call that enqueues boots. The number could be stored to pay cobblers on the basis of number of boots repaired.

Cobbler_12.

Purpose: To illustrate the use of an agent task (created through the use of an allocator) to serve as a "mailbox"

Problem: The agent or mailbox is a buffer, being called by both the server and (later) by the client. This is the second of the three client-server paradigms to be illustrated.

The customers are complaining; they want their own boots back after all. Use COBBLER_6 as a starting point. Have the customers create agent tasks as mailboxes and give both the boots and the address of the mailbox to the cobbler shop. The mailbox is to be of the form of a buffer, storing a single item. The cobblers return the repaired boots to the mailbox, rather than a storage area in the cobbler shop. The customer later calls his agent to retrieve the boots.

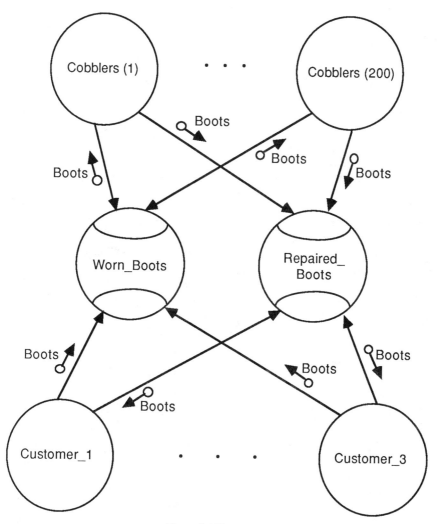

Figure Cobbler__11.

The agent is to get the item from a cobbler, return it to its customer, and then terminate.

This problem brings us back to the usual assumption of the client-server model that the product is associated with the request. You may wish to revise problems 6–11 to use this method.

Must the customers be all of the same type? Can the customer do other things while the boots are being repaired? Would it make sense for the customer to poll his mailbox? What happens to the mailbox when its function is complete?

Approach: We need to define an "agent" task as we did in Chapter 13. We will put it, along with needed definitions, in a separate package. The essential element of the agent is that it serves as a mailbox to which the cobblers can post the boots when they are done with the repairs. Therefore, we will pass the address of the agent to the cobbler. We must make sure that the address stays with the boots. (You might think of this as the address being written on a ticket attached to the boots.)

Each customer will create its own agent (using an allocator). We will use disposable agents that do one store, then one retrieve, then terminate. Therefore, an agent must be created for each pair of boots sent to the cobbler shop. The cobbler shop now has a storage area for the worn boots with the address ticket. (The two items are bundled and stored as a "Repair_Job"). The cobblers take jobs, repair the boots, and then mail them to the owner. Each customer now gets back his own pair of boots.

Solution: Here is the package that defines the agent. The definition of the agent needs some boot definitions, so we place these definitions in this package. (We will see an alternative approach later.)

```
package Define_Mailbox_Access is
   type Boot_Status is (Brand_New, Worn, Repaired);
   type Boots_Style is (Cowboy, Ski, Waders);

   type Pair_Of_Boots is
     record
       Style  : Boots_Style;
       Status : Boot_Status;
     end record;

   task type Mailbox is
     entry Store    (Boots : in  Pair_Of_Boots);
     entry Retrieve (Boots : out Pair_Of_Boots);
   end Mailbox;

   type Mailbox_Access is access Mailbox;
end Define_Mailbox_Access;
```

The Cobbler_Shop package now needs only a Deliver_Boots procedure, with a parameter for the address to which the boots are to be returned.

```
with Define_Mailbox_Access; use Define_Mailbox_Access;
package Cobbler_Shop is
   procedure Deliver_Boots (Boots   : in Pair_Of_Boots;
                            Mailman : in Mailbox_Access);
   -- Calls
     -- Mailman.Store
end Cobbler_Shop;
```

The package Customers shows its new calls.

```
package Customers is
   -- Calls
     -- Cobbler_Shop.Deliver_Boots
     -- Mailman.Retrieve
end Customers;
```

The Mailbox is very simple; it stores and retrieves a pair of boots.

```
package body Define_Mailbox_Access is
   task body Mailbox is
     Boots : Pair_Of_Boots;
   begin
     accept Store   (Boots : in  Pair_Of_Boots) do
       Mailbox.Boots := Boots;
     end Store;

     accept Retrieve (Boots : out Pair_Of_Boots) do
       Boots := Mailbox.Boots;
     end Retrieve;
   end Mailbox;
end Define_Mailbox_Access;
```

The Cobbler_Shop entrance procedure stores jobs in the buffer for worn boots.

```
package body Cobbler_Shop is
   type Repair_Job is
     record
       Boots   : Pair_Of_Boots;
       Mailman : Mailbox_Access;
     end record;
```

```
package Worn_Boots is
   procedure Enqueue (Job : in     Repair_Job);
   procedure Dequeue (Job :    out Repair_Job);
end Worn_Boots;

task type Cobbler is
   -- Calls
     -- Worn_Boots.Dequeue
     -- Mailman.Store
end Cobbler;

Dick, Jane : Cobbler;
task body Cobbler is separate;
package body Worn_Boots is separate;

procedure Deliver_Boots (Boots   : in Pair_Of_Boots;
                         Mailman : in Mailbox_Access) is
begin
   Worn_Boots.Enqueue ((Boots, Mailman));
end Deliver_Boots;
end Cobbler_Shop;
```

We used a record aggregate to build the Job out of its components
Boots and Mailman. If we wished to make this more explicit (to
help the reader) we might have done the following:

```
procedure Deliver_Boots (Boots   : in Pair_Of_Boots;
                         Mailman : in Mailbox_Access) is

   Job : Repair_Job;
begin
   Job.Boots   := Boots;
   Job.Mailman := Mailman;
   Worn_Boots.Enqueue (Job);
end Deliver_Boots;
```

However, the first formulation is preferred.

The cobblers take jobs from the buffer, repair the boots, and mail
the boots to the owner.

```
separate (Cobbler_Shop)
   task body Cobbler is
      Job : Repair_Job;
```

```
begin
  loop
    Worn_Boots.Dequeue (Job);

    if Job.Boots.Status = Worn then
      Job.Boots.Status := Repaired;
    end if;

    Job.Mailman.Store (Job.Boots);
  end loop;
end Cobbler;
```

The body of Customer is little changed. It needs visibility to Define_Mailbox_Access since that package contains definitions for Pair_Of_Boots used in Purchase_Boots and Abuse_Boots.

```
with Cobbler_Shop;
with Define_Mailbox_Access; use Define_Mailbox_Access;
package body Customers is
  task type Customer is
    -- Calls
      -- Cobbler_Shop.Deliver_Boots
  end Customer;

  Customer_1, Customer_2, Customer_3 : Customer;

  procedure Purchase_Boots ...
  procedure Abuse_Boots    ...

  task body Customer is separate;
end Customers;
```

The Customers define a Mailman, create the agent using the allocator, and pass the address to the Cobbler_Shop. The customer is free to take other actions while waiting for the boots to be repaired, but still gets back his own boots.

```
separate (Customers)
  task body Customer is
    Boots   : Pair_Of_Boots;
    Mailman : Mailbox_Access;
```

```
begin
  Purchase_Boots (Boots);

  loop
    Abuse_Boots (Boots);
    Mailman := new Mailbox;
    Cobbler_Shop.Deliver_Boots (Boots, Mailman);

    -- do work that does not depend upon boots

    Mailman.Retrieve (Boots);
  end loop;
end Customer;
```

Notice that the customer could also poll his agent to see if the boots are ready, i.e. as,

```
select
  Mailman.Retrieve (Boots);
else
  -- do other work
end select;
```

Presuming the other work is of some significance, this is likely to be a useful form of polling (rather than only looping and checking of the form of "busy-wait"). Notice that the agent will never be cross-polling with its creator; the agent exists only to pass on the repaired boots.

Discussion: Figure Cobbler_12 illustrates the multiple customer/agent interaction.

We have chosen to create a new agent for each pair of boots to be repaired. The agent terminates when its simple job is complete. This has certain reliability advantages in that erroneous multiple stores (in the Cobbler_Shop) will not adversely affect the operation of the customers. If the run-time environment does not collect the storage no longer needed by terminated tasks (typically called "garbage collection"), a long-running system will eventually run out of storage. The issue of garbage collection is controversial in real-time systems (since it is time-consuming and may occur unpredictably), and is highly implementation-dependent.

It is also appropriate to simply create a single agent for each customer (the statement Mailman := new Mail_Box) is moved to before

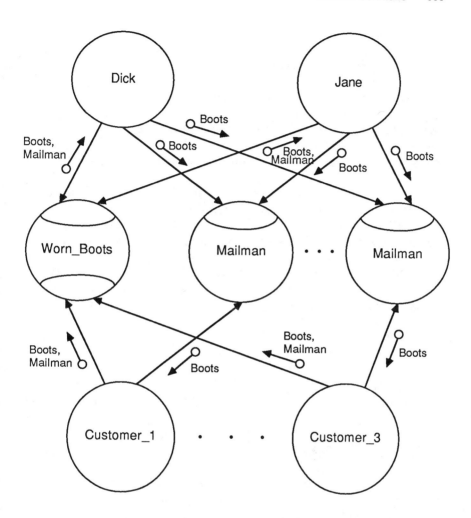

Figure Cobbler__12.

the loop. The agent body then must be changed to contain an infinite loop with the accepts for Store and Retrieve.

A larger issue is the visibility of the definition of the type Mailbox_Access. It needs visibility to the type Pair_Of_Boots. We have provided the visibility by placing the definitions associated with Pair_Of_Boots in the package Define_Mailbox_Access. This made it simple to explain the use of agents, but actually is somewhat awkward. A slightly better solution is to place the definitions associated with Pair_Of_Boots in an entirely distinct package, made generally available throughout the cobbler/customer system.

A second approach is to nest the package Define_Mailbox_Access within the Cobbler_Shop. This allows visibility to the needed definitions and provides the customers with visibility to the type Mailbox_Access.

However, this is still somewhat awkward with respect to compilation issues. We should not have to recompile Define_Access_Mailbox (which is sort of a "helper" package), when we recompile the Cobbler_Shop (a "client"). It is also conceptually clumsy to have such a general-purpose helper inside the package it is helping.

The best solution is a third alternative illustrated in COBBLER_13. The helper package is made generic, and instantiated with the needed type definition in the body of Cobbler_Shop. This solves the recompilation issue, and makes the package a useful reusable software component.

Let's summarize the three alternatives. The situation is that a "client" needs the services of a "helper", while the helper needs visibility into type definitions in the client. The alternatives are:

1. Move the types – The type definitions are moved out of the client package, either into the helping package or into a separate "definitions"package.

2. Nest the helping package – The helping package is nested in the client, thereby inheriting visibility to the needed types.

3. Make the helper generic – The helping package is instantiated in the client, gaining visibility to the needed types via a generic parameters.

The last approach is generally desired for large software systems, particularly when the helper package is a potentially reusable software component.

Cobbler_13.

Purpose: To illustrate the use of a generic approach to allow a helper package to gain visibility to a type definition in the unit requiring the help

Problem: Use a generic package to define the agent used in COBBLER_12. Instantiate the package in the Cobbler_Shop.

Approach: The generic package defining the agent is to be a library unit. It will be instantiated in the specification of the Cobbler_Shop. The generic parameter will be the type, Pair_Of_Boots.

Solution: Here is the generic package.

```
generic
  type Stored_Type is private;
package Generic_Mailbox_Access is
  task type Mailbox is
    entry Store   (Object : in  Stored_Type);
    entry Retrieve (Object : out Stored_Type);
  end Mailbox;

  type Mailbox_Access is access Mailbox;
end Generic_Mailbox_Access;
```

The package body is unchanged except for the package name and the name/type of the stored object.

```
package body Generic_Mailbox_Access is
...
end Generic_Mailbox_Access;
```

The Cobbler_Shop now withs and instantiates the generic package.

```
with Generic_Mailbox_Access;
package Cobbler_Shop is
  type Boot_Status is ...
  type Boots_Style is ...
  type Pair_Of_Boots is ...

  package Post_Office is new Generic_Mailbox_Access
                              (Stored_Type => Pair_Of_Boots);
  use Post_Office;
  ...
  ...
end Cobbler_Shop;

package Customers is ... end Customers;
package body Cobbler_Shop is ... end Cobbler_Shop;
```

The package body Customers now withs only the Cobbler_Shop.

```
with Cobbler_Shop;
package body Customers is ... end Customers;
```

In the task body Customer, we will use subtypes (a form of renaming) to obtain visibility to needed type definitions.

```
separate (Customers)
   task body Customer is
      subtype Mailbox_Access is Cobbler_Shop.Post_Office.Mailbox_Acce:
      subtype Mailbox is Cobbler_Shop.Post_Office.Mailbox;

      Boots   : Cobbler_Shop.Pair_Of_Boots;
      Mailman : Mailbox_Access;
   begin
      ...
   end Customer;
```

Discussion: The type of the object to be stored is now the formal generic parameter Stored_Type. The package is instantiated with the actual parameter, Pair_Of_Boots, thereby gaining the needed visibility.

Cobbler__14.

Purpose: To combine several aspects of previous problems

Problem: Combine problems 8, 9, and 13, i.e., have each customer create its own mailbox, with the cobbler shop using a generic type manager. Establish a coordinating task in the cobbler shop to take the boots from the customers and place them in the buffer for the cobblers. The coordinating task need not time out when no boots have arrived.

Since we have changed the problem so much, it is worth restating the cobbler problem in its entirety.

A cobbler shop has a clerk to take orders from customers, and two cobblers who actually do the repairs. The clerk takes the address of the customer, attaches it to the boots, and puts the job (boots and address ticket) on a shelf of boots to be repaired. The shop has storage for 100 pair of boots awaiting repair. Each cobbler takes jobs from the shelf, repairs the boots, and mails the repaired boots to the address on the ticket.

(This problem is essentially the same as a problem in Barnes, [BAR84, page 251]. The problem generated so much spirited discussion in an advanced tasking class, that I began to use modifications of it to illustrate various issues and paradigms. Hence, this problem is the foundation for the cobbler series. Since we are using the problem to illustrate more points than did Barnes, our solution is somewhat more elaborate.)

Approach: Combine the appropriate aspects of problems 8, 9, and 13; add a generic type manager buffer (as in COBBLER_8), and a coordinating task (similar to COBBLER_9), to the solution in COBBLER_13.

Solution: The generic package Monitor_Type_Manager is the same as in COBBLER_8.

```
generic
  Buffer_Size : Natural := 100;
  type Buffered_Type is private;
package Monitor_Type_Manager is
  type Bounded_Buffer is limited private;

  procedure Enqueue (Buffer   : in out Bounded_Buffer;
                     In_Item  : in      Buffered_Type);
  procedure Dequeue (Buffer   : in out Bounded_Buffer;
                     Out_Item : out     Buffered_Type);
  private
    ...
end Monitor_Type_Manager;

package body Monitor_Type_Manager is ... end Monitor_Type_Manager;

separate (Monitor_Type_Manager)
  task body Bounded_Buffer is ... end Bounded_Buffer;
```

The generic package Generic_Mailbox_Access is the same as in COBBLER_13.

```
generic
  type Stored_Type is private;
package Generic_Mailbox_Access is
  task type Mailbox is
    entry Store    (Object : in  Stored_Type);
    entry Retrieve (Object : out Stored_Type);
  end Mailbox;

  type Mailbox_Access is access Mailbox;
end Generic_Mailbox_Access;

package body Generic_Mailbox_Access is ... end Generic_Mailbox_Access
```

The package Cobbler_Shop must "with" Generic_Mailbox_Access. It then instantiates its own package with the appropriate access type.

```
with Generic_Mailbox_Access;
package Cobbler_Shop is
  type Boot_Status is ...
  type Boots_Style is ...
  type Pair_Of_Boots is ...

  package Post_Office is new Generic_Mailbox_Access
                                  (Stored_Type => Pair_Of_Boots);
  use Post_Office;
  procedure Deliver_Boots ...
end Cobbler_Shop;
```

The package Customers, both specification and body, is unchanged and will not be shown.

The main change to the Cobbler_Shop is withing and instantiating the Monitor_Type_Manager to buffer objects of type Repair_Job.

```
with Monitor_Type_Manager;
package body Cobbler_Shop is
  type Repair_Job is ...

  package Worn_Boots is new Monitor_Type_Manager
                                  (Buffer_Size   => 100,
                                   Buffered_Type => Repair_Job);

  Worn_Boots_Shelf : Worn_Boots.Bounded_Buffer;
```

```
task type Cobbler is
  -- Calls
    -- Worn_Boots.Dequeue
    -- Mailman.Store
end Cobbler;
```

We also add the Clerk, that now stores jobs rather than boots.

```
task Clerk is
  entry Store_Job (Job : in Repair_Job);
end Clerk;

Dick, Jane : Cobbler;

task body Cobbler is separate;
task body Clerk   is separate;

package body Worn_Boots is separate;
```

The procedure Deliver_Boots now calls the clerk with a job.

```
procedure Deliver_Boots (Boots   : in Pair_Of_Boots;
                          Mailman : in Mailbox_Access) is
begin
  Clerk.Store_Job ((Boots, Mailman));
end Deliver_Boots;
end Cobbler_Shop;
```

The Clerk now stores jobs, using the instantiated type manager.

```
separate (Cobbler_Shop)
  task body Clerk is
    Job : Repair_Job;
  begin
    loop
      accept Store_Job (Job : in Repair_Job) do
        Clerk.Job := Job;
      end Store_Job;

      Worn_Boots.Enqueue (Worn_Boots_Shelf, Job);
    end loop;
  end Clerk;
```

Discussion: We have already discussed the individual components of this solution.

Cobbler__15.

Purpose: To allow the customer to be a called task, while still using a mailbox agent to receive the boots from the cobbler shop

Problem: Suppose each customer has two pair of boots, and was able to proceed on his task if either pair was mended. Modify the code of the customer to wait for either of two mailboxs. Is this as general and flexible as the previous scheme—For the customer? For the cobbler? For the interaction in general? What sort of changes did you have to make to the customers?

Approach: Since the Customer task is to be called, it must have an entry. We will call this "Repaired_Boots". We will give the customer two Helpers. (These are not agents created by the execution of an allocator.) The Helpers will be declared internal (nested) to the Customer task. Therefore, they have visibility to call the Repaired_Boots entry. The Cobbler_Shop need not be concerned with these details; the Customer/Cobbler_Shop interaction is unchanged. However, now the Helper (instead of the customer) calls the mailbox, gets the boots, and then calls the customer to deliver the boots.

Solution: All changes are limited to the body of the Customer task. There is no change to the Cobbler_Shop or the specification or body of the Customers package.

```
separate (Customers)
  task body Customer is
    subtype Mailbox_Access is Cobbler_Shop.Post_Office.Mailbox_Access;
    subtype Mailbox      is Cobbler_Shop.Post_Office.Mailbox;
```

The Helper is of the style "transporter". Since we need two identical Helpers, we will make a task type.

```
    task type Transporter is
      entry Get_Boots (Mail_Man : in Mailbox_Access);
    end Transporter;
```

We need storage for the boots.

```
Boots        : Pair_Of_Boots;
Other_Boots : Pair_Of_Boots;
Any_Boots    : Pair_Of_Boots;
```

Here is the Mailman (as before) and the new Helper tasks.

```
Mailman : Mailbox_Access;
My_Helper       : Transporter;
My_Other_Helper : Transporter;
task body Transporter is separate;
begin
  Purchase_Boots (Boots);
  Purchase_Boots (Other_Boots);

  loop
    Abuse_Boots (Boots);
    Abuse_Boots (Other_Boots);

    Mailman := new Mailbox;
    Cobbler_Shop.Deliver_Boots (Boots, Mailman);
    My_Helper.Get_Boots (Mailman);

    Mailman := new Mailbox;
    Cobbler_Shop.Deliver_Boots (Other_Boots, Mailman);
    My_Other_Helper.Get_Boots (Mailman);

    -- do work that does not depend upon boots
    ...
    ...

    accept Repaired_Boots (Boots : in Pair_Of_Boots) do
      Any_Boots := Boots;
    end Repaired_Boots;

    -- do the work that depends upon having either pair of boots
    ...
    ...
```

We should make sure we eventually get the other pair of boots.

```
            accept Repaired_Boots (Boots : in Pair_Of_Boots) do
              Other_Boots := Boots;
            end Repaired_Boots;
        end loop;
    end Customer;
```

The transporter is as we have seen in previous examples. It uses the address of the Mail_Man to get the boots.

```
    separate (Customers.Customer)
        task body Transporter is
          Mail_Man : Mailbox_Access;
          Boots    : Pair_Of_Boots;
        begin
          accept Get_Boots (Mail_Man : in Mailbox_Access) do
            Transporter.Mail_Man := Mail_Man;
          end Get_Boots;

          Mail_Man.Retrieve (Boots);

          Customer.Repaired_Boots (Boots);
        end Transporter;
```

Discussion: Figure Cobbler_15 shows the multiple tasks involved in implementing this solution. The "Customer_*" represents any one of the customers. There are actually still multiple customers.

There are several interesting aspects to this problem. First of all, the Customer gets to wait for either pair of boots, then go about its business. It could also wait for interaction with other tasks by the use of a selective wait. It has the various advantages that we have discussed for called tasks.

Second, this is a very general and flexible scheme. The interaction with the Cobbler_Shop is unchanged, and we have all the advantages previously discussed for using a mailman style agent to uncouple the task interaction.

Third, we are using two tasks (the mailman agent which is of style "buffer" and the transporter Helper) to achieve the effect of a loosely coupled "relay". We have seen this sort of interaction before. Note that if we changed the mailman to be a relay as a single task, we would lose some of the advantages of the loosely coupled interaction. Specifically, the users of the Cobbler_Shop would have to be only a single type.

Fourth, there are alternate ways to have the Customer's Helpers know who to call to deliver the boots. The customers could be

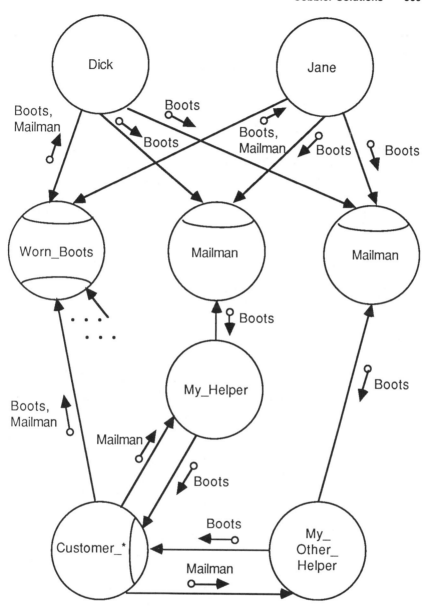

Figure Cobbler__15.

established as an array of tasks, passing their own index to the
transporter when they pass the address of the mailman. Alternatively, the customers could be created through the evaluation of an
allocator. Then they could pass their own address (a pointer to
themselves) to the transporter when they pass the address of the

mailman. In either of these two cases, the customers would need an additional entry for some initializing code to tell them what their index or address is. These alternative approaches make interesting additional exercises.

Finally, we note that we have allowed the first Mail_Man task to become anonymous when we created the second Mail_Man. This is generally a bad idea, since we loose visibility to a potentially wayward task. It is appropriate here since the task performs such a simple chore, then terminates. If we wish to avoid the anonymous task, we need a second object of an access type to point to the second Mail_Man.

Cobbler_16.

Purpose: To illustrate the "receipt" model of task interaction

Problem: Get rid of the mailbox task. Instead, give each customer a receipt for each pair of boots. Make the receipt secure so that you are certain the proper customer is getting the boots (i.e., the receipt cannot be copied). This is the third of the three client-server paradigms to be illustrated.

This involves major changes to the structure of the solution. For example, there must be consideration of generation or storage of receipts, the method of controlling and validating receipts, the sort of exceptions that are to be raised in certain circumstances, and so on.

Approach: This is essentially the same problem as the MTS case study in Chapter 14. We will add a status "Unrepairable" and a procedure called "Repair_The_Boots" to accomplish repair. These aspects make the problem even closer to the MTS case study.

We will not discuss the approach further (since essentially the same problem was discussed in the case study), but will present the completely coded solution since it is so different from the previous solutions.

Solution:

```
-- This is a cobbler solution at the same level of complexity
-- as the MTS case study.
```

```
package Cobbler_Shop is
   type Boot_Status is (Brand_New, Worn, Repaired, Unrepairable);
   type Boots_Style is (Cowboy, Ski, Waders);

   type Pair_Of_Boots is
     record
       Style  : Boots_Style;
       Status : Boot_Status;
     end record;

   type Receipt_Type is limited private;
   procedure Deliver_Boots (Boots   : in     Pair_Of_Boots;
                            Receipt : in out Receipt_Type);

   procedure Pick_Up_Boots (Receipt : in out Receipt_Type;
                            Boots   :    out Pair_Of_Boots);

   Receipt_Is_In_Use,
   Boots_Do_Not_Need_Repair,
   Invalid_Receipt,
   Cobbler_Shop_Is_Full,
   Boots_Are_Not_Ready : exception;
private
   Max_Number_of_Boots : constant := 100;
   type Boots_ID is range 1 .. Max_Number_of_Boots;

   type Receipt_Type is
     record
       Number   : Boots_ID;
       Assigned : Boolean := False;
     end record;
end Cobbler_Shop;

package Customers is
   -- Calls
   -- Cobbler_Shop.Deliver_Boots
   -- Cobbler_Shop.Pick_Up_Boots
end Customers;
```

```
package body Cobbler_Shop is
  Number_Of_Cobblers : constant := 200;

  type Job_Ticket is
    record
      Number : Boots_ID;
      Boots  : Pair_Of_Boots;
    end record;

  task Clerk is
    entry Deliver_Boots (Boots   : in     Pair_Of_Boots;
                         Receipt : in out Receipt_Type);
    entry Pick_Up_Boots (Receipt : in out Receipt_Type;
                         Boots   :    out Pair_Of_Boots);
    entry Get_A_Job          (Current_Job : out Job_Ticket);
    entry Return_Finished_Job (Current_Job :  in Job_Ticket);
  end Clerk;

  task type Typical_Repairman is
    -- Calls
      -- Clerk.Get_A_Job
      -- Clerk.Return_Finished_Job
  end Typical_Repairman;

  Cobbler : array (1 .. Number_Of_Cobblers) of Typical_Repairman;

  task body Clerk             is separate;
  task body Typical_Repairman is separate;

  procedure Deliver_Boots (Boots   : in     Pair_Of_Boots;
                           Receipt : in out Receipt_Type) is
  begin
    if Receipt.Assigned then
      raise Receipt_Is_In_Use;
    elsif Boots.Status /= Worn then
      raise Boots_Do_Not_Need_Repair;
    end if;

    Clerk.Deliver_Boots (Boots, Receipt); -- may raise
                                -- Cobbler_Shop_Is_Full
  end Deliver_Boots;
```

```
procedure Pick_Up_Boots (Receipt : in out Receipt_Type;
                         Boots   :    out Pair_Of_Boots) is
begin
  if not Receipt.Assigned then
    raise Invalid_Receipt;
  end if;

  Clerk.Pick_Up_Boots (Receipt, Boots); -- may raise
                                -- Boots_Are_Not_Ready
  end Pick_Up_Boots;
end Cobbler_Shop;

package body Customers is
  Number_Of_Customers : constant := 3;

  task type Customer_Type is
    -- Calls
      -- Cobbler_Shop.Deliver_Boots
      -- Cobbler_Shop.Pick_Up_Boots
  end Customer_Type;

  Customer : array (1 .. Number_Of_Customers) of Customer_Type;

  task body Customer_Type is separate;
end Customers;

with Queue_Object_Manager;
separate (Cobbler_Shop)
  task body Clerk is

    Boots_Storage : array (Boots_ID) of Pair_Of_Boots;
    Boots_Number  : Boots_ID;

    -- Boots_Storage contains the Boots, both
    -- those awaiting Repair and those that have
    -- been Repaired.

    -- Boots_Number, Receipt.Number, and Job_Ticket.Number are all
    -- equivalent names for Boots, and are of type Boots_ID

    package Receipt_Store is new Queue_Object_Manager
                      (Buffered_Type => Boots_ID,
                       Buffer_Size   => Max_Number_of_Boots);
```

```
-- Receipt_Store holds the set of receipts that are
-- ready for use. When it is empty, the cobbler shop
-- is full.

package Job_Number_Store is new Queue_Object_Manager
                    (Buffered_Type => Boots_ID,
                     Buffer_Size   => Max_Number_of_Boots);

-- Job_Number_Store holds the set of jobs that are yet to be
-- Repaired. (A job is an index to where the Boots are
-- stored in the Boots store.)  When it is empty, the
-- cobbler shop has no work to do.


-- USE OF THE RECEIPT AND JOB NUMBER STORES:

-- (1) When Boots are delivered (entry Deliver_Boots), a
-- number is taken out of the
-- receipt store, used to store the Boots, given to the customer
-- as a receipt, and stored in the job number store.

-- (2) Cobblers take Boots (entry Get_A_Job)
-- and repair them. The clerk takes the job number
-- out of the job number store.

-- (3) Repaired Boots are returned by the
-- Cobblers (entry Return_Finished_Job). The clerk returns the
-- Boots to the Boots storage.

-- (4) After a customer picks up the Boots,
-- (entry Pick_Up_Boots), the number is returned to the
-- receipt store.

function Awaiting_Repair (Boots : Pair_Of_Boots)
                                        return Boolean is
begin
   return Boots.Status = Worn;
end Awaiting_Repair;
begin -- Clerk

Initialize_The_Receipt_Store:
for I in Boots_ID loop
   Receipt_Store.Enqueue (I);
end loop Initialize_The_Receipt_Store;
```

```
loop
  Handle_Exceptions_For_Select:
  begin
    select
      accept Deliver_Boots (Boots    : in      Pair_Of_Boots;
                            Receipt : in out Receipt_Type) do

        Handle_Empty_Receipt_Store:
        begin
          Receipt_Store.Dequeue (Boots_Number);

          Boots_Storage (Boots_Number) := Boots;

          Receipt := (Number   => Boots_Number,
                      Assigned => True);
        exception
          when Receipt_Store.Buffer_Empty =>
            raise Cobbler_Shop_Is_Full;
        end Handle_Empty_Receipt_Store;
      end Deliver_Boots;

      Job_Number_Store.Enqueue (Boots_Number);
    or
      accept Pick_Up_Boots (Receipt : in out Receipt_Type;
                            Boots   :    out Pair_Of_Boots) do
        if Awaiting_Repair (Boots_Storage (Receipt.Number)) then
          raise Boots_Are_Not_Ready;
        end if;

        Boots := Boots_Storage (Receipt.Number);
        Receipt_Store.Enqueue (Receipt.Number);
        Receipt.Assigned := False;
      end Pick_Up_Boots;
    or
      when not Job_Number_Store.Empty =>
        accept Get_A_Job (Current_Job : out Job_Ticket) do
          Job_Number_Store.Dequeue (Boots_Number);

          Current_Job := (Number => Boots_Number,
                          Boots  => Boots_Storage (Boots_Number));
        end Get_A_Job;
    or
```

```
            accept Return_Finished_Job (Current_Job : in Job_Ticket) do
               Boots_Storage (Current_Job.Number) := Current_Job.Boots;
            end Return_Finished_Job;
          end select;
       exception
         when Cobbler_Shop_Is_Full |
               Boots_Are_Not_Ready    => null;
       end Handle_Exceptions_For_Select;
     end loop;
   end Clerk;


separate (Cobbler_Shop)
   task body Typical_Repairman is
     Mended      : Boolean;
     Current_Job : Job_Ticket;

     procedure Repair_The_Boots (Boots  : in Pair_Of_Boots;
                                 Mended : out Boolean) is separate;
     -- Repair_The_Boots repairs the boots if possible,
     -- appropriately setting the status of Mended
     -- We will not provide a proper body (complete solution)
     -- for Repair_The_Boots.

   begin
     loop
       Clerk.Get_A_Job (Current_Job);
       Repair_The_Boots (Current_Job.Boots, Mended);

       if Mended then
         Current_Job.Boots.Status := Repaired;
       else
         Current_Job.Boots.Status := Unrepairable;
       end if;

       Clerk.Return_Finished_Job (Current_Job);
     end loop;
   end Typical_Repairman;

with Cobbler_Shop; use Cobbler_Shop;
separate (Customers)
   task body Customer_Type is
     Boots   : Pair_Of_Boots;
     Receipt : Receipt_Type;
```

```
      procedure Purchase_Boots (Boots : out Pair_Of_Boots)
                                                 is separate;
      procedure Abuse_Boots (Boots : in out Pair_Of_Boots)
                                                 is separate;
   begin
      Purchase_Boots (Boots);

      loop
        Handle_Exceptions:
        begin
          Abuse_Boots (Boots);
          Cobbler_Shop.Deliver_Boots (Boots, Receipt);

          -- may do alternate work

          Cobbler_Shop.Pick_Up_Boots (Receipt, Boots);

        exception
          when
            Receipt_Is_In_Use           |
            Boots_Do_Not_Need_Repair    |
            Invalid_Receipt             |
            Cobbler_Shop_Is_Full        |
            Boots_Are_Not_Ready         =>
              null; -- or do whatever is necessary
                    -- in each case
        end Handle_Exceptions;
      end loop;
   end Customer_Type;
```

Discussion: The solution was extensively discussed as part of the case study. An important aspect of the relationship between this problem (dealing with cobblers) and the MTS (dealing with messages in a real-time system), is that all the cobbler problems are actually real-time systems in disguise.

Additional Problems

There are many additional possibilities and paradigms to explore using the cobbler problems. Here are a few variations that you may wish to think about and implement. Solutions are not provided here.

Additional__1.

Purpose: To show the use of an agent as a transporter

Problem: Modify COBBLER_16. The customer wants to be a called task with respect to having the boots returned, but the cobbler is still to be called, implying the use of a receipt. Use an agent task to fetch the boots from the cobbler using the receipt originally provided to the customer. The agent (or some combination of tasks comprising the customer-cobbler intermediary) is essentially a transporter. The customer must pass the receipt to the agent, hence modifying slightly the type and use of the receipt.

Additional__2.

Purpose: To illustrate a pool of reusable agents/mailboxes

Problem: Instead of having each customer create its own mailbox, establish a new package that maintains and provides a pool of reusable agents. The customers check out a mailbox, use it to help have the boots repaired, and allow the agent to return itself to the pool. Should the pool be a fixed size?

Additional__3.

Purpose: To illustrate the use of the address/identification of the customer task for returning of a result

Problem: Returning to COBBLER_12, modify the interactions so that the customer gives the cobbler *his own* address rather than the address of a mailbox. Is this as flexible as with the use of a mailbox? Can the customers be of any type?

Additional__4.

Purpose: To illustrate the "helper" model of task interaction. This is essentially a fourth client-server paradigm.

Problem: Now change things around so that the cobbler shop assigns a customer a personal cobbler until the shoes are mended. (The cobblers must now be created by the evaluation of an allocator). This modifies the structure of the problem a great deal. Should the cobblers be created as needed, or should they be allocated from a pool of cobblers? If a pool, how should the pool be organized?

Bibliography

ABB82   Abbott, R., and G. Booch, *A Usage Guide for Ada*, The Aerospace Corporation, 11 January 1982.

ABB83   Abbott, R., Program Design by Informal English Descriptions, *Comm. ACM*, vol. 26, no. 11, November 1983.

ALL81   Allworth, S. T., *Introduction to Real-Time Software Design*, Springer-Verlag, New York, 1981.

AND83   Andrews, G. R., and I. B. Schneider, Concepts and Notations for Concurrent Programming, *ACM Computing Surveys*, vol. 15, no. 1, March 1983.

ANS83   *Reference Manual for the Ada Programming Language*, ANSI/MIL-STD 1815A, January 22, 1983.

BAC82   Bach, I., On the Type Concept of Ada, *Ada Letters*, vol. II, no. 3, November/December 1982.

BAK85   Baker, T. P. and Riccardi, G. A., Ada Tasking: From Semantics to Efficient Implementation, *IEEE Software*, March 1985.

BAR84   Barnes, J. G. P., *Programming in Ada*, Addison-Wesely, London, 1984.

BEN82   Ben-Ari, M., *Principles of Concurrent Programming*, Prentice-Hall International Inc., London, 1982.

BOE81   Boehm, B. W., Software Engineering Economics, Prentice-Hall Inc., Englewood Cliffs, N.J., 1981.

BOO87   Booch, G., *Software Engineering with Ada* Second Edition, Benjamin/Cummings, Menlo Park, Calif., 1987.

BOO86   Booch, G.: Object-Oriented Development, *IEEE Transactions on Software Engineering*, vol. SE-12, no. 2, February 1986.

BOW82   Bowles, K. L., Linked Ada Modules Shape Software Systems, *Electronic Design*, July 22, 1982.

BRI73a   Brinch Hansen, P., Concurrent Programming Concepts, *Computing Surveys*, vol. 5, no. 4, December 1973.

BRI73b   Brinch Hansen, P., *Operating System Principles*, Prentice-Hall Inc., Englewood Cliffs, N.J., 1973.

BRI77   Brinch Hansen, P., *The Architecture of Concurrent Programs*, Prentice-Hall Inc., Englewood Cliffs, N.J., 1977.

BRI78   Brinch Hansen, Distributed Processes: A Concurrent Programming Concept, *Comm. ACM*, vol. 21, no. 11, November 1978.

BUH84   Buhr, R. J. A., *System Design with Ada*, Prentice-Hall Inc., Englewood Cliffs, N.J., 1984.

BUR85   Burns, A., *Concurrent Programming in Ada*, Cambridge University Press, Cambridge, England, 1985.

BUR86   Burger, T. M., and K. W. Nielsen, An Assessment of the Overhead Associated with Tasking Facilities and Task Paradigms in Ada, *Ada Letters*, vol. VII, no. 1, January/February 1987.

CEN84   *Real Time Ada*, Center For Tactical Computer Systems (CENTACS), Fort Monmouth, N.J., July 1984.

CHA82   Chase, A., and M. Gerhardt, The Case for Full Ada as a Design Language, *Ada Letters*, vol. II, no. 3, November/December 1982.

CHE84   Cherry, G. W., *Parallel Programming in ANSI Standard Ada*, Reston Publishing Company, Reston, Virginia, 1984.

CHE86a   Cherry, G. W., *Ada Graph, The Ada Productivity Tool, Volume 1: Commentary and Ada PDL and Code*, The Analytic Sciences Corporation, Reading, Mass., 1986.

CHE86b   Cherry, G. W., *Ada Graph, The Ada Productivity Tool, Volume 2: Figures and Graphs*, The Analytic Sciences Corporation, Reading, Mass., 1986.

CLA80   Clarke, A., C. Wileden, and L. Wolf, Nesting in Ada is for the Birds. Proceedings of the ACM-SIGPLAN Symposium on the Ada Programming Language, Boston, Mass., December 1980, published as SIGPLAN Notices 15, no. 11, November 1980.

DAH72   Dahl, O. J., E. W. Dijkstra, and C. A. R. Hoare, *Structured Programming*, Academic Press, New York, 1972.

DEI84   Deital, H. M., *An Introduction to Operating Systems*, rev. 1st ed., Addison-Wesely, Reading, Mass., 1984.

DEM78   DeMarco, T., *Structured Analysis and System Specification*, Yourdon Inc., New York, 1978.

DER76   DeRemer, F., and H. H. Kron, Programming-in-the-Large Versus Programming-in-the Small, *IEEE Transactions on Software Engineering*, vol. SE-2, no. 2, June 1976.

DIJ68   Dijkstra, E. W., Cooperating Sequential Processes, in *Programming Languages*, edited by F. Genuys, Academic Press, New York, 1968.

DIJ71   Dijkstra, E. W., Hierarchical Ordering of Sequential Processes, *Acta Informatica*, vol. 1, no. 2, 1971.

DIJ72   Dijkstra, E. W., Notes on Structured Programming, in Ref. DAH72.

DOD78   Department of Defense Requirement for High Order Computer Programming Languages, *STEELMAN*, June 1978.

DOD80   Requirements for Ada Programming Support Environments, Stoneman, DoD, February 1980.

EVA81   Evans, A., Jr., A Comparison of Programming Languages: Ada, Pascal, C, Lawrence Livermore Laboratory Technical Report UCRL-15346, April 1981.

FEU84   Feuer, A. R., and N. Gehani, *Comparing and Assessing Programming Languages: Ada, C, and Pascal*, Prentice-Hall Inc., Englewood Cliffs, N.J., 1984.

FOS83   Foster, C. C., *Real Time Programming: Neglected Topics*, Addison-Wesely, Reading, Mass., 1983.

FRE83   Freedman, R. S., "The Common Sense of Object Oriented Languages", *Computer Design*, February 1983.

GEH84   Gehani, N., *Ada: Concurrent Programming*, Prentice-Hall Inc., Englewood Cliffs, N.J., 1984.

GOM84   Gomaa, H., A Software Design Method for Real-Time Systems, *Comm. ACM*, vol. 27, no. 9, September 1984.

GOO81   Goos, G. and W. Wulf, DIANA Reference Manual, Carnegie-Mellon University, March 1981.

GLA83   Glass, R. L., *Real-Time Software*, Prentice-Hall Inc., Englewood Cliffs, N.J., 1983.

HAB76   Habermann, A. N., *Introduction to Operating System Design*, Science Research Associates Inc., Chicago, Ill., 1976

HAB80   Habermann, A. N., and Nassi, I. R., Efficient Implementation of Ada Tasks, Technical report CMU-CS-80-103, Department of Computer Science, Carnegie-Mellon University, January 1980.

HAB83   Habermann, A. N., and Perry, D. E., *Ada for Experienced Programmers*, Addison-Wesely, Reading, Mass., 1983.

HAR85   Harbaugh A., XAda, An Executable Ada Design Language Methodology, *Ada Letters*, vol. IV, no. 6, 1985.

HIL82   Hilfinger, P. N., Implementation Strategies for Ada Tasking Idioms, Proceedings of the AdaTEC Conference on Ada, Arlington, Va., October 1982.

HIL83   Hilfinger, P. N., *Abstraction Mechanisms and Language Design*, MIT Press, Cambridge, Mass., 1983.

HOA74   Hoare, C. A. R., Monitors: An Operating System Structuring Concept, *Comm. ACM*, vol. 17, no. 10, October 1974.

HOA78   Hoare, C. A. R., "Communicating Sequential Processes" *Comm. ACM*, vol. 21, no. 8, August 1978.

HOA81   Hoare, C. A. R., The Emperor's Old Clothes, *Comm. ACM*, vol. 24, no. 2, February 1981.

HOA85   Hoare, C. A. R., *Communicating Sequential Processes*, Prentice-Hall Inc., Englewood Cliffs, N.J., 1985.

ICH79   Ichbiah, J., et al., Rationale for the Design of the Ada Programming Language, *SIGPLAN Notices*, vol. 14, no. 6, part A, June 1979.

ICH83   Ichbiah, J., et al., Ichbiah, Barnes, and Firth On Ada, Video Tapes, Alsys, Waltham, Mass., 1983.

ICH84   Ichbiah, J., Ada: Past, Present, Future, *Comm. ACM*, vol. 27, no. 10, October 1984.

IIT84   *Catalog of Resources for Education in Ada and Software Engineering*, IIT Research Institute, Lanham, Maryland, May 1986.

JAC75   Jackson, M. A., *Principles of Program Design*, Academic Press, New York, 1975.

LIS86   Liskov, B., and J. Guttag, *Abstraction and Specification in Program Development*, MIT Press, Cambridge, Mass., 1986.

LOR72   Loren, H., *Parallelism in Hardware and Software: Real and Apparent Concurrency*, Prentice-Hall Inc., Englewood Cliffs, N.J., 1972.

MAC83   MacLaren, L., Evolving Toward Ada in Real-Time Systems, in *Real-Time Software*, edited by R. L. Glass, Prentice-Hall Inc., Englewood Cliffs, N.J., 1983.

MIC80   Mick, J., and Brick, J., *Bit-Slice Microprocessor Design*, McGraw-Hill, New York, 1980.

MIT84   Preliminary Program Manager's Guide to Ada, ESD-TR-83-255, WP-25012, The MITRE Corporation, February 1984.

MYE76   Myers, G. J., *Composite/Structured Design*, Van Nostrand Reinhold, New York, 1976.

NIE86   Nielsen, K. W., Task Coupling and Cohesion in Ada, *Ada Letters*, vol. VI, no. 4, July/August 1986.

NIE88   Nielsen, K. W., and K. C. Shumate, *Designing Large Real-Time Systems with Ada*, Mc Graw-Hill, New York, 1988.

NIS84   Nissen, J., and P. Wallis, *Portability and Style in Ada*, Cambridge University Press, Cambridge, England 1984.

ORR77   Orr, K. T., *Structured Systems Development*, Yourdon Press, New York, 1977.

PAG80   Page-Jones, M., *The Practical Guide to Structured Systems Design*, Yourdon Press, New York, 1980.

PAR72   Parnas, D. L., On the Criteria to be Used in Decomposing Systems Into Modules, *Comm. ACM*, vol. 15, no. 12, December 1972.

PAR79   Parnas, D. L., *Designing Software for Ease of Extension and Contraction*, IEEE Transactions on Software Engineering, Volume SE-5, Number 2, March 1979.

PET83   Peterson, J. L., and A. Silberschatz, *Operating System Concepts*, Addison-Wesley, Reading, Mass., 1983.

PYL85   Pyle, I. C., *The Ada Programming Language*, Prentice-Hall Inc., Englewood Cliffs, N.J., 1985.

ROU85   Roubine, O., Programming Large and Flexible Systems in Ada, in *Ada in Use: Proceedings of the Ada International Conference* (Paris, May 14–16, 1985). Cambridge University Press, Cambridge, England 1985.

SHA81   Shaw, M., et al, A Comparison of Programming Languages for Software Engineering, Software-Practice and Experience, Volume 11, Number 1-52, 1981.

SHU82   Shumate, K. C., The Programming Language Ada, Auerbach portfolio ACPM 12-01-09, August/September 1982 (revised 1985).

SHU84   Shumate, K. C., *Understanding Ada*, Harper & Row, New York, 1984.

SIM79   Simpson, H. R., and K. L. Jackson, Process Synchronization in Mascot, *Computer Journal*, vol. 22, no. 4, 1979.

SOF80   Ada Compiler Validation Implementer's Guide, 1067 - 2.3, Contract Number MDA 903-79-C-0687, SofTech Inc., October 1, 1980.

WAR85   Ward, P. T., and S. J. Mellor, *Structured Development for Real-Time Systems, Volume 1: Introduction and Tools, Volume 2: Essential Modeling Techniques, Volume 3: Techniques of Implementation Modeling*, Yourdon Press, New York, 1985

WEG84   Wegner, P., Capital-Intensive Software Technology, Part 1: Software Components, *IEEE Software*, July 1984.

WEI71   Weinberg, G. M., *The Psychology of Computer Programming*, Van Nostrand, New York, 1971.

WEL81   Welsh, J., and A. Lister, A Comparative Study of Task Communication in Ada, *Software Practice and Experience*, vol. 11, 1981.

WIC80   Wichmann, B. A., A Comparison of Pascal and Ada, *Computer Journal*, May 1980.

WIE83   Wiener, R., and R. Sincovec, *Programming in Ada*, John Wiley & Sons Inc., New York, 1983.

WIE84   Wiener, R., and R. Sincovec, *Software Engineering with Modula-2 and Ada*, John Wiley & Sons Inc., New York, 1984.

WIR71   Wirth, N., Program Development by Stepwise Refinement, *Comm. ACM* vol. 14, no. 4, April 1971.

WIR76   Wirth, N., *Algorithms + Data Structures = Programs*, Prentice-Hall Inc., Englewood Cliffs, N.J., 1976

WIR77   Wirth, N., Programming Languages: What to Demand and How to Assess Them, *Software Engineering*, ed. by R. H. Perrott, Academic Press, New York, 1977.

YOU79   Yourdon, E., and L. L. Constantine, *Structured Design*, Prentice-Hall Inc., Englewood Cliffs, N.J., 1979.

YOU82   Young, S. J., *Real Time Languages: Design and Development*, Ellis Horwood Limited, Chichester, England, 1982.

YOU83   Young, S. J., *An Introduction to Ada*, Ellis Horwood Limited, Chichester, England, 1983.

Index

Many items in the index are the principal subject of an entire chapter. They are noted as "activation (Chapter 11), 24, 2.6.1 (52), Figure (310)." This example also illustrates that activation is the primary topic of section 2.6.1 starting on page 52, and is illustrated with a Figure on page 310. The Cobbler problems are frequent examples of indexed items, noted as "agent task Cobbler_12 (552)." Exercises and Solutions to exercises are also referenced.